This book brings clarity and coherence to what the Bible is and is not trying to tell us about the nature and origins of spiritual evil. Reading Heiser's work has a way of exposing just how much we have unconsciously rewritten the Bible to fit our modern sensibilities, and how we've muddled the biblical storyline by underestimating the themes explored in this book. Get ready for many lightbulb moments, and for a whole new appreciation of biblical texts you thought you already understood. This book is highly recommended!

Tim Mackie, PhD
Co-creator of *The Bible Project*

Dr. Michael Heiser is a master guide into the unseen realm of angels and demons, making accessible to a wider audience the findings of top Hebrew and Semitic scholars. And his newest book focusing on demons—in keeping with his recent bestselling books—will challenge you to rethink many of your common assumptions. Let all things be tested by the truth of the word! You are in for an enlightening read.

Michael Brown, PhD
Host of the Line of Fire radio broadcast, president of FIRE School of Ministry, and author of *Jezebel's War with America*

Michael Heiser has done a great service to all who want to understand the biblical theology of demons, the supernatural powers in rebellion against God. He gives a detailed exploration of the biblical materials as well as the best of the literature of ancient Jewish writers. He correctly believes that we must read the biblical accounts in the context of their ancient worldview. Reviewing all this material, helpfully gathered into this book, will challenge most everyone's understanding of demons. His work is controversial so he brings the work of those who differ with him into his discussions. The study will correct widely-held errors in modern demonology and make us more faithful followers of the One who has won the decisive victory over the devil.

Gerry Breshears, PhD
Professor of Theology, Western Seminary, Portland

Is it right to say that you love a book about demons? If so, I love this book about demons! Dr. Michael Heiser brilliantly unveils more of the unseen realm, this time the mysterious and misunderstood forces of darkness that made the death and resurrection of Christ necessary. *Demons* will not only answer your most difficult questions about the underworld, but it will help you realize why your role in the Great Commission is so important. Get this book now!

Frank Turek, PhD
CrossExamined.org and co-author, *I Don't Have Enough Faith to Be an Atheist*

DEMONS

More from Michael S. Heiser

Angels:
What the Bible Really Says about God's Heavenly Host

The Unseen Realm:
Recovering the Supernatural Worldview of the Bible

Supernatural:
What the Bible Teaches about the Unseen World

The World Turned Upside Down:
Finding the Gospel in Stranger Things

The Bible Unfiltered:
Approaching Scripture on Its Own Terms

I Dare You Not to Bore Me
with the Bible

Reversing Hermon:
Enoch, the Watchers & the Forgotten Mission of Jesus Christ

The Façade

The Portent

DEMONS

WHAT THE BIBLE REALLY SAYS
ABOUT THE POWERS OF DARKNESS

MICHAEL S. HEISER

LEXHAM PRESS

Demons: What the Bible Really Says about the Powers of Darkness

Copyright 2020 Michael S. Heiser

Lexham Press, 1313 Commercial St., Bellingham, WA 98225
LexhamPress.com

Print ISBN 9781683592891
Digital ISBN 9781683592907
Library of Congress Control Number 2020930219

Lexham Editorial: Douglas Mangum, Abigail Stocker, Jim Weaver, Danielle Thevenaz
Cover Design: Brittany Schrock
Interior Design and Typesetting: Beth Shagene

Contents

Abbreviations

ABD	*Anchor Yale Bible Dictionary.* Edited by David Noel Freedman. 6 vols. New York: Doubleday, 1992
Ant.	Josephus, *Jewish Antiquities*
APOT	*The Apocrypha and Pseudepigrapha of the Old Testament.* Edited by Robert H. Charles. 2 vols. Oxford: Clarendon, 1913
AYB	Anchor Yale Bible
BAR	*Biblical Archaeology Review*
BASOR	*Bulletin of the American Schools of Oriental Research*
BBR	*Bulletin for Biblical Research*
BCOT	Baker Commentary on the Old Testament
BDAG	Bauer, Walter, Frederick W. Danker, William F. Arndt, and F. Wilbur Gingrich. *Greek-English Lexicon of the New Testament and Other Early Christian Literature.* 3rd ed. Chicago: University of Chicago Press, 2000
BECNT	Baker Exegetical Commentary on the New Testament
BNTC	Black's New Testament Commentaries
BSac	*Bibliotheca Sacra*
CAD	*The Assyrian Dictionary of the Oriental Institute of the University of Chicago.* 21 vols. Chicago: The Oriental Institute of the University of Chicago, 1956–2006

DCH	*The Dictionary of Classical Hebrew.* Edited by David J. A. Clines. 9 vols. Sheffield: Sheffield Academic Press, 1993–2014
DDD	*Dictionary of Deities and Demons in the Bible.* Edited by Karel van der Toorn, Bob Becking, and Pieter W. van der Horst. Leiden: Brill, 1995. 2nd rev. ed. Grand Rapids: Eerdmans, 1999
DNTB	*Dictionary of New Testament Background.* Edited by Craig A. Evans and Stanley E. Porter. Downers Grove, IL: InterVarsity Press, 2000
DNWSI	*Dictionary of the North-West Semitic Inscriptions.* Edited by Jacob Hoftijzer and Karel Jongeling. 2 vols. Leiden: Brill, 2003
DOTHB	*Dictionary of the Old Testament: Historical Books.* Edited by Bill T. Arnold and H. G. M. Williamson. Downers Grove, IL: InterVarsity Press, 2005
DOTP	*Dictionary of the Old Testament: Pentateuch.* Edited by T. Desmond Alexander and David W. Baker. Downers Grove, IL: InterVarsity Press, 2003
DOTWPW	*Dictionary of the Old Testament: Wisdom, Poetry & Writings.* Edited by Tremper Longman III and Peter Enns. Downers Grove, IL: InterVarsity Press, 2008
DPL	*Dictionary of Paul and His Letters.* Edited by Gerald F. Hawthorne and Ralph P. Martin. Downers Grove, IL: InterVarsity Press, 1993
DSD	*Dead Sea Discoveries*
DULAT	*A Dictionary of the Ugaritic Language in the Alphabetic Tradition.* Edited by Gregorio Del Olmo Lete and Joaquín Sanmartín. 2 vols. Leiden: Brill, 2015
EHLL	*Encyclopedia of Hebrew Language and Linguistics.* Edited by Geoffrey Khan. 4 vols. Leiden: Brill, 2013
ERE	*Encyclopedia of Religion and Ethics.* Edited by James Hastings. 13 vols. New York: Scribner's Sons, 1908–1927

GBH	*A Grammar of Biblical Hebrew*. Paul Joüon and Takamitsu Muraoka. Rev. English ed. Roma: Pontificio istituto biblico, 2006
GKC	*Gesenius' Hebrew Grammar*. Edited by Emil Kautzsch. Translated by Arthur E. Cowley. 2nd ed. Oxford: Clarendon, 1910
HALOT	*The Hebrew and Aramaic Lexicon of the Old Testament*. Ludwig Koehler, Walter Baumgartner, and Johann J. Stamm. Translated and edited under the supervision of Mervyn E. J. Richardson. 5 vols. Leiden: Brill, 1994–2000
HTR	*Harvard Theological Review*
HUCA	*Hebrew Union College Annual*
ICC	International Critical Commentary
JBL	*Journal of Biblical Literature*
JESOT	*Journal for the Evangelical Study of the Old Testament*
JNES	*Journal of Near Eastern Studies*
JPS	Jewish Publication Society. *Tanakh: The Holy Scriptures*. Philadelphia: Jewish Publication Society, 1985
JSOT	*Journal for the Study of the Old Testament*
JSP	*Journal for the Study of the Pseudepigrapha*
JTS	*Journal of Theological Studies*
KAI	*Kanaanäische und aramäische Inschriften*. Edited by Herbert Donner and Wolfgang Röllig. 2nd ed. Wiesbaden: Harrassowitz, 1966–1969
KTU	*Die keilalphabetischen Texte aus Ugarit*. Edited by M. Dietrich, O. Loretz, and J. Sanmartín. Neukirchen-Vluyn, 1976. KTU² = 2nd enlarged ed. of *KTU: The Cuneiform Alphabetic Texts from Ugarit, Ras Ibn Hani, and Other Places*. Edited by M. Dietrich, O. Loretz, and J. Sanmartín. Münster, 1995 (= *CTU*)
LBD	*The Lexham Bible Dictionary*. Edited by John D. Barry. Bellingham, WA: Lexham Press, 2016

LES	*The Lexham English Septuagint.* Edited by Ken M. Penner. Bellingham, WA: Lexham Press, 2019
LSJ	H. G. Liddell, R. Scott, and H. S. Jones. *A Greek-English Lexicon.* 9th ed. with rev. supp. Oxford: Clarendon, 1996
NAC	New American Commentary
NICOT	The New International Commentary on the Old Testament
NIDNTTE	*New International Dictionary of New Testament Theology and Exegesis.* Edited by Moisés Silva. 5 vols. Grand Rapids: Zondervan, 2014
NIDOTTE	*New International Dictionary of Old Testament Theology and Exegesis.* Edited by Willem A. VanGemeren. 5 vols. Grand Rapids: Zondervan, 1997
NIGTC	New International Greek Testament Commentary
NovT	*Novum Testamentum*
OTL	Old Testament Library
OTP	*The Old Testament Pseudepigrapha.* Edited by James H. Charlesworth. 2 vols. New York: Doubleday, 1983, 1985
TDNT	*Theological Dictionary of the New Testament.* Edited by Gerhard Kittel and Gerhard Friedrich. Translated by Geoffrey W. Bromiley. 10 vols. Grand Rapids: Eerdmans, 1964–1976
TDOT	*Theological Dictionary of the Old Testament.* Edited by G. Johannes Botterweck and Helmer Ringgren. Translated by John T. Willis et al. 8 vols. Grand Rapids: Eerdmans, 1974–2006
TLOT	*Theological Lexicon of the Old Testament.* Edited by Ernst Jenni, with assistance from Claus Westermann. Translated by Mark E. Biddle. 3 vols. Peabody, MA: Hendrickson, 1997
TNTC	Tyndale New Testament Commentaries
TOTC	Tyndale Old Testament Commentaries

TWOT	*Theological Wordbook of the Old Testament.* Edited by R. Laird Harris, Gleason L. Archer Jr., and Bruce K. Waltke. 2 vols. Chicago: Moody Press, 1980
TynBul	*Tyndale Bulletin*
VT	*Vetus Testamentum*
WBC	Word Biblical Commentary
ZAW	*Zeitschrift für die alttestamentliche Wissenschaft*

What You Know
May Not Be So

As familiar as the subject matter of demons might seem, *Demons: What the Bible Really Says about the Powers of Darkness* will surprise you. Most readers will expect a lot of discussion on Satan, demons, and the "principalities and powers" of Paul's writings. We'll certainly cover those subjects, but I need to prepare you at the outset that a good bit of what you'll read in this book about those (and other) divine enemies of God will not conform to what you're already thinking. There will be material in here that you've never heard in church or perhaps even in a seminary class.

OBSTACLES TO OVERCOME

I'm announcing this at the outset because, when I decided to write this book, I did so despite knowing that there were serious obstacles to overcome. To be blunt, Christians embrace a number of unbiblical ideas about the powers of darkness. The reasons are twofold and are related. First, most of what we claim to know about the powers of darkness does not derive from close study of the original Hebrew and Greek texts. Second, much of what we think we know is filtered through and guided by church tradition—not the original, ancient contexts of the Old and New Testaments.

Taken collectively, these two realities mean that our beliefs about Satan and the dark powers are not rooted in these powers' own original contexts. Bible teachers (including some scholars) are prone to write about the powers of darkness on the basis of English translation. That undermines the nuance found in the original languages. Substituting traditions that emerged *after* the biblical period for ancient context and conflating ancient-language terms into the vocabulary of English translations produces an incomplete and occasionally misleading portrait of the supernatural forces hostile to God and his children. As a step toward rectifying this situation, this book seeks to root a theology of the powers of darkness in the original text, understood on the text's own terms.

You might be wondering what sort of unbiblical ideas I'm referencing. A few illustrations will suffice. Most English translations use the term "demon" three times in the Old Testament (Lev 17:7; Deut 32:17; Ps 106:37). Christian readers might wonder why demons are mentioned so infrequently in the Old Testament compared to the New Testament Gospels. But that very question erroneously presumes that the "demons" of the Old Testament are the same as those encountered in the Gospels. They are not. Another assumption is that the *śāṭān* figure of Job 1–2 is the devil of the New Testament. That conclusion is not feasible exegetically. Another example is the oft-repeated belief that Satan and one-third of the angels of heaven rebelled against God before the creation of humankind. This idea is prevalent throughout Christian tradition despite the fact that such an episode appears nowhere in the Bible. The only passage that comes close is Revelation 12:4, a passage dealing with the birth of the Messiah, thousands of years after the primeval period.

Aside from certain assumptions reflexively brought to our study, there is also the issue of what we mean by "darkness" and, by extension, the "powers" of that darkness. As with the terminology for hostile supernatural powers, the meaning of "darkness" isn't self-evident. While it is obvious that the literal physical circumstance of the absence of light is *not* in view, considering what the Bible seeks to communicate by its references to darkness matters for framing what it says about certain supernatural powers. In Scripture, darkness is a metaphor for negative, fearful human experiences. There are roughly two hundred references to darkness in Scripture, nearly all of which are used as a contrast to the God of the Bible—the source of love and life. It is no surprise, then, that death, the threat of death, and the realm of the dead itself are linked to supernatural entities expelled from God's presence and service.

THE ROADMAP FOR OUR STUDY

Despite the fact that it will challenge some cherished assumptions, this book does not focus on criticism of such ideas. Rather, it seeks to inform and intrigue.

The first of four sections examines the Bible's vocabulary for the powers of darkness. The goal is to alert readers to how the Septuagint (the ancient Greek translation of the Hebrew Bible) conflates the wide variety of terms for supernatural powers in rebellion against God, a set of terms inherited by New Testament writers. At the same time, Jewish authors writing in Hebrew and Aramaic in the Second Temple ("inter-testamental") period were introducing new terms. Navigating these developments is essential for understanding the meaning (or lack thereof) of New Testament vocabulary.

The second section focuses on how the evil cast of characters in the Old Testament came to be in an adversarial posture against their Creator. Contrary to many popular Christian traditions, there were three divine rebellions, not just one; of these, the first two framed ancient beliefs about Satan, the problem of human depravity, and the origin of demons. The third is the point of reference for the "princes" of Daniel 10 and Paul's teaching on the principalities and powers. These divine rebels are *distinct*—the rebellions were not committed by the same entities.

Our third section focuses on the powers of darkness in the New Testament with a view toward how the material of the Old Testament was processed by New Testament writers. The Gospels, for example, put forth the notion that the Messiah was identified in part by his ability to cast out demons—but no Old Testament passage proposes this idea. Equally mysterious is the connection Paul explicitly draws between the delegitimization of the authority of the principalities and powers to the resurrection of Christ. Once again, there is (apparently) no Old Testament passage that connects these two ideas.

Lastly, the book addresses imprecision and points of confusion in modern Christian demonology. In some respects, this last section will merge and summarize earlier points of discussion, but in other instances, it anticipates new questions that arise from the material covered in the book.

My hope is that *Demons: What the Bible Really Says about the Powers of Darkness* will not only demonstrate why reading the Bible in its own context matters, but how doing so can lead to the excitement of rediscovering Scripture.

BIBLICAL VOCABULARY FOR THE POWERS OF DARKNESS

OVERVIEW

Our study of the powers of darkness logically begins with the Old Testament. From the perspective of English Bible translations, the word "demons" seldom occurs in the Old Testament. The ESV, for example, uses the term only three times. "Evil spirit" occurs only once (Judg 9:23), a passage that may or may not involve a supernatural entity. This creates the impression (and drives the flawed conclusion) that the Old Testament has little to say about supernatural powers of darkness. We simply cannot depend on English translations for an Old Testament study of demons or the infernal powers.

As I noted in the Introduction, the metaphor of darkness is crucial to understanding how Israelites thought about the fearful experiences of life. The Old Testament writers linked the rebellion of supernatural beings with the mirror-opposition to the eternal, joyful life intended by the creation of earth and humanity. A loving God created the earth as his own abode-temple,[1] intending humanity to be part of his family. Supernatural

---

1. In regard to understanding the creation narratives as temple building, see John H. Walton, *The Lost World of Genesis One: Ancient Cosmology and the Origins Debate* (Downers Grove, IL: IVP Academic, 2009). A more scholarly version of this content is: John H. Walton, *Genesis 1 as Ancient Cosmology* (Winona Lake, IN: Eisenbrauns, 2011).

mutinies brought death, disaster, and disease to earth. Instead of all the earth becoming sacred space, darkness permeated the world.

For the ancient Israelite, the threats of the natural world and the perils of life were consequences of divine rebellions that were in turn catalysts to rebellion, treachery, and idolatry in humanity. Anyone in ancient Israel who heard or read the story of Eden knew that wasn't where they were living. Creation was far from perfect. Life on earth wasn't remotely idyllic.[2] An Old Testament theology of the powers of darkness connects sinister spiritual beings with death, the realm of the dead, and an ongoing assault on the harmony, order, and well-being the good God of all the earth desired in the world he had created for humankind.

This first section of our study briefly surveys how the Old Testament describes hostile supernatural powers of darkness against that backdrop. Chapter 1 covers a range of Hebrew terms, considered in their wider ancient Near Eastern context, that identifies a supernatural being hostile to God whose rebellion led to fear, calamity, depravity, and death in God's world. Chapter 2 explains how the terms of the preceding chapter were translated in the Septuagint (LXX), the ancient Greek translation of the Hebrew Old Testament. Our examination of the Septuagint will show us clearly that the translators often chose one Greek term to render many *different* Hebrew terms. Since the New Testament was written originally in Greek, the vocabulary of the Septuagint often finds its way into the New Testament. The result is that the New Testament has fewer words for the powers of darkness and loses some of the nuanced presentation of evil spirits found in the Old Testament.

A word on the limits of our study: first, while our investigation will include terms like (plural) *'elohim* ("gods"), we won't be concerned with discussing specific gods and goddesses (Baal, Molech, Chemosh, Asherah, etc.). Any rival deity (i.e., other than Yahweh) that was worshiped in antiquity was considered an evil power in the biblical worldview. Eventually we will encounter the Old Testament explanation for the appearance

---

2. Christians often presume that the entire earth was Eden, but this runs contrary to what we read in Genesis. For a brief discussion of this material, see Michael S. Heiser, *The Unseen Realm: Recovering the Supernatural Worldview of the Bible* (Bellingham, WA: Lexham Press, 2015), 49–50. For full treatments of this issue, see Hulisani Ramantswana, "God Saw That It Was Good, Not Perfect: A Canonical-Dialogic Reading of Genesis 1–3," (PhD diss., Westminster Theological Seminary, 2010), and Eric M. Vail, "Using 'Chaos' in Articulating the Relationship of God and Creation in God's Creative Activity" (PhD diss., Marquette University, 2009).

of these rival gods. For our study of vocabulary, profiling individual deities is not necessary. We will also not profile specific deities whose mythic
story lines are drawn upon by biblical writers (e.g., Typhon for Dan 7–12;
Athtar or Phaethon for Isa 14:12–15).

Second, we are not concerned with terms that *might* point to demonic
entities that occur in personal names or geographical names. In the
ancient world it was common to include names of deities in personal
names (e.g., Daniel = "El/God is my judge") and places (Baal-zephon,
Exod 14:2). While those examples are clear, others are only speculative.
For example, Sismai in 1 Chronicles 2:40 may have been named for a
deity known from ancient Syria (Ugarit) and Phoenicia, but there is no
way to establish this with certainty. Other intentional omissions include
names that could point to sinister divine beings but may only point to
humans thought to be empowered by dark powers (e.g., Gog).

Section I therefore aims to introduce Old Testament vocabulary in
the Hebrew Bible (chapter 1) and to survey what the Septuagint does
with that vocabulary (chapter 2). This will set the stage for subsequent
sections of the book, which will focus on understanding the supernatural
rebellions in the Old Testament and the inheritance in the New Testament of that dark landscape.

CHAPTER 1

Hebrew Terms
for Evil Spiritual Beings

OUR TASK IN THIS CHAPTER IS TO BRIEFLY STUDY HEBREW TERMS IN the Old Testament that describe evil spirits—supernatural entities that oppose God. English Bible readers will presume this means a study of demons. That presents us with an immediate obstacle. Scholars who have devoted considerable attention to this topic have long pointed out that "there is no equivalent expression for the word 'demon' in the Semitic languages."[1] This is indeed the case, which may sound odd. John Walton summarizes the situation concisely:

> No general term for "demons" exists in any of the major cultures of the ancient Near East or in the Hebrew Bible. They are generally considered one of the categories of "spirit beings" (along with gods and ghosts). The term *demons* has had a checkered history; in today's theological usage the term denotes beings, often fallen angels, who are intrinsically evil and who do the bidding of their master, Satan. This definition, however, only became commonplace long after the Hebrew Bible was complete.[2]

---

1. Henrike Frey-Anthes, "Concepts of 'Demons' in Ancient Israel," *Die Welt des Orients* 38 (2008): 38–52.

2. John H. Walton, "Demons in Mesopotamia and Israel: Exploring the Category of Non-Divine but Supernatural Enemies," in *Windows to the Ancient World of the Hebrew Bible: Essays in Honor of Samuel Greengus*, ed. Bill T. Arnold, Nancy L. Erickson, and John H. Walton (Winona Lake, IN: Eisenbrauns, 2014), 229–46 (esp. page 229). Walton's study is useful, particularly since he is a trusted evangelical scholar. However, as the title of his essay makes clear, his focus is limited to Mesopotamia. Consequently, some of his discussion could unintentionally mislead readers. He excludes, for example, comparative Ugaritic material in his understanding of certain Israelite concepts and Old

Despite this reality, we are not without material! A variety of terms in the Hebrew Bible are relevant to our topic. But in order to understand why the plethora of terms exists and their relationship to one another, they need to be framed in accord with the ancient Israelite worldview.

As noted in the preview to this section, Old Testament writers linked the rebellion of supernatural beings to the hazards and calamities they experienced. The life God desired for human beings on earth had been diverted and corrupted. The fears and threats of the natural world were consequences of divine rebellions, from which death and chaos over-spread the world of humanity. For this reason most of the terms we find in the Old Testament can be categorized as either (1) terms that are associated with the realm of the dead and its inhabitants, with fearful places associated with that realm, or with the threat of death itself, or (2) terms associated with geographical dominion by supernatural powers in rebellion against Yahweh, the God of Israel. But before we get to those two categories, we should begin with some general terms related to what an evil spirit is, ontologically speaking.

TERMS DESCRIBING THE NATURE OF EVIL SPIRITS

Ontology refers to what a thing *is*, a thing's nature. By definition, an evil spirit *is* a spirit. What I wrote in another volume about the good members of God's heavenly host is pertinent here, for evil spirits are members of God's heavenly host who have chosen to rebel against his will. Passages such as 1 Kings 22:19–23 make it clear that "the members of God's heavenly host are spirits (Hebrew: *rûḥôt*; singular: *rûaḥ*)—entities that, by nature, are not embodied, at least in the sense of our human experience of being physical in form."[3]

The point of "spirit" language is contrast with the world of human-kind. The members of God's heavenly host are not, by nature, embodied,

---

Testament passages related to divine beings in opposition to Yahweh. Including that material would at times lead to quite different conclusions than he draws.

3. Michael S. Heiser, *Angels: What the Bible Really Says about God's Heavenly Host* (Bellingham, WA: Lexham Press, 2018), 2. See pages 2–7 in that source for a discussion of the "spirit" terminology of this passage and its relationship to Pss 103:20–22; 104:4. Note that in 1 Kgs 22:19–23 the spirit being that steps forward with a workable solution to deceive Ahab is never called evil. God's judgment of evil (supernatural or human) is not to be construed as evil itself. There is neither indication nor logical requirement that divine agents who carry out God's judgment of the wicked are themselves evil.

physical beings of our terrestrial world.[4] This is why the Old Testament writers occasionally use Hebrew *šamayim* ("heavenly ones"), *kōkebîm* ("stars"), and *qedōšîm* ("holy ones"). The first two terms typically refer to the visible sky and celestial objects in that sky. Using such language of entities in God's service metaphorically places them in the nonterrestrial spiritual realm, the plane of reality in which God exists (Ps 115:3; Isa 66:1; Job 38:7–8). A designation such as "holy ones" situates these beings in God's presence—as opposed to the world of humankind (e.g., Ps 89:5–7; Job 15:15).

One frequently misunderstood term that identifies a being as a member of the nonhuman, nonterrestrial world is *'elōhîm* ("god"; "gods"). I've written extensively on this term and how the biblical writers affirmed the existence of multiple *'elōhîm*—that is, a populated spiritual world.[5] Since the biblical writers identify a range of entities as *'elōhîm* that they explicitly differentiate from Yahweh and emphasize as lesser beings than Yahweh, it is clear that the term *'elōhîm* is not a label for only one Supreme Being. As I have noted elsewhere:

> A biblical writer would use *'elōhîm* to label any entity that is not embodied by nature and is a member of the spiritual realm. This "otherworldliness" is an attribute all residents of the spiritual world possess. Every member of the spiritual world can be thought of as *'elōhîm* since the term tells us where an entity belongs in terms of its nature.[6]

---

4. In a footnote in *Angels*, I wrote: "This point is not contradicted by passages that refer to angels as men and that have them performing physical acts (e.g., Gen 6:1–4; 18:1–8, 16, 22; 19:1, 10–11, 16; 32:24 [compare Hos 12:4]). When angels interact with human beings, appearance in human form or actual embodiment is normative in Scripture. Without taking some form that could be detected and parsed by the human senses, angelic presence and interaction would be incomprehensible" (*Angels*, 2, note 2). For how this relates to passages like Gen 6:1–4 and Matt 22:23–33, see Heiser, *Unseen Realm*, chapters 12–13, 23, and Heiser, *Reversing Hermon: Enoch, the Watchers, and the Forgotten Mission of Jesus Christ* (Crane, MO: Defender, 2017), 37–54.

5. Heiser, *Unseen Realm*, 21–27. For my peer-reviewed work on the subject, see Michael S. Heiser, "Monotheism, Polytheism, Monolatry, or Henotheism? Toward an Assessment of Divine Plurality in the Hebrew Bible," *BBR* 18.1 (2008): 1–30; Heiser, "Should *'elohim* with Plural Predication Be Translated 'Gods'?" *Bible Translator* 61.3 (July 2010): 123–36; Heiser, "Does Deuteronomy 32:17 Assume or Deny the Reality of Other Gods?" *Bible Translator* 59.3 (July 2008): 137–45.

6. Heiser, *Angels*, 12.

The term *'elōhîm* simply means "divine beings"—residents of the supernatural world.[7] By choosing *'elōhîm* to describe a particular being, the biblical writer was not denying the uniqueness of Yahweh, the God of Israel. Rather, the term helped them affirm that there was an animate, spiritual world, of which Yahweh was a member. Yahweh was, of course, unique in that he was the uncreated Creator of these other spiritual beings and superior to them in his attributes.

The word *'elōhîm* is vocabulary that works in concert with terms such as *rûḥôt* ("spirits"). Some of the spirit beings created by God to serve him in the spiritual realm rebelled against him.[8] Their rebellion did not mean they were no longer part of that world or that they became something other than what they were. They are still spiritual beings. Rather, rebellion affected (and still characterizes) their disposition toward, and relationship to, Yahweh.

Beyond these ontological terms, it is helpful to group terms describing evil spirits in the Old Testament. These can be broadly categorized as: (1) terms that are associated with the realm of the dead and its inhabitants; (2) terms that denote geographical dominion of supernatural powers in rebellion against Yahweh; and (3) preternatural creatures associated with idolatry and unholy ground. The vocabulary explored in these categories derives from the divine rebellions described in the early chapters of Genesis.

It is important to note that the vocabulary for evil spirits in the Old Testament appears to have no unifying principle. Recognizing and understanding the supernatural nature of what unfolds in Genesis 3; 6:1–4; and 11:1–9 (compare Deut 32:8–9) provides the framework for how Old Testament writers thought about the unseen spirit world and its relationship to the terrestrial world.[9] We will also need to consider the matter of "pseu-

---

7. The term *'elōhîm*, while morphologically plural, is used over two thousand times in the Hebrew Bible to describe the singular God of Israel. This is not unique to the Hebrew Bible. For example, the Amarna tablets, written in Akkadian, use the morphologically plural *'ilāni* ("gods") to address the singular pharaoh of Egypt. For some discussion, see Aubrey R. Johnson, *The One and the Many in the Israelite Conception of God* (Eugene, OR: Wipf & Stock, 2006), 24; Walter Eichrodt, *Theology of the Old Testament*, vol. 1 (Philadelphia: Westminster John Knox, 1961), 185.

8. We will examine those rebellions and how the supernatural rebels are differentiated in Scripture in Section II of the present study.

9. See chapters 3–7 of the present study.

do-demons" in the academic discussion of certain terms in the Hebrew Old Testament.

Terms Associated with the Realm of the Dead and Its Inhabitants

The coherence of this category extends from divine rebellions described in Genesis 3 (the fall) and Genesis 6:1–4 (the transgression of the sons of God). We must content ourselves at this point with cursory observations in that regard. The fall brought death to humankind. Its supernatural antagonist, described with the term *nāḥāš* ("serpent") in that passage, was cast down to *'ereṣ*, a term most often translated "earth" but which is also used for the domain of the dead (Jonah 2:6; Jer 17:13; Ps 71:20). Jonah 2:6 is especially instructive in this regard, in that the word *'ereṣ* is found in parallel with the term *šaḥat* ("pit"), a term frequently employed to speak of the grave or underworld (Job 33:18, 22, 24, 28, 30; Ps 30:9; Isa 51:14).

The most familiar evil supernatural figure in the biblical underworld is the serpent of Eden—known later, beginning in the Second Temple period, as "Satan." My wording here suggests that the serpent is never called "Satan" (*śāṭān*) in any verse of the Old Testament. That is, indeed, the case. The subject of why this is so, how the characterization of this figure developed, and how passages other than Genesis 3 contribute to a theology of this figure is very complicated and controversial, and it will be addressed in more detail later.[10]

The realm of the dead—that afterlife destination for all mortals—is referred to by a variety of terms in the Hebrew Old Testament, including *she'ôl* ("Sheol"; "the grave"), *māwet* ("death"), *'ereṣ* ("land [of the dead]"), and *bôr* ("pit").[11] As the realm of the disembodied dead, this place has no literal latitude and longitude. Nevertheless, the association of death with burial led biblical writers to describe the dead as "going down" (Heb. *y-r-d*) to that place (Num 16:30; Job 7:9; Isa 57:9). Lewis summarizes this conception: Sheol "represents the lowest place imaginable (Deut 32:22;

---

10. See chapters 3–4 and 9.

11. The term "Sheol" is used the most frequently, "occurring some 66 times" (Theodore J. Lewis, "Dead, Abode of the," *ABD* 2:101).

Isa 7:11) often used in contrast with the highest heavens (Amos 9:2; Ps 139:8; Job 11:8)."[12]

In Old Testament theology this realm was populated by spirit inhabitants in addition to the disembodied human dead. While the Old Testament credits God with sovereign oversight over the dead and the power to raise the dead, the realm of the dead is not equated with the presence of God. In fact, the domain of God (the "heavens") was *opposite*, far above, that of the dead. It was the hope of the righteous to be removed from the underworld. Consequently, these nonhuman residents of Sheol were understandably perceived as sinister and fearful.[13]

1. "Rephaim" (*rěpā'îm*)[14]

As Lewis has noted, "A great deal of literature has been written on the nature of the Rephaim especially since the publication of Ugaritic texts where they are mentioned extensively."[15] The biblical conception of the *rěpā'îm* was related to, but differed from, their characterization (*rp'um*) at ancient Ugarit.

The English Standard Version renders *rěpā'îm* as "giants," "shades" (meaning "spirits of the dead"), or "the dead," depending on context (see,

---

12. Lewis, "Dead, Abode of the," *ABD* 2:102. On the connections between Sheol and the physical grave, Lewis adds: "Sheol is intimately connected with the grave, although the degree to which it is identified with the grave has been debated. On one extreme we have those who see the grave behind every reference to Sheol, while on the other extreme Sheol and the grave are kept totally separate" (103).

13. The nature of the Old Testament afterlife (positive and negative) is a matter of scholarly debate. For a recent overview of the topic, see Philip S. Johnston, *Shades of Sheol: Death and Afterlife in the Old Testament* (Downers Grove, IL: IVP Academic, 2002). I am on the side that argues that biblical writers had a positive view of the afterlife for the righteous—that, though all mortals wind up in Sheol, the righteous hoped for removal from it to be with their Lord. Sheol was perceived as oppositional to the presence of God. It is the realm of death, not life. To be in the presence of the Lord was life, not death. While God is not prevented from being in Sheol (or any place), it is not his abode. That is, there is biblical evidence that the righteous hoped to be with the Lord upon death—they did not presume there was no positive alternative to the cadaverous existence in the underworld. Any view that seeks to exclusively equate Sheol with a generic realm of the dead and argue that biblical writers had no view of the positive afterlife must demonstrate that Sheol was the home of Yahweh in the Old Testament mind. For further discussion, see Michael S. Heiser, "Old Testament Theology of the Afterlife," in *Faithlife Study Bible* (Bellingham, WA: Lexham Press, 2012, 2016).

14. This Hebrew term is often translated "the dead" (ESV: Job 26:5; Prov 21:16) or "the shades" (ESV: Isa 14:12; 26:19) in English Bibles. We will use the transliterated term here. For more information on the Rephaim, see Michael S. Heiser, "Rephaim," *LBD*.

15. Lewis, "Dead, Abode of the," 103–4. See his article for textual references in the Ugaritic material. Cho points out that at Ugarit, due to their clear association with the underworld, the *Rapi'uma* are "warrior deities or divinized dead kings," pointing out that some scholars regard them as "minor gods who serve the higher gods." See Sang Youl Cho, *Lesser Deities in the Ugaritic Texts and the Hebrew Bible: A Comparative Study of Their Nature and Roles* (Piscataway, NJ: Gorgias Press, 2008), 218–19.

e.g., 1 Chr 20:4; Isa 26:14; and Job 26:5, respectively). This variation in translation highlights the main interpretive difficulty surrounding the term: were the Rephaim humans (whether living or dead), quasi-divine beings, or disembodied spirits? Biblical usage ranges across all of these possibilities while extrabiblical sources like the Ugaritic tablets do not present the Rephaim as giants. The Ugaritic *rp'um* are clearly divine residents of the underworld. The term *rp'um* occurs in parallel to *'ilnym* ("underworld gods") and *'ilm* ("gods"), and other tablets place the *rp'um* in the underworld.[16] The English translation of *rĕpā'îm* as "shades" captures the "otherworldly, shadowy nature of the living-dead residents of the underworld."[17]

For the purposes of the present study, the point to be made is that the biblical Rephaim are supernatural residents of the underworld, a place in the spiritual plane of reality dissociated with the presence of God.[18] To

---

16. The parallel usage is in *KTU* 1.6 vi:45–49. Texts that place the Rephaim in the underworld include *KTU* 1.20–22; *KTU* 1.108; *KTU* 1.161.

17. Michael S. Heiser, "Rephaim," *LBD*, n.p. Elsewhere in this article I note: "Scholars believe the most likely Semitic root for *repha'im* is רפא (*rp'*). This is the consensus despite the transparent links between the term and Hebrew רפה (*rph*). For example, in 2 Sam 21:16–22, Goliath is linked to other giants, other "descendants of the giants" (ESV; the latter term in Hebrew being הָרָפָה, *haraphah*). However, in the parallel account in 1 Chr 20:6–8, the term rendered 'giants' is הָרָפָא (*harapha'*). This makes clear that, at least for these biblical writers, רפא (*rp'*) and רפה (*rph*) were alternate spellings of the same root."

Note that the Hebrew root *r-p-'* means "to heal" in the vast majority of instances where it is used in Old Testament Hebrew. According to Michael L. Brown, the root *r-p-'* "occurs 67 times in verbal conjugations … and 19 times in derived nominal forms" (Brown, "I Am the Lord, Your Healer": A Philological Study of the Root RAPA' in the Hebrew Bible and the Ancient Near East" [PhD diss., New York University, 1985], 37). While most scholars accept the root *r-p-'* as underlying *rĕpā'îm*, the connection does not help us determine the meaning of Rephaim in the Bible. Brown asks the obvious questions that seem to have evaded others: Are there any biblical, Ugaritic, or other Northwest Semitic texts that cast the Rephaim/*rp'um* as healers? Was the Canaanite deity *rāpiu* a healer? The answer to both questions is no (Brown, "I Am the Lord, Your Healer," 124–27).

Aubrey Johnson offers one of the more coherent discussions of the alternative roots for *rĕpā'îm* (Johnson, *The Vitality of the Individual in the Thought of Ancient Israel* [Cardiff: University of Wales, 1964], 89). While noting the uncertainty of the Ugaritic material, Johnson first discusses Biblical Hebrew *rph* as an option. Among the glosses offered in the *Hebrew and Aramaic Lexicon of the Old Testament [HALOT]* for the verb *rph* are "to grow slack," "wither, collapse," and "to slacken, let loose" (*HALOT*, s.v. רפה). Other sources include "sink down" as a possible gloss (*TWOT*, s.v. רָפָה). Since ancient Israel, along with other surrounding cultures, considered the dead inhabitants of the underworld to still be experiencing some sort of subterrestrial life, the rationale for this root as the basis for *rĕpā'îm* is that the term denotes "weakness or loss of energy" (Johnson, *Vitality of the Individual*, 89). This would aptly describe the cadaverous existence of life in the underworld; passages like Job 26:5 describe the dead (*rĕpā'îm*) beneath the surface of the cosmic waters under the earth, sinking listlessly in the realm of the dead.

18. The Rephaim are further associated with the underworld in less obvious ways. For example, the geographical area that includes Oboth and Abarim in the Transjordan (Num 21:10–11; 33:43–48)

remain in that place was to be separated from life with God. That idea is evident in passages like Proverbs 21:16: "One who wanders from the way of good sense [i.e., one who is a fool, defined in Scripture as a wicked person or unbeliever] will rest in the assembly of the dead [rĕpā'îm]." The fool misled by the wicked woman Folly into keeping company with her in her home "does not know that the dead [rĕpā'îm] are there, that her guests are in the depths of Sheol" (Prov 9:18).

It is noteworthy that, unlike the material from Ugarit, the Old Testament at times uses the term rĕpā'îm for the giant clans of the days of Moses and Joshua. Og, king of Bashan, was said to be the last vestige of the Rephaim (Deut 3:11, 13; Josh 12:4; 13:12). The Rephaim are linked to the Anakim in Deuteronomy 2:10–11: "The Emim formerly lived there, a people great and many, and tall as the Anakim. Like the Anakim, they are also counted as Rephaim." According to Numbers 13:33, the Anakim were "from the Nephilim." As we will see in chapters 5 and 6, biblical writers saw the origin of the Nephilim as extending from the rebellion of divine "sons of God" (Gen 6:1–4) before the flood. This became the basis for the Jewish theology of the origin of demons in the Second Temple era.[19] Consequently there is a dark, sinister element to the Israelite conception of the Rephaim as inhabitants of the underworld.[20] The literature and religion of ancient Ugarit lacked a divine rebellion story comparable to Genesis 6:1–4. That element is at the heart of the divergence between Ugarit and the Old Testament with respect to the Rephaim.

---

was associated with ancient cults of the dead. These place names mean, respectively, "spirits of the dead" and "those who have passed over [to the Netherworld]" (K. Spronk, "Travellers," *DDD* 876–77). See the discussion of these terms below under "Spirits" on pages 15–17.

19. Genesis 6:1–4 was a theological polemic against the tale of the *apkallu* in Mesopotamian religion. In both the biblical and Mesopotamian material, the divine offenders whose rebellion produced quasi-divine giants are consigned to the underworld as punishment. Second Temple Jewish texts draw on both traditions as the explanation for the origin of demons. New Testament writers were familiar with these Second Temple sources, as well as the classical Greek story of the Titans and the giants. This matrix of texts and ideas are the wellspring from which Peter and Jude draw their theology of "angels that sinned" in the New Testament (2 Pet 2:4–5; Jude 6).

20. This is why it is incorrect to say, as many do, that the Old Testament has no conception of a terrifying afterlife. It is true that the idea of hell—a place designed for punishment of the wicked—is not systematically presented in the Old Testament. But later notions, such as that found in the first century, that there was a place "prepared for the devil and his angels" (Matt 25:41) connects the realm of death with supernatural rebels. While the data points for the idea of hell are not connected in the Old Testament, the data points are nevertheless to be found there. Later Judaism is not contriving the idea.

2. "Death" (*māwet/mōt*)

Since a connection between the realm of the dead and death is obvious, it should be no surprise that death is at times personified in the Old Testament. The less-obvious point is the inclusion in the ancient Canaanite pantheon of the deity known as Mōt ("Death").[21]

Some Old Testament passages referring to death have "mythological overtones in texts which could, however, be read in a totally demythologised way."[22] In Canaanite mythology, Mōt is depicted as "a voracious consumer of gods and men" with an enormous appetite who "dwells in the underworld, which is an unpleasant (muddy) place of decay and destruction."[23]

The observation about Mōt being "demythologised" is appropriate.[24] The biblical writers did not have a "god of death" distinct from Yahweh. Life and death were the purview of the true God alone (Deut 32:39; 1 Sam 2:6; 2 Kgs 5:7). Death (*mōt*) was under the authority of Yahweh. Nevertheless, biblical writers drew on broad Semitic notions that there was a spirit entity who was lord over the realm of the dead. God may sovereignly send someone to the underworld, but certain texts put forth the idea that the dead would be under the authority of its master.[25]

---

21. Some scholars associate Mōt (personified "Death") with the "King of Terrors" (*mlk blhwt*) of Job 18:14 since the preceding verse contains the line "firstborn of death" (Job 18:13). As Rüterswörden notes, the identification is controversial and depends in large part on whether there is an ancient Near Eastern background for "firstborn of death" as a supernatural entity. Efforts have been made to identify the phrases with Mesopotamian Namtar, god of plague and pestilence, Nergal, the god of the Netherworld, and Mōt from the Canaanite pantheon. All these approaches have significant problems. See U. Rüterswörden, "King of Terrors," *DDD* 486–88. It should also be noted that neither the term *mashḥît* ("destroyer") nor *mal'akê rā'îm* ("angels of destruction") are cast by Old Testament writers as denizens of the underworld or evil spirits. Rather, though signifying supernatural agents of plague and death (Ps 78:48–49), they are loyal members of the heavenly host sent to judge the wicked. A good case can be made that the *mashḥît* of Passover's judgment is Yahweh himself as the angel of Yahweh. See Heiser, *Unseen Realm*, 150–52; Heiser, *Angels*, 65–68.

22. J. F. Healey, "Mot," *DDD* 599.

23. Ibid.

24. Some scholars use this term to propose that biblical writers, in some sort of religious epiphany, came to deny the existence of all other divine beings besides Yahweh. This proposition is not coherent. See Heiser, "Monotheism, Polytheism, Monolatry, or Henotheism," 1–30; Heiser, "Does Divine Plurality in the Hebrew Bible Demonstrate an Evolution from Polytheism to Monotheism in Israelite Religion?" *JESOT* 1.1 (2012): 1–24; Heiser, "Monotheism and the Language of Divine Plurality in the Hebrew Bible and the Dead Sea Scrolls," *TynBul* 65.1 (2014): 85–100. Another perspective of "de-mythologizing" is to acknowledge that biblical writers stripped foreign deities of autonomy or independent personality without denying their existence. This describes the situation with Mōt.

25. Healey ("Mot," 601) summarizes how the biblical writers accomplished this portrayal: "Death appears, for example, in a personified guise in Hos 13:14: 'Shall I ransom them (Ephraim) from the power of Sheol? Shall I redeem them from Death? Death, where are your plagues? Sheol, where is

The Old Testament does not specifically associate death with the serpent figure or the term *śāṭān*. The New Testament's reference to the devil having "the power of death" (Heb 2:14) does have roots in Canaanite (and Israelite) thought. In Canaanite religion, the sons of El must fight for the position of coregent with their father. In the Baal Cycle, Mōt initially conquers Baal, so Baal appears to be dead. However, Baal revives and conquers Mōt. "Prince Baal" (Ugaritic: *ba'al zebul*) ascends to the coregency and becomes lord of the underworld in the process. This Canaanite title is the backdrop for Beelzebul, a name for Satan/the devil in the New Testament.[26]

An important idea extends from Mōt's vanquishing of Baal. The latter deity was a storm god and, as such, the bringer of rain, which in turn sustained life and made the land fertile.[27] This meant that Mōt was associated with the opposite—the barren, desert wilderness, which itself was a metaphor of the realm of the dead.[28] In his detailed study of the wilderness motif, Alston observes,

> There is considerable evidence in the Old Testament that an intimate relationship exists between the concept of the "wilderness" and that

your destruction?' Here the personification is very clear, but there is no need to assume a mythological overtone or to rule it out. … In other texts there is mention of specific characteristics of Death which have some sort of parallel in the picture of Mot painted by the Ugaritic texts. Thus in Hab 2:5 the insatiability of personified Death is mentioned ('whose greed is as wide as Sheol, and like Death he is never satisfied'). … The same idea, though applied to a personified Sheol, is found in Isa 5:14 ('Therefore Sheol has enlarged its appetite, and opened its mouth beyond measure': and cf. Prov 1:12; 27:20; 30:15–16; Ps 141:7). … Isa 25:8 on the other hand has Yahweh swallowing up Death and this indicates more clearly a parallel with Canaanite mythology: normally it was Mot who did the swallowing, but in this case Yahweh makes nonsense of the law of Canaanite myth by himself swallowing the swallower. … Another case in which there is a close parallel with the Ugaritic texts is Ps 49:15, which says of the over-confident: 'Like sheep they are appointed for Sheol; Death shall be their shepherd; straight to the grave they descend.' Here we have Death leading people into Sheol and this reflects the way the Ugaritic texts convey the idea that it is necessary to beware of Mot, since he can entrap the innocent and is specifically mentioned as consuming sheep (*KTU* 1.4 viii: 17–20)."

26. J. C. de Moor and M. J. Mulder, "בַּעַל (ba'al) ("lord")," *TDOT* 2:194. For Baal as *zbl* ("prince") in Ugaritic texts, see *KTU* 1.5.VI:9–10; 1.6.I:41–43; 1.6.III:2–3, 8–9, 20–21; 1.6.IV:4–5, 15–16; 1.9:18; 1. Mulder and de Moor write: "*Baal-zebub* is mentioned as the god of the Philistine city of Ekron (2 K. 1:2f., 6, 16). The only discernible function of this deity is that of giving advice and help in cases of illness or injury. Baal-zebub ("lord of the flies") is probably a deliberate distortion of *b'l zbl* or *zbl b'l*" (194). More will be said about Baal-zebul and Baal-zebub in relation to Beelzebul later in our study. As was noted earlier, while the data points for the later idea of hell are not connected in the Old Testament, the data points are nevertheless present. See Charles F. Fensham, "A Possible Explanation of the Name Baal-Zebub of Ekron," *ZAW* 79.3 (1967): 361–64 (esp. 363).

27. Daniel Schwemer, "The Storm Gods of the Ancient Near East: Summary, Synthesis, Recent Studies: Part II," *Journal of Ancient Near Eastern Religions* 8.1 (2008): 8–16.

28. See the ensuing discussion for more on the wilderness association with evil spirits.

of the primordial chaos … that part of reality which cares not for human life and provides not for its sustenance, posing instead the constant threat of extinction.[29]

More specific to Mōt ("Death"), Talmon notes, "In Ugaritic myth it is Mot, the god of all that lacks life and vitality, whose 'natural habitation is the sun-scorched desert, or alternatively, the darkling region of the netherworld.'"[30]

There are other terms in the Old Testament for spirits who reside in the realm of the dead with the *rĕpā'îm*. If the hope of the righteous was removal from Sheol to everlasting life with God, then by definition those left to remain in Sheol would abide there with the evil spirits, whose underworld residency is traced to supernatural rebellion.[31] The underworld was therefore quite logically a place where spirits of the wicked human dead and supernatural evil spirits would be found.

3. "Spirits" (*'ôb*; plural: *'ōbôt*, also *'ōbĕrîm* ["those who have passed over"])

Some of the terminology for these fearful spirits derives from place names. For example, the geographical area that includes Oboth and Abarim in the Transjordan (Num 21:10–11; 33:43–48) was associated with ancient cults of the dead. These two place names mean, respectively, "spirits of the dead" and "those who have passed over [to the Netherworld]."[32] The Hebrew root '-b-r, behind the name Abarim, means "to cross over [from one side to another]," so the Qal participle *'ōbĕrîm* means "those who cross over."

Spronk notes that this participle "seems to have a special meaning in the context of the cult of the dead, denoting the spirits of the dead crossing the border between the land of the living and the world of the dead."[33] The Ugaritic parallels make this association clearly. The Ugaritic cognate of *'ōbĕrîm* is *'brm* found in *KTU*[2] 1.22 i:15.

---

29. Wallace M. Alston, "The Concept of the Wilderness in the Intertestamental Period" (ThD diss., Union Theological Seminary in Virginia, 1968), 2–3.

30. Talmon quotes Gaster here. Shemaryahu Talmon, "The 'Desert Motif' in the Bible and in Qumran Literature," in *Biblical Motifs: Origins and Transformations*, vol. 3, ed. Alexander Altmann (Cambridge: Harvard University Press, 1966), 31–64 (esp. 43).

31. See chapters 5 and 6.

32. Spronk, "Travellers," 876–77.

33. Spronk, "Travellers, 876.

In the Ugaritic text *KTU*² 1.22 describing a necromantic session, the king invokes the spirits of the dead (Rephaim) and celebrates a feast, probably the New Year Festival, with them. It is told that they came over traveling by horse-drawn chariots. As they are taking part in the meal served for them, they are explicitly called "those who came over."[34]

The geographical associations with ʿōbĕrîm are evident in Ezekiel 39:11, which indicates the "Valley of the Travelers [ʿōbĕrîm]" is "east of the sea" (ESV). According to Spronk, the sea "is probably the Dead Sea. So it was part of Transjordan. This is a region which shows many traces of ancient cults of the dead, such as the megalithic monuments called dolmens and place names referring to the dead and the netherworld, viz. Obot, Peor, and Abarim."[35]

The Hebrew term "Oboth" (ʾōbôt) likewise has an otherworldly overtone and is associated with the spirits of the dead and those who worked to communicate with those departed spirits. Tropper explains that ʾôb is now more commonly understood to refer to the spirits of the dead, deriving the meaning from the Arabic cognate ʾāba, "return."[36] Other possible etymologies suggest interpreting ʾôb "as 'hostile' (a derivation of the root ʾyb 'to be an enemy'); or as 'ancestral.'"[37] According to Tropper, those who argue for the meaning "ancestral"

> assume an etymological connection between ʾôb and ʾāb "father, ancestor". The meaning "ancestral spirit" for ʾôb is based on a number of considerations. In the ancient Orient, necromancy was part of the Cult of the Ancestors. This essentially involved the invocation and interrogation of the dead patriarch from whom a family could seek advice and assistance. Several times in the OT, the Heb term ʾābôt "fathers", similar to ʾōbôt, designates dead ancestors.[38]

Certain places removed from Canaan, the Holy Land, like Oboth and Abarim, were deemed the destination of those who have passed over to

---

34. Ibid.
35. Ibid.
36. J. Tropper, "Spirit of the Dead," *DDD* 807.
37. Ibid.
38. Ibid. Clearly, to say that the Old Testament has no concept of a threatening afterlife fails to do justice to the data.

the realm of the dead.[39] The reference to the "cult of the dead" or "ancestor cults" is an important aspect of an Old Testament theology of evil spirits. The realm of the dead was filled with the spirits of the human wicked and other evil supernatural spirits. In addition to *'ôb* ("spirit"; pl: *'ōbôt*) and *'ōběrîm* ("those who have passed over"), members of that fearful, motley assembly went by various terms associated with ongoing contact with the living.

4. "Knowing One" (*yiddě 'ōnî*)

Deuteronomy 18:9–14 lists a number of "abominable practices" forbidden to Israelites. One prohibition is utilizing the services of *šō 'ēl 'ôb wě-yiddě 'ōnî* (literally, "one who inquires of a spirit or a knowing one"; Deut 18:11).[40] The term *yiddě 'ōnî* (from *y-d-*', "to know") means "knowing (one)" and occurs eleven times, always with the term *'ôb*.

English translations at times render this word as "medium," which obscures something of note about its meaning. Several passages clearly have the terms referring to the spirit entities being channeled, not to the human channeler. Passages in Leviticus illustrate the point:

> Do not turn to the spirits [*'ôbôt*], to the ones who have knowledge [*yiddě 'ōnî*]; do not seek them out, and so make yourselves unclean by them: I am Yahweh your God. (Lev 19:31)

> If a person turns to the spirits [*'ôbôt*], to those who have knowledge [*yiddě 'ōnî*], whoring after them, I will set my face against that person and will cut him off from among his people. (Lev 20:6)

> A man or a woman who has a spirit [*'ôb*] or knowing one [*yiddě 'ōnî*] in them shall surely be put to death. They shall be stoned with stones; their blood shall be upon them. (Lev 20:27)[41]

The point made here should not escape the reader. While *yiddě 'ōnî*, "knowing (one)," and *'ôb* may at times be used of human mediums, the

---

39. This belief is very likely behind the strange New Testament passage that has the devil fighting with Michael for the body of Moses (Jude 9). For a discussion of that passage, see Heiser, *Angels*, 122–23.

40. The literal rendering is the author's. I take the conjunctive *waw* as "or" due to the use of *'ô* (Heb. "or") in other passages where these terms occur in tandem (Lev 20:27).

41. These three translations are the author's.

failure to note that they also refer specifically to supernatural entities results in missing Old Testament terminology for evil spirits.[42]

5. "The Dead" (*mētîm*)

We can now look at the rest of Deuteronomy 18:11. It contains another term relevant to our study. Israelites were forbidden the services of "one who inquires of a spirit or a knowing one or one who inquires of the dead [*mētîm*]." The word *mētîm* is distinguished from the two preceding terms. Isaiah 8:19, the only other passage where *mētîm* occurs with *yiddĕʿōnî* and *ʾōb*, could be read that way, but it could also be understood as associating the terms:

> And when they say to you, "Inquire of the spirits [*ʾōbôt*] and the knowing ones [*yiddĕʿōnî*] who chirp and who mutter," should not a people inquire of their God? Should they inquire of the dead [*mētîm*] on behalf of the living?[43]

The term *mētîm* could therefore be a distinct reference to spirit entities in the realm of the dead or perhaps a subset of *yiddĕʿōnî* and *ʾōb*. The latter choice would still allow the term to retain distinctiveness.

I raise the semantic issue for a reason. Hebrew *mētîm* with definite article (as in the two verses above) occurs twelve times.[44] In all instances where the context does not have divination in view, the clear reference is dead human beings (Num 17:13–14; 25:9; Judg 16:30; Ruth 1:8; 2:20; Ps 115:17; Eccl 4:2; 9:3). The two passages from Ecclesiastes have the afterlife dead in view. I suggest, then, that *mētîm* in passages forbidding divinatory contact refer specifically to the disembodied spirits of dead people as opposed to nonhuman supernatural spirits. This must be the case as well for reasons of logic. It would make sense that "the dead" refers to human beings who have died, for all humans die. The same idea is not applicable to nonhuman spirit beings. There is nothing in the Bible to

---

42. Examples where these terms are used of the human conduits would include 1 Sam 28:3, 9, where *ʾōbôt* and *yiddĕʿōnî* are both marked accusative objects of the verb *k-r-t* ("cut off"). Saul could not "cut off" spirit entities through any ability of his own, and so he must have the human conduits in view. There are other phrases that have the human conduit in focus, such as *ʾēshet baʿalat ʾōb* ("mistress of the spirit"; i.e., a female medium) in 1 Sam 28:7.

43. The translation is the author's.

44. The definite article is the word "the," expressed in Hebrew most often as *ha-*. For example, *ha-mētîm* = "*the* dead" as opposed to merely "dead," which could be construed in various ways. "The dead" refers to dead humans whose spirits have now passed over to the realm of the dead.

indicate a belief that spirits had determinate lifespans.[45] Their demise would take a specific decision from their creator (Ps 82:6–7).[46] Consequently, a term like 'ôbôt may refer to either kinds of disembodied spirit, but mētîm speaks of the human dead in the underworld.[47]

6. "Hidden One" (ḥabî; ḥebyôn)

Our final terms (ḥabî and the related ḥebyọn) are indeed obscure, occurring only two times in the Old Testament. In both instances the meaning of each term is debated. Nevertheless, both have importance for the development of the underworld and a devil figure in subsequent Jewish thinking.

Isaiah 26:20 reads as follows in the ESV:

45. As I have discussed elsewhere, heavenly spirits (in rebellion or not) share God's attributes as his imagers. There is, in biblical theology, only one eternal being—God—who is the source of all other things, visible and invisible, in the heavens or on earth (Col 1:15–16). This means that "[Spirit beings] are not 'timeless' in the sense of being eternal beings. They had a beginning as created beings. They are immortal (Luke 20:36), but that immortality is ultimately contingent, based on God's authority and pleasure" (Heiser, Angels, 170).

46. As we will see in chapters 7 and 11, the judgment in Psalm 82 is eschatological (cp. Isa 24:21–24; 34:1–5) and applies very specifically to one group of supernatural rebels.

47. As Kennedy notes, "There is abundant evidence for cults of the dead in the pagan world that surrounded Israel. ... Whether a cult of the dead existed in Israel is more problematic" (Charles A. Kennedy, "Dead, Cult of the," ABD 2:106). The term "cult" can be confusing. Its use in this context refers to the practice of leaving offerings of food and drink for the departed dead—i.e., ritual/religious acts that presume the ongoing life of the dead in Sheol. Leaving flowers or favorite objects at a grave is perhaps a useful analogy, though in ancient Israel there would have been more religious significance to the act. Much of the debate focuses on archaeological data (e.g., tombs that have structural features like chapels for food and drink offerings). Textual evidence from the Hebrew Bible for an ancestor cult is scant. Kennedy writes: "In Judg 17:5 an 'ēpôd and tĕrāpîm are installed in a family shrine at which the son will serve as priest, a combination of factors that strongly suggests an ancestral memorial. The tĕrāpîm were ancestral images that could be life-size (1 Sam 19:13) or as small as a mask. Rachel's theft of the tĕrāpîm (Gen 19:31) is interpreted as her way of maintaining a controlling influence in her family's affairs. ... Food offerings to the dead are specifically condemned (Deut 26:14; Ps 106:28) and yet there are biblical narratives describing family shrines and yearly sacrifices for all the family (1 Sam 20:6). That David can use this excuse to leave Saul's table at the time of the new moon suggests that family sacrifices were more highly regarded than royal feasts" ("Dead, Cult of the," 106–7). That food offerings for the dead are clearly condemned tells us at least that some Israelites engaged in the practice. It also seems clear that funeral banquets involving some sort of "communion" with the dead were also disallowed (Jer 16:5–8; Ezek 43:7–9), likely because such things were similar to death cult practices of pagan religions, such as invoking the Rephaim to mime the dynastic death cult of Ugarit. See Theodore J. Lewis, "Ancestor Worship," ABD 1:241; Baruch A. Levine and Jean-Michel de Tarragon, "Dead Kings and Rephaim: The Patrons of the Ugaritic Dynasty," Journal of the American Oriental Society 104.4 (1984): 649–59. David's excuse is, however, not condemned (1 Sam 20:6). Godly Israelites would have avoided, on the basis of passages like Deut 18:11, contacting the dead for divinatory purposes, but it is an open question as to whether food and drink offerings were disallowed in totality. When an Israelite participated in such things, the act should not be necessarily be interpreted as an attempt to contact a wicked disembodied human spirit for idolatrous or nefarious purposes.

Come, my people, enter your chambers,
and shut your doors behind you;
hide yourselves [*ḥabî*] for a little while
until the fury has passed by.

On the basis of an Ugaritic parallel, Cyrus Gordon proposed that *ḥabî* ought to be understood as a divine name.[48] Xella notes that one Ugaritic text (*KTU* 1.114:19–20) refers to a figure called *ḥby* (likely a divine name here) and describes the figure as possessing horns and a tail:

> This difficult text deals with the *marzēaḥ* of the god El and with his drunkenness. … The Father of the gods, full of wine, has an infernal vision and sees this *ḥby*, a divine or demonic entity, who perhaps soils him with his excrements and urine. El's condition is that of the dead in the Netherworld and this may suggest that *ḥby* is here a chthonic deity. It is not unlikely that this personage, who appears to El in an alcoholic trance during a feast related to the cult of the dead, is really an infernal god; horns and tail may allude to his bovine/ taurine form.[49]

The *marzēaḥ* of Ugaritic was part of the Ugaritic cult of the dead, "a feast for and with departed ancestors."[50] This provides a context for Xella and other scholars to see *ḥby* as a chthonic or infernal deity, meaning a deity related to the underworld.[51] That Ugaritic *ḥby* also has horns and

---

48. C. H. Gordon, "The Devil, ḥby," *Newsletter for Ugaritic Studies* 33 (1985): 15; Gordon, "ḤBY: Possessor of Horns and Tail," *Ugarit Forchungen* 18 (1986): 129–32.

49. P. Xella, "Haby," *DDD* 377.

50. Lewis, "Ancestor Worship," 240–41. Amos 6:4–7 contains a reference to the feast. For brief discussion, see Bruce E. Willoughby, "Amos, Book of," *ABD* 1:209.

51. The horns and tail description have generated debate about the meaning of *ḥbî*. Gordon presumed that *ḥbî* corresponded to Ugaritic *ḥby*, which is considered by specialists to be a deity name. See *DULAT* 1:354; Pierre Bordreuil and Dennis Pardee, *A Manual of Ugaritic* (Winona Lake, IN.: Eisenbrauns, 2009), 314. This decision forced Gordon to juxtapose *ḥbî* with "wrath" (Heb. *za'am*) in Isa 26:20 for grammatical and syntactical coherence. Other scholars have noted that such a meaning does nothing to explicate the horns and tail. If *ḥbî* derives from Hebrew *ḥbh* it may also be translated "hidden (one)" (*HALOT*, s.v. אבה), in which case the meaning would not be "invisible" (cf. the horns and tail), but a deity seldom seen due to its abode in the realm of the dead. In his detailed study of the Ugaritic text *KTU* 1.114, Cathcart prefers "the crawler" on the basis of Arabic *ḥabā* ("to creep, crawl"), seeing in the horns and tail the pincers and tail of a crawling scorpion. See Kevin J. Cathcart, "Ilu, Yariḫu, and the One with the Two Horns and Tail," *Ugarit, Religion, and Culture: Essays Presented in Honour of John C. L. Gibson*, ed. N. Wyatt, W. G. E. Watson, and J. B. Lloyd (Münster: Ugarit-Verlag, 1996), 5. Cathcart goes on, citing Pardee, Liverani, and Xella, to further speculate that *ḥby* might be the Ugaritic counterpart to Egyptian *ḥpy* ("the [Apis] bull"). Apis was identified with Osiris, lord of the dead, in Egyptian religion. In a different article, Cathcart and Watson also propose "the embracer"

a tail has prompted some scholars to see a conceptual precursor to the devil of later Jewish and Christian thought.[52]

Habakkuk 3:4 is another Old Testament text that factors into this discussion. The preceding and following verses are relevant to the rationale used by some scholars in the interpretation of verse 4:

> [3] God came from Teman,
>   and the Holy One from Mount Paran. *Selah*
> His splendor covered the heavens,
>   and the earth was full of his praise.
> [4] His brightness was like the light;
>   rays [*qarnayim*] flashed from his hand;
> and there he veiled [*ḥebyôn*] his power.
>   [5] Before him went pestilence,
> and plague followed at his heels.

The word translated "rays" in Habakkuk 3:4 (*qarnayim*) means "horns" elsewhere, literally in terms of parts of an animal's head (Gen 22:13), or figuratively for the edges of an object (1 Kgs 1:50). Gordon believed *qarnayim* in Habakkuk 3:4 should be rendered "horns" in part because the verse also references *ḥebyôn*, which he took to be the name of a Canaanite deity *ḥby*:

> And Brilliance shall be as the light; he has horns [*qarnayim*] from his hand; and there is Hebyôn. (Hab 3:4, author's translation)

Gordon's approach is not as far-fetched as it seems. As we will discuss below, Habakkuk 3:5 contains two terms that may well be Canaanite deities (*deber, rešep*). Nevertheless, other scholars are skeptical.[53] Despite the uncertainty, if these references do bear witness to an underworld denizen

---

(Kevin J. Cathcart and W. G. E. Watson, "Weathering a Wake: A Cure for Carousal: A Revised Translation of *Ugaritica V* text I," *Proceedings of the Irish Biblical Association* 4 [1980]: 35–58). Wyatt opts for "creeping monster" in his translation of the text (N. Wyatt, *Religious Texts from Ugarit: The Words of Ilimilku and his Colleagues* [Sheffield: Sheffield Academic Press, 1998], 411).

52. On Jewish and Christian writings that contribute to this portrayal, see Alexander Kulik, "How the Devil Got His Hooves and Horns: The Origin of the Motif and the Implied Demonology of 3 Baruch," *Numen* 60 (2013): 195–229.

53. Xella ("Haby," 377) cites Spronk's criticisms (K. Spronk, *Beatific Afterlife in Ancient Israel and in the Ancient Near East* [Neukirchen-Vluyn: Neukirchener Verlag, 1986], 199, note 4). Tsumura is likewise skeptical, at least with respect to Hab 3:4. He proposes the "horns" be understood as "rays" and translates: "The brightness shall be as the light; he has rays/horns from his hand, where his power is hidden." See David Toshio Tsumura, "Janus Parallelism in Hab 3:4," *VT* 54.1 (2004): 124–28.

conceptually akin to Mōt ("Death"), that figure (like Mōt) is not autono-mous. The infernal *ḥby* is on Yahweh's leash, subservient to his authority. He is therefore "demythologized" in terms of independent status.

Terms That Denote Entities with Geographical Dominion

1. "Territorial Spirits (Shedim; *šēdîm*)

As noted earlier, Deuteronomy 32:8 informs us that the division of human-ity into disparate nations at Babel occurred in tandem with allotting those nations to lesser *'elōhîm*, the "sons of God" (and vice versa). This event is the Old Testament explanation for the devolution from human-ity's corporate relationship with the true God to individual nations with rival pantheons. The "sons of God" of the Babel event are the gods of the nations in Old Testament theology (cf. Deut 4:19–20; 17:1–3; 29:23–26). The focus of Psalm 82 is the corruption of these *'elōhîm*. The *'elōhîm* being judged in council in Psalm 82:1 are called "sons of the Most High" in Psalm 82:6. In that context, Deuteronomy 32:17 provides us with an important term for consideration:

> They [the Israelites] sacrificed to demons [*šēdîm*] that were no gods [*'ělōah*], to gods [*'elōhîm*] they had never known.

Earlier passages in Deuteronomy show that the "sons of God" allot-ted to the nations in Deuteronomy 32:8 were considered gods (*'elōhîm*).[54] This is indicated as well by the use in Deuteronomy 32:17 of *'elōhîm* who are also called *šēdîm*.[55] The coupling of these two terms is consistent with related terms in other Semitic languages. The Balaam inscription of Deir-'Alla (line 5, combination I) refers to the *šaddayyîn* as *'ělāhîn* ("gods").[56] The Akkadian *šēdū(m)* is prefixed with the DINGIR sign, which marked

---

54. These *'elōhîm* were not merely idols, as a comparison of the "host of heaven" language in Deut 4:19–20; 17:3 with the "spirit" language of 1 Kgs 22:19–23 (part of the Deuteronomistic History) shows. On the reading "sons of God," see Michael S. Heiser, "Deuteronomy 32:8 and the Sons of God," *BSac* 158 (2001): 52–74; Jeffrey Tigay, *Deuteronomy* (JPS Torah Commentary; Philadelphia: Jewish Pub-lication Society, 1996), 513–17; Peter C. Craigie, *The Book of Deuteronomy* (NICOT; Grand Rapids: Eerdmans, 1976), 379.

55. Despite the clarity of the Hebrew text of Deut 32:17, the ESV creates an internal contradiction in the passage, perhaps to misguidedly protect readers from a presumed polytheism in the text. Deu-teronomy 32:17, when rendered correctly and understood in context, does not promote polytheism. There is no need to obscure the Hebrew text. See Heiser, "Does Deuteronomy 32:17 Assume or Deny the Reality of Other Gods," 137–45.

56. See "Deir 'Alla Plaster Text," in *The Aramaic Inscriptions*, ed. H. H. Hardy II and Charles Otte III (Bellingham, WA: Lexham Press, 2008).

divinity.[57] The Akkadian term provides the semantic nuance for our purposes, as *šēdū(m)* were perceived as territorial spirits.[58]

2. "Prince" (*śar*; plural: *śārîm*)

Daniel 8–12 is one of the more familiar Old Testament passages relating to Old Testament angelology. The angel Gabriel is mentioned twice (Dan 8:16; 9:21), while Michael is part of the narrative on three occasions (Dan 10:13, 21; 12:1). In three of the instances where Michael is mentioned, he is referred to as "prince" (*śar*). That he is not the only "angelic prince" is indicated by Daniel 10:13, where he is said to be "one of the chief princes."

The speaker who labels Michael thus is not explicitly identified, though his identity can be discerned from the context as a divine figure superior to Michael.[59] Since Michael assists this heavenly figure (Dan 8:4–6) in his conflict against "the prince of the kingdom of Persia" (Dan 10:13), it is clear that there are adversarial divine "princes" (*śārîm*) in biblical thought.

As I noted in *The Unseen Realm*, in concert with other scholars, the notion of hostile divine princes (i.e., evil territorial spirits) in Daniel 10 derives from the allotment of the nations in Deuteronomy 32:8–9 to lesser *'elōhîm*.[60] John Collins affirms this connection in his article on "Prince" (*śar*):

---

57. Frey-Anthes, "Concepts of 'Demons' in Ancient Israel," 42.

58. Frey-Anthes thinks that a problem exists in aligning the biblical *šēdîm* with the Akkadian *šēdu(m)* because "the [*šēdîm*] in the Old Testament have got a completely different function than the DINGIR *šēdu(m)* in Mesopotamia" (42). Unfortunately, Frey-Anthes never tells us what the presumed "function" of the biblical *šēdîm* was. Instead, noting Ps 106:37, the only other instance of the term in the Hebrew Bible, she refers to the biblical *šēdîm* as "bloodthirsty creatures that demand the sacrifice of children," a note that says nothing about the "function" of *šēdîm* (43). HALOT (s.v. שֵׁד) cites W. von Soden's *Akkadisches Handwörterbuch* (Wiesbaden: Harrassowitz, 1965–1981) and the *Chicago Assyrian Dictionary* (*CAD*) in support of its own identification. I suggest that the missing "function" Frey-Anthes seeks can be found in the *CAD*. According to the *CAD* entry, a *šēdu* was, generally, a guardian spirit (no. 1), but more particularly (no. 2) the guardian spirit of a temple, a palace, or a city (*CAD*, s.v. "šēdu A"). This aspect of territoriality fits quite well with the notion that, outside Yahweh's own possession, the land of Israel, other places were under the dominion of other *'elōhîm/ šēdîm*.

59. I take the speaker to be the "prince of the host" (Dan 8:11), who is later described as the "prince of princes" (Dan 8:25). See Heiser, *Angels*, 68–73.

60. Heiser, *Unseen Realm*, 118–19. This connection to Deut 32:8–9 is why scholars often refer to the princes of Daniel 10 as "patron angels" of the nations. The most complete recent scholarly survey of Michael in Jewish and Christian tradition is Darrell D. Hannah, *Michael and Christ: Michael Traditions and Angel Christology in Early Christianity* (Tübingen: Mohr Siebeck, 1999). See also Gillian Bampfylde, "The Prince of the Host in the Book of Daniel and the Dead Sea Scrolls," *Journal for the Study of Judaism in the Persian, Hellenistic, and Roman Periods* 14.2 (1983): 129–34; Benedikt Otzen, "Michael and Gabriel: Angelological Problems in the Book of Daniel," in *The Scriptures and*

The notion that different nations were allotted to different gods or heavenly beings was widespread in the ancient world. In Deut 32:8–9 we read that "When the Most High gave to the nations their inheritance, when he separated the sons of men, he fixed the bounds of the peoples according to the number of the sons of God". ... The origin of this idea is to be sought in the ancient Near Eastern concept of the Divine Council ... Sirach reaffirms Deuteronomy 32: "He appointed a ruler over every nation, but Israel is the LORD's own portion" (Sir 17:17; cf. Jub 15:31–32). In the *Animal Apocalypse* (*1 Enoch* 89:59) the angels or gods of the nations are represented by seventy shepherds, to whom Israel is handed over.[61]

Preternatural Creatures Associated with Idolatry and Unholy Ground

The supernatural outlook of Deuteronomy 32:8–9 contributed to the cosmic-geographical worldview of the biblical psyche. Ground not occupied by the presence of God—whether that meant the Israelite camp during the journey to Canaan or the temple in Jerusalem—was not holy ground. This could be an innocuous opposition. God's glory was "here but not there." One must maintain separation from some areas, but others would not be violated by human presence. But forbidding, uninhabitable places in lands associated with other gods were *unholy* in the sense of sinister and evil. This was especially true of the desert wilderness, whether literal or used metaphorically to describe places ravaged by divine judgment. As Alston notes, "Darkness [is] closely related to the concept of the wilderness. ... The mythical understanding of the wilderness is often denoted by the notion that it is the habitat of strange animals and hostile demons."[62]

1. "Azazel" (*ăzāzēl*); "He-Goats"/ "Goat Demons" (*śā ʿîr; śĕ ʿîrîm*)[63]

Leviticus 16 and its Day of Atonement (Yom Kippur) ritual is the backdrop for these fascinating terms.

---

the Scrolls: Studies in Honor of A. S. van der Woude on the Occasion of his 65th Birthday, ed. F. Garcia Martinez, A. Hilhorst, and C. J. Labuschagne (Leiden: Brill, 1992), 114–24.

61. John J. Collins, "Prince," *DDD* 663; see also Ronnie Goldstein, "A New Look at Deuteronomy 32:8–9 and 43 in the Light of Akkadian Sources," [Hebrew] *Tarbiz* 79.1 (2010): 5–21.

62. Alston, "The Concept of the Wilderness," 6–7.

63. Frey-Anthes objects to the term "goat demons" on the grounds that these creatures have no real powers that merit their being worshiped ("Concepts of 'Demons' in Ancient Israel," 47). Why

⁷And [Aaron] shall take the two goats, and he shall present them before Yahweh at the tent of assembly's entrance. ⁸Then Aaron shall cast lots for the two goats: one lot for Yahweh and one for Azazel. ⁹And Aaron shall present the goat on which the lot for Yahweh fell, and he shall sacrifice it as a sin offering.¹⁰But he must present alive before Yahweh the goat on which the lot for Azazel fell to make atonement for himself, to send it away into the desert to Azazel. (LEB)

Many English translations have "scapegoat" or "the goat that goes away" where the LEB reads "Azazel."⁶⁴ While the Hebrew *ăzāzēl* may be translated these ways, there are good reasons to opt for "Azazel" in the passage. The word *ăzāzēl* is actually a proper name. Leviticus 16:8–10 explains that one goat is designated *"for* Yahweh" and one *"for* Azazel." The parallel phrasing indicates that "Azazel" is a proper name here just like "Yahweh." But if Azazel is a proper name, then who is Azazel?

Azazel is regarded as the name of a demon in the Dead Sea Scrolls and other ancient Jewish books. In fact, in one scroll (4Q 180, 1:8) Azazel is the leader of the angels that sinned in Genesis 6:1–4. The same description appears in the book of 1 Enoch (8:1; 9:6; 10:4–8; 13:1; 54:5–6; 55:4; 69:2).⁶⁵

In his detailed study of the etymology of the name "Azazel," Hayim Tawil draws attention to ancient Near Eastern comparative evidence that makes considering Azazel a demonic entity comprehensible.⁶⁶ Specifically, Tawil explores Mesopotamian texts dealing with demons ("children

---

this matters isn't clear, especially since elsewhere in her article Frey-Anthes wants to deny "demonic" status to any term or entity for which there is no evidence of cult. Here, there is clear evidence of cult (Lev 17:7), but demonic status is denied because she sees no logic in an Israelite sacrificing to that cult. Requiring a cult for divine or "demonic" status is a specious criterion. Israelites had no cult for the *rĕpā'îm*, but it is clear they were thought to be sinister supernatural spirits of/from the underworld. Likewise Israelites believed in angels, and believed that some of them fell from holiness, but there is no biblical evidence that they worshiped them (fallen or holy). Cult was no prerequisite to believing in the existence of a supernatural being.

64. For example, NIV, NASB, KJV.

65. Heiser, *Unseen Realm*, 177. See also B. Janowski, "Azazel," *DDD* 128; Hayim Tawil, "'Azazel, the Prince of the Steepe: A Comparative Study," *ZAW* 92.1 (1980): 43–59; Dominic Rudman, "A Note on the Azazel Goat Ritual," *ZAW* 116.3 (2004): 396–401. Tawil notes that the notion that Azazel was a demon (or even Satan) was the dominant view "from the early Post Biblical period till the very late Midrashim ... [and] was likewise advocated by both medieval commentators, the rationalist Ibn-Ezra and the mysticist Ramban, respectively" (Tawil, "Azazel," 45–46).

66. Hanson also took note of some of this evidence in his work on 1 Enoch: P. D. Hanson, "Rebellion in Heaven, Azazel, and Euhemeristic Heroes in 1 Enoch 6–11," *JBL* 96 (1977): 221–22. Hanson's

of the netherworld") who were believed to exit the realm of the dead through holes and fissures in the earth.[67] Once in the world of the living, "demons and other powers of hostility most common dwelling place is the 'steepe-land' (Sumerian *EDIN* = Akkadian *ṣēru*) ... also to be understood as one of the symbolic designations of the netherworld."[68] Tawil cites numerous examples of this terminology to make the telling observation that certain magical rituals and incantations bear striking similarities to both the vocabulary in Leviticus 16 and Azazel passages in the Semitic (Ethiopic) text of 1 Enoch. Further, he traces the Sumerian-Akkadian netherworld language to the domain of Mōt, the god of death at Ugarit. Tawil's research establishes that both biblical vocabulary and later Second Temple Jewish discussion of Azazel were firmly rooted in early Mesopotamian material about demonic powers of darkness.[69]

The association of the desert wilderness as a place connected to the realm of the dead also lurks behind Leviticus 17:7: "So they shall no more sacrifice their sacrifices to goat demons, after whom they whore." This passage's immediate proximity to Leviticus 16 is striking. A conceptual connection seems evident:

> In the Day of Atonement ritual, the goat for Yahweh—the goat that was sacrificed—purges the impurities caused by the people of Israel and purifies the sanctuary. The goat for Azazel was sent away after the sins of the Israelites were symbolically placed on it.
>
> The point of the goat for Azazel was not that something was owed to the demonic realm, as though a ransom was being paid. The goat for Azazel banished the sins of the Israelites to the realm *outside*

---

discussion took note of the links between Akkadian magical texts and 1 Enoch 10's description of the binding of Azazel in connection with the ritual of the Day of Atonement.

67. Tawil, "'Azazel," 48–49.

68. Ibid., 49.

69. This sort of elucidation in Second Temple texts of a context for earlier biblical material arises out of familiarity that Second Temple writers had with Mesopotamian material. The connection to Hebrew content in Leviticus 16 suggests strongly that those responsible for the final form of the Torah during the Babylonian period were aware of the same Mesopotamian texts. As we will see in chapter 5, recovering the original context for Gen 6:1–4 follows the same path. Readers should note that just because the Mesopotamian content was lost upon modern commentators does not mean it was lost to ancient scribes. The clear linkages between certain Second Temple texts (e.g., 1 Enoch, the "Book of Giants") and Mesopotamian material that predated the Torah demonstrates that Second Temple writers were much more in tune with what was going on in these passages than scholars of modern eras who did not have access to the literature of Qumran and Mesopotamia.

Israel. ... The high priest was not sacrificing *to Azazel*. Rather, Azazel was getting what belonged to him: sin.[70]

Milgrom likewise notes the connection between demons and the wilderness in Mesopotamian thought and explains the relevance of that connection for understanding Azazel in Leviticus 16:

Elimination rites are therefore employed to drive the demons from human habitations and back to the wilderness, which is another way of saying that the demons are driven back to their point of origin. ... Thus, in Israel, the goat for Azazel bearing the sins of Israel, though it is bound for the wilderness, is in reality returning evil to its source, the netherworld.[71]

2. "Howling Creature" (*'iyyîm*); "Wild Beasts" (*ṣiyyîm*); "Lilith" (*lîlît*)
The terminology of this section will no doubt be unfamiliar and strange.[72] But to a culture that held the desert wilderness to be a place of frightful beings associated with the underworld, "the desert [was] populated by phantom-like creatures."[73] Frey-Anthes summarizes the association of wild, deserted places with perceived dark powers:[74]

The concept of a subdivided world which is present in the Old Testament texts leads to the idea of animals and not clearly definable creatures, who are the inhabitants of a counterworld to human civilisation. Included among the eerie and dangerous animals who haunt deserted places. ... The following are mostly called "desert-demons": Those who live in the ruins ... As the name of the [*ṣiyyîm*] explains where they dwell ("those who belong to the dry landscape/desert dwellers"), the expression [*'iyyîm*] has rather got an onomatopoeic nature, it defines a howling creature ("howler"). ... The pair [*'iyyîm*] and [*ṣiyyîm*] belongs to the description of a destroyed city in Isa 13:21f.; Isa 34:14 and Jer 50:39. ... The texts, however, speak of ghosts

---

70. Heiser, *Unseen Realm*, 177–78.

71. Jacob Milgrom, *Leviticus 1–16: A New Translation with Introduction and Commentary* (AYB; New Haven, CT: Yale University Press, 1991), 1072. See also M. Louise Holbert, "Extrinsic Evil Powers in the Old Testament" (ThM thesis, Fuller Theological Seminary, 1985), 124–29.

72. The terminology here is selective due to space constraints. Other lemmas associated with wild creatures in the passages considered could be added.

73. Talmon, "The 'Desert Motif,'" 43.

74. I have substituted transliteration (in brackets) for Hebrew in the excerpt.

living at the periphery but they avoid a clear identification, which would be needed for an incantation, to identify the evil forces it wants to drive away. The creatures are described ambiguously in order to underline the vagueness of the peripheral counterworld.[75]

Two of the passages noted above deserve some attention. In Isaiah 13:21–22, a description of the impending devastation of Babylon, the terms ṣiyyîm and 'iyyîm occur in tandem with the śě'îrîm (Isa 13:21) associated with illegitimate sacrifices in Leviticus 17:7 (cf. Deut 32:12). The same grouping is present in Isaiah 34:14, a passage that adds lîlît to the assemblage—the Hebrew spelling of the well-known Mesopotamian demon-goddess Lilith:[76]

> The "wind-demoness" Lilith, who can already be found in the Sumerian Epos "Gilgames, Enkidu and the Underworld" does not seem to have had any special importance outside Mesopotamia. Interpretations of supposed findings from Ugarit and Phoenicia are very uncertain. It is astonishing, however, that, according to Isa 34:14, Lilith belongs to the inhabitants of the counter world together with owls and other birds of prey, ostrich, jackals, snakes, desert dwellers, howlers and he-goats. The description of the ruins of Edom in Isa 34:11–15 is a subtly composed literary text with close connections to Isa 13,21f. and Jer 50,39, which are similar descriptions of the deserted Babylon. Isa 34,11–15 intensifies the descriptions of Isa 13,21f. and Jer 50,39 by listing the inhabitants of the periphery in a detailed way and by introducing Lilith.[77]

As Janowski notes, these terms could very naturally speak of "zoologically definable animals, i.e. nocturnal consumers of carrion, who appear in pairs or in packs," but "their association with theriomorphic demons

75. Frey-Anthes, "Concepts of 'Demons' in Ancient Israel," 43.

76. On Lilith as a goddess, see Jeremy Black and Anthony Green, *Gods, Demons and Symbols of Ancient Mesopotamia: An Illustrated Dictionary* (Austin: University of Texas-Austin, 2003), 118; D. R. West, *Some Cults of Greek Goddesses and Female Daemons of Oriental Origin Especially in Relation to the Mythology of Goddesses and Daemons in the Semitic World* (Neukirchen-Vluyn: Neukirchener Verlag, 1995), 126–27; M. Hutter, "Lilith," *DDD* 520.

77. Frey-Anthes, "Concepts of 'Demons' in Ancient Israel," 45. For additional information on *lîlît*/Lilith in these and other biblical passages, see Judit M. Blair, *De-Demonising the Old Testament: An Investigation of Azazel, Lilith, Deber, Qeteb, and Resheph in the Hebrew Bible* (Tübingen: Mohr-Siebeck 2009), 63–95; Peter D. Miscall, *Isaiah 34–35: A Nightmare/A Dream* (Sheffield: Sheffield Academic Press, 1999).

... and the demon Lilith, is intended to place the aspect of the counter-human world in the foreground."[78]

Why does the biblical writer cast the judgment of Babylon in this way? Babylon was, in many ways, a metaphor for evil and chaos in the Old Testament, "one of the dread images of the Bible, stretching from OT history to the apocalyptic vision of Revelation."[79] Talmon adds, "The presence of such monsters in fact indicates that a place had been reduced to the primeval state of chaos."[80] But Babylon was merely the primary point of reference to a much more comprehensive threat.

In his study of "desolation passages" in the prophets, John Geyer draws on Milgrom's observation that the biblical vocabulary for desolation has secure Mesopotamian cognates that "refer to the netherworld."[81] This frames the context for the "strange creatures" found in the prophetic desolation oracles. He writes:

> Psalm 74 explicitly links the *ṣyym* with creation mythology. They devour the carcass of Leviathan. ... [In Isa 13:21] it is not quite clear what LXX is translating as what, but the Greek list includes *seirēnes* ["sirens"], *daimonia* ["demons"], and *onokentauroi* ["donkey centaurs"] showing a tradition which associated the terms with mythology. Other scholars have come down firmly on the side of those who count the *ś 'yrym* as demonic and monstrous inhabitants of the desert among them.[82]

Biblical writers were not expressing the notion that night birds and animals were actually demons any more than modern people who entertain superstitions about black cats think those animals are not members of the animal kingdom. An owl might be the symbol of Lilith, but owls were nevertheless birds. The vocabulary of nocturnal presence and behavior allowed the prophets to communicate the notion that some places are the jurisdiction of cosmic evil and therefore occupied by evil spirits.

---

78. B. Janowski, "Jackals," *DDD* 459.

79. "Babylon," in *Dictionary of Biblical Imagery*, ed. Leland Ryken et al. (Downers Grove, IL: InterVarsity Press, 2000), 68.

80. Talmon, "The 'Desert Motif'," 43.

81. John B. Geyer, "Desolation and Cosmos," *VT* 49.1 (1999): 58. Both Geyer and Milgrom reference the work of Tallquist in this regard: K. Tallquist, "Sumerisch-Akkadische Hymnen der Totenwelt," *Studia Orientalia* 4 (1934): 17–22.

82. Geyer, "Desolation and Cosmos."

Earlier in our study, we noted that part of the logic undergirding the sinister, supernatural character of Sheol was its "mirror opposition" to the place where Yahweh dwelled (the heavens). The same principle is in operation here. The most unholy ground is Babylon. It is no coincidence that the disinheritance of the nations to other 'elōhîm (Deut 32:8–9), thereby creating the fundamental contrast between Yahweh's people and "portion" (Deut 32:9) and other peoples and places under other dark lords, occurs at Babylon (Gen 11:1–9). There are clear Babylonian elements in the framing of the other two supernatural rebellions that produce evil spirits (Gen 3; 6:1–4).

As one scholar puts it, for Old Testament theology, the harmony of creation was "broken and permanently threatened by disorderly, supernatural beings and forces, hostile to God and humankind."[83]

Demythologized Pseudo-Demons

General Considerations

Israelites were not unique among the peoples of antiquity—or now, for that matter: death was a fearful thing. While the righteous hoped to be released from Sheol to be with God and other loved ones who worshiped the true God, there is no indication in the Old Testament that Israelites presumed that would happen immediately at death. The hope of the righteous for deliverance from the realm of the dead is often (but not exclusively) found in passages dealing with eschatological judgment and vindication. In other words, the Old Testament theology of afterlife included hope but conveyed uncertainty about when the hoped-for release would occur.

As a result, for Israelites, anything that threatened death might be associated with the realm of the dead and the disembodied spirits therein. This presents interpretive and theological difficulties that require careful navigation.

Ancient Near Eastern texts make it quite clear that people living in biblical times parsed natural disasters mythically. Storms, earthquakes, diseases, famines, and the like were outbursts of divine wrath from a range of deities. Calamity, illness, or death might occur either because

---

83. R. Murray, *The Cosmic Covenant: Biblical Themes of Justice, Peace, and the Integrity of Creation* (London: Sheed & Ward, 1992), 17.

some deity didn't like you or your people, or as a side effect of a conflict with another deity. The question of whether biblical writers thought this way is one that arises from the text.

The short answer is "yes and no." On the one hand, in biblical thought, everything that threatens life is the result of such rebellion. Natural disaster, disease, and death extend from humanity's failure to fulfill the Edenic mandate, a failure provoked through the deception of a divine rebellion. The earth was under a curse. Eden was lost. Demonic spirits derivative from the transgression in Genesis 6:1–4 became an ongoing scourge of human well-being. God disinherited humanity at the Babel event, assigning the nations to lesser gods who sowed chaos among their charges (Deut 32:8–9; Ps 82).[84] For Israel, raised up by divine intervention on the part of Yahweh after Babel's judgment, things like plague, infertility, sickness, natural disasters, and external threats of violence were only to be feared in the wake of apostasy (Exod 15:26; Lev 26:14–39; Deut 28:15–68).[85]

This broad-stroked worldview put supernatural causation of natural disaster, illness, and death on the table, so to speak. But it would be an exaggeration to presume that all such things—or even most—would have been viewed as having divine causation. Ancient people, especially in complex societies, would have known that common sense and wisdom were behind undesirable circumstances as well. Their outlook was not wholly enchanted.[86] The terms that follow, then, do not name demons but reflect the biblical worldview that the threats of the natural world were somehow tied to a cosmic struggle involving the spiritual world.

---

84. See Heiser, *Unseen Realm*, 110–15.

85. For discussion on these and related matters, Michael L. Brown, *Israel's Divine Healer* (Grand Rapids: Zondervan, 1995), 72–78, 99–104, 122–25, 133–48.

86. Given our modern scientific knowledge of germs, viruses, bacteria, and genetics, we of course cast a much wider net when it comes to common sense (knowledge) and wisdom. But if we are not materialist atheists or deists, divine causation and intervention is part of our worldview. For an ancient Israelite, if you didn't plant enough food or didn't keep animals away from crops, you were going to go hungry—not because of evil spirits, but because of stupidity. If you failed to build walls to protect your city, your poor thinking was the reason for your vulnerability. If you didn't nurse your child or abandoned it to the elements, you could expect it to die. The entire world wasn't enchanted, but if there was no *apparent* reason for tragedy, you would look to the supernatural for an explanation. Modern people who believe in God and the spiritual world do the same. We ask God to heal. We pray for a drought to end or for protection from the elements. We do not do so because we believe such things are in the job descriptions of particular entities. We do so to show dependence on God's sovereignty.

1. Chaos Symbols

One of the major themes in Old Testament literature, particularly in its poetic material, is that of life's difficulties. One aspect of this was humanity's struggle against a fallen creation, not only in terms of its violence and deadliness but also in terms of the challenges it presented for human subsistence. One could meet death by virtue of earthquake or famine, storms at sea or eating the wrong plant. The human plight meant depending on the very thing that could kill you in hundreds of ways. Scholars describe this situation and its biblical expression with terms like "chaos." Chaos imagery in ancient literature explains humanity's fundamental struggles by relating them to comparable struggles in the divine realm.[87]

Biblical writers framed this situation in light of their belief in God's sovereign control and the involvement of evil spirits in the threats they faced. The metaphor of violent, untamed monsters was common in both biblical and ancient Near Eastern literature. These chaos beasts hailed from the sea (Leviathan, Rahab) and land (Behemoth).[88] These monsters "represented the forces of chaos held in check by the power of the creator deity."[89] When Leviathan is mentioned in the Old Testament, the text is generally asserting Yahweh's power over the sea monster (see Job 3:8; 41:1; Pss 74:14; 104:26; Isa 27:1). The conflict between Yahweh and these creatures is fundamentally different than the similar conflicts in Canaanite and Mesopotamian mythology.

> The mythological background of the deity battling and defeating a sea monster (i.e., the Chaoskampf motif) is most evident in Psa 74:14 and Isa 27:1. … Unlike the mythological stories of struggle between Ba'al and Yam or Marduk and Tiamat, Yahweh and Leviathan are not both divine creatures and equals. Yahweh is the sole divine creator, and

---

87. Mabie explains, "The imagery associated with chaos and death in the literature of the ancient world functions to inform human understanding of the realities of life under the principle of divine activity and design. Such texts are a reflex of cultural etiology—the search to understand and express primary causes and overarching structures in the divine and human realm" (see F. J. Mabie, "Chaos and Death," *DOTWPW* 41–42).

88. See C. Uehlinger, "Leviathan," *DDD*, 511–15; J. Day, *God's Conflict with the Dragon and the Sea* (Cambridge: Cambridge University Pres, 1985); B. F. Batto, "Behemoth," *DDD* 165–68; J. V. Kinnier Wilson, "A Return to the Problems of Behemoth and Leviathan," *VT* 25 (1975): 1–14; K. William Whitney, *Two Strange Beasts: Leviathan and Behemoth in Second Temple and Early Rabbinic Judaism* (Winona Lake, IN: Eisenbrauns, 2006); K. Spronk, "Rahab," *DDD* 684–85. On Rahab (not the woman of Jericho story!), see Isa 51:9; Ps 89:11; Job 9:13; 26:12.

89. Douglas Mangum and Matthew James Hamilton, "Leviathan," *LBD*, n.p.

Leviathan is mere creation. ... The physical description of Leviathan in Job 41 clearly depicts a creature that cannot be tamed or subdued by human power. In this case, the writer of Job clearly appropriated imagery to make the rhetorical point that only Yahweh is powerful enough to keep the forces of chaos in check.[90]

These monsters were not considered real animals one could encounter with unfathomably large dimensions and powers.[91] The metaphor communicated the fearful (and often fatal) struggle with earthly and heavenly rebellion and chaos. The entire world might irrupt in chaos, defying the restraint of a good God.

2. Demythologized Forces of Nature

In addition to symbols representing the encompassing reach of chaos, biblical writers used the names of deities from Canaanite religion attached to specific natural phenomena and illnesses. Unlike their polytheistic counterparts, they did not have distinct deities acting independently of the true God in charge of those forces.[92] Just as death (*mōt*) itself was

---

90. Ibid.

91. The biblical imagery draws on the mythological literature of Mesopotamia (the dragon Tiamat from Enuma Elish) and Canaan (Yamm and Litānu from the Baal Cycle). Tiamat, together with her consort Apsu (the watery deep) produces the first generation of gods and goddesses in Mesopotamian religion. Tiamat is cast as a literal beast, slain by Marduk, from whose body heaven and earth are made. The Bible endorses no such mythology. Litānu is an opponent of Baal in his struggle for supremacy among the children of El, the goal of which was to become El's coregent. This struggle has more to do with kingship than creation order, though there are elements of latter in play due to Baal's status as giver of rain and crops. The biblical writers did not assign sovereignty over nature to deities other than Yahweh. Note that this imagery follows all the way through the Bible, even to the book of Revelation, where we find a beast, a dragon rising from the chaotic sea and a land beast (Rev 13).

92. The fact that the gods assigned to the nations at Babel (Deut 32:8–9; see chapter 7) eventually abused their populations (Ps 82) is a different circumstance. Psalm 82 nowhere links the crimes of the *ʾelōhîm* being judged (Ps 82:1) and natural disasters, plagues, etc. Rather, they have caused chaos among their populations via injustice. The judgment of the gods in the divine council is made coherent by virtue of over-arching themes in biblical theology. Once God chose Israel, the well-being of humanity became intertwined with covenant relationship. The point is not that God no longer acted on behalf of humans in general, but that his special care was directed toward his own children (Israel) and those who would be blessed through them or by them (Gen 12:3). Ultimately, this is in turn connected to the appearance of the Messiah and the eschatological restoration of Eden. The fall and subsequent dispersion of the nations to lesser "sons of God" (Deut 32:8) who would abuse those nations links the Old Testament concepts of creation, justice, righteousness, human suffering, death, and alienation from God for those outside his family. Patrick D. Miller, referencing the work of Schmid, writes in this regard: "H.H. Schmid has made an effective case for the view that the notion of 'righteousness' (*ṣedeq/ṣedāqāh*) in the Old Testament is fundamentally an all-encompassing world order. Starting from an examination of *maʿat* in Egyptian thought and looking at the close connection between the cosmic and the ethical-social order that is a common feature of ancient Near Eastern thought, Schmid contends that ' "righteousness" is not understood narrowly as a legal

under the authority of Yahweh, so were disease and natural disaster. Yahweh was the lone sovereign. For example, when Egypt was punished with plagues, it wasn't because Yahweh had to request the services of a deity or demon. The Most High either acts unilaterally or dispatches a supernatural underling to dispense judgment through such disasters (Ps 78:49–50).[93]

In our earlier discussion of the term *ḥby* I noted that Habakkuk 3:5 contains two terms that may well be Canaanite deities (*deber, rešep*). In the prophet's description of God's victory march from the area south of the promised land, "in terms reminiscent of the theophany at Mt Sinai,"[94] *deber* ("pestilence") and *rešep* ("plague") follow at his heels.

Scholars have long noted that both terms are Canaanite deities. Baker observes, "Yahweh has his two personified attendants who are subject to

---

matter, but as universal world order, as comprehensive salvation'. … Such an understanding of the close association between the Old Testament concepts of righteousness and justice and the mainte-nance of the world order that is set forth in the creation and demonstrated in nature and history. … It is against this background that one must look at one of the texts in which the council of Yahweh is most explicitly present, Psalm 82. It takes place entirely in the world of the gods, although what is clear from the story is that that world is totally ruled and controlled by the Lord. The psalm depicts a meeting of the 'divine council' (v. 1) in which God rises and pronounces judgment on the gods." See Miller, *Israelite Religion and Biblical Theology: Collected Essays* (Sheffield: Sheffield Academic Press, 2000), 438. See also H. H. Schmid, "Creation, Righteousness, and Salvation: 'Creation Theology' as the Broad Horizon of Biblical Theology," in *Creation in the Old Testament*, ed. Bernhard W. Ander-son (Philadelphia: Fortress Press, 1984), 102–17.

93. See the brief discussion in Heiser, *Angels*, 66–67, 136–37. The resulting theology is important. Disease and calamity happen neither because God is at the mercy of other supernatural beings who control such things nor because he is capricious in his control over such things. Natural disaster is a byproduct of either a fallen creation or God's righteous judgment. Knight summarizes the ideas: "The once-conquered chaos has broken forth again, and God will intervene at some future point to subdue chaos or dissolve the present creation and will then re-recreate the world and the chosen people. … Consequently, whenever there is an apparent dysfunction of this global entity, the people make their complaint directly to God, the creator, for immediate deliverance and restitution during their lifetime. … Natural disaster is as a rule attributed to the action of the deity, both among Israel-ites and among their neighbors. Earthquakes, volcanoes, storms, devouring fires, plagues, rampaging animals, warming insects—such things do not 'just happen.' … Since the divine sphere is held to be the cause of all that is inexplicable in the human sphere, these go to the account of the gods. In polytheistic religions demons or malicious gods are typically held responsible for the bizarre occurrences. Yahwism, however, could not tolerate any divine or semi-divine rivals to God. … As amoral as YHWH's wrath may at times appear, it became increasingly interpreted—especially by the prophets and the Deuteronomists—as punishment for human evil. In this manner, disorders lose their anomalous character. They become understandable as expressions of divine power and will, the same sort that marked the creation of the world." See Douglas A. Knight, "Cosmogony and Order in the Hebrew Tradition," in *Cosmogony and Ethical Order: New Studies in Comparative Ethics*, ed. Robin W. Lovin and Frank Reynolds (Chicago: University of Chicago Press, 1985), 136, 144, 146.

94. David W. Baker, *Nahum, Habakkuk and Zephaniah: An Introduction and Commentary* (TOTC; Downers Grove, IL: InterVarsity Press, 1988), 69.

his control (cf. Ps. 91:6), exemplifying his power. Both are also Canaanite deities, leading here to a hidden polemic against pagan worship."[95] The term *deber* is commonly used in the Old Testament alongside terms for warfare and famine, all depicting the causes of widespread death (especially in the books of Jeremiah and Ezekiel). While this is the most common usage for *deber*, del Olmo Lete notes the term "seems to be used a number of times in a personified sense as a demon or evil deity (Hab 3:5; Ps 91:3, 6; cf. Hos 13:14)."[96] In Habakkuk 3:5, *deber* ("pestilence") and *rešep* ("plague") are presented "marching at Yahweh's side as His helpers. This follows the ancient Mesopotamian tradition according to which 'plague' and 'pestilence' are present in the entourage of the great god Marduk."[97]

Some scholars object to *deber* as a true deity name,[98] but its partnering with *rešep* in Habakkuk 3:5 strongly suggests this is the case, "given the presence of [Resheph] in the Ugaritic texts as a god of destruction (*KTU* 1.14 I 18–19; 1.82:3)."[99] *Rešep* appears in Deuteronomy 32:23–24, where Yahweh threatens his apostate people:

> [23] And I will heap disasters upon them;
>   I will spend my arrows on them;
> [24] they shall be wasted with hunger (*rāʿāb*),
>   and devoured by plague (*rešep*)
>   and poisonous pestilence (*qeṭeb*).

As noted above, Resheph is a deity of destruction at Ugarit. He is portrayed as an archer there (*KTU* 1.82:3), and so the phrase "spending my arrows" is interesting. Resheph is accompanied by *qeṭeb* and *rāʿāb*. The former appears in an Ugaritic text as a kinsman of Mōt ("Death"). The latter appears to be an epithet of Mōt.[100]

95. Ibid., 70.

96. G. del Olmo Lete, "Deber," *DDD* 231–32. For other passages and commentary related to *deber*, see Blair, *De-Demonising the Old Testament*, 96–176.

97. Del Olmo Lete, "Deber," *DDD* 232.

98. Frey-Anthes opines that "there are no safe sources identifying either *deber* or *qeṭeb* as ancient Oriental gods" ("Concepts of 'Demons' in Ancient Israel," 41). She provides little in the way of a rationale for her skepticism. She does not interact with texts cited by other scholars. Instead she notes that in later (Second Temple) literature only *qeṭeb* (see the discussion) is called a demon, and that, in the Old Testament *deber*, *rešep*, and *qeṭeb* are not "personal characters." Neither observation is directly relevant to how Canaanites thought nor the phenomena of their own literature.

99. Del Olmo Lete, "Deber," 232; See P. Xella, "Resheph," *DDD* 700–701; Blair, *De-Demonising the Old Testament*, 194–212.

100. N. Wyatt, "Qeteb," *DDD* 673. See Blair, *De-Demonising the Old Testament*, 177–93.

In Psalm 91:3–6, the psalmist writes that those who dwell in the shelter of the Most High and abide in the shadow of the Almighty will be delivered "from the deadly pestilence [*deber*]" (v. 3) and will not fear "the arrow that flies by day, nor the pestilence [*deber*] that stalks in darkness, nor the destruction [*qeṭeb*] that wastes at noonday" (v. 5–6). Why? Because these forces are not autonomous deities. Yahweh of Israel is in control of them. Consequently, he will protect his own from their lethal harm.

SUMMARY

We began this chapter acknowledging that the Old Testament has words for demons that align with common conceptions of that term, drawn as they are from episodes in the Gospels or church tradition, but that there were still plenty of data for consideration. We've covered considerable ground, but this is nevertheless our beginning point. As we proceed, we will learn how the mass of terms we discussed were muddled and merged by Greek translation of the Hebrew Bible in the Septuagint, the source for most of the passages from the New Testament quoted by its authors.

CHAPTER 2

It Was All Greek to Them, Too

We now have an idea of the variety of ways the Old Testament writers talked about evil spirits—supernatural beings in rebellion against God, who inhabited the realm of the dead or held dominion of unholy ground. In the preview to the first two chapters I noted that the Hebrew terms were eventually translated by learned Jewish translators into Greek—specifically, the Septuagint (LXX), the Old Testament most frequently quoted by New Testament writers. Since the translation language was Greek, this important project naturally is often discussed in the context of the Hellenistic age that began with Alexander's conquests. But we must not lose sight of the reality that this era itself is situated within the larger Second Temple period. We will be looking at Greek translations from the Septuagint in this chapter, but we will find that the translators were informed by the wider Jewish context as well.[1]

SEPTUAGINT TRANSLATION OF HEBREW TERMS FOR THE POWERS OF DARKNESS

Straightforward Literalism

The enterprise of Bible translation isn't always uniform. English translations of the Bible vary widely in vocabulary choice, sometimes dramatically. Those who venture beyond English to Hebrew and Greek word study know that English translations oscillate from straightforward

---

1. In Section II of our study we will widen the scope of how evil spirits are described and labeled in Second Temple Jewish literature (Greek, Hebrew, and Aramaic). The emphasis here is what the LXX does with the vocabulary of chapter 1.

word-for-word correspondence to interpretive translation of thought rather than vocabulary. Study Bibles and their footnotes will alert readers to another issue: divergence in ancient manuscripts that the translators followed (or could have followed).

The Septuagint was no different. In many respects its handling of Hebrew terminology for sinister spirit beings is predictably ordinary and regular. The following Hebrew terms, for example, are regularly translated with literal Greek glosses in the passages discussed or noted in the preceding chapter:[2]

- *rûḥôt* ("spirits"): *pneuma* ("spirit")
- *qedōšîm* ("holy ones"): *hagioi* ("holy ones")
- *māwet/mōt* ("death"): *thanatos* ("death")
- *mētîm* ("the dead"): *nekros* ("dead")

As noted in the previous chapter, *'ôb/ 'ōbôt* ("spirit"; "spirits") may speak of human or nonhuman spirits in the realm of the dead or, in some passages, those who conjure them. Not surprisingly, the LXX translators indiscriminately use *engastrimythos* ("familiar spirit[s]") for *'ôb/ 'ōbôt*, as the gloss is serviceable whether the context points to the spirits themselves or the human channel. The same is true of *yiddĕ'ōnî*, which the LXX is prone to translate with *epaoidos* ("one who knows [by way of sorcery or enchantment]").[3]

The literalistic tendency is also present with respect to how LXX translators render plural *'ēlîm* or *'elōhîm* and *benê 'ēlîm/ 'elōhîm* ("gods"; "sons of God"), though this reality is often missed by scholars, who often presume that LXX translators were enforcing a "monotheizing tendency."[4] This notion is based on a misunderstanding of divine plurality and a failure to examine the totality of the data.

---

2. By "literal" I mean that the translation is not interpretive but simply utilizes the most analogous word in the language of translation. The regularity of these Greek translation choices is demonstrated via *The Lexham Analytical Lexicon of the Septuagint* (Bellingham, WA: Logos Bible Software, 2012).

3. For example, Lev 19:31 in the LXX uses *epaoidos* for the Hebrew text's *yiddĕ'ōnî*. See LSJ, s.v. "ἐπαοιδός."

4. See C. H. Dodd, *The Bible and the Greeks* (London: Hodder & Stoughton, 1935). Mark S. Smith, a scholar of Israelite religion, claims that references to plural *'ēlîm* or *'elōhîm* and *benê 'ēlîm/ 'elōhîm* were subject to censoring in Second Temple Judaism and the LXX (Mark S. Smith, *God in Translation: Deities in Cross-Cultural Discourse in the Biblical World* [Tübingen: Mohr Siebeck, 2008], 200–201).

It is true that the LXX utilizes *angeloi* for translating plural *ʾēlîm* or *ʾelōhîm* and *benê ʾēlîm/ ʾelōhîm*. But it is a misrepresentation of the data to say that the LXX does this most of the time. As the table below illustrates, most of the time the LXX opts for the more literalistic *theoi* (or some other plural form of *theos*, "god").[5]

Hebrew Bible "gods"/"divine beings" (ʾelōhîm; ʾēlîm) "sons of God" (benê ʾēlîm/ʾelōhîm)	LXX renders the Hebrew terms with plural of *angelos* ("angel")	LXX preserves divine plurality by using a plural form of *theos* ("god")[1]
Torah references to other gods (ʾelōhîm). Examples: Exod 18:11 ("greater than all gods"; ʾelōhîm) Deut 8:19 ("go after other gods"; ʾelōhîm) Deut 10:17 ("God of gods"; ʾelōhîm) Deut 17:3 ("served other gods"; ʾelōhîm) Deut 29:26 ("served other gods ... gods whom they had not known and whom [God] had not allotted to them"; ʾelōhîm twice)[2]		Plural of *theos* is ubiquitous in Torah legal literature (over 60 times, including all the verse references to the left): Exod 18:11; Deut 8:19; 10:17; 17:3; 29:26
Exod 15:11 ("among the gods"; ʾēlîm)		Exod 15:11 (*theois*)
Ps 82:1 ("in the midst of the gods"; ʾelōhîm)		Ps 81:1 (*theous*)[3]
Ps 86:8 ("among the gods"; ʾelōhîm)		Ps 85:8 (*theois*)
Ps 95:3 ("great King above all gods"; ʾelōhîm)		Ps 94:3 (*theous*)
Ps 96:4 ("feared above all gods"; ʾelōhîm)		Ps 95:4 (*theous*)
Ps 97:9 ("you are exalted far above all gods"; ʾelōhîm)		Ps 96:9 (*theous*)
Ps 136:2 ("the God of gods"; ʾelōhîm)		Ps 135:2 (*theōn*)
1 Sam 28:13 ("I see a god/gods coming up out of the earth"; ʾelōhîm)		1 Sam 28:13 (*theous*)

1. Some versification numbers in LXX differ from those in the Hebrew Masoretic Text (MT).

2. On the allotment language, see the ensuing discussion of Deut 32:8.

3. See R. B. Salters, "Psalm 82:1 and the Septuagint," *ZAW* 103.2 (1991): 225–39.

Table continued on next page.

---

5. The table is drawn from Heiser, *Angels*, 80–81.

Hebrew Bible "gods"/"divine beings" (ʾelōhîm; ʾēlîm) "sons of God" (benê ʾēlîm/ʾelōhîm)	LXX renders the Hebrew terms with plural of *angelos* ("angel")	LXX preserves divine plurality by using a plural form of *theos* ("god")
Gen 6:2 ("sons of God"; *benê hā-ʾelōhîm*		Gen 6:2 ("sons of God"; *hoi huioi tou theou*)[4]
Ps 29:1 ("sons of God"; *benê ʾēlîm*)		Ps 28:1 ("sons of God"; *huioi theou*)
Ps 89:7 ("sons of God"; *benê ʾēlîm*)		Ps 88:7 ("among the sons of God"; *en huioi theou*)
Ps 8:5 ("you have made him a little lower than God/the gods"; *ʾelōhîm*)	Ps 8:6 ("less than the angels"; *brachy ti par' angelous*)	
Ps 97:7 ("worship him all you gods"; *ʾelōhîm*)	Ps 96:7 ("all his angels"; *pantes hoi angeloi autou*)	
Job 1:6; 2:1 ("sons of God"; *benê hā-ʾelōhîm*)	Job 1:6; 2:1 ("the angels of God"; *hoi angeloi tou theou*)	
Deut 32:8 ("sons of God"; *benê ʾelōhîm*)[5]	Deut 32:8 ("angels of God"; *angelōn theou*)	
Deut 32:43 ("bow down to him, all gods"; *ʾelōhîm*)[6]	Deut 32:43 ("angels of God"; *angeloi tou theou*)[7]	
Job 38:7 ("sons of God"; *benê ʾelōhîm*)	Job 38:7 ("all my angels"; *pantes angeloi mou*)	
Ps 138:1 ("before the gods I sing your [Yahweh's] praise"; *ʾelōhîm*)	Ps 137:1 ("before the angels"; *enantion angelōn*)	

4. Scholars will often note that this phrase (like its Hebrew counterpart) can be rendered "sons of the gods." Wright notes in regard to the LXX rendering in Gen 6:2: "The 'sons of the gods' are well known in Greek mythology and many have argued that they are the figures that lie behind the *bene elohim* and the giants of Genesis 6:1–4. Hesiod describes a generation of beings in *Works and Days* 110–25 that could easily be identified as the *bene elohim* in Early Judaism. They are said to have lived upon the earth ὥστε θεοί (as gods) and after the earth had covered their generation, they lived upon the earth as 'pure spirits.' ... The fourth generation created by Zeus fits a similar description of the *gibborim* of Genesis 6:4. This was a race of 'hero men' known as demigods. This race appears to have fallen to the same fate as the giants in *1 Enoch* tradition." See Archie T. Wright, *The Origin of Evil Spirits: The Reception of Genesis 6:1–4 in Early Jewish Literature* (Tübingen: Mohr Siebeck, 2013), 73. The issue of identification is complicated by the fact that the Greek giant/Titan stories are not uniform in content because the traditions were composed and edited over the course of several centuries. See Walter Scott, "Giants (Greek and Roman)," *ERE* 6:194–96.

5. The oldest Hebrew text of this verse, found among the Dead Sea Scrolls, reads *benê hā-ʾelōhîm*. The Masoretic Text reads "sons of Israel." For a lengthy discussion of why the scroll reading is superior, see Heiser, "Deuteronomy 32:8 and the Sons of God," 52–74.

6. This wording is absent from the Masoretic Text but present in Dead Sea Scroll material. For a discussion, see Heiser, "Monotheism, Polytheism, Monolatry, or Henotheism," 9–10; Tigay, *Deuteronomy*, 516–17.

7. The LXX adds "sons of God" to the first stanza of this verse, a phrase not present in the Hebrew material from Qumran. See the ensuing discussion for the implications and Tigay, *Deuteronomy*, 516–17, for an explanation.

The data clearly show that only in a minority of passages does the LXX opt for a plural of *angelos* instead of a plural of *theos*.[6] Of those instances, half have divergent LXX manuscript readings that bear witness to a plural form of *theos* in place of a plural form of *angelos*.[7]

It is simply not correct, then, to suppose that LXX data indicate trepidation on the part of Second Temple period Jewish translators with respect to alleged polytheistic language in the Hebrew Bible.[8] For the present purpose, though, the choice of *angelos* as a gloss is noteworthy in that it is clear evidence that the rebellious *'elōhîm* and *benê 'ēlîm* were construed as evil spirits, not mere idols of wood or stone.

---

6. As I have noted elsewhere, "Some of those instances (Pss 29:1; 82:1 89:7; Exod 15:11) are among the most frequently cited passages by scholars seeking to argue that the Hebrew Bible preserves vestiges of polytheism. If Jews of the Second Temple period were concerned that such language might be taken as polytheism, it makes little sense to leave passages like these intact—undisguised as angels. The unevenness of what we find shows that the LXX cannot be regarded as proof for a campaign to erase polytheistic language and downgrade instance of divine plurality to angels." See Heiser, *Angels*, 81–82.

7. For "angels of God" in Job 1:6; 2:1, the Greek text of Aquila reads "sons of God" (*hoi huioi theou* and *hoi huioi tou theou* respectively). Aquila and Theodotion also have "sons of God" in place of "all my angels" in Job 38:7. Lastly, for "before the angels" in LXX Ps 137:1 Aquila and the Heptapla column E' have "before the gods" (*enanti theōn*).

8. Construing multiple *'elōhîm* as polytheism is to read a modern theological conception back into ancient thought. Divine plurality is no obstacle to adherence to the uniqueness of Yahweh in the minds of the writers of the Hebrew Bible. Modern scholars mistakenly presume that the multiple *'elōhîm* must have been construed as sharing essentially the same attributes, but this is not the case. See Michael S. Heiser, "The Divine Council in Late Canonical and Non-Canonical Jewish Literature" (PhD diss., University of Wisconsin-Madison, 2004); Heiser, "Monotheism, Polytheism, Monolatry, or Henotheism," 1–30; and Heiser, "Divine Plurality in the Hebrew Bible," 1–24. The ultraconservative scribes of the Qumran community also had no problem with divine plurality. See Heiser, "Monotheism and the Language of Divine Plurality," 85–100. Other scholars have noted the same incongruity between such claims and terminology in the scrolls. Though I believe that connecting the vocabulary of divine plurality with polytheism (especially in the Qumran material) is misguided, see Peter Hayman, "Monotheism—A Misused Word in Jewish Studies?" *Journal of Jewish Studies* 42.1 (1991): 1–15 (esp. 8–9); and Jonathan Ben-Dov, "The Resurrection of the Divine Assembly and the Divine Title El in the Dead Sea Scrolls," in *Submerged Literature in Ancient Greek Culture: Beyond Greece: the Comparative Perspective: Vol. 3, The Comparative Perspective*, ed. Giulio Colesanti and Manuela Giordano (Berlin: De Gruyter, 2016): 9–31. Ben-Dov makes the surprising mistake of assigning the epithet *'lyn* ("Most High") to El when discussing Ugaritic sources (Ben-Dov, 11). That epithet is never used of El at Ugarit.

Some Interpretive Renderings

However, the Septuagint's translation consistency starts to break down with the Hebrew lemmas *śar* ("prince") and *rĕpā'îm*.

1. "Commander" (*śar*)

Supernatural figures are described in the Hebrew with the lemma *śar* in eight verses (Josh 5:14–15; Dan 8:11, 25; 10:13, 20–21; 12:1).[9] The LXX is not always consistent in its treatment of the term nor in its perspective of the supernatural character of the figure in question:[10]

- Joshua 5:14–15—*archistratēgos* ("commander")
- Daniel 8:11—*archistratēgos* ("commander")
- Daniel 8:25—*apōleias andrōn* ("destruction of men")[11]
- Daniel 10:13—*stratēgos* ("commander")
  Theodotion LXX—*archōn* ("ruler")[12]
- Daniel 10:20—*stratēgos* ("commander")
  Theodotion LXX—*archōn* ("ruler")
- Daniel 10:21—*angelos* ("angel, messenger")
- Daniel 12:1—*angelos* ("angel, messenger")

Setting aside Daniel 8:25, which contains a text-critical issue with the LXX rendering of *śar*,[13] we can proceed with some observations.

---

9. See the discussion in chapter 1.

10. Unless otherwise noted, LXX readings in this chapter come from Randall Tan and David A. deSilva, *The Lexham Greek-English Interlinear Septuagint* (Bellingham, WA: Logos Bible Software, 2009). Theodotion readings come from Randall Tan and David A. deSilva, *The Lexham Greek-English Interlinear Septuagint: Alternate Texts* (Bellingham, WA: Logos Bible Software, 2010).

11. The LXX translator may have had a Hebrew text that was different than the Masoretic Text. See the following note.

12. The Greek text of Theodotion was thought for many years to have been a second century AD revision of the existing LXX. Jobes and Silva comment: "This traditional understanding of the Theodotionic recension is problematic because certain renderings once thought distinctive to it are now known to have existed a century or two before he lived. … [R]ecent discoveries, especially the Greek Minor Prophets scroll [from Qumran], have confirmed the view that, for at least parts of the Hebrew Bible, a translation containing elements once attributed to Theodotion was already in use prior to NT times." See Karen H. Jobes and Moisés Silva, *Invitation to the Septuagint*, 2nd ed. (Grand Rapids: Baker Academic, 2015), 28.

13. Tov suggests a reading of *šēd rabbîm* ("destruction of many [men]") to explain the Greek reading. The first term *šēd* (שֵׁד) would be an example of graphic confusion in transmission (in place of *śar*, שַׂר). See Emanuel Tov, *The Parallel Aligned Hebrew-Aramaic and Greek Texts of Jewish Scripture: Alexandrinus and Theodotion Variants* (Computer Assisted Tools for Septuagint Studies; Bellingham, WA: Logos Bible Software, 2003).

Regardless of disagreement on the identity of the *śar* in Joshua 5:14–15, the context makes it quite clear that the figure is supernatural.[14] Echoing the wording of the burning bush incident (Exod 3:1–3), Joshua is commanded by the *śar* to remove his sandals because he is standing on holy ground. Daniel 10:21 and 12:1 are equally as obvious. The writer's use of *angelos* for Michael, a figure that Jewish tradition unanimously considered supernatural, removes any ambiguity as to his thinking.

Daniel 8:11, a reference to the "prince [*śar*] of the host [*ṣābā'*]," is not as explicit, but the preceding verse's reference to "the host [*ṣābā'*] of heaven" makes a host of humans (and therefore a human prince) very unlikely. While there is a human host elsewhere in the vision (Dan 8:12, 13), the phrase "prince of the host" (*śar haṣṣābā'*) is basically identical to the description of the supernatural commander in Josh 5:14–15 (*śar ṣĕbā'*).[15] That the LXX translator saw a divine figure in Daniel 8:11 is quite reasonable.

This clarity notwithstanding, there is ambiguity as to whether the LXX translator(s) presumed the *śar* in Daniel 10:13, 20 was a divine being. In the LXX these verses have, respectively, *ho stratēgos basileōs Persōn* ("the commander of the king of the Persians") and *meta tou stratēgou basileōs Persōn* ("with the commander of the king of the Persians"). The Masoretic Text (MT) does not have the word "king" (*melek*) in the phrase in either instance. The presence of this word serves to orient the prince in service of the human king of Persia. Either the LXX translator was looking at a Hebrew text different from the MT or made an interpretive insertion on his own.

However, Septuagint readings are not uniform in these passages.[16] Theodotion's rendering of Daniel 10:13 reads *ho archōn basileias Persōn* ("the ruler of the kingdom of the Persians"). The switch from "king" to "kingdom" allows one to see either a human or divine being as the ruler. Similarly, Daniel 10:20 has *meta touarchontos Persōn* ("with the

---

14. See the comments in chapter 1.

15. The only difference is the lack of the definite article in the Joshua instances.

16. Curiously, the Theodotion text of Daniel reads *ho archōn basileias Persōn* ("the ruler of the kingdom of Persia") in Dan 10:13 but *tou archontos Persōn* ("the ruler of Persia") in Dan 10:20. Other texts have *tou stratēgou basileōs Persōn* ("the ruler of the king of Persia"). See Alfred Rahlfs and Robert Hanhart, eds., *Septuaginta: SESB Edition (Alternate Texts)* (Stuttgart: Deutsche Bibelgesellschaft, 2006).

ruler of the Persians"). Both instances in the Theodotion text permit a divine prince/ruler.

Some scholars argue that these two instances in (non-Theodotion) LXX Daniel overturn the notion of "patron angels" for Second Temple period Judaism. Presuming Daniel was written during that period (the "late" date), these scholars then suggest that the interpretive translations here in Daniel 10 reveal a move away from earlier polytheistic Israelite religion. We have already seen how this thesis is incoherent in light of how the LXX handles plural *'ēlîm* or *'elōhîm* and *benê 'ēlîm/'elōhîm* ("gods"; "sons of God"). The same incoherence plagues the idea here, as a number of Second Temple Jewish texts bear witness to the idea that the nations were governed by supernatural beings allotted to them at the Babel debacle (Deut 32:8–9).[17] We will consider those data in more detail later. At this point it is adequate merely to note two passages:

> He appointed a leader for each nation, and Israel is the portion of the Lord. (Wisdom of Sirach 17:17; LES)

> [God] chose Israel that they might be a people for himself. And he sanctified them and gathered them from all of the sons of man because (there are) many nations and many people, and they all belong to him, but over all of them he caused spirits to rule so that they might lead them astray from following him. But over Israel he did not cause any angel or spirit to rule because he alone is their ruler. (Jubilees 15:30b–32a; *OTP*, 2:87)

Again, it is evident that Jewish religious writers and thinkers of the Second Temple period suffered no offense from the theology of their own sacred Scriptures.

2. "Rephaim" (*rĕpā'îm*) and "Nephilim" (*nĕpîlîm*)

When encountering *rĕpā'îm*, Septuagint translators diverged from each other in their translation decisions.

---

17. Darrell D. Hannah, "Guardian Angels and Angelic National Patrons in Second Temple Judaism and Early Christianity," in *Angels: The Concept of Celestial Beings—Origins, Development and Reception*, ed. Friedrich V. Reiterer, Tobias Nicklas, Karin Schöpflin (Berlin: De Gruyter, 2007), 413–35.

Septuagint translation of Rephaim	Passages[1]
Plural forms of *gigas* ("giants")[2]	Gen 14:5; Josh 12:4; 13:12; Job 26:5; Prov 21:16; Isa 14:9; 1 Chr 11:15; 14:9; 20:4
Raphaein, Raphain, Raphaeim (transliteration of Hebrew *rĕpā 'îm*)[3]	Gen 15:20; Deut 2:11, 20 (twice); Deut 3:11, 13; Josh 15:8; 18:16;[4] 2 Sam 23:13
Plural form of *iatros* ("healers")	Ps 88:10 (LXX 87:11); Isa 26:14
Plural form of *gēgenēs* ("earth-born")[5]	Prov 2:18; 9:18
Plural form of *Titan* ("Titans")	2 Sam 5:18, 22
Plural form of *asebēs* ("ungodly, impious, irreverent")[6]	Isa 26:19

1. The LXX translator of Joshua either chose to not translate the term in Josh 17:15 or had a Hebrew text that differed from the Masoretic Text, where *rĕpā 'îm* is present. The same problem may be behind Isa 17:5, thought that instance is likely a case where the translator saw Hebrew *ēmeq rĕpā 'îm* ("Valley of the Rephaim") and interpreted the phrase as "solid ravine" (LXX: *sterea pharangi*).

2. LSJ, s.v. "Γίγας."

3. All these transliterations occur in the LXX text.

4. This instance combines *rĕpā 'îm* with the preceding word *ēmeq* ("valley"), resulting in Greek *Emekraphain*.

5. BDAG, s.v. "γηγενής."

6. BDAG, s.v. "ἀσεβής."

Septuagint translation of Nephilim	Passages
Plural form of *gigas* ("giants")	Gen 6:4; Num 13:33 (once)[1]

1. In the Hebrew Bible, *nĕpîlîm* occurs twice in Num 13:33. It also apparently did in the text used by the LXX translator, who chose to render the term *andres hypermēkeis* ("men of great stature") in one instance.

Some of these translation choices are immediately understandable. Transliteration of proper nouns is a common choice in modern English Bibles, so it is no surprise to see that in an ancient translation. There is also little mystery behind the fact that *rĕpā 'îm* were understood as giants since passages in which that Hebrew term occurs describe the Rephaim as such (Deut 3:11, 13; Josh 12:4; 13:12; cp. Deut 2:10–11; Num 13:33).[18] The

---

18. It is noteworthy that, unlike the material from Ugarit, the Old Testament at times uses the term *rĕpā 'îm* of the giant clans of the days of Moses and Joshua. Og, king of Bashan, was said to be the last vestige of the Rephaim (Deut 3:11, 13; Josh 12:4; 13:12). The *rĕpā 'îm* are linked to the Anakim in Deut 2:10–11: ("The Emim formerly lived there, a people great and many, and tall as the Anakim. Like the Anakim, they are also counted as Rephaim"). According to Num 13:33, the Anakim were "from the Nephilim." As Seeman notes, it is clear that the LXX translator understood the link between the Nephilim of Genesis 6, the Anakim of Numbers 13, and the Rephaim via the use of *gigantes* in the relevant places (Chris Seeman, "The Watchers Traditions and Gen 6:1–4 [MT and LXX]," in *The Watchers in Jewish and Christian Traditions*, ed. Angela Kim Harkins, Kelley Coblentz Bautch, and John C. Endres, S.J. [Minneapolis: Fortress Press, 2014], 33). The LXX also used *gigas* ("giant") for Hebrew *gibborîm* in Gen 6:4 and elsewhere. For our purposes in that regard, the LXX uses of plural

two instances of "healers" reflect the translator's attempt to render the word in accord with what he thought was the meaning of the basic Hebrew root. As noted in the preceding chapter, many modern scholars also think *rĕpā'îm* derives from the root *r-p-'* ("to heal"), despite evidence to the contrary.[19] "Ungodly" (*asebēs*) is likewise comprehensible given the context of Isaiah 26, as part of what scholars call the "little apocalypse" of Isaiah (24–27).[20] Watts breaks down this section of Isaiah:

1. The Present World Order is dissolved: 24:1–20.
2. The Place of Jerusalem in the coming order: 24:21–26:6.
3. The necessity of YHWH's judgment: 26:7–21.
4. Conditions for Israel's deliverance: 27:1–13.[21]

Isaiah 26:14 calls for judgment on God's enemies, so translating *rĕpā'îm* as "the ungodly" is not out of line, though it obscures the various circumstances of that term in its role in opposing God's plan for Israel and humanity.

The choice of "earth-born" and "Titans" are probably the most unusual choices, at least to us. In the Second Temple period, however, such a rendering would have made good sense. The LXX bears witness to the fact that its Jewish translators recognized the term's association with giants. The giants (*gigantes*) of Hellenistic (Greek) religion were described as "earth-born" since their mother was Earth (Gaia). Gaia's children were the Titans:

[The Titans' origin] is described in the *Theogony* of Hesiod, specifically in connection with what scholars term the Titanomachy ("Wars

---

forms of *gigas* in Ezek 32:12, 21,27 are of interest. The relevant portion of Ezek 32 references the underworld where other passages have *rĕpā'îm*. In all three verses the MT reads *gibbôrîm*. In Ezek 32:27 the Hebrew text has both *gibbôrîm* and *no'pelîm*. Some construe the latter as a reference to the *nĕpîlîm* but the LXX translator did not (correctly in my view), choosing to translate the form as *peptōkotōn* ("fallen"). Aramaic texts from Qumran (Aramaic Book of the Watchers and the Book of Giants) also connect Gen 6:4 and Num 13:33. See Samuel Thomas, "Watchers Traditions in the Dead Sea Scrolls," in *The Watchers in Jewish and Christian Traditions*, ed. Angela Kim Harkins, Kelley Coblentz Bautch, and John C. Endres, S.J. (Minneapolis: Fortress Press, 2014), 137.

19. As I pointed out in an earlier footnote in chapter 1, scholars like Michael L. Brown have noted the problems with this understanding. He asks the obvious questions that seem to have evaded others: Are there any biblical, Ugaritic, or other Northwest Semitic texts that cast the Rephaim/*rp'um* as healers? Was the Canaanite deity *rāpiu* a healer? The answer to both questions is no (Brown, "I Am the Lord, Your Healer," 124–27).

20. William R. Millar, "Isaiah, Book of: Isaiah 24–27 (Little Apocalypse)," *ABD* 3:488–89.

21. John D. W. Watts, *Isaiah 1–33*, rev. ed. (WBC; Nashville: Thomas Nelson, 2005), 371.

of the Titans"). The Titans (Gk. pl. *titanes*) were the children of the gods Uranos ("Heaven") and Gaia ("Earth"). Gaia became infuriated after Uranos cast certain of the Titans into Tartarus. Gaia successfully incited the remaining Titans (save for Oceanus) to rebel against Uranos. Gaia gave one of them, Kronos, a sickle, by which he castrated Uranos (*Theog.* 134–207). Blood from the wound fell into the soil of Earth, an impregnation of Gaia that produced the *gigantes*, along with the Eriyanes (the Roman Furies) and the ash-tree Nymphs. The Titans were later overthrown by the Olympians, led by Zeus, who cast the Titans into Tartarus. This angered Gaia once more, and she incited her children the *gigantes* to rise up against the Olympians, a conflict known as the Gigantomachy. This second conflict is preserved mainly via Apollodorus (b. ca. 180 BC) whose works were compiled in the 2nd cent. CE. The Olympians defeated the *gigantes* and confined them to Tartarus.[22]

Martin West's monumental work on the connections between ancient Near Eastern and Greek myth and literature took note of this connection.[23] As Doak comments, the Septuagint's use of the lemmas *titan* and *gēgenēs* thus creates a conceptual link between the biblical Rephaim and these figures of Greek mythology:

> The very references to the Giants and Titans already suggest a world which is in some way comparable to Greek myth. … [T]he effect of the introduction of Greek mythological vocabulary in suggestive and enigmatic places can only, in effect, serve to make the Greek Giants and Titans part of the biblical story.[24]

The takeaway for our purposes is that LXX translators clearly associated *rephāîm* both with giants and supernatural inhabitants of the realm of the dead.

---

22. M. S. Heiser, "Giants—Greco-Roman Antiquity," in *Encyclopedia of the Bible and Its Reception*, vol. 10 (Berlin: de Gruyter, 2015). See also Scott, "Giants (Greek and Roman)," 193–97.

23. Martin L. West, *The East Face of the Helicon: West Asiatic Elements in Greek Poetry and Myth* (Oxford: Clarendon, 1997), 117, 163, 166, 205.

24. Brian R. Doak, *The Last of the Rephaim: Conquest and Cataclysm in the Heroic Ages of Ancient Israel* (Boston: Ilex Foundation, Center for Hellenic Studies, 2012), 58.

SEPTUAGINT USE OF GREEK *DAIMONION* IN HEBREW BIBLE TRANSLATION

The most significant observation with respect to Septuagint translation decisions is the use of *daimonion*. The lemma occurs seventeen times, nine of which are found in the apocryphal (or "deuterocanonical") books of Tobit and Baruch.[25] The related *daimōn* is used once.[26]

The LXX use of this lemma is an important factor in understanding how the demons of the Gospels were conflated with the gods ('*ēlîm* or '*elōhîm* and *benê* '*ēlîm*/'*elōhîm*; "gods" or "sons of God") allotted to the nations at Babel (Deut 32:8–9). Later chapters will show why Old Testament and later Jewish theology would distinguish these two groups of divine beings. It is sufficient here to note the problem: LXX translators used *daimonion* in certain passages that speak of the sons of God allotted to the nations, and later New Testament authors use the same term for spirit entities that harm people. Consequently, two groups of sinister divine beings that have completely different origins in Old Testament and Second Temple Jewish thought get lumped together.

While this conflation is unfortunate, the vocabulary (*daimonion*) is still quite serviceable. Greek *daimōn* and *daimonion* broadly refer to a divine being (good or evil). It can also be used of divine beings at different places in the divine hierarchy or supernatural pecking order. Rexine summarizes:

> The word *daimōn* reflects the dynamism of the Greek vocabulary operating throughout the various periods of Greek literature. There is, of course, no single English equivalent. It is a word of tremendous range and significance. ... It is a word more generalized and less personalized than *theos*. ... [A]n investigation of classical Greek literature would lead to the discovery of the following meanings for *daimōn*: (1) the use of the word to signify a god or goddess or

---

25. The LXX utilizes the related *daimōn* only once (Isa 65:11). See the discussion.

26. The terms overlap semantically, especially when the adjective lemma (*daimonion*) is used substantively. The lemma *daimōn* is a noun. One cannot argue that the use of *daimonion* somehow makes the *šēdîm* or "sons of God" less divine or not supernatural at all. Though it probably presses the semantics too far, the fact that *daimonion* could be used to describe "intermediate" divinity (essentially, "divinity rank") could make it quite a useful term for establishing the lesser rank of the sons of God relative to Yahweh. For further discussion, see Werner Foerster, "Δαίμων," *TDNT* 2:8; BDAG, s.v. "δαιμόνιον."

individual gods and goddesses. This would be a rare use of the term; (2) more frequently, we would find it used of the Divine Power (the Latin *numen*). This would signify a superhuman force, impersonal in itself, but regularly belonging to a person (a god of some kind); (3) the Power controlling the destiny of individuals and then one's fortune or lot; (4) it could be further specialized as the good or evil *genius* of a person or family; (5) a more special use would reveal the *daimones* as titular deities, the "souls" of the men of the golden age of Hesiod; (6) general spiritual or semi-divine creatures who are less than gods, but intermediate between the gods and men (cf. Plato); (7) finally, "devil," and "bad spirit" in the Christianized sense (of course this last is not classical).[27]

As a result, the Greek translator of the LXX could use these terms without *intending* the categories of divine rebels in the Old Testament to be merged into one ontological class. Unfortunately, we have lost the knowledge of the term's range of nuance. This has led some scholars to drive a theological wedge between the testaments, charging that New Testament writers would not view the gods allotted to the nations as "real" deities, just "demons."

The thinking is curious since a demon would indeed be a supernatural entity. It also misses the fact that the divine plurality language of the Hebrew Bible doesn't point to polytheism but to rank and hierarchy of other supernatural entities with respect to Yahweh.[28] The driving assumption seems to be that more than one divine being means polytheism for the Old Testament but does not in the New Testament, so long as one avoids using a term like "gods" in any context that might construe them as real.

This imaginary line is one that the LXX crosses quite transparently.[29] Recall that our earlier table indicated that the LXX translates *benê 'elōhîm*

---

27. John E. Rexine, "*Daimon* in Classical Greek Literature," *Greek Orthodox Theological Review* 30.3 (1985): 336. I have transliterated the Greek words present in the excerpt.

28. See the bibliographic sources used in chapter 1's discussion of *'elōhîm*.

29. The New Testament does as well, by virtue of its use of LXX and other points of connection with Old Testament divine plurality passages. The New Testament writers were not ignorant of the nuances of the terms. They in fact use other terminology that shows their knowledge of the demonology of Second Temple Judaism and its differentiation between divine rebels. A term like *daimonion* was simply flexible enough to apply broadly. See chapter 10.

("sons of God") in Deuteronomy 32:8 as *angelōn theou* ("angels of God"), but uses plural forms of *theos* elsewhere when the gods allotted to the nations are mentioned (Deut 17:3; 29:26; Ps 82:1, 6).[30] In Deuteronomy 32:17 these gods (*'elōhîm*) are described as *šēdîm*, guardian spirits. The LXX chooses to translate *šēdîm* of Deuteronomy 32:17 with *daimonion* but also refers to these same beings as gods (*theoi*):

> They sacrificed to demons (*daimoniois*) and not to God,
> to gods (*theois*) whom they had not known (LES).

The vocabulary is neither inconsistent nor confused. There is no effort on the part of the translators to deny the reality of the divine beings allotted to the nations, or perhaps make them less than gods by calling them *daimonion*. LXX Deuteronomy 32:17 shows the flaw in such thinking.

The following instances of *daimonion* are instructive in this regard. The *'elōhîm/šēdîm* allotted to the nations are *daimoniois* ("demons") in Deuteronomy 32:17. The LXX translator made the same translation choice in the only other Old Testament passage where we find *šēdîm* (Ps 106:37; LXX Ps 105:37). LXX Psalm 95:5 (Heb. 96:5) reads, "For all the gods (*theoi*; Heb. *'elōhîm*) of the nations are demons (*daimonia*), but the Lord made the heavens" (LES). Here the LXX chose to translate Hebrew *'elōhîm* literally, but the ensuing term is not *šēdîm* but *'ĕlîlîm* ("idols"). The Hebrew Bible here draws a close association between the spirit beings and the objects of worship they were believed to inhabit. In ancient Near Eastern thought, the two were not the same, though closely associated. Construing this as meaning that the biblical writers thought the gods of the nations were merely handmade objects does not reflect the reality of ancient beliefs about idols. Michael Dick, whose research focuses on idolatry in the ancient Near East, cites ancient texts that reveal the idol maker using deity language for the idol that he made with his own hands while still maintaining a conceptual distinction between the image he made and the deity it represented. The deity would come to reside in the

---

30. The Ps 82 references are relevant because the psalm ends with the psalmist crying out to God to take back the nations. The judgment of the gods in the psalm is the judgment of the sons of God (Ps 82:6) allotted to the nations at Babel. This is the context for other eschatological judgment passages, such as Isa 34. See Joel Reemtsma, "The Punishment of the Powers: Deuteronomy 32 and Psalm 82 as the Backdrop for Isaiah 34" (paper presented at the Annual Meeting of the Evangelical Theological Society, San Diego, CA, Nov 19, 2014).

statue, but it was distinct from the statue. Dick notes one occasion where "the destruction of the statue of Shamash of Sippar was not regarded as the death of Shamash. Indeed, Shamash could still be worshiped."[31]

Gay Robins, another scholar of ancient cult objects and idolatry, explains the conceptual distinction between deity and image maintained in the ancient Near Eastern worldview:

> When a non-physical being manifested in a statue, this anchored the being in a controlled location where living human beings could interact with it through ritual performance. ... In order for human beings to interact with deities and to persuade them to create, renew, and maintain the universe, these beings had to be brought down to earth. ... This interaction had to be strictly controlled in order to avoid both the potential dangers of unrestricted divine power and the pollution of the divine by the impurity of the human world. While the ability of deities to act in the visible, human realm was brought about through their manifestation in a physical body, manifestation in one body did not in any sense restrict a deity, for the non-corporeal essence of a deity was unlimited by time and space, and could manifest in all its "bodies," in all locations, all at one time.[32]

The point is that, for ancient people—including Israelites—gods and their idols were closely related but not identical. This is important because Paul cites Deuteronomy 32:17 in 1 Corinthians 10:21–22 to warn the Corinthians about fellowshipping with demons. Paul obviously believed *daimonia* were real. Paul would not be contradicting the supernatural worldview of his Bible.[33] As we will see below, the LXX authors behind the books of Tobit and Baruch would side with Paul, as their books certainly assign reality to *daimonia*. Against this backdrop, it is somewhat difficult to discern what the LXX translator of Isaiah 65:3, 11 was thinking.

---

31. Heiser, *Unseen Realm*, 36, note 14. See Michael B. Dick, "Prophetic Parodies of Making the Cult Image," in *Born in Heaven, Made on Earth: The Making of the Cult Image in the Ancient Near East*, ed. Michael B. Dick (Winona Lake, IN: Eisenbrauns, 1999), 33–34.

32. Gay Robins, "Cult Statues in Ancient Egypt," in *Cult Image and Divine Representation in the Ancient Near East*, ed. Neal H. Walls (Boston: American Schools of Oriental Research, 2005), 1–2.

33. This did not prevent at least one Jewish LXX translator from inserting his own theological preference. See LXX Ps 90:6 (Heb. 91:6).

This people who provokes me is before me always; they sacrifice in their gardens and burn incense on their bricks to demons [*daimoniois*] that do not exist. (Isa 65:3 LES)

But you who have forsaken me and who forget my holy mountain and who prepare a table for a demon [*daimoniō*; Heb. *gad*] and fill up a mixture to Fortune [*tychē*; Heb. *mēnî*] … (Isa 65:11 LES)

The first thing to point out is that the phrase "to demons that do not exist" is not present in the Masoretic Text (MT). The translator either had a different text or, more likely, added the phrase in light of the content of verse 11 to follow. While it might seem obvious that the translator was inserting a theological point, the content of verse 11 creates some confusion for the translator's thought process. The LXX uses *daimoniō* in Isaiah 65:11 for Hebrew *gad*, a well-known deity name in Canaanite, Phoenician, and Punic texts.[34] Gad was a god (or goddess) of good luck, which is why Gad often appears in texts with a goddess (or god) of destiny, Tyche (*Tychē*), as here in LXX Isaiah 65:11.[35] Why the translator recognized one deity name but generalized the other with the lemma *daimonion* is not clear. He may not have cared, since he inserted the line "do not exist" earlier in Isaiah 65:3.

The remaining instances where *daimonion* was used by LXX translators in passages from the Hebrew Bible make it clear that if the translator of Isaiah 65 had a theological predilection for denying the reality of other gods, his cohorts did not share it.

Part of our discussion in the preceding chapter exposed how biblical writers used terms for preternatural creatures to convey the idea of unholy ground—territory associated with evil spirits.[36] Two of the most important passages in that regard were Isaiah 13:21–22 and Isaiah 34:14. The LXX translator used the plural of *daimonion* in both instances:

---

34. S. Ribichini, "Gad," *DDD* 339. See also F. L. Benz, *Personal Names in the Phoenician and Punic Inscriptions* (Rome: Biblical Institute Press, 1972), 294–95; J. Teixidor, *The Pantheon of Palmyra* (Leiden: Brill, 1979) 88–100.

35. L. H. Martin, "Tyche," *DDD* 877. See also S. D. Sperling, "Meni," *DDD* 566–67; W. C. Greene, *Moira. Fate, Good, and Evil in Greek Thought* (Cambridge, MA: Harvard University Press, 1944); L. B. Radford provides an extended discussion of Tyche (Radford, *The Epistle to the Colossians and the Epistle to Philemon* [London: Methuen, 1931], 127–43, 324–26).

36. The prominent Hebrew terms in that discussion were ṣiyyîm ("wild beasts"), 'iyyîm ("howling creatures"), and śĕ'îrîm ("he-goats" or "goat demons").

And wild animals will rest there, and the houses will be filled with sound; and Sirens [*seirēnes*] will rest there, and divine beings [*daimonia*] will dance there. And donkey-centaurs will settle there, and hedgehogs will make dens among their houses. It is coming quickly, and it will not delay. (Isa 13:21–22 LES)

And demons [*daimonia*] will meet donkey-centaurs [*onokentaurois*], and one will cry out to the other. There donkey-centaurs [*onokentauroi*] will rest, since they have found a rest for themselves. (Isa 34:14 LES)

The choice of "sirens" (*seirēnes*) for Hebrew *ʾōḥîm* ("howling creatures") in Isaiah 13:21 indicates that something other than the animal kingdom was in view to the translator.[37] In Greek mythology, sirens were beings who lured sailors to their deaths with their beautiful singing. In their earliest depictions in Greek art, they are shown with a woman's head and a bird's wings and body.[38] Shorey describes their role in mythology and the Greek word's use in the LXX:

[Sirens] are in a sense sea-nymphs inhabiting a lonely ocean isle, somewhere in the western fairyland of Odyssean adventure. ... Ovid merely says that the Sirens were playmates of Proserpine, and that the gods granted them wings that they might continue their search for her over the sea also. In the legend of the Argonauts, as the mythographs Apollodorus and Hyginus tell us, Orpheus sang against the Sirens who, being defeated, cast themselves into the sea and were transformed into hidden rocks. ... In the language of the LXX (Job 30:29, Is 34:13; 43:20, Jer 27:39) Siren is a synonym for the wild creatures and spirits that inhabit waste places.[39]

Remaining in Isaiah 13:21, the translator chose *daimonia* to render Hebrew *śeʿîrîm*. Recall from our earlier discussion of Azazel that *śeʿîrîm*

---

37. This is the only occurrence of this lemma in the Hebrew Bible. *HALOT* (s.v., אֹחַ) notes that it may speak of eagles or owls.
38. Paul Shorey, "Sirens," *ERE* 11:578.
39. Shorey, "Sirens," 578.

was translated "goat demons" in passages like Leviticus 17:7. The translator of LXX Isaiah therefore went a supernatural direction.[40]

What is meant by "donkey centaur" must remain speculative. In both passages (Isa 13:22; 34:14) this odd creature corresponds to *'iyyîm*. Again, the choice makes it evident that the writer did not have the normative animal world in view. His use of *daimonia* at the beginning of Isaiah 34:14 (for *ṣiyyîm*; "wild animals") points us in the direction of sinister supernatural entities.[41] Martin observes:

> Initially, it seems clear that *daimonian* translates *ṣiyyîm* and that *'iyyîm* is rendered as *onokentauroi* (doubtless here meaning some kind of ass-human hybrid, such as a "donkey-centaur"). ... The ancient referents of *ṣiyyîm* and *'iyyîm* are uncertain, and it is impossible at this time to identify their species. Fortunately, for our purposes it is enough to figure out what the translator thought they meant. *Daimonia* was taken to represent either the *ṣiyyîm* in particular or to include that word and others in the list, so at least *he* thought the Hebrew words referred to daimons, and *'iyyîm* to be ass-human hybrids. Since the term *śeʿîr* also occurs in the context (if the translator's Hebrew was like ours), it is tempting to imagine our translator picturing daimons, such as Dionysus, cavorting with satyrs and centaurs. Both satyrs and centaurs were regularly in the entourage of Dionysus, as was portrayed in Greek art. At any rate, *daimonia* here refers to mythological beings, perhaps including gods, who inhabit a deserted place.[42]

Moving on from the preternatural vocabulary, the LXX translator also apparently took the references to chaos forces such as *deber* ("pestilence") and *qeṭeb* ("destruction") as evil supernatural entities. Compare Psalm 91:3–6 in English translations of both the Hebrew Masoretic Text (ESV) and the Greek Septuagint (90:3–6 LES):

---

40. This was apparently the case in Isa 34:14, though it evades detection in the English translation above. The phrase "one will cry out to the other" occurs where the Masoretic Text has *śeʿîr* ("goat" or "goat demon"), which is the subject of the following verb *yiqrà* ("calls out"). The translator does not repeat *daimonia* here (or its singular form), choosing instead to have the donkey centaurs play the role of the goat demon ("one will cry out to the other").

41. It seems that the translators of Lev 17:7 and 2 Chr 11:15 sought to either obscure or denigrate the supernatural nuance. In both passages Hebrew *śeʿîrîm* is translated with *mataiois* ("worthless things").

42. Dale Basil Martin, "When Did Angels Become Demons?" *JBL* 129.4 (2010): 661. I have transliterated the Greek and Hebrew characters in the excerpt.

Masoretic Text (translated in ESV)	Septuagint (translated in LES)
3 For he will deliver you from the snare of the fowler and from the deadly pestilence [*deber*]. 4 He will cover you with his pinions, and under his wings you will find refuge; his faithfulness is a shield and buckler. 5 You will not fear the terror of the night, nor the arrow that flies by day, 6 nor the pestilence [*deber*] that stalks in darkness, nor the destruction [*qeṭeb*] that wastes at noonday.	3 because he will rescue from the trap of hunters and from a terrifying word. 4 With his shoulders he will overshadow you, and under his wings you will have hope; with a shield his truth will surround you. 5 That one will not be afraid from fear by night, from the arrow flying by day, 6 from the deed carried out in darkness, from mishap and demon [*daimonou*] at midday.

There are several items to notice in the LXX rendering, particularly the appearance of a "midday demon." Riley explains:

> The Midday Demon is found in the Septuagint version of Ps 91:6 (LXX 90:6). In Ps 91:5–6, the Hebrew psalmist declares that the one who takes refuge in the Almighty will not fear: "The Terror of the night nor the Arrow that flies by day, nor the Pestilence (*Deber*) that stalks in darkness nor the Destruction (*Qeṭeb*) that wastes at noonday."
>
> The parallelism of the verses twice balances a night and a daytime Evil, each of which was understood by rabbinic interpreters to refer to a demonic spirit: the day-time *Qeṭeb* is balanced by the night demon, Pestilence, *Deber*. In Deut 32:24 the "poisonous *Qeṭeb*" is parallel to Resheph, the well-known Canaanite demon of plague. Thus the *Qeṭeb* is the personified destruction or disease, riding the hot desert wind (cf. Isa 28:2 and the wind demons of Mesopotamia). In Ps 91:6b … the Septuagint translators confronted a different Hebrew text (with Aquila and Symmachus), reading *wšd* for *yšwd*, meaning "Destruction and the demon (*šed*) of noontime," which the LXX rendered as "Misfortune and the Midday demon. …" This variant violated the parallelism of the original, and added a fifth Evil (*ṣhrym šd*), the Midday demon.[43]

From the psalm's rendering alone it is not possible to tell if the translator moved away from the sort of demythologization we discussed in chapter 1, where such deity names were used to communicate the notion that natural forces were at the behest of autonomous deities but Yahweh

---

43. G. J. Riley, "Midday Demon," *DDD* 572. I have transliterated the Greek and Hebrew characters in the excerpt.

of Israel held sovereign sway over all other powers. While the language here certainly includes supernatural powers, their relationship to Yahweh can't be discerned from the translation.

DAIMONION IN TOBIT AND BARUCH

Tobit and Baruch are two Second Temple Jewish literary works that were part of the LXX, the contents of which, therefore, extend beyond the books of the Hebrew Bible.[44] *Daimonion* occurs seven times in Tobit and twice in Baruch.[45] Some of the references are generic and made in the context of magical acts to thwart demons (Tobit 6:8, 18; 8:3). Others, however, have the story's demonic villain Asmodeus in view. Asmodeus has taken the lives of a series of men married to a woman named Sarah (Tobit 3:8 LES: "She was given seven husbands but Asmodeus the evil demon killed them before they could be with her"). Asmodeus must be bound in order to protect Tobias, the son of Tobit, who is destined to be Sarah's next (and final) husband (Tobit 3:17; 6:15–16).

The fact that magical means are necessary to deal with Asmodeus makes it clear that he is a supernatural figure. The demon draws interest from scholars because the story of Tobit attributes a range of tragedies, including death, to demons. Some scholars view this as a theological innovation:

> In the Book of Tobit the *daimōn* Asmodai (*aēsma daēuua*, "Demon of Wrath") allows us to catch a glimpse of the beginnings of the

---

44. Scholars believe that Greek was not the original language of Tobit. Hebrew and Aramaic are both candidates for the original composition. As deSilva notes: "Scholars had long debated whether the original language was Greek or a Semitic language (Aramaic or Hebrew). Pfeiffer (1949: 272–73) correctly notes the Semitisms behind the Greek and so posits a Semitic original, favoring Aramaic (given the author's familiarity with Aramaic literature such as the tale of Ahiqar). His opinion has been confirmed by Fitzmyer (1995a: 671), whose examination of the five Qumran manuscripts proved that Greek was not the original language but rather, that the original was Semitic and probably Aramaic. The Qumran manuscripts have helped less than scholars had hoped with regard to settling the question of a Hebrew or Aramaic original." See David A. deSilva, *Introducing the Apocrypha: Message, Context, and Significance* (Grand Rapids: Baker Academic, 2002), 68. [His cited sources are R. H. Pfeiffer, *History of New Testament Times, with an Introduction to the Apocrypha* (New York: Harper & Brothers, 1949); J. A. Fitzmyer, "The Aramaic and Hebrew Fragments of Tobit from Cave 4," *Catholic Biblical Quarterly* 57 (1995): 655–75.] In regard to Baruch, deSilva writes: "Although no ancient Hebrew manuscript of any part of Baruch has surfaced, scholars are agreed that at least 1:1–3:8 was composed originally in Hebrew (Whitehouse 1913: 571–72; Tov 1975: 3–7). ... Several scholars argue that 3:9–5:9 was also composed in Hebrew..., but here there is greater debate" (201).

45. Tobit 3:8, 17; 6:8, 15–16, 18; 8:3; Baruch 4:7, 35.

development of a demonology, in which the demons act as independent opponents of God respectively of the angels in order to relieve the monotheistic God from threatening evil features on the one hand, and, on the other hand, to transfer him from his transcendental world into the world of man.[46]

It is not clear why this would be viewed as an innovation. Other Second Temple literature clearly has divine beings choosing to rebel against God.[47] The content of the two references in Baruch will sound familiar:

> [5]"Be courageous my people, memorial of Israel. [6]You were sold to the nations not for annihilation, but because you angered God; you were given over to adversaries. [7]For you provoked the one who made you, by sacrificing to demons [*daimoniois*] and not to God. (Baruch 4:5–7 LES)

The language and theology of Baruch 4:7 echoes Deuteronomy 32:17, a passage on which we spent considerable time. The reference is to Israel's apostasy, rejecting its status as Yahweh's portion and people (Deut 32:8–9) in sacrificing to the gods allotted to other nations. The result of this apostasy is described later in the chapter:

> [30]"Be confident, O Jerusalem! The one who named you will comfort you. [31]Wretched will be the ones who mistreated you and rejoiced at your fall. [32]Wretched be the cities in which your children were enslaved, wretched the one who received your sons. [33]Just as she rejoiced at your fall and was cheerful in your calamity, so will she grieve at her own desolation. [34]I will remove her satisfaction at her great population and turn her pride into grief. [35]Fire will come upon her from the Eternal One for many days, and she will be occupied by demons [*daimoniōn*] for a long time." (Baruch 4:30–35 LES)

After castigating Jerusalem for her apostasy, the narrative shifts in verse 30 to comfort and the declaration of impending catastrophe upon

---

46. Frey-Anthes, "Concepts of 'Demons' in Ancient Israel," 49.

47. Perhaps the possibility of Zoroastrian influence on the author of Tobit moves her in this direction (Frey-Anthes' etymology in the excerpt is Avestan). The point of her observation, of course, is the notion that demons could kill. But what then of demons like Lilith, feared as a night demon who would strangle children? The Lilith demon goes all the way back to Sumerian sources. A number of Mesopotamian demons whose names and etymologies show up in the Hebrew Bible threatened life. See M. Hutter, "Asmodeus," *DDD* 107; M. Hutter, "Lilith," *DDD* 520.

"the ones who mistreated you and rejoiced at your fall ... and [were] cheerful in your calamity" (Baruch 4:31, 33). Given the description of rejoicing and the reference to being "occupied by demons" (Baruch 4:35), it is very likely that the unnamed target of God's wrath is Babylon. As we saw earlier, Babylon was described as being occupied by preternatural creatures in the wake of its destruction.[48]

SUMMARY

This brief survey of how the Septuagint (LXX) translates the Hebrew Bible's vocabulary for evil spirits enables us to draw some broad conclusions. While some semantic nuancing is lost to readers, LXX translations are consistent with the content of the Hebrew Bible. While no one would claim LXX translators thought as one, the translators were not trying to amend or obscure the theological worldview of their predecessors. As we will see as we proceed, Jewish thinkers of the Second Temple period presumed the supernatural worldview of their forefathers.

---

48. See the discussion in Sean A. Adams, *Baruch and the Epistle of Jeremiah: Commentary* (Septuagint Commentary Series; Leiden: Brill, 2014), 139. Adams does not favor Babylon as the referent, arguing that the author of Baruch would not have had access to the Hebrew text of Isaiah. This trajectory fails logically. The author could have known Baruch from a targum or the LXX itself (prior to Baruch being included in a codex with the rest of LXX). If so, the description of Babylon in Isaiah 34 as being filled with demons and preternatural creatures would still have been clear.

THE POWERS OF DARKNESS IN THE OLD TESTAMENT AND SECOND TEMPLE JUDAISM

OVERVIEW

At several points of the initial chapters of our study, our survey of Old Testament vocabulary for the powers of darkness, I alluded to the subject matter of this next section: the three supernatural rebellions described in the Old Testament. In this second section we will drill down into each rebellion to accomplish three goals: (1) to understand the Old Testament theological framework for explaining the origin of the dark powers; (2) to show how that Old Testament framework was both embraced and developed by Second Temple (intertestamental) Jewish writers; and (3) prepare readers for discerning how a New Testament theology of the powers of darkness partakes of both the Old Testament and Second Temple period thought.[1]

---

1. In light of this third goal, our study intentionally excludes pseudepigraphical works very likely composed after the first century AD and interpolations post-dating the first century AD added to earlier Second Temple texts. Other studies on the powers of darkness that have cast a wider net in regard to the figure of Satan, the rebellion of the Watchers (the sons of God of Gen 6:1–4) and the sons of God allotted to the nations include: Tae Whoe (David) Chung, "The Development of the Concept of Satan in Old Testament and Intertestamental Literature" (PhD diss., Southwestern Baptist Theological Seminary, 2000); Zane D. Hodge, "A Historical and Grammatical Examination of Azazel in Biblical and Extra-biblical Sources with Special Emphasis Given to Its Meaning with the Hebrew Preposition ל" (PhD diss., Mid-American Baptist Theological Seminary, 2004); and Ryan Evan Stokes, "Rebellious Angels and Malicious Spirits: Explanations of Evil in the Enochic and Related Literature" (PhD diss., Yale University, 2010).

We will devote two chapters to each rebellion: the serpent of Genesis 3 (chapters 3–4), the sons of God of Genesis 6:1–4 (chapters 5–6), and the sons of God allotted to the nations at Babel, described in Deuteronomy 32:8–9 (chapters 7–8). It will quickly become evident that the interaction of Second Temple writers with the Old Testament is both informative and confusing. These authors at times conflated the villains of separate divine rebellions. They felt free to add details, weaving their own speculations into the fabric of their texts. Consequently, their literary works are simultaneously rooted in the Old Testament and are the products of fertile imaginations.

For example, some Second Temple authors have the rebellious sons of God from Genesis 6:1–4 led by a lead rebel, who is described in ways that would remind the reader of the Hebrew Bible of the rebel in Eden, the serpent, or the śāṭān of Job 1–2. The Old Testament makes no such associations, but that didn't stop these later writers from doing so.

While the linkages in this example are, in Old Testament terms, incorrect, they are valuable for showing us how Second Temple Jewish writers were thinking about the evil spirit beings in these episodes.

Our study will show that, while some Second Temple Jewish material is certainly purely speculative, it is an overstatement to caricature the relationship of Second Temple demonology as severely disconnected from the Old Testament. It is not. While writers of the period take the liberty to answer questions raised in Old Testament stories, we'll discover that in places they do so because they have a firmer grip on the context of Old Testament passages than we do.

It may sound odd, but we'll see that in some instances, Second Temple period writers had access to material that provides context to Old Testament rebellion episodes that Old Testament writers assumed their audience would know and, therefore, did not include. While they do speculate and unnecessarily conflate material, some of the gaps filled by these later writers is quite consistent with the Old Testament and makes the New Testament comprehensible. In other words, certain ideas in the New Testament about Satan and other powers of darkness cannot be found in the Old Testament but *are* found in Second Temple Jewish texts. New Testament writers were not averse to letting such material inform their thinking and even including it in what they wrote. That is perfectly consistent with God's providential oversight in inspiration.

CHAPTER 3

The Original Rebel—
I Will Be Like the Most High

THE GOAL OF THIS CHAPTER IS TO ESTABLISH THE PROFILE OF SCRIP-
ture's first supernatural rebel. As we saw in our discussion of the Old
Testament vocabulary for evil spirit beings, their portrayals share par-
ticularities, certain aspects that set them in binary opposition to their
Creator. The presence of God means life and light. The latter metaphor
is used in the Old Testament to speak of God's saving presence, his truth
and righteousness, and the blessing of being in harmony with God's order
and design.[1] Evil spirits represent death and darkness. As their rebellions
demonstrate, they traffic in deceit, injustice, and chaos.

TROUBLE IN GOD'S HOUSE

The contrasts of good versus evil and life versus death were never more
pronounced than in Scripture's portrayal of the first defection from God's
will. I speak here of the fall (Gen 3). We tend to think of that episode primarily in human terms. That's understandable, since the fall affected the
entirety of the human race. But behind the decisions of Adam and Eve
to violate God's command about the tree of the knowledge of good and

---

1. For example, 2 Sam 23:2–4; Pss 27:1; 119:130; Isa 5:20; Mic 7:8b. In the New Testament, "believers
are commanded to 'cast off the works of darkness and put on the armor of light' (Rom 13:12 RSV).
Equally evocative is the picture in Ephesians 5:8–9: 'Once you were darkness, but now you are light
in the Lord; walk as children of light'" ("Light," *Dictionary of Biblical Imagery*, ed. Leland Ryken et
al. [Downers Grove, IL: InterVarsity Press, 2000], 511).

evil, there was another created being, supernatural in nature, who had decided his own will was preeminent.

Most readers will acknowledge that the serpent (Heb. *nāḥāš*) was not simply a member of the animal kingdom.[2] This conclusion seems obvious, since the New Testament identifies the serpent as Satan or the devil (Rev 12:9). The devil is certainly not a zoological specimen (2 Cor 11:14; cf. Matt 4:1–11; John 8:44). Put simply, if we agree with the New Testament that a supernatural being (Satan) tempted Eve in Eden, then by definition the serpent must be more than a mere animal. We can only oppose this conclusion if we reject the New Testament assessment.[3]

Ancient readers—without the New Testament—would be able to draw the same conclusion, though they didn't necessarily use the same vocabulary.[4] They of course knew that animals did not talk, and so when that sort of thing was encountered in storytelling, they knew supernatural power was at play or a divine presence had taken center stage.

Ancient readers would have thought about Eden in such a way that the supernatural nature of the serpent would have been conspicuous. We think of the garden of Eden like we think of earthly gardens. We know God was there, but a garden is a garden; Eden was a *perfect* garden, but, at the end of the day, it was just a garden. People from the biblical period would have had a different perception, one that was more transcendent. They would have thought of Eden as a temple.[5] After all, temples are where gods live. Eden was the abode of God, "an earthly archetype of the heavenly reality."[6] "Because Adam communed with God in Eden,"

---

2. The writer's choice of the lemma *nāḥāš* may have been designed to convey double or triple entendre. The root consonants (*n-ḥ-š*) are the base of a noun ("serpent"; Num 21:6, 9), verb ("to foretell omens, do divination"; Deut 18:10), and "shining" (1 Chr 4:12, the name Ir-Nachash = "city of bronze"; cp. the "bronze serpent" = *nĕḥōšet nāḥāš*). The term in Genesis 3 is prefixed with the definite article (*hannāḥāš*) and could be translated "the serpent," "the one who performs divination," of "the shining one." See *HALOT*, s.v. נָחַשׁ. I have discussed these options in more detail in *Unseen Realm* (Heiser, *Unseen Realm*, 73–75, 87–92), but see the discussion to follow.

3. The biblical text does not say a divine being "entered" the serpent as though we have a possession here. That would be to read into the passage. The text is clear—it is the serpent that deceives Eve, initiating the cascade of events that leads to the loss of everlasting life for humanity. The New Testament affirms this (2 Cor 11:3; Rev 12:9; 20:2), also using "devil" or "Satan" to make the same point (Rev 12:9; 20:2; cf. Heb 2:14; John 8:44; cp. Gen 3:15; Rom 16:20).

4. We will discuss Satan in Second Temple literature in the next chapter.

5. This idea is well presented for a broad, popular audience by Walton, *Lost World of Genesis One*.

6. Ryken et al., *Dictionary of Biblical Imagery*, 849.

Wenham adds, "the latter was the temporal analog for the celestial archetype."[7]

The archetypal nature of Eden as the house-temple of God is why Eden is described as a well-watered garden (Gen 2:6, 8–9, 10–16; Ezek 28:2, 13) and a holy mountain (Ezek 28:14). There is no contradiction. An ancient reader would have embraced both descriptions. Both were common characterizations for divine dwellings. The motif of the garden as an abode of the gods is common in ancient Near Eastern literature.[8] Several Old Testament passages depict rivers flowing from God's dwelling in Jerusalem to water the desert (Ezek 47:1–12; Zech 14:8; Joel 3:18).[9] Wallace notes that "the main feature of the garden of God theme is the presence of the deity. The divine council meets there and decrees of cosmic importance are issued."[10]

Wallace's observation that the cosmic dwelling (garden or mountain) was also home to the divine council would have been expected by an ancient reader. The scholarly literature on the divine council[11] and the meeting place of the council as a garden or a mountain[12] is extensive.

---

7. Gordon J. Wenham, "Sanctuary Symbolism in the Garden of Eden Story," in *I Studied Inscriptions before the Flood: Ancient Near Eastern, Literary, and Linguistic Approaches to Genesis 1–11*, ed. R. S. Hess and D. A. Tsumura (Winona Lake, IN: Eisenbrauns, 1994), 399–404 (esp. 400).

8. Representative examples include Epic of Gilgamesh V, i, lines 6–9; Enki and Ninhursag, lines 55–64; and the Baal Cycle (KTU 1.3:5:4–9). For further discussion of this imagery, see Heiser, *Unseen Realm*, 44–48.

9. Howard N. Wallace, "Garden of God (Place)," *ABD* 2:906.

10. Ibid.

11. See for example, Miller, *Israelite Religion and Biblical Theology*, 422–44; E. Theodore Mullen Jr., *The Divine Council in Canaanite and Early Hebrew Literature* (Chico, CA: Scholars Press, 1980); Mullen, "Divine Assembly," *ABD* 2:215–16; Lowell K. Handy, *Among the Host of Heaven: The Syro-Palestinian Pantheon as Bureaucracy* (Winona Lake, IN: Eisenbrauns, 1994); S. B. Parker, "Sons of (the) God(s)," *DDD* 798; Michael S. Heiser, "Divine Council," *DOTWPW* 112–16; David Marron Fleming, "The Divine Council as Type Scene in the Hebrew Bible" (PhD diss., Southern Baptist Theological Seminary, 1989); Min Suc Kee, "The Heavenly Council and Its Type-Scene," *JSOT* 31.3 (2007): 259–73; Ellen White, *Yahweh's Council: Its Structure and Membership* (Tübingen: Mohr Siebeck, 2014); Matitiahu Tsevat, "God and the Gods in Assembly," *HUCA* 40–41 (1969–70): 123–37.

12. For example, see Richard J. Clifford, *The Cosmic Mountain in Canaan and the Old Testament* (Cambridge, MA: Harvard University Press, 1972); Clifford, "The Temple and the Holy Mountain," in *Cult and Cosmos: Tilting Toward a Temple-Centered Biblical Theology*, ed. L. Michael Morales (Leuven: Peeters, 2014), 85–98; Michael Morales, *The Tabernacle Pre-Figured: Cosmic Mountain Ideology in Genesis and Exodus* (Leuven: Peeters, 2012); Daniel T. Lioy, "The Garden of Eden as a Primordial Temple or Sacred Space for Humankind," *Conspectus* 10 (2010): 25–57; Ronald E. Clements, "Sacred Mountains, Temples, and the Presence of God," in *Cult and Cosmos: Tilting Toward a Temple-Centered Biblical Theology*, ed. L. Michael Morales (Leuven: Peeters, 2014), 69–85.

The divine council, the assembly of the heavenly host, was perceived as an administrative bureaucracy. In biblical thought, the members of the divine council participate in issuing and executing divine decrees.[13] Just as a king has a court, God was his own administration. Where he lives, he conducts business.

Genesis 2–3 portray Eden as a divine garden and mountain. But what indication do we have from Genesis 3 that there is a group of divine beings (a council) in Eden? In Genesis 3:5, the serpent told Eve, "God knows that when you eat of it your eyes will be opened, and you will be like God ['elōhîm], knowing good and evil." We discover that 'elōhîm in this verse should actually be read as a plural when we reach Genesis 3:22, where God—speaking not to Adam, Eve, or the serpent—says, "Behold, the man has become like one of us in knowing good and evil. Now, lest he reach out his hand and take also of the tree of life and eat, and live forever." The violation resulted in Adam and Eve becoming like "one *of us*," which obviously requires plurality. The fact that their sin did indeed result in knowing good and evil tells us the serpent did not lie in that component of his deception. God himself confirmed the result in verse 22. This means the 'elōhîm of verse 5 points to a group—God's heavenly council.[14]

The implication of seeing Eden through ancient Near Eastern eyes is that God was not the only divine being. God had created humankind as his imagers and tasked them with bringing the rest of the world outside Eden under control—in effect, expanding Eden through the rest

---

13. We briefly mentioned the divine council in chapter 1. On the participation of the heavenly host with God's rule, see Heiser, *Angels*, 32–46.

14. This plurality is not an indication of the Trinity. The other instance of this sort of plural language in the creation account (Gen 1:26, "let *us* create humankind in/as *our* image") makes that certain. I have discussed this passage in detail elsewhere (Heiser, *Unseen Realm*, 38–43). The most significant problem with this identification is that Gen 1:26 describes God announcing a decision to a group. If the group was actually the other two members of the Trinity, this announcement is nonsensical, because the members of the Trinity are co-eternal and co-omniscient. God (the Father) never needs to inform them of anything. The divine plurality language of Genesis (Gen 1:26; 3:5, 22; 11:7) has been analyzed extensively. The most exhaustive scholarly treatment is that of W. Randall Garr, *In His Own Image and Likeness: Humanity, Divinity, and Monotheism* (Leiden: Brill, 2003), especially 17–94. While the Old Testament does bear evidence of the Godhead (see Heiser, *Unseen Realm*, 127–48), the Trinity is never transparently expressed in the Old Testament. The plurality language is also not explainable as the "plural of majesty." As Joüon-Muraoka notes, "The *we* of majesty does not exist in Hebrew" (*GBH* §114e, note 2). The plural of majesty does exist for nouns (see *GBH* §136d), but Gen 1:26 is not about the nouns—the issue is the verbal forms. See also John C. Beckman, "*Pluralis Majestatis*: Biblical Hebrew," *EHLL* 3:145–46.

of creation.[15] God's will was disrupted when an external supernatural tempter, acting autonomously against God's wishes, succeeded in deceiving Eve.[16]

THE ORIGINAL REBEL OUTSIDE GENESIS 3

We know the basics of the fall story from Genesis 3. One of God's heavenly-council servants presents himself to Eve as a serpent with the intent to deceive. Many incorrectly presume, however, that the language of Genesis 3 can be parsed only as a talking snake. There are other options, particularly after the full text of the Hebrew Bible existed. Other passages contribute elements to the story.

For example, the divine being of Eden is referred to as a cherub (*kĕrûb*) in Ezekiel 28:14—specifically a "guardian" (*hassōkēk*) cherub.[17] This is not surprising, since *kĕrûb* comes from Akkadian *kurību*, a term for a throne guardian. As Launderville points out:

> The cherub in the OT ... had three distinctive roles: (1) to guard the source of life (Gen 3:24); (2) to draw the chariot of God (Ps 18:11 = 2 Sam 22:11; 4 Ezek 1:5–20; 10:1–22); and (3) to serve as the throne for God (1 Kgs 6:23–28; 8:6–8). ... In [Ezek] 28:14 an "anointed cherub" (*kĕrûb mimšaḥ*) functioned as a guardian (*hassōkēk*) within the garden of Eden. ... In the Mesopotamian tradition, there were numerous composite supernatural beings with human and animal characteristics, for example, the Snake dragon.[18]

---

15. The image of God is not a thing put within the human being. It is not an attribute or quality. Rather, it is a status—being created as God's imager, his proxy. The concept of humanity imaging God is one that runs through both Testaments and connects to the concept of Jesus being the "express image of God" (Heb 1:3; cf. 2 Cor 4:4) and the image to which believers are being conformed (Rom 8:29). See Michael S. Heiser, "The Image of God," *LBD*.

16. This divine defection was made possible because of God's decision to also create the supernatural beings of his heavenly council as his imagers in the spiritual realm—an observation that extends from the plurality language of Gen 1:26. The image is a concept that connects God, humanity, and the audience to whom God was speaking ("*our* image"). To accomplish the task of imaging him, God shared his attributes with *both* his human and divine creations (what theologians call "communicable" attributes). One of those attributes was freedom (i.e., free will). See Heiser, *Unseen Realm*, 61–67; Heiser, "The Image of God."

17. As *HALOT*, s.v. סכך, notes, this lemma speaks of protection and shutting off access.

18. Dale Launderville, "Ezekiel's Cherub: A Promising Symbol or a Dangerous Idol?" *Catholic Biblical Quarterly* 65.2 (2003): 165–83.

That a divine Mesopotamian *kurību* might be depicted as a "snake dragon" is striking. Other divine throne guardians, such as those in Egyptian religion, might also be cast as serpentine. Bernard Batto describes the Edenic rebel this way: "The 'serpent' [was] a semi-divine creature with wings and feet like the seraphs in Isa 6:2, whose function was to guard sacred persons and sacred objects such as the tree of divine wisdom."[19] Some would object that *śĕrāpîm* of Isaiah 6:2, 6 are fiery beings, an idea that presumes the noun derives from the verb *śārap* ("to burn").[20] As Provençal's study demonstrates, it is more likely that *śĕrāpîm* is simply the plural of the Hebrew noun *śārāp* ("serpent"), which in turn is drawn from Egyptian throne-guardian vocabulary (depictions of which can also include fire).[21]

Now we can take a closer look at two key passages from Ezekiel and Isaiah. Ezekiel 28:13–16 has transparent references to Eden, the garden mountain of God, the place of the divine council, and a divine rebel. Isaiah 14:12–15 also describes a divine being cast out of the divine council's meeting place (the *har mô ʿēd*, "mount of assembly"; Isa 14:13), whose offence was the thirst for autonomy, to be "like the Most High" over the council ("the stars of God"; Isa 14:13).[22] These portions of Isaiah 14 and Ezekiel 28 provide more details for thinking about what happened in Genesis 3.

---

19. Bernard F. Batto, *In the Beginning: Essays on Creation Motifs in the Bible and the Ancient Near East* (Winona Lake, IN: Eisenbrauns, 2013), 47.

20. *HALOT*, s.v. שׂרף.

21. Philippe Provençal, "Regarding the Noun שׂרף [*śārāp*] in the Hebrew Bible," *JSOT* 29.3 (2005): 371–79. As I have observed elsewhere, Provençal shows that "the Egyptian Uraeus serpent, drawn from two species of Egyptian cobras, fits all the elements of the supernatural seraphim who attend Yahweh's holy presence in Isaiah 6. The relevant cobra species spit 'burning' venom, can expand wide flanges of skin on either side of their bodies—considered 'wings' in antiquity—when threatened, and are (obviously) serpentine" (Heiser, *Angels*, 26–27). Joines adds that "a function of the uraeus is to protect the pharaoh and sacred objects by breathing out fire on his enemies." See Karen R. Joines, "Winged Serpents in Isaiah's Inaugural Vision," *JBL* 86.4 (1967): 410–15. Hendel further raises the possibility that the flame of Gen 3:24 may actually describe an individual divine being. See Ronald Hendel, " 'The Flame of the Whirling Sword': A Note on Genesis 3:24," *JBL* 104.4 (1985): 671–74.

22. In Isa 14:13 the "mount of assembly" (*har mô ʿēd*) is in the "far reaches of the north" (ESV; *yarkĕtę ṣāphôn*). The "north" (*ṣāphôn/tsāphôn*) is the parallel to Ugaritic Ṣapanu, the location of Baal's council. Biblical writers removed the council lead from Baal, attributing it to Yahweh, in passages like Ps 48:1–2, where Zion is in "the heights of the north." See H. Niehr, "Zaphon," *DDD* 927; Clifford, *The Cosmic Mountain in Canaan and the Old Testament*, 57–79; C. Grave, "The Etymology of Northwest Semitic *ṣapānu*," *Ugarit Forschungen* 12 (1980): 221–29; N. Wyatt, "The Significance of ṢPN in West Semitic Thought," *Ugarit: Ein ostmediterranes Kulturzentrum im Alten Orient*, ed. M. Dietrich and O. Loretz (Münster: Ugarit-Verlag, 1995), 213–37; E. Lipiński, "צפון," *TDOT* 12:435–43.

This perspective is not without controversy. I have discussed the relationship of these passages to Genesis 3 in detail elsewhere.[23] For present purposes, I will summarize parts of that lengthier treatment but also add relevant material.

It is useful to first note that the content of Isaiah 14:12–15 and Ezekiel 28:1–19 overlaps in a variety of ways. This is not in dispute among scholars. There is also consensus that both passages are aimed at human kings (Babylon and Tyre, respectively) and share elements of the literary genres of a mocking taunt (*māšāl*) and a lament (*qînà*) in their characterizations of those kings.[24] When it comes to the original context (or source) of the material used in both passages to mock/lament the demise of these kings, scholars disagree sharply.

Some scholars (this writer included) believe that, while each prophetic taunt/lament is directed at a human king, both passages draw on a primeval tale of a *divine* rebellion to portray the respective kings the way they do.[25] Since Genesis 3 clearly has the inaugural disruption of

---

23. Heiser, *Unseen Realm*, 73–92. On the "star" language for members of the divine council, see F. Lelli, "Stars," *DDD* 809–10; I. Zatelli, "Astrology and the Worship of the Stars in the Bible," *ZAW* 103 (1991): 86–99; Ulf Oldenburg, "Above the Stars of El: El in Ancient South Arabic Religion," *ZAW* 82 (1970): 187–208.

24. Commenting on Isaiah 14 Wildberger notes: "Verse 4a describes the song as a מָשָׁל [*māšāl*]. The word actually means 'likening, comparison' (see Akkadian *mašâlu*, 'be like'; Arabic *miṯlun*, 'the equivalent'); it can be used as a neutral term, 'saying, proverb,' but can also be used in the special, technical sense of a 'mocking saying'; the מֹשֵׁל is the one who speaks mocking words (Num. 21:27; see also Isa. 28:14). By their very nature, such sayings are short (see the מִשְׁלֵי שְׁלֹמֹה, 'proverbs of Solomon,' Prov. 1:1); simply for these reasons, the designation מָשָׁל does not adequately describe the poem in vv. 4b–21 as a whole. Modern scholars have known for a long time that the song obviously contains elements from the song of the lament for the dead. … However, the term מָשָׁל (mocking saying) is certainly used appropriately to identify certain elements of the song. As a comparison with Isa. 37:22–29 shows, Israel also knew about the mocking song that heaped scorn on disempowered enemies. It is easy to see that both songs have the same motifs (cf. particularly 37:24 with 14:13). This poet who fashioned 14:4bff. was certainly not the first to use *Qina* (lament) meter in a *mashal* (comparison, proverb, mocking saying) and direct this against a people or a political opponent. On this point as well, the clearest examples are in Ezekiel: 19:1–4; 27:2–10, 25b–36; 28:1–19; see also 31:1–18. It is significant that what Isaiah calls a מָשָׁל (mocking saying) in 14:4 is termed a קִינָה (*Qina*, lament) in Ezek. 27:2; 28:12; 32:2, 16 (and that מָשָׁל, "taunt song," and נהי [*nĕhî*], 'bitter lamentation,' are used together in Mic. 2:4)." See Hans Wildberger, *A Continental Commentary: Isaiah 13–27* (Minneapolis: Fortress, 1997), 51.

25. Examples of scholars who take this position, or at least are not hostile to it, include: H. J. van Dijk, *Ezekiel's Prophecy on Tyre (Ez. 26:1–28:19): A New Approach* (Rome: Pontifical Biblical Institute, 1968); Peter C. Craigie, "Helel, Athtar, and Phaethon (Isa 14:12–15)," *ZAW* 85 (1973): 223–25; W. Gallagher, "On the Identity of *Helel Ben Shaher* in Is. 14:12–15," *Ugarit Forschungen* 26 (1994): 131–46; J. W. McKay, "Helel and the Dawn-Goddess—A Re-examination of the Myth in Isa 14:12–25," *VT* 20 (1970): 450–64; Clifford, *The Cosmic Mountain in Canaan and the Old Testament*, 160–68.

God's good world, beginning with a divine entity who tempts Eve to sin, and since Genesis 3 has so many connections to these other passages (see following pages), these scholars ask whether all three passages (Isa 14:12–15; Ezek 28:1–19; Gen 3) might be drawing from the same literary well.[26] For these scholars, the chronological order of these three biblical passages does not matter. It is also not a requirement that all three draw from the same text. The issue is whether these texts ultimately have a divine rebel in view and, if so, whether these three passages can inform each other. If so, then Isaiah 14 and Ezekiel 28 have something to contribute to the content of Genesis 3—specifically, to its characterization of the divine rebel.

The tables on pages 69–70 present the terms or motifs associated with the divine council, its members, its meeting place, and divine rebellion in Genesis 3, Isaiah 14:12–14, and Ezekiel 28:1–19.[27] Nearly every term in this table has a secure cognate (parallel) in ancient Near Eastern texts about a divine rebellion.

---

26. As the scholarly work on these passages has shown, there are a number of texts from the ancient Near East about a singular divine rebel seeking to usurp supreme authority in the divine assembly. The studies referenced in the earlier footnotes establish coherent textual connections to ancient Near Eastern stories about Athtar, Phaethon, and Enlil/Illil. In one of my scholarly publications I opt for the Athtar myth of Ugarit as being the best reference point: Michael S. Heiser, "The Mythological Provenance of Isaiah 14:12–15: A Reconsideration of the Ugaritic Material," VT 51.3 (2001): 354–69. Athtar is "the brilliant," highlighting his astral/shining status, just as Helel's ("shining one, son of the dawn"). He is also a source of conflict in the council. While noting a number of scholars see the Athtar myth as an important backdrop to Isa 14:12–15, Ugaritic scholar N. Wyatt recently dismissed an Athtar connection. Wyatt's article did not interact with mine. I would only note here that my notion of rebellion was Athtar's snubbing of El's decision, not that Athtar sought the highest position. I read Athtar's action as the presumption of autonomy. Any member of the Israelite divine council (such as Helel in Isa 14:12–15) who sought autonomy by definition sought to "be like the Most High" in Israel's Yahwistic religion. To be the autonomous deity in the council would mean displacement of Yahweh as supreme authority. Genesis 3 portrays its rebel in this way—the *nāḥāš* is cast not as one sent by another authority to deceive the humans, but as acting on his own. His purpose is easily discerned by the reader: persuade the humans to violate the lone prohibition they'd be given so as to have them removed from the garden, God's domicile. Given the number of connections between Isa 14:12–15 and Ezek 28:1–19 and Ugaritic religious literature, it stands to reason that the biblical writers saw this as noteworthy. Even Baal had to seek El's permission to have his own house-temple. Athtar, on the other hand, rebuffs El's decision and then chooses (more likely, resumes) rule over the earth (*'arṣ*; in *KTU* 1.6.i.56–67, Athtar "went up" to the throne El chose for him and then "came down" to rule the earth). Not only does Athtar refuse to do as El desires, he presumes his previous dominion is his to return to. No permission of El is sought at any point.

27. The tables are adapted from Heiser, *Unseen Realm*, 75, 86, 90.

DIVINE COUNCIL ELEMENTS SHARED IN GENESIS 3, ISAIAH 14, EZEKIEL 28			
Hebrew Term	**English Meaning**	**Concept**	**Important Verses**
elim, ʾelōhîm (plural)	"gods"	divine council and members; shining appearance[1]	Gen 3:5, 22, 24; Ezek 28:2, 16; Isa 14:12–13; (cp. Pss 29:1; 82:1, 6; 89:6–7; Job 38:7)
kôkĕbê-ʾēl	"stars of God"		
hêlēl ben-šāḥar	"shining one, son of the dawn"		
kĕrûb, kĕrubîm	"cherub"; "cherubim"		
gan	"garden"	divine abode, council meeting place: a well-watered garden	Gen 2:6, 8–9, 10–16; Ezek 28:2, 13–14 (cp. Ezek 47:1–12 [Jerusalem temple]; Zech 14:8)
ʾēd	"(watery) mist"		
nāhār	"river"		
yammîm	"seas, waters"		
ṣāphôn	"north"	divine abode, council meeting place: a mountain	Ezek 28:2, 13–14; Isa 14:13–14 (cp. Pss 48:1–2; 68:15–17 [Zion]; Exod 24:15; Deut 33:1–2 [Sinai]; Ezek 40:2; 47:1–12 [Jerusalem temple])
yarkĕtȩ ṣāphôn	"heights of the north"		
bāmôt	"heights"		
har	"mount, mountain"		
har môʿēd	"mount of assembly"		
môšab ʾelōhîm	"seat of the gods"		

1. Those who want the rebel in Ezekiel 28 to be Adam draw attention to the bejeweled description of the rebel, presuming that the analogy of the high priest's breastplate proves the rebel is a man. The list of gemstones, however, does not precisely correspond to the high priest's wardrobe. A better alternative is to take the description of the rebel's "covering" not as a garment, but as a reference to his environment or setting. Luminosity of these gems (and cf. the "stones of fire" reference in Ezek 28:14) often indicates divinity and a divine place. The garden of Gilgamesh, for instance, is a jeweled garden. I think it significant that the list of gemstones *does* correspond quite well to the description of the new, supernatural Jerusalem in Rev 21. See Heiser, *Unseen Realm*, 77–80; Keith Dickson, "The Jeweled Trees: Alterity in Gilgamesh," *Comparative Literature* 59.3 (2007): 193–208; James A. Harrell, "Gemstones," *UCLA Encyclopedia of Egyptology*, ed. Willeke Wendrich (Los Angeles: UCLA, 2012), http://digital2.library.ucla.edu/viewItem.do?ark=21198/zz002czx1r; Harrell, "Old Testament Gemstones: A Philological, Geological, and Archaeological Assessment of the Septuagint," *BBR* 21.2 (2011): 141–71; F. Petrie, "Precious Stones," *Dictionary of the Bible*, vol. 4, ed. J. Hastings (New York: Scribner, 1919), 619–21; J. L. Myres, "Stones (Precious)," *Encyclopedia Biblica*, vol. 4, ed. T. K. Cheyne and J. S. Black (New York: Macmillan, 1903), 4799–4812; and E. F. Jourdain, "The Twelve Stones in the Apocalypse," *Expository Times* 22 (1911): 448–50.

DIVINE REBEL IMAGERY AND PUNISHMENT			
Hebrew Term	**English Meaning**	**Concept**	**Important Verses**
nāḥāš	"serpent" (noun); "to do divination" (verb)	divine being cast as either supernatural guardian of the divine presence or shining appearance associated with divinity	Gen 3:1, 2, 4, 13–14; Ezek 28:12 (*ḥwtm* = *ḥ-w-t* + silent [enclitic] *mem*)[1]; Isa 14:12; Ezek 28:13 (gems = brilliant, luminous appearance)
ḥawwat	"serpent"		
hêlēl ben-šāḥar	"shining [bronze]" (adj.); "shining one, son of the dawn"		
yārad	"brought down"	expulsion from the divine presence and former service role to Yahweh	Ezek 28:8, 17; Isa 14:11, 12, 15
gādaʻ	"cut down"		
šālak	"cast down"		
ʼereṣ	"earth, ground" (abstractly): "underworld"; "realm of the dead"	underworld, realm of the dead	Ezek 28:17; Isa 14:9, 11–12, 15; Gen 3:14–15[2]
sheʼôl	"Sheol"; "realm of the dead"		
rĕpāʼîm	underworld occupants	underworld occupants	Ezek 28:17; Isa 14:9
mĕlākîm[3]			

1. Earlier I noted the observations of Batto and Launderville that guardian cherubs can have a serpentine or dragon appearance. H. J. van Dijk argues that the word *ḥôtēm* in Ezek 28:12 (*ch-w-t-m*) may actually be the word *ḥwt* ("serpent") with enclitic *mem*. "Enclitic *mem*" is a rare phenomenon in ancient Semitic languages where the final letter *m* is silent. If van Dijk is correct in his suspicion (and he is influenced by other connections between Genesis 3 and Ezekiel 28), the Ezekiel passage may include a serpent. See van Dijk, *Ezekiel's Prophecy*, 113–14. For examples of *ḥ-w-h* (fem sing form *ḥ-w-t* = *ḥwt*) meaning "serpent" in Semitic languages, see *DNWSI* 1:353 (s.v. ḥwh₁). Scholars have debated the reality of the enclitic *mem* in Biblical Hebrew. See Horace D. Hummel, "Enclitic mem in Early Northwest Semitic, Especially Hebrew," *JBL* 76 (1957): 85–107; Mitchell Dahood, "Enclitic mem and Emphatic *lamedh* in Psalm 85," *Biblica* 37.3 (1956): 338–40; J. A. Emerton, "Are There Examples of Enclitic mem in the Hebrew Bible?" in *Texts, Temples, and Traditions: A Tribute to Menahem Haran*, ed. Michael V. Fox et al. (Winona Lake, IN: Eisenbrauns, 1996), 321–38; C. Cohen, "The Enclitic mem in Biblical Hebrew: Its Existence and Initial Discovery," in *Sefer Moshe: The Moshe Weinfeld Jubilee Volume: Studies in the Bible and the Ancient Near East, Qumran, and Post-Biblical Judaism*, ed. Chaim Cohen, Avi Hurvitz, and Shalom Paul (Winona Lake, IN: Eisenbrauns, 2004), 231–60. One clear example is the *mem* at the end of the phrase *bny ʼlm* in Ps 29:1. This phrase was long considered to read "sons of El/God" (*bny ʼlm*) with enclitic *mem* but has recently been changed in modern editions of the Hebrew text to "sons of the gods" (*bny ʼlm*). David Noel Freedman writes: "The *elîm* in the first line is to be read as El with enclitic *mem*: eli-m, i.e., the sons of El, the gods" (Freedman, "Archaic Forms in Hebrew Poetry," *ZAW* 31 [1960]: 101–7 [esp. 104]).

2. In these verses the serpent (*nāḥāš*) is cursed. Instead of his close proximity to the throne of God, this divine council member is made lower than all the beasts of the field. The curse metaphorically speaks of casting down to the ground.

3. This term ("kings" or "rulers") included underworld dead and divine beings in the wider Semitic world. Several biblical references make it clear that the *m-l-k-m* in view are supernatural. As Heider notes, there are "beings called *mlkm* in connection with the royal cult of the dead." See G. C. Heider, "Molech," *DDD* 585. Regarding the "kings" of Ps 68:12, 14, 29, "the opponents of Yahweh are precisely, according to Ps 68, the same divine dwellers of Bashan whom the Ugaritic tradition records: the *mlkm/mēlākîm* (*rpum*/Rephaim)." See G. del Olmo Lete, "Bashan," *DDD* 162. The same point is made in John F. Healey, "MALKŪ : MLKM : ANUNNAKI," *Ugarit Forschungen* 7 (1975): 235–38; Lowell K. Handy, "A Solution for Many MLKM," *Ugarit Forschungen* 20 (1988): 57–59. Handy focuses on the relationship between earthly *mlkm* and supernatural *mlkm*: "It would appear that the gods who hold these titles (*mlk, mlkt, ṭpṭ, ʼrẓ, zbl*) were all understood to be rulers of their respective spheres of the universe in the same manner as several human rulers (each *mlk, mlkt*) would simultaneously rule areas within an empire. The title *mlk* among the deities was used to designate rulers, not set rank. In the cosmic hierarchy, which was envisioned for the universe, several levels on both the human and divine planes were designated by the title *mlk*. With this in mind, *mlk* should be understood more in terms of English 'ruler' than English 'king.'"

The data show that the connections between the passages are numerous and specific. A member of the divine council rebelled and was expelled from the council. No scholar argues that any ancient Near Eastern text gives us all the elements of Genesis 3, Isaiah 14:12–15, or Ezekiel 28:1–19. Rather, the point is that these biblical passages do have undeniable similarities to each other and to divine rebellion episodes found elsewhere.

ADAM AS THE REBEL IN ISAIAH 14 AND EZEKIEL 28?

As I noted earlier, other scholars disagree with this approach. They assert that Isaiah 14:12–15 and Ezekiel 28:1–19 are *only* about the kings of Babylon and Tyre and cannot inform us about the fall in Genesis 3. For them, Adam's sin serves as an analogy for the downfall of these two kings. Adam becomes the focus of the hubris and fall described by the two prophets. These passages do not inform our understanding of the divine rebel in Eden.[28]

---

28. Scholars who lean this direction or state their rejection more forcefully include: Norman C. Habel, "Ezekiel 28 and the Fall of the First Man," *Concordia Theological Monthly* 38 (1967): 516–24; H. G. May, "The King in the Garden of Eden," in *Israel's Prophetic Heritage* (New York: Harpers, 1962), 166–76; J. L. McKenzie, "Mythical Allusions in Ezekiel 28:1–28," *JBL* 75 (1956): 322–27; Marvin A. Sweeney, "Myth and History in Ezekiel's Oracle Concerning Tyre (Ezekiel 26–28)," in *Myth and Scripture: Contemporary Perspectives on Religion, Language, and Imagination*, ed. Dexter Callender (Atlanta: Society of Biblical Literature Press, 2014): 129–48; Daniel I. Block, *The Book of Ezekiel, Chapters 25–48* (NICOT; Grand Rapids: Eerdmans, 1997), 103–15; Mark R. Shipp, *Of Dead Kings and Dirges: Myth and Meaning in Isaiah 14:4b–21* (Leiden: Brill, 2002); Matthias Albani, "The Downfall of Helel, Son of Dawn: Aspects of Royal Ideology in Isa 14:12–13," in *The Fall of the Angels*, ed. Christoph Auffarth and Loren T. Stuckenbruck (Leiden: Brill, 2004), 129–68. A more recent study proposes that "*helēl ben-šaḥar*, literally the 'shining one, son of the dawn', might better be identified as a reference to the sun. … [By virtue of] a hitherto overlooked relation to the conception of the chthonic sun as found in Ugaritic texts; it was proposed that the author of Isa 14:12–15 was aware of these associations between sun and underworld, and utilized them in the production of his passage. Thus the author could present an image of the sun soaring in the heavens before falling to the underworld, but unlike the Ugaritic Šapšu this sun had no authority over either territory. Instead the text descends into an ironic lament for this pitiful figure, totally subsumed under the power of Yahweh. The dual imagery of the sun as psychopomp and the sun as Mesopotamian king work together to further affirm the fall of the hubristic oppressor established already in vv. 4b–11" (Laura Quick, "*Helēl ben-šaḥar* and the Chthonic Sun: A New Suggestion for the Mythological Background of Isa 14:12–15," *VT* 68 [2017]: 1–20 (esp. 19–20). The significant study of Page (based on his Harvard University dissertation) is an example of this: Hugh R. Page, *The Myth of Cosmic Rebellion: A Study of Its Reflexes in Ugaritic and Biblical Literature* (Leiden: Brill, 1996). Page does more than anyone else to marshal the evidence that

Scholars of this persuasion articulate their case in different ways. For our purposes, we are interested in the broad strokes, which have variations. The argument is made that Isaiah 14:12–15 and Ezekiel 28:1–19 portray a human king craving dominion over God to the point of considering himself a god (Isa 14:13–14; Ezek 28:2). It is *Adam's* expulsion from the garden of God and loss of immortality, not the serpent's being cast down to earth/the underworld, that is the point of the expulsion language in these passages (Isa 14:11, 15; Ezek 28:16). Others take a slightly different approach, suggesting that Adam was the king of Eden and, like other ancient Near Eastern kings, was considered to be divine as the god's representative on earth. The king of Tyre (and, by analogy, Adam) transgressed by wanting more exaltation—to actually be considered a god or (in concert with Isa 14:13–14) rule the divine council.[29]

Many readers will no doubt wonder about the coherence of this "Adam option" in several respects. The most obvious puzzle is where, exactly, Adam appears in Isaiah 14 or Ezekiel 28. No English Bible will contain that name in either passage. Surely Adam has to be found in at least one of those texts in order to read both as analogous to the original human rebel and not the serpent. But where is Adam?

The answer has to do with differences between the traditional Hebrew Masoretic Text (MT) and Septuagint (LXX) in verses 11–19. There are several difficult grammatical forms in the MT that the LXX translator "resolved" when rendering the passage into Greek. If one prefers the LXX

---

the literary background to both Isa 14:12–15 and Ezek 28:1–19 has a divine rebellion in view. Nevertheless, he does not utilize that background to inform our reading of the episode in Eden. Rather, he veers toward Gen 6 in that regard.

29. This notion of course presumes that biblical Israel viewed its kings as divine, a very tenuous proposition. As Whitelam notes, some scholars have "tried to identify a common cultic pattern of divine kingship throughout the ANE. ... Their conclusions, however, have been challenged by subsequent scholarship." See Keith W. Whitelam, "King and Kingship," *ABD* 4:47. Whitelam cites the work of Engnell as representative of those scholars who want to find a common pattern of divine kingship in the ancient Near East, one that included the Israelite monarchy (Ivan Engnell, *Studies in Divine Kingship in the Ancient Near East* [Uppsala, 1943]). This view was challenged by Henri Frankfort, *Kingship and the Gods* (Chicago: University of Chicago Press, 1948). Curtis remarks, "On the whole, however, suggestions that the Israelites believed in some form of sacral or even divine kingship have not been widely accepted" (A. H. W. Curtis, "Canaanite Gods and Religion," *DOTHB* 142). In that regard, see A. R. Johnson, *Sacral Kingship in Ancient Israel*, 2nd ed. (Cardiff: University of Wales Press, 1967). The notion that biblical writers and their contemporary readers would have viewed Adam as divine suffers from internal problems as well. See the discussion.

over the traditional MT, Adam appears in Ezekiel 28:11–19. This no doubt sounds odd, so it is best to illustrate how this is the case.[30]

Ezekiel 28:13b–14 takes us directly to the heart of the matter. Here are the alternatives:

MT [13]On the day that you were created they were prepared. [14]You were an anointed guardian cherub. I placed you; you were on the holy mountain of God; in the midst of the stones of fire you walked. (ESV)

LXX [14]From the day you were created, I placed you with the cherub in the holy mountain of God; you came to be in the middle of fiery stones. (LES)

It is easy to see that the LXX has God "placing" another figure in the garden "with" the cherub. Scholars preferring the LXX naturally see this

---

30. There are three ways to approach the text of Ezekiel 28:11–19: (1) accept the consonants of the traditional Masoretic Text (MT) and its vowels ("vowel pointing") added by the Masoretic scribes. This would be the Hebrew text as we currently have it in printed editions, which is what the MT translations in the ensuing discussion followed; (2) accept the consonants of the Masoretic Text (MT) and change the vowels in places; (3) follow the Septuagint (LXX), which at times suggests the translator was working with a Hebrew text different than MT or engaged in loose translation. The most important recent study on the textual differences in this passage is that of Hector M. Patmore, *Adam, Satan, and the King of Tyre: The Interpretation of Ezekiel 28:11–19 in Late Antiquity* (Leiden: Brill, 2012). Patmore analyzes MT and LXX thoroughly, along with the Targums, on his way to discussing the reception/interpretation of the chapter in the church fathers and the rabbinic literature. As Lydia Lee observed in her study of the passage, "Patmore has recently come up with a reading of v. 14 similar to the LXX, one which does not perceive the Tyrian king as an anointed covering cherub. Interestingly enough, he suggests that 'Ezek xxviii 12–19 has been misread (deliberately or otherwise) by the scribe(s) who added the vocalization and accentuation,' and that the Hebrew text, stripped of its vowels and cantillation marks, identifies the Tyrian king not as a cherub, but as a god (אלהים היית)." See Lydia Lee, "'You Were the (Divine) Cherub': A Potential Challenge to Yahweh's Sole Divinity in Ezek 28:14," *JSOT* 41.1 (2016): 99–116 (esp. 101). Patmore's translation in this regard is: "When you were created the stretched out cherub, who covers, was established, then I set you on the Holy Mountain, you were a god, in the midst of fire stones you walked about" (Patmore, *Adam, Satan, and the King of Tyre*, 197–201). Patmore articulates his view in two other sources: Hector M. Patmore, "Did the Masoretes Get It Wrong? The Vocalization and Accentuation of Ezekiel XXVIII 12–19," *VT* 58 (2008): 45–57; Patmore, "Adam or Satan? The Identity of the King of Tyre in Late Antiquity," in *After Ezekiel: Essays on the Reception of a Difficult Prophet*, ed. A. Mein and P. M. Joyce (London: T&T Clark, 2011), 59–69 (esp. 60, 62). It is difficult to see how this translation contributes to any negative portrayal of the king (or Adam), or how (suggested by Lee) this was any threat to Yahweh. Given the divine council motifs, it is obvious there were other *'elōhîm* in Eden. Genesis 3:22 affirms that. It is also not clear why Patmore pairs "when you were created" of v. 13 with what follows in v. 14 when "they were prepared" (*kônānû*) at the end of v. 13 appears before the beginning of v. 14. This verb form is omitted in Patmore's translation, and it is difficult to see how its inclusion would not undermine the interpretive implication of his translation.

figure as Adam (the only alternative is Eve), and then align what is said about the human king of Tyre with this human in Eden.

This is not the place for a detailed analysis of the morphological forms and grammatical difficulties that either led the LXX translator to improvise the MT or that were absent from the text the translator used. These issues neither represent errors in the text nor are they anomalies. The issues are well known and have been addressed cogently decades ago. There is no need to abandon the MT.[31]

The unnecessary preference for the LXX is not the only weakness of disallowing Isaiah 14:12–15 and Ezekiel 28:1–19 any contribution to the understanding of the divine rebel in Genesis 3. There are more straightforward problems.

First, there is a methodological problem. If Isaiah 14:12–15 and Ezekiel 28:1–19 are dismissed as contributing to our understanding of the divine rebel, one wonders on what basis those two passages are permitted to comment on Adam. It is a biased method to have these passages serve to enlighten our understanding of Adam but not the serpent. Second, the "Adam option" requires presuming things about Adam that are not in the Genesis episode of the fall. Unlike the wording of Isaiah 14:13–14 and Ezekiel 28:2, Adam is never described as being part of the decision-making council of God nor desiring to be lord of the divine assembly. There is also no hint that Adam fancied himself a god.[32]

---

31. For careful analysis of points in Ezek 28:11–19 in defense of the unusual features of the Masoretic Text, see: James Barr, "'Thou Art the Cherub': Ezekiel 28.14 and the Post-Ezekiel Understanding of Genesis 2–3," in *Priests, Prophets, and Scribes: Essays on the Formation and Heritage of Second Temple Judaism in Honour of Joseph Blenkinsopp*, ed. Eugene Ulrich et al. (Sheffield: Sheffield Academic Press, 1992), 213–13; James E. Miller, "The Maelaek of Tyre (Ezekiel 28,11–19)," *ZAW* 105.3 (1993): 497–501; Lena-Sofia Tiemeyer, "Zechariah's Spies and Ezekiel's Cherubim," in *Tradition in Transition: Haggai and Zechariah 1–8 in the Trajectory of Hebrew Theology*, ed. Mark J. Boda and Michael H. Floyd (London: T&T Clark, 2008), 95–119; Knud Jeppesen, "You Are a Cherub, but No God!" *Scandinavian Journal of the Old Testament* 5:1 (1991); 83–94. I have sketched the grammatical problems and their resolution (i.e., a defense of MT) at my website: http://www.moreunseenrealm. com (ch. 11). Readers should also note there is no possible appeal to LXX to find Adam in Isa 14:12–15.

32. Regarding the "seat of the gods" that was "in the heart of the seas," both phrases point to the throne room of the divine council. There is a transparent parallel to *moshab elohim* ("seat of the gods") in Ugaritic (*m[t]b il*, "seat of El"; *KTU* 1.4.i.13). See Clifford, *The Cosmic Mountain in Canaan and the Old Testament*, 170; Mullen, *Divine Council in Canaanite and Early Hebrew Literature*, 150–55. Wyatt notes that a Canaanite king could (and would) claim to be ruling on behalf of El, but "to claim identity with El goes beyond acceptable limits." See N. Wyatt, *Space and Time in the Religious Life of the Near East* (Sheffield: Sheffield Academic Press, 2001), 155.

In this last regard, interpreters cannot intelligibly argue that Adam was a divine king so as to strike analogies with Isaiah's and Ezekiel's king-villains. Genesis 3:5, 22 clearly tells us that Adam (and Eve) would become "like gods" (kē 'lōhîm) only if and when they ate from the tree of the knowledge of good and evil. This obviously means they were not gods. The meaning of the phrase also does not speak of divinity, for after the two humans eat, they are "like gods" in only one aspect: "knowing good and evil." In this respect they were *like* the gods—the divine beings of God's council host in Eden—but they were not gods. Being *like* a divine being in a new way is not equivalent to *being* gods.[33]

Another coherence problem for the "Adam view" concerns the crimes described in Isaiah 14:12–15 and Ezekiel 28:1–19. These crimes are extreme pride, hubris at the level of presuming to be a god or like the Most High, or fitness to govern the divine council (Isa 14:13–14; Ezek 28:2, 6).[34] Where in Genesis 3 do we read of such traits or behavior with respect to Adam?[35] In other words, where is the coherence of the analogy?

In Genesis 3, Adam's transgression is never cast as a *defiant* act. Rather, he reacts to Eve's enjoyment of the fruit and partakes. There is no hint he wanted to be "above the stars of God," lord of the divine council, or saw himself so magnificent as to think himself divine. If this sort of thinking is lurking in his heart, the reader is never told. These details must be read into the text by those who, as noted above, want these passages to describe one character in Genesis 3 (Adam) but not another (the serpent).

---

33. By virtue of being God's imaging representatives (Gen 1:26–27) Adam and Eve were already like God/the divine beings of God's council before they ate from the forbidden tree. This is transparent proof that being *like* a divine being doesn't mean being a divine being. They were human and nothing more both before and after the fall. Lastly, amid all the talk (on the part of some) about how Adam's divinity helps connect Adam to Isa 14 and Ezek 28, Eve is conveniently left out. She fully shares the imaging status and the attributes God shared to accomplish their imaging task. She is also included in Gen 3:5, 22. Yet there is no talk of *her* divine kingship in "Adam option" commentary on Isa 14:12–15 and Ezek 28:1–19. This inequity shows the "Adam option" trajectory to be artificial and collapses the argument.

34. Other crimes (Ezek 28:16–18) are those of the king of Tyre, the other side of the analogy.

35. Because there is no suggestion that God remained in Eden on earth after the fall (i.e., that Eden persisted as a unique place on earth after the fall), both Adam and the serpent can be thought of as "cast out" of the divine presence. Hence the language of Ezek 28:16 in that regard can be utilized by either view of the rebel (human or divine). The verb translated "I destroyed you" in this verse ('abad) in ESV can be understood as "turned over to disaster" in the sense of being made to suffer one's fate. See *HALOT*, s.v. אבד (I).

WHAT ABOUT SATAN?

Most readers will likely presume that everything discussed in this chapter is about Satan. That would be incorrect ... and correct. I've actually avoided using the term until this point, mentioning only briefly at the beginning to note that Revelation 12:9 equates the serpent with the devil and Satan. Those familiar with my earlier work *The Unseen Realm* will know why. The Hebrew word *śāṭān*, commonly transformed into the personal name "Satan," is actually no such thing: this Hebrew term is not a proper personal noun and therefore does not point to the specific figure we know from the New Testament as Satan.

The reason this is indeed the case is straightforward, as it is based on the grammar of Biblical Hebrew. In Biblical Hebrew, the definite article (the word "the") is a single letter (*heh*; "h"). The definite article, as its name suggests, makes an otherwise common noun ("man") more specific—more definite ("*the* man"). English puts the definite article before the noun to be made definite. Hebrew works the same way, though it directly attaches the definite article to a noun (letter *h* + noun = "the [noun]." Hebrew is also like English in that, as a rule, it does not tolerate the definite article to precede a proper personal name. For example, I am not "the Mike." We don't go around calling each other by name with the word "the" preceding our name. By rule of Hebrew grammar, a noun preceded with a definite article is *not* a proper personal name.[36]

The Hebrew lemma *śāṭān* occurs twenty-seven times in the Hebrew Bible, ten of which are without the definite article.

definite article (*ha-*) + *śāṭān* (17 instances)	*śāṭān* without definite article (10 instances)
Zech 3:1, 2 (twice); Job 1:6, 7 (twice), 8, 9, 12 (twice); 2:1, 2 (twice), 3, 4, 6, 7	Num 22:22, 32; 1 Sam 29:4; 2 Sam 19:23; 1 Kings 5:18; 11:14, 23, 25; 1 Chr 21:1; Ps 109:6

Without exception, every rendering of *śāṭān* as "Satan" in English translations of Job 1–2 and Zechariah 3 has the definite article. The term should therefore not be rendered as a proper personal name in those passages—passages presumed by English readers to be critically important for a doctrine of the original rebel of Eden (Satan). This would mean that

---

36. *GBH* §137b; GKC §125d.

we don't have the serpent (or "devil," in New Testament language) in Job 1–2 and Zechariah 3.

The correct translation of *śāṭān* in these famous scenes is "the adversary" or "the accuser."[37] These options are based on usage in context—both with respect to humans, who are in view when the word is used, and divine beings. For example, in Psalm 109:6–7 we read:

> [6] Appoint a wicked man against him;
>> let an accuser (*śāṭān*) stand at his right hand.
> [7] When he is tried, let him come forth guilty;
>> let his prayer be counted as sin!

Goldingay observes that the accusers (cf. vv. 1–5) are "arguing their case before the heavenly court" and that they "ask for the appointment of someone to stand by the accused as an accuser or prosecutor (a *śāṭān*; cf. the heavenly accuser in Zech. 3)."[38] Like other commentators, he views their request as perverse, asking "for a faithless person, someone like them (cf. v. 2). ... They perhaps wanted justice to be done, but they have a twisted view of what this would mean."[39] Goldingay's reference to Zechariah 3 is noteworthy, as that famous passage has the *śāṭān* accusing Joshua, the high priest of Israel.[40]

Passages like these, along with Job 1–2, have led some scholars to view the *śāṭān* as "a member of the heavenly court with a role similar to a district attorney."[41] God expects the *śāṭān* to respond to his question about

---

37. *HALOT*, s.v. שָׂטָן. See also *DCH*, s.v. שָׂטָן.

38. John Goldingay, *Psalms, Vol. 3: Psalms 90–150* (BCOT; Grand Rapids: Baker Academic, 2006), 280.

39. Ibid., 280.

40. Of the *śāṭān* "standing before the Lord" Meyers and Meyers write: "This technical language (ʿmd lpny; cf. v 4 below) reveals the setting of the prophetic vision, the Heavenly Court over which Yahweh presides as chief judge. ... The concept of an assembly or council of the gods was a common motif throughout the ancient Near East. The issue before the Court concerns Joshua and the office of the high priesthood. The adversary is *haśśāṭān* or the accuser; the advocate is the *malʾāk*, Yahweh's messenger or herald. The appropriateness of the Heavenly Court scene derives from the gravity of the issue being considered" (Carol L. Meyers and Eric M. Meyers, *Haggai, Zechariah 1–8: A New Translation with Introduction and Commentary* [AYB; New Haven, CT: Yale University Press, 2008], 182).

41. Bruce Baloian, "שָׂטָן," *NIDOTTE* 3:1231. Handy refers to him as an "officer" of the heavenly court (Lowell K. Handy, "The Authorization of Divine Power and the Guilt of God in the Book of Job: Useful Ugaritic Parallels," *JSOT* 18.60 (1993): 107–18 (esp. 109). The language of Job 1:6; 2:1 lacks the sort of precision needed to answer whether the *śāṭān* is one of the sons of God or is merely appearing in a divine council meeting among them. Hartley asks, "Was the Satan one of the sons of God? The majority of scholars assume that he was. Driver-Gray understands the preposition *among*

Job's character. He presumes the *śāṭān* has something to report.[42] There is no hint that this task or the obedience of the *śāṭān* is to be wicked or out of place at a meeting of the divine council. Report he does, but it is at that point the *śāṭān* challenges God's assessment of Job (and, therefore, either God's omniscience or his truthfulness), leading to the events of the rest of the book. God's character must be validated.[43]

Consequently, translations that transform *śāṭān* with a definite article into proper personal names like "Satan" violate Hebrew grammar and, therefore, the intended meaning of these passages.[44] The only passages that might speak of a personalized Satan figure would be those ten where *śāṭān* lacks the definite article. I say "might" because the absence of the definite article does not require that the noun be a proper personal name. It may very well be (and I will argue, is) "an adversary."[45] All but three of those, however, have a human being in view (i.e., a human adversary).

(Heb. *baṯôk̲*) to indicate that he had a prominent place in this assembly. But some recent scholars understand the text to portray the Satan as an intruder. They come to this position either by taking the term *also* (Heb. *gam*) to mean 'other than' or by understanding the preposition *among* to indicate someone who is an outsider. This casting seems to put him as a distinct member of the assembly with a role that stands over against that of the other members." See John E. Hartley, *The Book of Job* (NICOT; Grand Rapids: Eerdmans, 1988), 72.

42. The occurrence of *śāṭān* in clear accusatorial/prosecutorial contexts no doubt contributed to the later Second Temple concept of many "satans" in God's presence, there to report on good and evil human behavior (1 En. 40:7).

43. This is why the *śāṭān* is permitted to do anything he wants to Job, short of taking his life. The council cannot be left with the impression that, had the *śāṭān* not been leashed, he would have succeeded in making Job curse God, thereby showing God's assessment incorrect. The *śāṭān* cannot be leashed, and Job must remain alive. Both are needed to show the *śāṭān* to be wrong and God to be right.

44. In addition, the alert reader will discern from the table that the lemma *śāṭān* does not occur in Genesis 3. In fact, the *nāḥāš* of Genesis 3 is never called *śāṭān* anywhere in the Hebrew Bible. See Peggy Day, *An Adversary in Heaven: śāṭān in the Hebrew Bible* (Atlanta: Scholars Press, 1988); John H. Walton, "Satan," *DOTWPW* 714–17. As I noted in *Unseen Realm*, "The *function* of the office of the *śāṭān* is why later Jewish writings began to adopt it as a proper name for the serpent figure from Genesis 3 who brought ruin to Eden. That figure opposed God's choices for his human imagers. The dark figure of Genesis 3 was eventually thought of as the 'mother of all adversaries,' and so the label *śāṭān* got stuck to him. He deserves it. The point here is only that the Old Testament doesn't use that term for the divine criminal of Eden" (57). See chapter 4 of the present study for how the Hebrew lemma *śāṭān* became used as a proper personal noun in later Jewish literature and the New Testament.

45. By way of illustration, Hebrew *'ādām* is often prefixed with the definite article and translated "the man" (Gen 2:15: "The Lord God took the man [*ha-'ādām*] and put him in the garden of Eden"). Hebrew *'ādām* without the article might be "Adam" (proper personal name; Gen 5:1: "These are the generations of Adam [*'ādām*]"), but may also best be translated in context as "mankind, humankind" (Gen 1:26: "let us make humankind [*'ādām*] as our image"). Context dictates such choices.

The exceptions are Numbers 22:22, 32 and 1 Chronicles 21:1. The *śāṭān* references in the book of Numbers are both to the angel of the LORD (Yahweh) and are part of the story of Balaam and his donkey:

> But God's anger was kindled because he went, and the angel of the LORD took his stand in the way as his adversary [*śāṭān*]. Now he [Balaam] was riding on the donkey, and his two servants were with him. (Num 22:22)

> And the angel of the LORD said to him, "Why have you struck your donkey these three times? Behold, I have come out to oppose [*śāṭān*] you [lit., "I have come as a *śāṭān*"] because your way is perverse before me." (Num 22:32)

Obviously, the angel of the LORD is not the rebel of Eden, the "Satan" of later Judaism and the New Testament. This leaves us with 1 Chronicles 21:1 as a possible reference to Satan, the devil. 1 Chronicles 21 is the infamous passage where "Satan" provokes David to take a census that leads to God's judgment and the loss of life of many Israelites. Some scholars propose that this lone reference is indeed pointing to Satan. This is a difficult position to defend. The incident is recorded elsewhere in the Hebrew Bible, in 2 Samuel 24. In that account, it is Yahweh himself who provokes David. Is Yahweh Satan?

Scholars have struggled with understanding the incident in light of the two accounts and have come up with amazingly creative ways to have both Yahweh and Satan behind the same provocation. I would suggest that the solution is not complicated if 1 Chronicles 21:1 is interpreted in light of Numbers 22:22, 32, the only other instance where we have *śāṭān* without the article used to describe a divine being. The wider context validates that approach. We begin with the parallel passages:

1 Chronicles 21:1–2	2 Samuel 24:1–2
Then Satan stood against Israel and incited David to number Israel. So David said to Joab and the commanders of the army, "Go, number Israel, from Beersheba to Dan, and bring me a report, that I may know their number."	Again the anger of the LORD was kindled against Israel, and he incited David against them, saying, "Go, number Israel and Judah." So the king said to Joab, the commander of the army, who was with him, "Go through all the tribes of Israel, from Dan to Beersheba, and number the people, that I may know the number of the people."

Who incited David—Satan or Yahweh (the LORD)? The resolution of this apparent contradiction is surprisingly straightforward. In Numbers 22:22, 32, it is the angel of Yahweh who stood in the way of Balaam and his donkey. This angel served as Yahweh's "adversary" (*śāṭān*) to oppose Balaam. The angel was, in effect, a divinely appointed adversary. Furthermore, as I have detailed at length elsewhere, this particular angel *was* Yahweh in human form.[46]

In light of the related account in Numbers 22, 1 Chronicles 21:1 ought to be translated, "Then an adversary stood against Israel …" This adversary is later identified as the angel of Yahweh *in both accounts* (1 Chr 21:14–15; 2 Sam 24:15–16). If, as evident in other Old Testament accounts, Yahweh and his angel were identified with each other or their distinct identities were blurred (e.g., Gen 48:15–16; Exod 3 [cp. Josh 5:13–15]; Judg 6), then there is no contradiction between the passages. The angel and Yahweh can be coidentified. The answer to the question of who incited David is "Yahweh" in both accounts.[47]

IMPLICATIONS

What have we learned about the original divine rebel? While ancient Israelites did not use the Hebrew term *śāṭān* for the *nāḥāš* of Genesis 3, it is clear that he was an adversarial figure in the flow of biblical history—a hostile entity to the purposes of God. His rebellion resulted in humanity's forfeiture of everlasting life with their Creator in the divine abode. Yahweh had, of course, warned Adam and Eve of this consequence, but even his warning reflected his love for his creatures. God never told Eve that, if they violated his command, he would kill them. Rather, he said

---

46. See Heiser, *Angels*, 57–63; Heiser, "Old Testament Godhead Language" and "The Name Theology of the Old Testament," *Faithlife Study Bible* (Bellingham, WA: Lexham Press, 2012, 2016). For a scholarly presentation of the Israelite Godhead concept, see Michael S. Heiser, "Co-Regency in Ancient Israel's Divine Council as the Conceptual Backdrop to Ancient Jewish Binitarian Monotheism," *BBR* 26.2 (2016): 195–226.

47. Readers will naturally wonder why God did this. As I noted in another publication, "Why would Yahweh incite David to do something for which He would later punish him? Both accounts begin by saying Yahweh was angry with Israel, not David. Yahweh chose to use David as His instrument of judgment against the nation, similar to the way He would use Nebuchadnezzar centuries later. As the Babylonian king was still accountable for His actions, so was David. Judgment (and its means) both belong to the LORD, but human agents are still accountable." See Michael S. Heiser, *I Dare You Not to Bore Me with the Bible* (Bellingham, WA: Lexham Press, 2014), 73.

simply, "You will surely die." Divorced from the source of life, God's own presence, their expulsion from Eden ensured that circumstance.[48]

Thankfully, the story did not end there. God promised redemption for Adam, Eve, and their descendants, and so the story of salvation history began from the shame of humanity's failure—a failure precipitated by a divine throne guardian who wished to rule instead of being ruled.

For being the first divine rebel, the villain of Eden would become perceived as "the god of this world" (2 Cor 4:4). This Pauline phrase is as much a theological statement as a play on words. In all three passages we've looked at (Isa 14:12–15; Ezek 28:11–19; Gen 3), the original supernatural rebel was "cast down" to the earth, expelled from membership in the divine council.[49] As I discussed in detail in *The Unseen Realm*, the Hebrew term for "earth" (*'ereṣ*) is also a term for the realm of the dead:

> The "ground" to which this haughty divine being is cast and where he is disgraced is also of interest. The Hebrew word translated "ground" is *'erets*. It is a common term for the earth under our feet. But it is also a word that is used to refer to the underworld, the realm of the dead (e.g., Jonah 2:6), where ancient warrior-kings await their comrades in death (Ezek 32:21, 24–30, 32; Isa 14:9). Adam, of course, was already on earth, so he couldn't be sentenced there. And he didn't wind up in the underworld. Yet this is the sort of language we would expect if the point was the expulsion of a heavenly being from the divine council.[50]

In biblical cosmology, the underworld (as its name suggests) is *in* or *under* the earth. It is consequently part of the earth. The rebel's sentence makes good sense in that light—he was plunged both to earth and under the earth. The serpent is associated with the realm of the dead because that is where he was sent. As we will see in the next chapter, the fact that this realm was thought by Israelites and, later, Jews to belong to Canaanite Baal, epithets and motifs attributed to Baal began to be applied to the

---

48. For a discussion on how the fall was possible and why God did not compel it, see Heiser, *Unseen Realm*, 56–70.

49. Recall that the *śāṭān* of Job 1–2 is not this figure, and so there is no inconsistency between those two chapters and the punishment of the divine rebel of Eden. For the "casting down" language in these passages, see Ezek 28:8, 17; Isa 14:9, 11–12, 15.

50. Heiser, *Unseen Realm*, 80–81.

demoted cherub of Eden. The Israelite lord of the underworld started resembling the Canaanite lord of the underworld.

Since the expulsion of humanity meant death passed to all humanity because of Adam's sin (Rom 5:12), death and the serpent became associated with each other in biblical thought. All of the motifs of darkness, death, disease, and chaos we discussed in preceding chapters would become part of that association, not because they are spelled out in Genesis 3 (they are not) but because all the conceptual roads lead to the realm of the dead.

What marks the profile of the first divine rebel? Hubris toward God, antipathy toward humanity, and dominion over the dark realm of the dead. All who die will abide in his realm absent the intervention by an even greater power. This Old Testament perspective is evident in later Second Temple Jewish literature but, as we will see in the next chapter, the profile undergoes development in that material.

CHAPTER 4

Satan in
Second Temple
Judaism

With respect to the Old Testament's original divine rebel, that data led to two observations. First, given a proper understanding of Job 1–2 and Zechariah 3, there are relatively few passages outside Genesis 3 that contribute to a profile of this supernatural villain.[1] Second, despite the limited data, what the Old Testament does say about the first defector from God's heavenly entourage is clear. The original rebel is consistently cast as haughty in the wake of a misguided attempt to exalt himself above God and the rest of God's council. He is a deceiver whose activities demonstrate antipathy toward God's human imagers. His punishment associates him with death, estrangement from God, and dominion in the realm of the dead.

In this chapter we will investigate Jewish writings that followed the Old Testament period for how writers thought about this figure.[2] We have already noted in our preview that we can expect continuity (Second Temple Jewish writers were not attempting to replace the content of their sacred Scriptures), but we will also encounter development. We will discern two trajectories with respect to this development. First, there was a propensity to conflate the story of the divine rebel of Eden with other

---

1. It is ironic that Old Testament scholars want to make the data pool even smaller by forbidding Isa 14:12–15 and Ezek 28:1–19 from having any voice in the matter.

2. For a convenient summary of what these writings contribute to the developing notion of Satan in this period, see Derek R. Brown, *The God of This Age* (Tübingen: Mohr Siebeck, 2015), 27–48.

divine rebellions in the Old Testament. We have yet to discuss those subsequent rebellions in detail, though we have already noted that they will concern the transgression of the sons of God before the flood (Gen 6:1–4) and the corruption of the sons of God allotted to the nations in the judgment at Babel (Deut 32:8–9; Ps 82). Second, some Second Temple writers felt quite free to invent content, to fill in the gaps of biblical episodes. The result was, to say the least, creative embellishment of Old Testament material.

The reader must also realize that Second Temple period writers will not always agree on the conflations and embellishments noted above.[3] Second Temple Judaism cannot be understood as a single, uniform religious outlook any more than modern Christianity is uniform. The latter's major representations (Roman Catholicism, Protestantism, and Orthodoxy) and dozens of smaller denominations and ethnically oriented variations do not agree on many aspects of Christian doctrine and practice. So it was with Second Temple Judaism, though the number of sects was far fewer than can be counted under the umbrella of Christianity today. Second Temple authors took liberties with Old Testament terminology and connected data points about evil spirits in different ways.

---

3. It is therefore inadvisable to presume a unified development leading to the New Testament Satan. It is much more secure to look for links back into the Old Testament and discuss why those links are at times repurposed or embellished. That discussion is naturally (more or less) informed speculation. I mention this because of the propensity of scholars to presume certain forces that need better proof than has heretofore been marshaled. Many who study the demonology of the Second Temple period uncritically assume a supposed breakthrough to monotheism motivated things like leaving demons unnamed or, as we saw in section 1, using *daimōn* for certain Hebrew vocabulary that reflect divine plurality. While a clearer profile of a "chief demon" who is essentially in charge of the other demons emerges in the Second Temple period, the textual basis for suggesting this was motivated by wanting to avoid divine plurality language is weak as is the coherence of the argumentation. For example, while the Qumran texts (apparently) seek to make demons minor players by not giving them names or personalities, books like 1 Enoch and Jubilees show little reticence in that regard. Jewish writings of a later period also show no fear in having named demons. Further, the idea on a neat evolutionary trajectory to what we think of as monotheism, finally achieved in the New Testament era, is not consistent with the data and depends on modern assumptions about how Israelites would have perceived Yahweh's relationship among other *ʾelōhîm*. See Heiser, "Monotheism, Polytheism, Monolatry, or Henotheism," 1–30; Heiser, "Monotheism and the Language of Divine Plurality in the Hebrew Bible and the Dead Sea Scrolls," 85–100; Hayman, "Monotheism—A Misused Word in Jewish Studies?" 1–15.

SATAN OR SATANS?

The term *śāṭān* provides a convenient point of entry for our discussion. In his essay on the demonologies of the Dead Sea Scrolls, Bennie Reynolds writes:

> It is well known that in the demonology of the New Testament one finds a powerful chief demon named Satan. ... As many studies have shown, the notion of Satan as a chief demon does not exist in the Hebrew Bible. ... Instead, one finds more generic conceptions of an adversary or accuser, who in some cases functions as an official or servant of the deity.[4]

This observation is true enough, given the fact that, as we saw in the preceding chapter, the Hebrew lemma *śāṭān* is never used of the serpent of Eden. The *śāṭān* was, rather, a divine officer tasked with reporting disobedience to God (Job 1–2).

During the Second Temple period, the prosecutorial role of the Job 1–2 figure shifted in the minds of certain authors. The behavior of the *śāṭān* could be (and was) parsed as opposing God's assessment of Job (effectively accusing God of error). This showdown in the divine council would naturally contribute to later perceptions of the villain of Genesis 3 as a being who opposed God's will.

The thinking is not hard to follow. It would take some time for the label "adversary" (i.e., the lemma *śāṭān*) to be applied to the serpent, but it would be. And it would stick. While the rebel of Genesis 3 is not cast as a "chief demon" in the Old Testament—even after other divine rebellions in the biblical story produced more villains—it would be unwarranted to conclude that Old Testament readers would not have thought of the serpent as God's archenemy. Second Temple writers certainly followed this line of thought. Reynolds's ensuing comment introduces us to the situation:

> Does the Satan known from the New Testament take the stage at Qumran? Several studies have demonstrated that the answer is no. ...

---

4. Bennie H. Reynolds III, "Understanding the Demonologies of the Dead Sea Scrolls: Accomplishments and Directions for the Future," *Religion Compass* 7.4 (2013): 103–14 (esp. 108).

What one does find, however, is a transformation of "satan" from an adversary into a category or species of demon.[5]

As evidence that the Qumran texts know a *category* of demon called a "satan," Reynolds cites two scrolls: Aramaic Levi 3:9 (= 4QLevi[b] ar 1 17, or 4Q213a) and 11QPsalms[a] XIX, 15 (= 11Q5). He translates the first as "let not any satan have dominion over me," and the second is similar: "Let no satan or unclean spirit have dominion over me."[6]

In both cases the lemma *śāṭān* lacks the definite article in the Hebrew text of the scrolls.[7] Consequently, we may translate the word in both texts as "Satan" (proper personal name), "a satan" (as Reynolds does), or simply "an adversary."[8] The second text (11QPsalms[a] XIX, 15) more clearly suggests a supernatural being, as *śāṭān* is mentioned in tandem with an evil ("unclean") spirit. Unlike Reynolds, who opts for "a satan" here, other scholars render the line, "Let not Satan rule over me, nor an unclean spirit."[9] The point is that Reynolds assumes that both texts are evidence of a demonic *category* of "satans," but neither text demands such a verdict.

The Hebrew lemma *śāṭān* occurs six other times in the Dead Sea Scrolls, all of which lack the definite article.[10] These instances, with translation, are as follows:

- "every adversary of holiness" (1Q28b [= 1QSb] col. i, line 8)
- "every destroying and murderous adversary" (1QH[a] col. xxii middle, line 2)
- "every adversary and destroyer" (1QH[a] col. xxiv middle, line 2)
- "he had neither adversary nor evil" (2Q20 frag. 1:2 [= Jub 46:2])
- "there was no adversary" (4Q504 frags. 1–2 iv, line 12)
- "let not an adversary rule over me, nor an evil spirit" (11Q6 frags. 4–5, line 16 [= 11QPsalms[b]])

---

5. Ibid., 108.

6. Ibid.

7. The Hebrew of the two scrolls is, respectively: *'l tšlṭ by kl śṭn* (4Q213a) and *'l tšlṭ by śṭn wrwḥ ṭm'h* (11QPsalms[a] XIX, 15).

8. "Adversary" is the decision of Florentino García Martínez and Eibert J. C. Tigchelaar, *The Dead Sea Scrolls Study Edition*, 2 vols. (Leiden: Brill, 1997–1998), 449.

9. García Martínez and Tigchelaar, *Dead Sea Scrolls Study Edition*, 1175.

10. This count is based on a search of the database by Martin G. Abegg, Jr., *Qumran Sectarian Manuscripts* (Bellingham, WA: Logos Bible Software, 2003). In 2Q20 and 11Q6, the word *śāṭān* is reconstructed based on other texts.

An examination of each of these mostly fragmentary texts reveals that 11QPsalmsᵃ is the only instance where context supports a supernatural adversary being in view.[11] That text allows either a translation that creates a demonic category of "satans" ("let not a *satan* rule over me, nor an evil spirit")[12] or a rendering that identifies the proper personal name ("let not Satan rule over me, nor an evil spirit"). Given the flexibility of translation and the paucity of the data, it is premature to conclude that a category of "satans" existed at Qumran.

There is no doubt, however, that multiple "satans" were part of the demonology of other Second Temple Jewish texts. The leading example is 1 Enoch.[13] At one point of his heavenly journey, Enoch describes seeing millions of supernatural beings standing before "the Lord of Spirits" (1 En 40:1). Enoch hears a series of four angelic voices, the fourth of which draws our interest:

> And I heard the fourth voice fending off the Satans and forbidding them to come before the Lord of Spirits to accuse them who dwell on the earth. (1 En 40:7)[14]

The Old Testament nowhere affirms multiple satans, but this verse not only does so but seems to envision multiple divine beings performing the office of the *śāṭān* evident in Job 1–2. If this is the case, they would not be evil. Yet it is curious that the fourth angelic voice—the archangel Phanuel (1 En 40:9)—seeks to impede their access to God.

The name Phanuel (*pnw'l*) is a play on Peniel (*pny'l*) from Genesis 32:30, the place name where Jacob wrestled with the "man" who was actually an angel (Hos 12:3–4). The biblical place name means "face of God"

---

11. 11Q6 is a parallel text to 11QPsalmsᵃ. The relevant phrase of line 16 is reconstructed based on the parallel in 11QPsalmsᵃ.

12. This is the choice of Torleif Elgvin, "Belial, Beliar, Devil, Satan," *DNTB* 154–55. García Martínez and Tigchelaar opt for "Satan" (García Martínez and Tigchelaar, *Dead Sea Scrolls Study Edition*, 1175).

13. This is the book popularly referred to as "the Book of Enoch." As the number implies, there is more than one book of Enoch known to scholars. 1 Enoch has chronological priority, hence the number.

14. R. H. Charles, "Book of Enoch," *APOT*, 2:211. I have preferred Charles's translation here because he more literally renders *sayṭān* as "satan." The translator of 1 Enoch for *OTP* inexplicably rendered the term "demons," only noting the literal reading of *sayṭān* in a footnote (see *OTP*, 1:32, note g). While Charles's translation used here capitalizes the translation ("Satans"), it is best understood as lower case ("satans") because the plurality rules out a proper personal name. Charles and other translators likely use the upper case because readers familiar with the New Testament would expect to see the capitalization.

(*pānîm* + *'ēl*), whereas *penû'ēl* (Phanuel) combines the verb *pānāh* ("to turn," literally or metaphorically in repentance) + *'ēl*. Nickelsburg notes that the result "often describes turning to other gods but can mean to turn *to* God."[15] It is for this reason that Phanuel can be construed as one "set over the repentance and hope of the inheritors of eternal life (v. 9)."[16] Phanuel, then, is tasked with impeding the satans because their accusation is false or ineffectual with respect to faithful believers. The satans of 1 Enoch 40:7 would therefore *not* be loyal servants of God.

These enemy satans reappear later in 1 Enoch—along with their leader, who is also called Satan. To process this odd circumstance, we need to consider several passages in 1 Enoch together.

In 1 Enoch 53, Enoch is shown "angels of plague co-operating and preparing all the chains of Satan" (1 En 53:3). The meaning of "chains of Satan" is not completely clear. Enoch asks in the next verse, "For whom are they preparing these chains?" The answer comes immediately: "For the kings and the potentates of this earth in order that they may be destroyed thereby" (1 En 53:4–5). Consequently, "chains of Satan" would not mean "chains *for* Satan."[17] Nickelsburg and VanderKam believe the idea to be in concert with other passages in 1 Enoch that have "angels of punishment" executing God's wrath:

> Angels of punishment ... prepare the places of punishment for the kings and the mighty (53:3) and the rebel angels (54:3 read in light of 56:1–4), and they drive the kings and the mighty to their destruction (62:11; 63:1, 11; see also 41:2, of "the sinners"). When God wishes to initiate the events of the eschaton, it is the angels who prod the kings into the war that will lead to their destruction (56:5–8; cf. 10:9 of the giants).[18]

This approach coheres with Old and New Testament passages that have angels carrying out God's judgment, apocalyptic and otherwise, where people who chose to follow Satan wind up sharing in his own eventual fate.[19] This idea does have possible correlation in the New

---

15. George W. E. Nickelsburg and James C. VanderKam, *1 Enoch 2: A Commentary on the Book of 1 Enoch, Chapters 37–82* (Hermeneia; Minneapolis: Fortress, 2012), 134.

16. Charles, "Book of Enoch," *APOT*, 2:211, note 7.

17. *OTP*, 1:37–38.

18. Nickelsburg and VanderKam, *1 Enoch 2*, 43.

19. Isa 13:4–13; 40:26; 45:12; Ps 78:48–51; Zech 14:5; Matt 16:27 [cp. Matt 25:31; 26:53; Mark 8:38; Luke 9:26]; Rev 7:1–2; 8:5–13; 9:1, 13–15; 10:1, 5, 7; 15:1, 6, 7, 8; 16:1, 5; 17:1; 18:1, 21; 19:11–16.

Testament (1 Cor 5:5; 2 Cor 12:7). "Chains of Satan" in effect would express the idea of a deserved fate brought on by being foolish enough to choose his way over God's. The conversation continues into 1 Enoch 54, with Enoch narrating:

> [1] Then I looked and turned to another face of the earth and saw there a valley, deep and burning with fire. [2] And they were bringing kings and potentates and were throwing them into this deep valley. [3] And my eyes saw there their chains while they were making them into iron fetters of immense weight. [4] And I asked the angel of peace, who was going with me, saying, "For whom are these imprisonment chains being prepared?" [5] And he said unto me, "These are being prepared for the armies of Azaz'el, in order that they may take them and cast them into the abyss of complete condemnation, and as the Lord of the Spirits has commanded it, they shall cover their jaws with rocky stones. [6] Then Michael, Raphael, Gabriel, and Phanuel themselves shall seize them on that great day of judgment and cast them into the furnace (of fire) that is burning that day, so that the Lord of the Spirits may take vengeance on them on account of their oppressive deeds which (they performed) as messengers of Satan, leading astray those who dwell upon the earth."[20]

The wording of verse 3 needs some explication. "Their chains" cannot refer to the earlier chains on the "kings and potentates" from the previous chapter (1 En 53:3–5), since the chains of 1 Enoch 54:3–4 are still being made. In chapter 54, the "kings and potentates" are getting what they deserve, being thrown into a "deep valley" burning with fire, as 1 Enoch 53:3–5 foreshadowed. The punishment of the "armies of Azaz'el" is yet future—the eschatological "great day of judgment."[21] Azaz'el's armies will be seized by the same four archangels from 1 Enoch 40, one of whom was tasked with preventing these accusers from access to God (1 En 40:7).

---

20. Nickelsburg and VanderKam, *1 Enoch 2*, 37–38.

21. As Nickelsburg and VanderKam note, "The 'great day' here is shorthand for 'the day of the great judgment' (10:6; see also 16:1; 19:1; 22:4; 25:4; 94:9; 98:10; 99:15; 104:5) or 'the great day of judgment' (22:11; 84:4)" (Nickelsburg and VanderKam, *1 Enoch 2*, 202–3).

AZAZ'EL/AZAZEL/ASAEL

The mention of Azaz'el (also spelled "Asael" in 1 Enoch) and the charac-terization of his supernatural armies as "messengers of Satan" are import-ant items. The juxtaposition of these elements means that either Azaz'el and his armies are under the command of Satan or that Azaz'el and Satan are to be identified with each other. Along with most other scholars of 1 Enoch, Nickelsburg and VanderKam prefer the latter: "The present con-text seems to identify Satan with Azazel. Perhaps the title reflects the developing identity of 'the satan' as the tempter and chief demon par excellence, as is attested, for example, in the New Testament."[22]

Readers will recall the name Azazel (= *ʿăzāʾzēl*) from our earlier dis-cussion in chapter 1. The goat sent away into the wilderness on the Day of Atonement was "for Azazel" (Lev 16:8, 10, 26). That the wilderness was associated with "goat demons" was apparent from Leviticus 17:7, where the Israelites wandering in the desert were told, "So they shall no more sacrifice their sacrifices to goat demons (*śĕʿîrîm*)." The wilderness was perceived as the place of chaos and the netherworld in the cosmic geog-raphy of Israel.

The passages under consideration here from 1 Enoch transform Azazel from a proper name associated with sacrifices on unholy ground to sinister entities (the "goat demons" of Lev 7:17) to the leader of evil supernatural forces.[23] Pinker observes that "only in pseudepigraphic lit-erature ... does Azazel appear as a full-fledged demonic being, and the

---

22. Nickelsburg and VanderKam, *1 Enoch 2*, 203.

23. Scholars of 1 Enoch have long noted the inconsistency in the book when it comes to identifying the leader of the Watchers. The difficulty extends to other Second Temple literature. Nickelsburg explains: "The identification of Asael as the archdemon marks the beginning of a tendency in most of the strata of 1 Enoch and in other Jewish literature: (a) to continue to mention the descent of the watchers and the procreation of giants; (b) to expunge the name of Shemihazah; (c) and to empha-size the name of Asael/Azazel, though not necessarily the sin of angelic instruction. 1 Enoch 12–16 emphasizes the sin attributed to Shemihazah and his associates, but his name is not mentioned. In what appears to be an interpolation made by the final interpolator of chaps. 6–11, however, Asael and his sin of revelation are mentioned (13:1–3). In the Animal Apocalypse (chaps. 85–90), Asael descends first and then a leaderless multitude of watchers, who mate with human women (chap. 86). The Book of Parables takes note of the giants but emphasizes the revelations of 'Azazel' and his asso-ciates. In 4Q180 1 6–8, the process of assimilation is complete: Azazel is identified as the leader of the angels who procreate giants. The sole exception to this tendency appears to have been the Book of Giants. The published Jewish and Manichaean texts uniformly mention Shemihazah as the father of the giants. Azazel is mentioned only once." See George W. E. Nickelsburg, *1 Enoch 1: A Commentary on the Book of 1 Enoch, Chapters 1–36; 81–108* (Hermeneia; Minneapolis: Fortress, 2001), 172.

scapegoat rite is viewed as a symbol of demonic expulsion and eschatological victory over demonic forces."[24]

How do we explain these innovations? There are two obvious questions. First, how is it that Azazel from Leviticus 16 could be perceived as a Satan figure? A complete answer is not possible via the data. However, the general coherence of such thinking is discernible.

Recall from chapter 1 that Tawil's detailed research on Azazel showed that the name may have been viewed in demonic terms by Israelites on the basis of Mesopotamian thought about demons and their desert home. He also shows that the language of Leviticus 16 had clear points of correlation with elements of Mesopotamian rituals against demons. In this regard it is interesting to note how Azazel's punishment is described in 1 Enoch 10:4–6:

> The Lord said to Raphael, "Bind Azaz'el hand and foot (and) throw him into the darkness!" And he made a hole in the desert which was in Duda'el and cast him there; he threw on top of him rugged and sharp rocks. And he covered his face in order that he may not see light; and in order that he may be sent into the fire on the great day of judgment.[25]

Azazel, the Satan figure of 1 Enoch, is thus sentenced to the deep recesses of the earth, cast into that pit by way of the desert hole, covered over by rough, jagged rocks to block off the light. Though the precise location of Duda'el is unknown, 1 Enoch 19:1 makes it clear that "goat demons" and a desert location are in view by linking the place name with Deuteronomy 32:17 and Leviticus 17:7:

> And Uriel said to me, "There stand the angels who mingled with the women. And their spirits—having assumed many forms—bring destruction on men and lead them astray to sacrifice to demons as to gods until the day of the great judgment, in which they will be judged with finality.[26]

---

24. Aron Pinker, "A Goat to Go to Azazel," *JHS* 7 (2007): 18. Pinker cites the following textual references: 1 Enoch 8:1; 9:6; 10:4–8; 13:1; cf. 54:5–6; 55:4; 69:2; Apocalypse of Abraham 13:6–14; 14:4–6; 20:5–7; 22:5; 23:11; 29:6–7; 31:5.

25. *OTP*, 1:17.

26. Nickelsburg, *1 Enoch 1*, 276. Deut 32:17 reads (LEB): "They sacrificed to the demons (*šēdîm*), not God, to gods whom they had not known," while Lev 17:7 has, "So they shall no more sacrifice their

First Enoch is centuries earlier than rabbinic material. It is significant, then, that Targum Pseudo-Jonathan has the goat "for Azazel" in Leviticus sent "to die in a rough and stony place which is in the desert of Soq, that is Beth Haduri (Lev 16:10, 21),"[27] a place name that Nickelsburg suggests may have come from the Greek word for "sharp" (*okseis*).[28] In other words, the rabbinic material had the goat for Azazel sent to a place that sounds like Duda᾽el and whose place name describes the location of rough, jagged rocks. Readers have no doubt noticed that the imagery and language is similar to Old Testament Sheol and the New Testament idea of Satan being cast into the lake of fire at the end of days (Rev 20:10).[29]

AZAZ᾽EL (SATAN) AS LEADER OF THE WATCHERS?

The second question that deserves consideration: How could Azazel be connected to the Watchers as their leader? Readers familiar with 1 Enoch's retelling of the episode of Genesis 6:1–4, where the sons of God violate the boundary between heaven and earth by cohabiting with women, will know that Azaz᾽el is cast as the leader of the transgressors, the Watchers (1 En 8:1; 9:1–6; 10:1–4).[30] This preflood episode is referenced in

---

sacrifices to goat demons, after whom they whore."

27. The translation is that of Michael Maher, "Targum Pseudo-Jonathan: Leviticus," in *Targum Neofiti 1: Leviticus and Targum Pseudo-Jonathan: Leviticus*, vol. 3 of *The Aramaic Bible*, ed. Kevin Cathcart, Michael Maher, and Martin McNamara (Collegeville, MN: The Liturgical Press, 1994), 167. Maher comments in a footnote on Lev 16:10: "Hebrew ṣwq ['Soq'] means 'peak, precipice,' but it also refers to the mountain from which the scapegoat was hurled; cf. *m. Yoma* 6,4–5" (167, note 30).

28. Nickelsburg, *1 Enoch 1*, 220–21. Nickelsburg and other scholars note that there are Aramaic variants for this place name that interchange "d" and "r" consonants (e.g., Stuckenbruck, *The Book of Giants from Qumran: Texts, Translation, and Commentary*, ed. Martin Hengel and Peter Schäfer [Tübingen: Mohr Siebeck], 1997). Barker adds this interesting sidebar: "Given the confusion possible in Hebrew script—'d' and 'r' look very similar—these three [place names] show that the scapegoat represented ('was') Azazel, banished to the desert on the Day of Atonement. ... Origen, the greatest biblical scholar of the early Church, knew that the scapegoat had represented Azazel (*Contra Celsum* 6.43)." Margaret Barker, *The Hidden Tradition of the Kingdom of God* (London: Society for Promoting Christian Knowledge, 2007), 37. Nickelsburg's full comment is: "The toponym, whatever its original form, could have derived from the 'sharp' (ὀξεῖς < Aram. חד/חדד) rocks." See Nickelsburg, *1 Enoch 1*, 222.

29. Nickelsburg suggests that "the author is implying the imagery of death, burial, and a resurrection to judgment (cf. [1 En] 22:10–11; 100:4; 103:6–8). Thus his grave is mythically identified with Sheol, the land of gloom or darkness, where one no longer sees the light." See Nickelsburg, *1 Enoch 1*, 221.

30. Those who have studied 1 Enoch with care will know that the book does not always present a consistent picture of the leadership of the Watchers. See the discussion and subsequent notes.

1 Enoch 65, where Noah despairs over the situation. Humankind will be judged because they have acquired the occult knowledge of the fallen angels—the "satans" (v. 6):

> [1]In those days, Noah saw the earth, that she had become deformed, and that her destruction was at hand. [2]And (Noah) took off from there and went unto the extreme ends of the earth. And he cried out to his grandfather, Enoch, and said to him, three times, with a bitter voice, "Hear me! Hear me! Hear me!" [3]And I said unto him, "Tell me what this thing is which is being done upon the earth, for the earth is struggling in this manner and is being shaken; perhaps I will perish with her in the impact." [4]At that moment, there took place a tremendous turbulence upon the earth; and a voice from heaven was heard, and I fell upon my face. [5]Then Enoch, my grandfather, came and stood by me, saying to me, "Why did you cry out so sorrowfully and with bitter tears? [6]"An order has been issued from the court of the Lord against those who dwell upon the earth, that their doom has arrived because they have acquired the knowledge of all the secrets of the angels, all the oppressive deeds of the Satans, as well as all their most occult powers, all the powers of those who practice sorcery, all the powers of (those who mix) many colors, all the powers of those who make molten images.[31]

This passage has the Watchers, the "armies of Azaz'el," under the dominion of Satan (i.e., Azaz'el) and also labels them as satans. First Enoch 69:5–6 follows this same trajectory. The chapter lists the rebellious fallen angels of 1 Enoch's retelling of Genesis 6:1–4. The description of one in particular (v. 6) is noteworthy for our discussion:

> [1]After this judgment, they shall frighten them and make them scream because they have shown this (knowledge of secret things) to those who dwell on the earth. [2]Now behold, I am naming the names of those angels! These are their names: The first of them is Semyaz, the second Aristaqis, the third Armen, the fourth Kokba'el, the fifth Tur'el, the sixth Rumyal, the seventh Danyul, the eighth Neqa'el, the ninth Baraqel, the tenth Azaz'el, the eleventh Armaros, the twelfth Betryal, the thirteenth Basas'el, the fourteenth Hanan'el, the fifteenth

---

31. *OTP*, 1:45.

Tur'el, the sixteenth Sip^{w}ese'el, (the seventeenth Yeter'el), the eigh-
teenth Tuma'el, the nineteenth Tur'el, the twentieth Rum'el, and the
twenty-first Azaz'el. [3] These are the chiefs of their angels, their names,
their centurions, their chiefs over fifties, and their chiefs over tens.
[4] The name of the first is Yeqon; he is the one who misled all the
children of the angels, brought them down upon the earth, and per-
verted them by the daughters of the people. [5] The second was named
Asb'el; he is the one who gave the children of the holy angels an evil
counsel and misled them so that they would defile their bodies by the
daughters of the people. [6] The third was named Gader'el; this one is
he who showed the children of the people all the blows of death, who
misled Eve, who showed the children of the people (how to make)
the instruments of death (such as) the shield, the breastplate, and
the sword for warfare, and all (the other) instruments of death to the
children of the people.[32]

After the offending sons of God are listed (the group previously called
satans in 1 Enoch 65:6) one of them (v. 6) is more specifically identified as
the divine being who deceived Eve. The effect is jarring, to say the least.
Previously (1 En 54:4–6) Azaz'el was identified as (uppercase) Satan, the
ultimate evil authority. The modern reader familiar with the Old Testament would assume Azaz'el was being equated with the serpent of Eden.
But in this chapter Azaz'el is relegated to the tenth angel listed, and a
different angel/satan is credited with deceiving Eve.[33]

By way of a preliminary summary, the Old and New Testaments
diverge from the thinking of 1 Enoch 65 and 69 in several respects. As we
saw earlier, the Old Testament does not refer to any evil spirit as a satan.
The New Testament does not witness a multiplicity of satans. It knows

---

32. *OTP*, 1:47.

33. Scholars of 1 Enoch have long known that its demonology evinces such inconsistencies. Our
purpose is not to unravel them, but to draw attention to connections to the Old Testament and
development that will inform our subsequent discussion of how the New Testament speaks of Satan
and demons. Nickelsburg and VanderKam try to discern the writer's logic: "The mention of Eve is
puzzling at first. She is not a significant figure in 1 Enoch, being mentioned elsewhere only in 32:6
along with Adam ('your father of old and your mother of old'). She does not fit well in a paragraph
that focuses on weaponry and war. Nonetheless, she is not out of place here for two reasons. First,
according to Genesis 3, it is her eating of the fruit that brings death into the world. Note the juxtaposition of 'serpent,' 'woman,' and 'die' in Gen 3:4. See also 2 Cor 11:3, 'the serpent led Eve astray'
(*eksapataō*; Eth. 'ashata as here), as well as Wis 2:24, where the envy of the devil (*diabolos*) brought
death into the world, and Rom 5:12–17, where death is the consequence of the sin of Eden." See Nickelsburg and VanderKam, *1 Enoch 2*, 301.

one satan, who is addressed by the proper name "Satan." Yet the New Testament does describe Satan as having authority over the other divine rebels and powers of darkness. He has a kingdom, an army of angels, and rules this world (Matt 25:41; John 12:31; 2 Cor 4:4; Rev 12:7–9; 20:7–9). These details are not present in the Old Testament, but they are consistent with statements in 1 Enoch and, as we will see, other Second Temple Jewish texts. Further, 1 Enoch describes a fiery end-of-days judgment for the unrighteous, Azazel (Satan), and the armies of Azazel (Satan). None of these ideas can be found in the Old Testament, but all of them echo New Testament theology about "the devil and his angels" (Matt 25:41) and the day of judgment's lake of fire (Rev 20:10–15).

LEADER OF EVIL SPIRITS BY OTHER NAMES

How did other Second Temple–period texts speak of a leader of the evil spirits? How did they use the term "satan"? What relationship did such a figure have to other divine rebels? Not surprisingly, other Second Temple works align at points with 1 Enoch but also depart from the thinking of its author.

One such literary work is the pseudepigraphical book of Jubilees.[34] Its tenth chapter is an instructive case in point. Jubilees 10 is set after the flood. Noah by this time has many grandchildren. Their fathers, Noah's sons, report to the aged patriarch that his grandchildren are being targeted by the demons that arose after the flood.[35] Noah prays,

---

34. Jubilees 10:11–13 references an apparently older "Book of Noah," which Sacchi speculates was rewritten as (Ethiopic) 1 Enoch 6–11. See Paolo Sacchi, *Jewish Apocalyptic and Its History*, trans. William J. Short, OFM (Sheffield: Sheffield Academic Press, 1990), 213. Writings of Noah are referenced elsewhere in Jubilees, and scholars of Second Temple Jewish literature have argued for the presence of a "Book of Noah" in certain Dead Sea Scrolls (1Q19, 4Q534–536) and as the basis for Jub 7:20–39; 10:1–7. See M. J. Bernstein, "Noah and the Flood at Qumran," in *The Provo International Conference on the Dead Sea Scrolls: Technological Innovations, New Texts, Reformulated Issues*, ed. D. Parry and E. Ulrich (Leiden: Brill, 1998), 199–231; D. Dimant, "Noah in Early Jewish Literature. Appendix: The So-Called *Book of Noah*," in *Biblical Figures Outside the Bible*, ed. M. E. Stone and T. A. Bergren (Harrisburg, PA: Trinity Press International, 1998), 123–50 (esp. 144–46); C. Werman, "Qumran and the Book of Noah," in *Pseudepigraphic Perspectives: The Apocrypha and Pseudepigrapha in Light of the Dead Sea Scrolls. Proceedings of the International Symposium of the Orion Center for the Study of the Dead Sea Scrolls and Associated Literature*, ed. E. G. Chazon and M. E. Stone with the collaboration of A. Pinnick (Leiden: Brill, 1999), 171–81; Dorothy M. Peters, *Noah Traditions in the Dead Sea Scrolls* (Atlanta: Society of Biblical Literature, 2008).

35. Note the wording, "your Watchers, the fathers of these spirits" (i.e., the spirits harassing Noah's grandchildren, the demons). These demons would be the disembodied Watcher-spirits released at

[O Lord] you know that which your Watchers, the fathers of these spirits, did in my days and also these spirits who are alive. Shut them up and take them to the place of judgment. And do not let them cause corruption among the sons of your servant, O my God, because they are cruel and were created to destroy. [6] And let them not rule over the spirits of the living because you alone know their judgment, and do not let them have power over the children of the righteous henceforth and forever.[36]

God responds by instructing the archangels to bind the evil spirits but is then approached by their lord with a request:

And the LORD our God spoke to us [the archangels] so that we might bind all of them. [7,8] And the chief of the spirits, Mastema, came and he said, "O Lord, Creator, leave some of them before me, and let them obey my voice. And let them do everything which I tell them, because if some of them are not left for me, I will not be able to exercise the authority of my will among the children of men because they are (intended) to corrupt and lead astray before my judgment because the evil of the sons of men is great." [9] And he said, "Let a tenth of them remain before him, but let nine parts go down into the place of judgment." [10] And he told one of us to teach Noah all of their healing because he knew that they would not walk uprightly and would not strive righteously. [11] And we acted in accord with all of his words. All of the evil ones, who were cruel, we bound in the place of judgment, but a tenth of them we let remain so that they might be subject to Satan upon the earth. [12] And the healing of all their illnesses together with their seductions we told Noah so that he might heal by means

---

the death of the giants (the Nephilim), who were fathered by the Watchers. See 1 Enoch 15–16 and chapter 6 of the present study. Stuckenbruck notes: "The way Jubilees accounts for the origin of evil spirits is similar to the view in both the Book of the Watchers and Book of the Giants that identifies such spirits with the spirits or souls of the dead giants (compare Jub 10:5 with 1 En 15:8–11). Another similarity is that, ultimately, the demonic forces behind evil in the world are regarded, in effect, as powers whose judgment is assured; in other words, they are already defeated beings whose complete destruction is only a matter of time (until the day of judgment; cf. Jub 10:7, 8, 11)." See Loren T. Stuckenbruck, "The Book of Jubilees and the Origin of Evil," in *Enoch and the Mosaic Torah: The Evidence of Jubilees*, ed. Gabriele Boccaccini et al. (Grand Rapids: Eerdmans, 2009), 302. VanderKam agrees noting that the spirits in Jubilees 10 "are, somewhat in line with *1 Enoch* 12–16, identified as the descendants of the Watchers (10.5)" See James C. VanderKam, *The Book of Jubilees* (Sheffield: Sheffield Academic Press, 2001), 131.

36. *OTP*, 2:76.

of herbs of the earth. [13] And Noah wrote everything in a book just as we taught him according to every kind of healing. And the evil spirits were restrained from following the sons of Noah.[37]

In Jubilees 10:11–13, we learn that nine-tenths of the sinning Watchers were imprisoned in the abyss for their crimes, but one-tenth were allowed to remain on earth "so that they might be subject to Satan." Is the "Satan" referred to in verse 11 by the archangel (who is the speaker from v. 10 onward) the "chief of the spirits" called "Mastema"? It would seem so, as this chief presumed jurisdiction in his request (vv. 7–8) and there is no indication the archangels altered the agreement.

What is Mastema? In 1 Enoch, Satan and Azaz'el are identified with each other in certain passages, but the name "Azaz'el" does not appear in Jubilees.[38] Instead, the name "Mastema" is used for Satan, and Mastema is never portrayed as being under the authority of a superior evil figure.[39] As VanderKam notes, Mastema appears in the Dead Sea Scrolls:

> [His] full title is now attested in Hebrew as śar-ham-maśṭmâ (e.g. 4Q225 2.2.13) ... the Prince of Mastema. ... [The] word "mastemah" is a noun which apparently emerged as a name or title at a later time. It is found twice in the Hebrew Bible (Hos. 9:7–8) where it means "animosity, hostility." The phrase "the Prince of Mastema" in *Jubilees* clearly designates an individual who bears this title, while Mastema alone seems to have become a name. In *Jub.* 10.11 the context implies that he is identified with the satan. It seems as if he is the counterpart to the angel of the presence.[40]

The identification of Mastema with Satan (or the use of those two terms for the same cosmic figure) seems driven by two factors. First, *maśṭēmâ* is a noun that derives from the verb *śṭm*, which means "to be at enmity with, be hostile towards."[41] This verb is linguistically related to *śṭn* (i.e., *śāṭān*; "accuser, adversary")—"In the OT the root *śṭn* forms the qal 'to be hostile to,' and the nom[inative]s *śāṭān* 'opponent' and *śiṭnâ*

---

37. *OTP*, 2:76.

38. Conversely, the term Mastema does not appear in 1 Enoch.

39. Aside from Jub 10:7–8 Mastema is referenced in Jub 11:5, 10–11; 17:16; 18:9, 12; 19:28; 48:2, 9, 12, 15; 49:2.

40. VanderKam, *The Book of Jubilees*, 43–44.

41. *HALOT*, s.v. שׂטם.

'hostility' … the by-form *śṭm* produces the qal [verb form] and the noun *maśṭēmâ* 'hostility.'"[42] Second, some Second Temple writers seem to be driven by the assumption that divine hostility is to be considered evil. The author of Jubilees alters several Old Testament episodes to make Mastema the instigator in the place of Yahweh, thereby creating a more pronounced cosmic duality than one finds in the Old Testament.[43]

Returning to Jubilees 10, before God approved this idea, he commanded one of the archangels tasked with punishing the Watchers to "teach Noah all of their healing because he knew they [the Watchers remaining on earth] would not walk uprightly and would not strive righteously" (Jub 10:10). This is followed by the statement, "Noah wrote everything in a book just as we taught him according to every kind of healing. And the evil spirits were restrained from following the sons of Noah."[44]

The passage is strange in terms of both Mastema's request and God's acquiescence to it. A casual reading might conclude that Mastema needs help in leading people astray and God permits it, reflecting perhaps a

---

42. *TLOT*, s.v. שָׂטַן. A "by-form" (also spelled "biform") is "a morphophonemic alternant of a uniform grammatical or lexical element" (Paul Korchin, "Biforms," *EHLL* 1:352).

43. As Fröhlich observes: "In Jubilees Mastema is the leader of the demons in Noah's time. Subsequently, in the Jubilees narrative Mastema appears alone, and always as the instigator: in the time of Ur, Kesed's son (Jub 11:5–6), and then in Terah's days (Jub 11:10–12). In the time of Abraham unclean demons, led by Mastema, ruled the world. These demons are described as descendants of the Fallen Angels (Jub 19:8–10). Abraham has power over the demons; the source of his power is his righteousness. He is not only unwilling to sacrifice to idols while living in the city of Ur, but he sets 'the house of idols' on fire (Jub 12:12). The biblical story of the binding of Isaac (ʿaqedah) is again reformulated in Jubilees: the attempt at sacrifice is here upon the request of Mastema. He is the one who asks God to test Abraham's faith (Jub 17:16). He intends to kill Moses on his way back from Midian (Jub 48.2–3), and Mastema helps the Egyptian wizards, Moses' rivals in Egypt (Jub 48.9–18)." See Ida Fröhlich, "Theology and Demonology in Qumran Texts," *Henoch* 32.1 (2010): 101–29 (esp. 122). Sacchi curiously has God "employing" Mastema in these scenes. While his suggestion that the author of Jubilees seems to desire to extricate God from evil has merit, he over-reads the texts in this regard. See Sacchi, *Jewish Apocalyptic and Its History*, 225. As Stuckenbruck notes (and Fröhlich's comments echo the thought), the Mastema passages in Jubilees could be read in such a way that it is possible the author "presupposes that these celestial rulers such as Mastema (*Jub.* 48:9, 12) are not always under God's control, whereas the angels who remain strictly obedient to God act on behalf of Israel (cf. *Jub.* 48:13)." See Loren T. Stuckenbruck, "Angels of the Nations," *DNTB* 30. It is misguided to presume that angels of destruction (*mashḥit*) and the angel Yahweh are evil entities (Exod 12:13, 21, 23; 1 Chr 21:15–16). This is not the way the Old Testament casts them. While they are God's agents to punish evil, the Old Testament does not include or endorse the idea that God chooses evil, fallen beings for such tasks, as though he or the loyal members of his host cannot perform the dirty work. God has the moral right to punish evil any way he deems fit. It is misguided to label divine testing of humans or judgment of evildoers as "evil" itself.

44. *OTP*, 2:76. The insertion in brackets is that of this author.

hardline predestinarian notion like that which dominated the sect at Qumran, which believed humanity was predestined to follow one of two "spirits" (good or evil supernatural influences). This is only part of the picture, though. The remaining one-tenth of the demons are cast as one means of judging and testing humankind:

> In Jubilees the spirits of the Watchers' sons cause sin, bloodshed, pollution, illness, and famine after the flood (esp. Jub 11:2–6). It is made explicit, however, that they do so as part of God's plan. During the lifetime of Noah, demons are diminished in number and subordinated to Mastema to help him in his divinely appointed task of destroying and misleading the wicked (10:8–9). Lest the reader imagine Mastema and his hosts as the dark side of a cosmic dualism and/or as evil forces in active conflict with God, Jubilees stresses that their existence on the earth is the result of God's acknowledgment of humankind's chronic wickedness (10:8–9). Demons may cause suffering, but the reader is assured that their actions are part of an unerringly fair system of divine justice (cf. Jub 5:13–14).[45]

Interestingly, as was the case with 1 Enoch—where Azaz'el, the leader of the demons, was *not* the deceiver of Eve—so in Jubilees Mastema is nowhere identified as the serpent, the original rebel of Genesis 3. The

---

45. Annette Yoshiko Reed, "Enochic and Mosaic Traditions in Jubilees: The Evidence of Angelology and Demonology," in *Enoch and the Mosaic Torah: The Evidence of Jubilees*, ed. Gabriele Boccaccini et al. (Grand Rapids: Eerdmans, 2009), 357–58. Jubilees 5:12–15, in part cited by Reed, is instructive in regard to the predestinarian thinking. After the flood God "made for all his works a new and righteous nature so that they might not sin in all their nature forever, and so that they might all be righteous, each in his kind, always. And the judgment of all of them has been ordained and written in the heavenly tablets without injustice. And (if) any of them transgress from their way with respect to what was ordained for them to walk in, or if they do not walk in it, the judgment for every (sort of) nature and every kind has been written. And there is nothing excluded which is in heaven or on earth or in the light or in the darkness or in Sheol or in the depths or in the place of darkness. And all their judgments are ordained, written, and engraved. He will judge concerning every one: the great one according to his greatness and the small one according to his smallness, and each one according to his way" (*OTP*, 2:65). Referencing 1QS 3:15–17, Sacchi writes of this Second Temple predestinarian outlook: "If God is omnipotent, such that in that omnipotence he foresaw and predetermined even the words that come out of the mouths of humans, he must also have determined angelic affairs. Essenism, at least that of the sect's great texts, does not use the myth of the fall of the angels. God from the beginning created two spirits, two angelic beings, and placed one as head of the light and the other as head of the darkness, one to love and the other to hate. This prince of darkness is yet another new interpretation of the devil; in this case, however, created as such by God with powers over all those, spirits and human beings, who have been assigned by God to his faction." See Sacchi, *Jewish Apocalyptic and Its History*, 225–26.

Jubilees fall story (Jub 3:17–31) has the serpent, but the names "Satan" and "Mastema" do not occur in its telling. Both books therefore know a figure, at times called "Satan," who is lord over demons (either the offending Watchers before the flood or their spirit children after the flood), but they do not actually associate that figure with the serpent.

The leader of the forces of darkness went by other names in Second Temple literature. More common than Mastema and Satan is Belial (Heb. *bĕliyya'al*), a term that in Hebrew means "wickedness." While Belial does not appear as a proper name for Satan in the Old Testament, it is used frequently in pseudepigraphic literature and the Dead Sea Scrolls.[46] It appears only once in the New Testament as a name for the devil (2 Cor 6:15). Some Old Testament references to *bĕliyya'al*, while not a proper name for personified evil, still have mythological overtones from close associations with Sheol and death, especially in passages like Psalm 18:4–5 and Psalm 41:8.[47]

Belial (or Beliar) is the most common name or title for the prince of darkness in the Dead Sea Scrolls and the Pseudepigrapha. His characterization as king of demonic hordes is unambiguous:

> Belial is called the angel of wickedness, the ruler of this world (*Mart. Is.* 2:4; 4:2). He is the head of the demonic powers (*Mart. Is.* 1:8). In dualistic fashion, his law and will are described as being set over against the law and will of the Lord (*T. Naph.* 2:6, 3:1). His way is one of darkness as opposed to light (*T. Levi* 19:1; cf. *T. Jos.* 20:2). Belial's angels are set over against the angels of the Lord (*T. Ash.* 6:4). He is master of the spirits of error (*T. Jud.* 25:3; *T. Zeb.* 9:8; *T. Levi* 3:3; cf. the spirit of truth and the spirit of error in *T. Jud.* 20:1). ... He is called the angel of enmity (CD 16:5; 1QM 13:11) who is the prince of the kingdom of wickedness (1QM 17:5–6). He heads the forces of darkness, often called "the army/troops or lot of Belial," against the

---

46. Lewis notes extensive references to Belial (or Beliar) in the pseudepigraphic literature (Theodore J. Lewis, "Belial," *ABD* 1:655). Examples can be found in Jubilees, the Testaments of the Twelve Patriarchs, the Sibylline Oracles, the Martyrdom of Isaiah, the Ascension of Isaiah, and the Lives of the Prophets. According to Lewis, "Belial is the most frequently used title for the leader of the forces of darkness in the Qumran material, occurring especially often in the *War Scroll* (1QM) and the *Thanksgiving Hymns* (1QH)" (Ibid.). References to Belial in the Dead Sea Scrolls are just as extensive as references in pseudepigraphic texts.

47. Lewis, "Belial," 655.

Sons of Light or "the lot of God" (1QM 1:1, 13; 11:8; 15:3; 1QS 2:2, 5). "All the spirits of his lot, the angels of destruction, walk according to the precepts of darkness, and towards them is their desire all together" (1QM 13:12). … The reign or dominion of Belial (*mmšlt bly 'l*) occurs frequently in the Qumran material (e.g., 1QM 14:9; 18:1; 1QS 1:18, 24; 2:19; 3:21–22; CD 12:2). It was believed that the present age was under his control (cf. 1QS 2:19 "year by year as long as the dominion of Belial endures").[48]

Nitzan's work on Belial in the Dead Sea Scrolls reveals the connection of Belial with Mastema.[49] In the War Scroll, Belial is found in parallel with Mastema:

You created Belial for the pit,
    the angel Mastemah (= the angel of enmity);
his [dom]ain is darkness,
    his counsel is for evil and wickedness.
All the spirits of his lot
    angels of destruction
        walk in the laws of darkness,
            towards them goes his only desire. (1QM XIII, 10–12)

A few lines earlier, the same text reads, "Accursed be Belial in his malicious [*maśṭēmâ*] plan" (1QM XIII, 4). Belial is also known as *Melchi-resha'* ("king of wickedness") in a few Dead Sea Scrolls (4QAmram [= 4Q544] 2.3; 4Q280 2.2). Nitzan observes that the name is connected to the curses of Belial and his lot (i.e., his followers). The name is thought by scholars to be a deliberate counterpart to Melchizedek, who appears in Qumran texts as the leader of the forces of good.[50] As Hamilton notes, "Ultimately [Beliar] will be chained by God's Holy Spirit (*T. Levi* 18:12), and cast into a consuming fire (*T. Jud.* 25:3)."[51]

---

48. Lewis, "Belial," 655.
49. Bilha Nitzan, "Evil and Its Symbols in the Qumran Scrolls," in *The Problem of Evil and Its Symbols in Jewish and Christian Tradition*, ed. Henning Graf Reventlow and Yair Hoffman (London: T&T Clark, 2004), 91. The translations of 1QM XIII that follow are Nitzan's.
50. Ibid., 91. Nitzan cites the work of Kobelski in this regard: P. J. Kobelski, *Melchizedek and Melchiresa* (Washington, DC: The Catholic Biblical Association of America, 1981). It should be noted that Azazel is mentioned by name in the Qumran Book of Giants (4Q203 frag. 7 i:5). Azazel also appears in 4Q180 Frag. 1:7–8, where he is referenced along with the rebellious angels and the giants.
51. Victor P. Hamilton, "Satan," *ABD* 5:988.

SERPENT, DECEIVER, AND TEMPTER

Several facts about Satan in Second Temple Judaism are apparent at this point. A number of texts have an archenemy of God in the form of a leader of evil spirits. That figure is called "Satan" (among other names or titles). Certain texts link that figure to the rebellious Watchers (sons of God) of Genesis 6 infamy instead of the serpent deceiver of Eden.[52] These features will not sound strange to someone familiar with the New Testament. However, they are absent in the Old Testament. There is no Old Testament passage that suggests that Satan was the leader of other divine rebels.

One might wonder, then, why Second Temple–period writers would make such connections. The answer is not that they simply are contriving content. These data points have abstract, though not textual, relationships to each other in the Old Testament. How Second Temple–period writers could have brought those points together is discoverable.

It is not preposterous to read Genesis 3 and conclude God has an ancient cosmic enemy who had evil intentions with respect to both God's authority and human destiny. The only way to avoid that conclusion would be to assume God had no qualms about the deception of Eve by the serpent and that the deception did no harm. Both propositions are obviously false. Consequently, viewing the serpent as a divine enemy hostile to God's intentions for humankind is a coherent conclusion.

To this conclusion another can coherently accrue. Despite the fact that the Old Testament does not identify the serpent as *śāṭān*, the confrontation between the *śāṭān* of Job 1–2 and God was adversarial, not collegial. That means that the *śāṭān* of Job 1–2 could be perceived as an enemy of God. That conclusion could be read back into Genesis 3 (and Second Temple material informs us that it was).

A third abstract trajectory concerns death and the realm of the dead. The serpent became associated with death because expulsion from Eden meant loss of immortality and because the divine rebel was cast down to

---

52. The matter whether Second Temple Judaism thought of Satan as the serpent of Gen 3 is necessarily distinguished from related questions, such as the effect of Adam's sin upon humanity and the impulse to sin (depravity) within human beings. These are related but distinct subjects in Second Temple Judaism as they are in historic Christianity. Human sinfulness had variegated explanations in Second Temple Judaism. One example is the "two spirits" doctrine at Qumran.

the underworld—Sheol, the pit.[53] Since Second Temple Jewish literature had the Watchers sent to the abyss for their transgression, they became connected conceptually to the realm of the dead as well.

Consequently, the profile of Satan one finds in Second Temple period literature is comprehensible. The measure of coherence the portrait sustains is not undermined by the manufacture of hierarchical relationships between these figures, where the original rebel emerges as the leader of subsequent rebels.

While the abstract paths taken by Second Temple Jewish writers are discernible, it is fair to ask if those writers speak of the serpent and, if so, in what ways. The serpent is indeed present in this material in ways that add to the conceptual matrix of Second Temple Jewish thinking about Satan.

Second Temple literature affirms the Genesis 3 story. For example, its retelling in Jubilees 3 follows the Old Testament very closely. The account in the Sibylline Oracles (1:55) has the serpent as "the cause of the deceit."[54] In the *Wisdom of Solomon* (Wis), readers learn that "by the envy of the devil death entered into the world, And they that belong to his realm experience it" (Wis 2:24).[55] Brown affirms the straightforward implication of passage: "The Wisdom of Solomon implies that the devil was responsible for the introduction of evil into the world."[56] Sacchi notes:

> Even if in the book of Wisdom the serpent is never named, the affirmation that God did not create death (1.14) and that this entered the world only by the work of the devil (2.24) can only be explained by thinking of a reference to the Eden story and the disobedience of Adam. In the book of Wisdom the devil remains only as the cause of death, which is the evil *par excellence*.[57]

---

53. This casting down is described as being to the "ground" or "earth" (*'ereṣ*; Isa 14:12; Ezek 28:17), to Sheol (*sheʾōl*; Isa 14:15), or to the "pit" (*bôr*; Isa 14:15). In Israelite cosmology, the realm of the dead was located in the earth. Hebrew *'ereṣ* is at times specifically associated with the realm of the dead, the "pit" (*shaḥat*) which has inescapable bars (Jon 2:6), the destination of those who have forsaken the Lord (Jer 17:13). Consequently, the term *'ereṣ* is appropriate for both. See Luis Stadelmann, *The Hebrew Conception of the World* (Rome: Biblical Institute Press, 1970), 165–76; Lewis, "Dead, Abode of the," 103; D. A. Neal, "Sheol," *LBD*.

54. *OTP*, 1:336.

55. *APOT*, 1:538.

56. Brown, *God of This Age*, 29.

57. Sacchi, *Jewish Apocalyptic and Its History*, 226–27.

It is no surprise, then, that some Dead Sea Scrolls associate the serpent with Sheol:

When the deeps boil over the springs of water, they rush forth to form huge waves, and breakers of water, with clamorous sound. And when they rush forth, Sh[eo]l [and A]bad[don] open; [al]l the arrows of the pit make their voice heard while going down to the abyss; and the gates of [Sheol] open [for all] the deeds of the serpent. (1QH^a XI, 15b–17)

The scroll continues to the thought that there are other spirits in the underworld: "And the doors of the pit close upon the one expectant with injustice, and everlasting bolts upon all the spirits of the serpent" (1QH^a XI, 18).[58] "Spirits of the serpent" could be construed as spirits in the service of the serpent. Another text (4Q525 frag. 15) associates the serpents with darkness, the "flames of death" and "flames of sulphur." Andersen notes, "At Qumran the souls of the righteous after death live with God 'like angels' while the souls of the wicked go to join the spirits of Belial (1QS 4:6–8, 11–13; 1QM 12:1–7)."[59] The "spirits of Belial" are the wicked human dead, other evil spirits, or both.[60] This sort of language draws the original Edenic rebel and his punishment into the Second Temple discourse of the powers of darkness.[61] It is reasonable to ask how it is coherent to exclude Genesis 3 when considering the meaning of such phrases and imagery. In addition, the fact that these texts precede the New Testament must not be missed.

In his statement above, Andersen does not cite the texts under consideration that link the realm of the dead with the serpent(s)—but he could have done so in support of his point. In the Old Testament, the realm of the dead is not only described with fire imagery but is also a watery abode (e.g., Job 26:5–6; 2:6).[62] 1QH^a column XI goes on to describe the

---

58. Some scholars would render the phrase *rwhy 'p 'h* in line 18 as "spirits of wickedness" instead of "spirits of the serpent." The lemma *'p 'h* clearly refers to a snake in other instances (Job 20:16; Isa 30:6; 59:5 [cp. 1QIsa^a: *'p '*]). See *HALOT*, s.v. אפעה.

59. F. I. Andersen, "2 (Slavonic Apocalypse of) Enoch," *OTP*, 1:139, note p (2 En 22:10).

60. See the predestinarian theology of the two spirits described above (see page 99, note 45).

61. Put another way, literate Second Temple Jews would have made Genesis 3 part of the matrix of ideas. The New Testament writers were literate. There is no reason to conclude that Jewish readers would *only* know of one book or corpus in their time.

62. Johnston is skeptical that water imagery can be properly related to Sheol. However, he does not cite Qumran material in the section where he expresses that skepticism. It seems clear that when

realm of the dead as a place inundated by "the torrents of Belial" (line 29) which "break into Abaddon" (line 32). Since Belial is so clearly a Satan figure, it is easy to see how Second Temple writers could have associated Belial with the serpent. All the particulars of the New Testament's association of the serpent, Satan, and the underworld and its other spirits can be found in these texts by means of their abstract relationships.

Other points of data can be included in this matrix of ideas that lead to New Testament thinking about "the devil and his angels" (Matt 25:41). The use of the term "devil" (*diabolos*) in Wisdom 2:24 is noteworthy in this regard. As deSilva notes, the date of this book has been long debated:

> [Its date] has been placed anywhere between 220 B.C.E. and 100 C.E. The *terminus a quo* is set by the author's use of the Greek translation of Isaiah, Job, and Proverbs, the first of which was probably available by 200 B.C.E. (Reider 1957: 14; Holmes 1913: 520). The *terminus ad quem* is set by the evident use of the work by several New Testament authors (Holmes 1913: 521; Reider 1957: 14). A date within the early period of Roman domination of Egypt, especially the early Roman Principate (or Empire), seems most likely.[63]

The Roman Principate began in 27 BC, so the *Wisdom of Solomon* likely predates the New Testament era. But it is deSilva's comment on this book's use of the Septuagint translation of Job that is the more important point. In LXX Job, *diabolos* ("devil") is used to translate *śāṭān* throughout Job 1–2. The translation choice makes sense. The term *diabolos* means

---

the writer of 1QHᵃ col. XI says that the "torrents of Belial break in Abaddon" and "overflow like a devouring fire" (note the deliberate reference to the more familiar metaphor) causing "cords of death" to allow no escape, that the underworld could be described with such language. See Johnston, *Shades of Sheol*, 114–23.

63. DeSilva, *Introducing the Apocrypha*, 132. On the verdict that LXX Job was completed circa 200 BC, Claude Cox agrees, pushing it toward the end of the second century BC: "The first attestation of LXX-Job is its use in Aristeas' *On the Jews*, a text excerpted by Alexander Polyhistor. That Aristeas is using LXX-Job is clear from the titles 'king' and 'tyrant' in the identification of the three friends. Since Polyhistor wrote around the middle of the first century B.C.E., Aristeas is to be dated to the first half of that same century. LXX-Job must belong somewhat earlier, probably the end of the second century B.C.E." See Cox, "11.3.1 Septuagint [of Job]," in *Textual History of the Bible: Volume 1C: Writings*, ed. Armin Lange and Emanuel Tov (Leiden: Brill, 2017), 176. Another second century BC text (Wisdom of Ben Sira) is ambivalent about using terms like *diabolos* or *śāṭān* of the serpent. On one hand, the author writes: "When the ungodly curses the satan, he curses his own soul" (Sirach 21:27). The use of the definite article suggests an impersonal figure. However, later in the book we read: "The beginning of sin was from a woman, and because of her we all die" (Sirach 25:24), which seems to presume a tempter in Eden.

"slanderer." As we discussed in an earlier chapter, while the *śāṭān* of Job had a legitimate prosecutorial function in the divine council, he over-stepped his bounds by challenging God's assessment of Job—essentially slandering God's integrity.

The ramifications should be apparent. We have already seen that Wisdom 2:24 uses *diabolos* to refer to the villain of Genesis 3 ("by the envy of the devil [*diabolos*] death entered into the world, And they that belong to his realm experience it"). The same author was well acquainted with LXX Job's use of the same term. It is not unreasonable to think that literate Jews of the Second Temple period were acquainted with this text along with the Qumran material that associated the same Genesis 3 rebel with the place where the unrighteous go after death.[64]

The pseudepigraphical work known as the Testaments of the Twelve Patriarchs, dated to the second century BC, refers to Satan as a personal evil spirit. Some of its references are neutral (Testament of Reuben 3:6) while others align with 1 Enoch's identification of Satan as the leader of evil spirits, particularly the Watchers (Testament of Dan 5:6; 6:1). This figure is apparently linked to the fall in Eden by virtue of its mortal con-sequences for humanity: "For among all men the spirit of hatred works by Satan through human frailty for the death of mankind" (Testament of Gad 4:7).[65] The same work also speaks of this villain as the devil (Tes-tament of Naphtali 8:4, 6; Testament of Asher 3:2). Texts from Qumran also speak of Belial in this manner, an entity that "rules over people … tempting them to transgress the rules of the community."[66]

---

64. Scholars often reference material that is contemporaneous with, or subsequent to, the New Testament in discussions of the identification of *śāṭān* with Genesis 3. The material under discussion here that chronologically precedes the New Testament and sets the conceptual precedent for the New Testament's presentation of Satan is rarely mentioned. Hamilton is representative: "Although *śāṭān* does not appear in Genesis 3, later rabbinic sources identified satan with the serpent in Eden (*Soṭa.* 9b; *Sanh.* 29a). He is identified in a more impersonal way with the evil inclination which infects humanity (*B. Bat.* 16a). In a more personal way, he is the source behind God's testing of Abraham (*Sanh.* 89b). Additionally, *śāṭān* is responsible for many of the sins mentioned in the OT. For exam-ple, it is *śāṭān* who was responsible for the Israelites worshipping the golden calf because of his lie that Moses would not return from Mount Sinai (*Šabb.* 89a). He is the driving force behind David's sin with Bathsheba (*Sanh.* 107a), and it is he who provokes the gentiles to ridicule Jewish laws, thus weakening the religious loyalties of the Jews (*Yoma* 67b). The sounding of the horn on the New Year is to confuse *śāṭān* (*Roš. Haš.* 16b). Only on the Day of Atonement is *śāṭān* without power. This is suggested by the numeral value of *śāṭān*, 364; i.e., there is one day in the year he is powerless (*Yoma* 20a)." Hamilton, "Satan," *ABD* 5:988.

65. *OTP*, 1:815.

66. Brown, *God of This Age*, 38.

Another Second Temple period Jewish book that could very well pre-date the New Testament is the Testament of Job. Scholars have dated this text at some time between the first century BC and the first century AD.[67] Scholars have noted that the doctrine of Satan found in this pseudepi-graphical work is more developed than other Second Temple texts and bears closer resemblance to the New Testament presentation of Satan. The book refers to the "devil" (Testament of Job 3:3) as one who tempts and harasses Job and his family. Sacchi notes:

> Here the devil, called by this name or that of Satan, appears more as the opponent of humans than of God. He is the one "by whom human nature is deceived" (3.3), in the sense that he attempts to deceive it. As a tempter, he has freedom of initiative and encounters an obstacle only in the human conscience; but if Satan wants to attack someone in a material way, he must request authorization from God (ch. 8).[68]

The Testament of Job also speaks of the devil as "Satan" (T. Job 3:6; 7:1; 16:2; 20:1; 22:2; 23:1–3; 27:1, 6; 41:5). It is Satan by whom men are deceived (T. Job 3:6). He is "the enemy" (T. Job 47:10; cf. 7:11).[69]

SUMMARY

As I noted at the beginning of our overview of the Second Temple–period perspective on Satan, we have restricted ourselves to works that, to the best standards of scholarship, lead to the New Testament and its own perspective.[70] We have seen that there is no single, unified presentation of Satan, the original divine rebel of Eden, in Second Temple Jewish

---

67. OTP, 1:833–34. Greater precision is not possible. The lengthy critical study of the work by Haralambakis led her to concede, "This monograph supports the view that it is difficult, if not impossible, to draw strong conclusions about issues related to the original context (such as date, author, setting and function)." Maria Haralambakis, *The Testament of Job: Text, Narrative and Reception History*, ed. Lester L. Grabbe (London: T&T Clark, 2012), 183. Brown references the recent study of Davila who seeks to push the date into the fifth century AD. See Brown, *God of This Age*, 39; James R. Davila, *The Provenance of the Pseudepigrapha: Jewish, Christian, or Other?* (Leiden: Brill, 2005), 195–99.

68. Sacchi, *Jewish Apocalyptic and Its History*, 230.

69. Brown notes that the Testament of Job has particular import for a Pauline theology of Satan.

70. Readers may have expected some discussion of the Life of Adam and Eve in regard to its fascinating portrayal of how the devil and his comrades refuse to worship Adam when commanded

literature. Nevertheless, all the particulars of the New Testament's theology of Satan are present in the literature of this earlier period. Those particulars are grounded in the Old Testament, though both Second Temple texts and the New Testament form a theological mosaic from those data in varied ways. The same sort of dynamic will be evident as we proceed to the second and third divine rebellions of the Old Testament.

---

to do so in Eden (LAE 14:3). Life of Adam and Eve dates to AD 100–600. See Marinus de Jonge and Johannes Tromp, *The Life of Adam and Eve and Related Literature* (Sheffield: Sheffield Academic Press, 1997), 77. Some scholars seek to push Life of Adam and Eve to early in the first century AD. Pinero is representative, who argues that the Latin version dates to before AD 70 and derives from a Greek composition. See A. Pinero, "Angels and Demons in the Greek *Life of Adam and Eve*," *Journal for the Study of Judaism in the Persian, Hellenistic and Roman Period* 24 (1993): 191–214 (esp. 192). De Jonge and Tromp dispute this in detail, and so I have excluded this work. The same chronological exclusion applies to texts mentioning Satanael (2 Enoch, 3 Baruch). They clearly derive from the Christian period.

CHAPTER 5

The Second Divine Rebellion—
Making Our Own Imagers

It's no secret that Genesis 6:1–4 is a controversial passage:

> ¹When man began to multiply on the face of the land and daughters were born to them, ²the sons of God saw that the daughters of man were attractive. And they took as their wives any they chose. ³Then the Lord said, "My Spirit shall not abide in man forever, for he is flesh: his days shall be 120 years." ⁴The Nephilim were on the earth in those days, and also afterward, when the sons of God came in to the daughters of man and they bore children to them. These were the mighty men who were of old, the men of renown.

The questions generated by these verses are obvious. Who are the sons of God? Are they divine or human? Who were the Nephilim? Why were they renowned?

Most interpreters, whether Jewish or Christian, consider the "sons of God" who have sexual relations with the "daughters of man" in the passage to be mere mortals, human men from the line of Seth or some other royal lineage. The usual strategy for defending the legitimacy of a nonsupernaturalist approach to Genesis 6:1–4 is to defer to the unity of Christian tradition on the passage.[1] This of course sidesteps the *earlier*

---

1. The earliest *unambiguous* Christian reference to the "human view" of the sons of God can be found in the writings of Julius Africanus (AD 160–240). A century later Augustine became the champion of this approach. His influence is still felt today. Newman observes: "Augustine (A.D. 354–430) discusses Gen 6:1–4 in his *City of God*. His basic approach is seen in 15.22: 'It was the order of this love, then, this charity or attachment, which the sons of God disturbed when they forsook God and were enamored of the daughters of men. And by these two names (sons of God and daughters

broad consensus in favor of a supernatural reading of the episode. Many readers will not know this earlier consensus ever existed. The "human view" of the sons of God, though dominant today, was once a minority position. The supernatural reading once reigned supreme for simple reasons. Biblical writers who allude to the passage take the sons of God to be divine beings, and Second Temple period Jewish writers overwhelmingly followed that trajectory.[2]

---

of men) the two cities [city of God and city of man] are sufficiently distinguished. For though the former were by nature children of men, they had come into possession of another name by grace.' Augustine goes on (15.23) to admit that angels do appear in bodies, and that stories were at his time being told of women being assaulted by sylvans and fauns, but he says 'I could by no means believe that God's holy angels could at that time have so fallen.' He interprets 2 Pet 2:4 as referring to the primeval fall of Satan. The word 'angel,' he points out, can with scriptural warrant be applied to men. Besides, the giants were already on earth when these things happened, and so not the offspring of the sons of God and daughters of men. Also the giants need not be of enormous stature but only so large as sometimes seen today. God's response in Gen 6:3 is directed against men, so that is what the 'angels' were. He dismisses with contempt 'the fables of those scriptures which are called apocryphal.' " See Robert C. Newman, "The Ancient Jewish Exegesis of Genesis 6:2, 4," *Grace Theological Journal* 5.1 (1984): 13–36 (quote from 25–26). There are serious flaws with Augustine's thinking here, no doubt colored by his antipathy toward the Manicheans, who revered the book of 1 Enoch. As this chapter demonstrates, Augustine has no awareness of the original Mesopotamian context of Gen 6:1–4. But it is difficult to fault him for that oversight, as the material was largely lost and could not have been translated anyway. Rather, he is to be faulted for imposing his own city of God hermeneutic on a biblical text, and he offers only a subjective opinion on how evil a divine being could have been. He also appeals to an event (the fall of Satan, presumably taking one-third of the angels with him) as the explanation for 2 Pet 2:4. There is no such event recorded in Scripture. As we saw in the preceding chapter, the first place one finds a plurality of angels under Satan's control or influence is 1 Enoch and similar texts—the ones Augustine calls fables. If one appeals to Rev 12:1–9 there is an immediate obstacle. The language of Rev 12:1–9 is clearly set at the first advent (Rev 12:4–5). There is no mention of the flood in the passage. Rather, 2 Pet 2:5 includes a reference to Noah and the flood. The only group of divine beings (angels) who sinned to which Peter could be referring is in Gen 6:1–4. Augustine's view is, frankly, contrived. On Manicheanism, see John C. Reeves, *Jewish Lore in Manichaean Cosmogony: Studies in the Book of Giants Traditions* (Cincinnati: Hebrew Union College Press, 1992). From the abstract: "Reeves demonstrates that the motifs of Jewish Enochic literature, in particular those of the story of the Watchers and Giants, form the skeletal structure of Mani's cosmological teachings, and that Chapters 1 to 11 of Genesis fertilized Near Eastern thought, even to the borders of India and China." As Van Oort notes: "It is well known that the life and the work of Augustine of Hippo (354–430), the most influential Father of the Western Church, were inextricably connected with Manichaeism." H. van Oort, "Augustine and Manichaeism: New Discoveries, New Perspectives," *Verbum et Ecclesia* 27.2 (2006): 709–28 (esp. 709).

2. Jewish targums (Aramaic translations of the Old Testament) flirt with the human view but do not completely move away from a supernatural view until roughly the same time period as the Christian departure (the third century AD). Newman writes in this regard: "It is difficult to know where to place the targumim. These Aramaic translations of Scripture (often paraphrases or even commentaries) have an oral background in the synagogue services of pre-Christian times, but their extant written forms seem to be much later. Among these, the *Targum Pseudo-Jonathan* [*Tg. Ps.-J.*] presents at least a partially supernatural interpretation. Although in its extant form this targum is later than the rise of Islam in the 7th century A.D., early materials also appear in it. … [Its translation] 'sons of the great ones' may reflect a non-supernatural interpretation, but the reference to Shamhazai and Azael falling from heaven certainly does not. The names given are close to those in *1 Enoch*, considering

All nonsupernatural views of Genesis 6:1–4 suffer the same ultimately insurmountable difficulty: they ignore the original Mesopotamian context of the passage and consequently forfeit the polemic intended by the biblical writer. In other words, they take the passage out of its original context and impose a foreign context that imbues the passage with an unintended meaning. This is not a sound hermeneutical method. The original Mesopotamian backdrop to Genesis 6:1–4 provides clarity on why the ancients did not adopt a human view of the sons of God, how Second Temple Jewish writings preserved that original context, and why Peter and Jude mention "angels that sinned" in conjunction with Noah and the flood (2 Pet 2:4–5).[3] It is also crucial for understanding the origin

---

that the latter has gone through two translations to reach its extant Ethiopic version. Notice also that the Nephilim are here identified with the angels rather than their offspring as in *Enoch*, *Jub.*, and Josephus. … *Targum Neofiti* [*Targ. Neof.*] is the only complete extant MS of the Palestinian Targum to the Pentateuch. The MS is from the 16th century, but its text has been variously dated from the 1st to the 4th centuries A.D. In place of the Hebrew בני האלהים is the Aramaic בני דייניא, 'sons of the judges,' using a cognate noun to the verb ידן appearing in the MT of Gen 6:3. Nephilim is rendered by גיבריה, 'warriors.' The text of the targum seems to reflect a nonsupernatural interpretation, unless we press the last sentence of 6:4—'these are the warriors that (were there) from the beginning of the world, warriors of wondrous renown'—so as to exclude human beings. However, the MS has many marginal notes, which presumably represent one or more other MSS of the Palestinian Targum. One such note occurs at 6:4 and reads: 'There were warriors dwelling on earth in those days, and also afterwards, after the sons of the angels had joined (in wedlock) the daughters of the sons.' Thus the text of *Targ. Neof.* seems to be nonsupernatural while a marginal note is clearly supernatural. … The *Targum of Onqelos* [*Tg. Onq.*] became the official targum to the Pentateuch for Judaism. According to the Babylonian Talmud [*Bab. Talm.*] (Meg. 3a) it was composed early in the 2nd century A.D., but this seems to be a confusion with the Greek translation of Aquila. Although the relations between the various targumim are complicated by mutual influence in transmission, *Onq.* was probably completed before A.D. 400 in Babylonia using Palestinian materials as a basis. In our passage *Onq.* reads בני רברביא, 'sons of the great ones,' probably referring to rulers." See Newman, "The Ancient Jewish Exegesis of Genesis 6:2, 4," 21, 23–24. It should be noted that the first-century writer Philo reflects *both* views. Newman also notes: "In his treatise *On the Giants*, the Alexandrian Jewish philosopher Philo (20 B.C.–A.D. 50) quotes the Old Greek version of this passage with the readings ἄγγελοι τοῦ θεοῦ and γίγαντες. Unfortunately Philo is not always a clear writer. Apparently he takes the literal meaning of the verses to refer to angels and women since, immediately after quoting Gen 6:2, he says: 'It is Moses' custom to give the name of angels to those whom other philosophers call demons [or spirits], souls that is which fly and hover in the air. And let no one suppose that what is here said is a myth.' After a lengthy discussion arguing for the existence of non-corporeal spirits, however, Philo proceeds to allegorize the passage: 'So, then, it is no myth at all of giants that he [Moses] sets before us; rather he wishes to show you that some men are earth-born, some heaven-born, and some God-born.'" See Newman, "Ancient Jewish Exegesis," 19.

3. Note the chronological flow of the Old Testament points of analogy for the ungodly in 2 Pet 2:4–6: the angels that sinned, followed by the flood, followed by the Sodom and Gomorrah incident. As noted in the preceding comments on Augustine, there is no other Old Testament passage that has a group of angels sinning. Genesis 6:1–4 is not only the obvious referent; it is the only referent.

of demons.[4] It is for this reason that we will devote most of our attention in this chapter to the Mesopotamian context of Genesis 6:1–4. However, before engaging in that discussion we will begin with some general observations on the inadequacies of nonsupernatural approaches.

THE SETHITE EXPLANATION

The Sethite interpretation of Genesis 6:1–4 argues that the sons of God are men from the genealogical line of Seth, the son born to Adam and Eve after Abel's murder (Gen 4:25–26; 5:3–4). In this view, the men of Seth's lineage are godly since in the days of Seth "people began to call upon the name of the LORD" (Gen 4:26). Seth essentially functions as a foil or counterpart to the evil Cain, who murdered Abel. It is further presumed that the women of Genesis 6:1–4 are (1) from Cain's ungodly line and (2) ungodly themselves by virtue of their genealogical ancestor. Genesis 6:1–4 therefore describes the intermarriage between the godly Sethite lineage and the ungodly Cainite lineage.[5]

The Sethite approach is deeply flawed. The view requires reading a number of data points into the narrative. Nowhere in Scripture is the line of Seth actually referred to as "sons of God." There is no reason to conclude that all the men of Seth's line were godly. On this point, Genesis 4:26 does not say that it was the people from the line of Seth, men or

---

4. As we will discuss in detail in the next chapter, a wide range of Second Temple Jewish texts put forth the idea that demons originated from the rebellion in Gen 6:1–4 (the rebellion of the Watchers). Specifically, the disembodied spirits released at the death of the giants, the offspring of the union of the sons of God and mortal women, are the demons known in Second Temple texts and the New Testament Gospels. Consequently, our discussion in this chapter is directly relevant to the question of the origin of demons.

5. This view was propounded by John Calvin, which naturally meant its wide adoption. See John Calvin, *Commentaries on the First Book of Moses Called Genesis*, trans. John King, 2 vols. (Edinburgh: The Calvin Translation Society, 1847), 1:238. For a modern example of its adoption, see K. A. Mathews, *Genesis 1–11:26* (NAC; Nashville: Broadman & Holman, 1996), 329. Mathews (and other defenders of the Sethite view) favor it in part because of the notion that "chaps. 4 and 5 contrast the two lines of descent from Adam—the Cainites and Sethites. … [The flood] is actually embedded within the Sethite genealogy, which is not completed until the notice of Noah's death (9:29)" (Mathews, *Genesis 1–11:26*, 329–30). It is obvious that there is a relationship between the flood and the descendants of Seth. They are alive when the flood happens. But why their existence should be used as a definitional hermeneutic for the phrase "sons of God"—used elsewhere in the plural for divine beings—is not at all clear. This trajectory also does nothing to address the other weaknesses of a Sethite approach, namely, that it must read crucial content items into the narrative. And, as our own discussion notes, the Sethite view cannot account for the comments of Peter and Jude and has no relationship to the original Mesopotamian context of Gen 6:1–4.

otherwise, who called "upon the name of the LORD." One also wonders how godly the Sethites could have been, since they were the ones who took all the ungodly women they desired. In like manner, the two references to the "daughters of man" in Genesis 6:2, 4 do not identify the women as descendants from the line of Cain. Further, there is no reason to conclude that the women were ungodly. There is also no prohibition against the intermarriage of the separate lines of humanity extending from Adam and Eve to be found in Genesis 1–5. All of the major elements of the Sethite view are, therefore, absent from the text. Lastly, the Sethite view cannot account for the nature of the Nephilim, the offspring of the forbidden union.[6]

POLYGAMOUS ROYAL MARRIAGES

In light of the obvious difficulties with the Sethite view, it should be no surprise that commentators who do not want to follow the supernatural view have sought an alternative. This approach suggests that the "sons of God" in Genesis 6:1–4 are human kings thought to be divine by ancient peoples. This view is argued by presuming that the "sons of the Most High" in Psalm 82:6 (also called 'elōhîm in that verse and Ps 82:1) are human beings and then reading that assumption back into Genesis 6:1–4. Passages like Exodus 4:23 and Psalm 2:7, where God refers to humans as his children, are offered in support. The marriages in question would then speak of the practice of polygamy on the part of these kings.

---

6. On the morphology and meaning of the term *nĕpîlîm*, see Heiser, *Unseen Realm*, 105–7. Many want this term to mean "fallen ones" (i.e., evil or fallen in battle). The Septuagint translators did not see the term this way and the morphology of the term is not in accord with this option. As I noted in *Unseen Realm*: "The spelling of the word *nephilim* provides a clue to what root word the term is derived from. *Nephilim* is spelled two different ways in the Hebrew Bible: *nephilim* and *nephiylim*. The difference between them is the 'y' in the second spelling. Hebrew originally had no vowels. All words were written with consonants only. As time went on, Hebrew scribes started to use some of the consonants to mark long vowel sounds. English does this with the 'y' consonant—sometimes it's a vowel. Hebrew does that with its 'y' letter, too (the *yod*). The takeaway is that the second spelling (*nephiylim*) tells us that the root behind the term had a long-i (y) in it before the plural ending (*-im*) was added. That in turn helps us determine that the word does not mean 'those who fall.' If that were the case, the word would have been spelled *nophelim*. A translation of 'fallen' from the verb *naphal* is also weakened by the 'y' spelling form. If the word came from the verb *naphal*, we'd expect a spelling of *nephulim* for 'fallen'" (*Unseen Realm*, 106). As the next chapter will make clear, the Second Temple Jews who inherited the Hebrew Bible as its sacred literature considered the Nephilim to be giants from whom would come demons.

We have already noted the incoherence of seeing the *'elōhîm* in Psalm 82 as humans.[7] The "sons of the Most High" are members of God's council in Psalm 82:1. They are called *'elōhîm* in both verses. That "sons of the Most High" is synonymous with "sons of God" ought to be evident, as only the God of Israel would be called "Most High" by the biblical writers. Psalm 89:5–7 explicitly situates the sons of God in Yahweh's council "in the skies" (i.e., the heavens, where God lives). Consequently, the sons of God in the divine council—the "sons of the Most High" in Psalm 82:6—are not men. It is much more coherent, and biblically consistent, to read "sons of God" as supernatural beings as elsewhere in the Old Testament (Job 1:6; 2:1; 38:7; Ps 29:1).

In addition to this fundamental flaw, the text of Genesis 6 never says the marriages were polygamous. The idea of polygamy must be read into the phrase, "they took as their wives any they chose" (Gen 6:2). As Mathews notes, this reading "is only inferential at best [and] there is no sense that coercion is taking place."[8] Further, ancient Near Eastern parallels offered in defense of this view restrict divine sonship language to *individual* kings. There is no precedent for a *group* of men of a royal household being considered (collectively) as divine children of a deity.[9]

---

7. See chapter 1.

8. Mathews, *Genesis 1–11:26*, 329.

9. The divinization of kings was linked to royal accession to the throne and its cultic procedures. It could also be achieved through propaganda. Scholars such as Frankfort have long noted that the belief in the king's "actual" divinity is more a part of Egyptian thought than Mesopotamian and Canaanite (H. Frankfort, *Kingship and the Gods: A Study of Ancient Near Eastern Religion as the Integration of Society and Nature* [Chicago: University of Chicago Press, 1948], 5–6). Michalowski notes that, in the ancient Near East, "all kings are sacred and mediate between sacred and profane, but not all kings are gods" (Piotr Michalowski, "The Mortal Kings of Ur: A Short Century of Divine Rule in Ancient Mesopotamia," in *Religion and Power: Divine Kingship in the Ancient World and Beyond*, ed. Nicole Brisch [Chicago: The Oriental Institute of the University of Chicago, 2008], 34). Divinized human kingship as a large collective is an *eschatological* concept in the Bible that cannot be read back into the pre-flood context of Gen 6:1–4. As I have written elsewhere, corporate divine kingship "was God's original design for his human children to be servant rulers over the earth under his authority as his representatives—*in the presence of his glory*. Restoring the loss of the Edenic vision eventually involves creating a people known as Israel and giving them a king (David), who is the template for messiah. In the final eschatological outcome, the messiah is the ultimate Davidic king, and all *glorified* believers share that rule in a new, global Eden. ... The idea of believers ruling over nations must be read in the context of the reclamation of the nations disinherited by God in Deut 32:8–9. ... The eschatological portrayal of glorified human rulers in a global Eden is why Hos 1:10 cannot be used to argue that the sons of God in Gen 6:1–4 are human. First, the phrase is not a precise parallel. Second, that passage must be viewed in the larger context of biblical theology. Hos 1:10 is *eschatological*. It looks to a distant future time when the *northern* kingdom of Israel will be restored as people of God. That eschatological event coincides with the ultimate glorification of believers—who are, and will be, children of the living God, ruling and reigning with Yahweh, as originally intended, in a new, global

Those who argue for the view that "sons of God" refers to divinized human kings sometimes appeal to the fact that no ancient Near Eastern sources depict divine beings marrying human women. There is a fundamental problem with this approach. Genesis 6:1–4 is not necessarily describing marriage at all. That idea is inferred from English translation. The Hebrew word often translated "wives" is the common word for "women" (*nāšîm*). The relevant phrase of Genesis 6:2 simply says, "They took for themselves women." The language of sexual euphemism is used in both v. 2 and v. 4 to describe the sons of God "taking" and "entering" the daughters of man. The text is making the point that the sons of God have sexual relationships with human women, not that they are marrying the women.[10]

The failure of these nonsupernatural approaches to Genesis 6:1–4 is made more acute by the fact that Peter and Jude presume that Genesis 6:1–4 is about supernatural beings. For our present discussion it is most convenient to first consider the ancient Mesopotamian context of Genesis 6:1–4 as a precursor to the descriptions of the "angels that sinned" in these New Testament passages.

THE MESOPOTAMIAN BACKSTORY TO GENESIS 6:1–4: An Overview

Genesis 6:1–4 draws on the Mesopotamian tale of the *apkallu*. Most Bible students and even scholars will never have heard of them. This is because it has only been since 2010 that a concerted effort was undertaken to revisit the familiar Mesopotamian flood stories with an eye toward the elements of Genesis 6:1–4.[11] Prior to that time, virtually no mention of

---

Eden. The fact that God will see his human family fulfill the original Edenic goal does not overturn the fact that God also has a divine family. At the last day, when human believers are glorified, the two families and councils *merge*. One family of God doesn't erase the other." See Heiser, *Unseen Realm*, 96 (including footnote 9).

10. Heiser, *Unseen Realm*, 96, note 8.

11. Since the late nineteenth century, it has been well known that the flood stories of Mesopotamia have clear, unmistakable parallels with the biblical flood story. For a general overview of the comparison, see Jack P. Lewis, "Flood," *ABD* 2:798–803. For a more detailed discussion of the relationship of the flood story to Mesopotamian material, see David Toshio Tsumura, "Genesis and Ancient Near Eastern Stories of Creation and Flood: An Introduction," in *I Studied Inscriptions from before the Flood: Ancient Near Eastern, Literary, and Linguistic Approaches to Genesis 1–11*, ed. Richard S. Hess and David Toshio Tsumura (Winona Lake, IN: Eisenbrauns, 1994), 44–57.

the *apkallu* can be found in an English commentary on Genesis.[12] Before 2010 only two scholarly essays specifically pursued the *apkallu* story as having an important relationship to Genesis 6:1–4.[13]

This situation changed with the work of Amar Annus, a cuneiform specialist.[14] Annus's work was followed by several other studies.[15] We will draw on Annus's work in this and the following chapter, as his aim was specifically to connect Second Temple Jewish material on the fallen sons of God (the Watchers) to the *apkallu*. It is convenient, though, to begin with Greenfield's summary to introduce the *apkallu*:

> In Mesopotamian religion, the term *apkallu* (Sumerian: *abgal*) is used for the legendary creatures endowed with extraordinary wisdom. Seven in number, they are the culture heroes from before the Flood. … In the myth of the "Twenty-one Poultices" the "seven *apkallu* of Eridu," who are also called the "seven *apkallu* of the Apsu," are at the service of Ea (Enki). … A variety of wisdom traditions from the antediluvian period were supposedly passed on by the

---

12. For example, a search of the leading commentary series most often used by evangelical pastors (such as NAC, WBC, NICOT, TOTC, AYB, and others) reveals that only the New American Commentary (Mathews), the JPS Torah Commentary (Sarna), and the Word Biblical Commentary (Wenham) contain the term *apkallu*. Of the ten total occurrences of the term in these three works, only once are the *apkallu* mentioned in connection with the flood. That single reference appears in a footnote, where *apkallu* appears in the title of an article (Mathews, *Genesis 1–11:26*, 323, note 81). Consequently, prior to recent years, pastors and other Bible students had little to no exposure to the actual context of Gen 6:1–4. It should be obvious that early church fathers and important figures like Luther and Calvin would also have had no exposure to the Mesopotamian background of the passage. The primary sources from Mesopotamian were unknown and, in any case, would not have been deciphered. As we will see, the Dead Sea Scrolls provide a link back to the Mesopotamian context, but these were only discovered in the mid-twentieth century.

13. Those two essays are Anne Draffkorn Kilmer, "The Mesopotamian Counterparts of the Biblical Nephilim," in *Perspectives on Language and Text: Essays and Poems in Honor of Francis I. Andersen's 60th Birthday*, ed. E. W. Conrad and E. G. Newing (Winona Lake, IN: Eisenbrauns, 1987), 39–44; Helge Kvanvig, "Gen 6: 1–4 as an Antediluvian Event," *Scandinavian Journal of the Old Testament* 16.1 (2002): 79–112.

14. Amar Annus, "On the Origin of the Watchers: A Comparative Study of the Antediluvian Wisdom in Mesopotamian and Jewish Traditions," *JSP* 19.4 (2010): 277–320.

15. David Melvin, "The Gilgamesh Traditions and the Pre-History of Genesis 6:1–4," *Perspectives in Religious Studies* 38.1 (2011): 23–32; Ida Fröhlich, "Mesopotamian Elements and the Watchers Traditions," in *The Watchers in Jewish and Christian Traditions*, ed. Angela Kim Hawkins, Kelley Coblentz Bautch, and John C. Endres, S.J. (Minneapolis: Fortress, 2014), 11–24; Henryk Drawnel, "The Mesopotamian Background of the Enochic Giants and Evil Spirits," *DSD* 21.1 (2014): 14–38; J. C. Greenfield, "Apkallu," *DDD* 72–74. Kvanvig, who published one of the essays before 2010 noted above, expanded on his study in his subsequent monograph: Helge Kvanvig, *Primeval History: Babylonian, Biblical, and Enochic: An Intertextual Reading* (Leiden: Brill, 2011).

apkallu. ... The seven sages were created in the river and served as "those who ensured the correct functioning of the plans of heaven and earth." Following the example of Ea, they taught mankind wisdom, social forms and craftsmanship. The authorship of texts dealing with omens, magic and other categories of "wisdom" such as medicine is attributed to the seven *apkallu.*[16]

Greenfield's opening comments inform us that the *apkallu* were divine beings who taught certain points of knowledge to humankind, including omens and magic. One of the passages we read in the previous chapter that used the term "satan" of the leaders of the Watchers had Noah lamenting that the judgment of the flood had come in part because humanity had "acquired the knowledge of all the secrets of the angels" (1 En 65:6). We will return to this point. For now, we note it as an initial point of connection between the Watchers, the fallen sons of God of Genesis 6:1–4, and the *apkallu.*

Greenfield also makes the observation that the seven *apkallu* were created in "the river," a reference to the primeval deep or underworld (or abyss, the realm of the dead) in Mesopotamian thought. Given the association of this cosmic location in Israelite thinking, this certainly would not have been a positive or neutral idea to the writer of Genesis. Annus writes of this point:

> The realm of Apsu is often confused with underworld in Mesopotamian literature. Evidence indicates that the reason for this was either a simple confusion, or Apsu itself was occasionally thought to be a netherworld inhabited by malevolent spirits. The second option seems more likely, as there are many literary references, which place underworld deities and demons in Apsu.[17]

Greenfield used the term "culture heroes" of the *apkallu.* This term refers to the idea (for Mesopotamian peoples) that the *apkallu* were responsible for the greatness of their civilization. As Kvanvig notes, the *apkallu* were "culture-heroes who brought the arts of civilization to the land. During the time that follows this period, nothing new is invented,

---

16. Greenfield, "Apkallu," 72.

17. Annus, "Origin of the Watchers," 302. See also Wayne Horowitz, *Mesopotamian Cosmic Geography* (Winona Lake, IN: Eisenbrauns, 1998), 342–43.

the original revelation is only transmitted and unfolded."[18] This belief motivated Mesopotamian scribes, the scholars of that culture, to seek to establish "physical ancestry and equality to antediluvian figures."[19] Establishing such links allowed the scribes to claim they were masters of knowledge held only by the gods, thus legitimizing their status, power, and influence.[20]

This Mesopotamian theological propaganda has importance for the present study. Babylonian scribal tradition held that the seventh antediluvian king, Enmeduranki, had received divine knowledge from the gods. Given the similarities between the Sumerian King List and the genealogies in Genesis 4–5, scholars have noted that the seventh patriarch in the period before the flood in the biblical material was Enoch (Gen 5:23–24).[21] Enoch was the seventh from Adam (Jude 14), the one who was taken from earth to the heavenly realm. This correspondence was one basis for the authority of Enoch in apocalyptic Jewish literature in the Second Temple period. Enoch, the seventh from Adam, had access to divine knowledge.

The *apkallu* were the key figures in making sure that the knowledge humanity obtained from the gods before the flood survived the deluge. For Mesopotamians, the entire repository of knowledge that was to prove indispensable for civilization—and thus their own greatness—"was traced back to the wisdom of *apkallu*s in its entirety."[22] Lenzi explains:

> The learned scribes received their secret texts in the same manner that all scribes received texts from before their own time: they inherited copies of them from other scribes. But how did they inherit copies *from the gods*? This is where another of Ea's associations assisted the scholars in their construction of secret corpora by providing a mechanism of reception. Ea from very early times was associated with the seven mythological sages called the *apkallu* who lived before the

---

18. Kvanvig, *Roots of Apocalyptic*, 201.

19. Annus, "Origin of the Watchers," 295.

20. On these claims see Alan Lenzi, *Secrecy and the Gods: Secret Knowledge in Ancient Mesopotamia and Biblical Israel* (Helsinki: The Neo-Assyrian Text Corpus Project, 2008).

21. Annus, "Origin of the Watchers," 278. On the complex issue of the biblical Enoch-Enmeduranki relationship, Annus directs attention to the two major studies: James C. VanderKam, *Enoch and the Growth of an Apocalyptic Tradition* (Washington, DC: Catholic Biblical Association of America, 1984); Helge S. Kvanvig, *Roots of Apocalyptic: The Mesopotamian Background of the Enoch Figure and of the Son of Man* (Neukirchen-Vluyn: Neukirchener Verlag, 1988).

22. Ibid., 289. On this subject, see also the monograph by William Hallo, *Origins: The Ancient Near Eastern Background of Some Modern Western Institutions* (Leiden: Brill, 1996).

flood. The scholars created a mythology in which the members of their guild became the professional continuation of the position of the ancient *apkallu*.[23]

Mesopotamian scribes propagandized their status by titling their scholarly writings according to names of *apkallu*. Writing about Mesopotamian astronomy/astrology, Francesca Rochberg adds:

> This gets to the root of the Mesopotamian scribal notion of knowledge, which is what unites divination, horoscopy, and astronomy in the learned cuneiform tradition. And this way of identifying the elements of knowledge, i.e., systematized, even to some extent codified knowledge, was connected with the gods from whom it was claimed such scholarly knowledge was derived in the days before the Flood.[24]

But Enoch (and Enmeduranki for the Mesopotamians) lived before the flood. Many readers will know that, according to various Mesopotamian flood traditions, the higher gods of the pantheon sent the flood to punish humanity for being a noisy nuisance. In the version of the flood story found in the Epic of Gilgamesh, the Mesopotamian god Ea warns a man named Utnapishtim that the gods are planning to destroy the city of Shuruppak. Ea warns him in a dream and instructs him to build a boat:

> Rather than warn his neighbors of the danger, Ut-napishtim was instructed to deceive them about the purpose of his boat if they asked him. He was to load into it "the seed of life of all kinds," his family, relations, and skilled craft workers, as well as beasts. They rode out a 7-day storm in which all the gods "cowered like dogs" (XI 115). The vessel came to rest on Mt. Nisir, and 7 days later Ut-napishtim sent out a dove, a swallow, and a raven. The raven did not return. Coming out of his vessel, he offered a sacrifice around which the gods, "having smelled the sweet odor," gathered "like flies" (XI 161). Enlil was angry that any humans had survived but was pacified by the other gods. Eternal life was bestowed on Ut-napishtim and his wife.[25]

---

23. Lenzi, *Secrecy and the Gods*, 106–7.

24. Francesca Rochberg, *The Heavenly Writing: Divination, Horoscopy, and Astronomy in Mesopotamian Culture* (Cambridge: Cambridge University Press, 2004), 17.

25. Lewis, "Flood," 799. The Roman numerals in the quotation (and others below) correspond to Gilgamesh Epic tablet numbers.

Several Mesopotamian versions of the flood story are known. In other versions, the hero is known as Atrahasis or Ziusudra. The discovery of a fragment of the Epic of Gilgamesh at Megiddo in 1956 suggests the Mesopotamian flood story was known to peoples living in Canaan.[26]

How could Mesopotamian scribes living after the flood have claimed inheritance of the knowledge of the *apkallu* in light of this destruction? A cuneiform tablet from Uruk provides the answer.[27] The tablet lists seven kings who lived before the flood. Each of their names is given along with an assisting *apkallu*. This divine figure (or "divine sage") was assigned to the king to provide him with the knowledge necessary for fostering and maintaining civilization. The list of preflood kings and their *apkallu* adviser teacher reads as follows:[28]

(*apkallu*) Uanna: King Aialu

(*apkallu*) Uannedugga: King Alalgar

(*apkallu*) Enmedugga: King Ammeluanna

(*apkallu*) Enmegalamma: King Ammegalanna

(*apkallu*) Enmebulugga: King Enmeušumgalanna

(*apkallu*) Anenlilda: King Dumuzi

(*apkallu*) Utuabzu: King Enmeduranki

After the flood four *apkallu* are also known from Mesopotamian texts.[29] It is noteworthy that the four post-flood *apkallu* are described as being "of human descent."[30] The fourth post-flood *apkallu* is further described as being only "two-thirds *apkallu*."[31]

If we recall from Greenfield's brief description that the *apkallu* were Mesopotamia's divine "culture heroes," the implication of this post-flood

---

26. Ibid.

27. The tablet (W.20030, 7) is from the Seleucid period, well after the Babylonian (or earlier) era. Nevertheless, as studies of the *apkallu* in other cuneiform material has confirmed, the ideas and names conveyed in this tablet have a much older history. See Lenzi, *Secrecy and the Gods*, 107–8.

28. The spellings are drawn from Kilmer, "Mesopotamian Counterparts," 40, and Seth L. Sanders, *From Adapa to Enoch: Scribal Culture and Religious Vision in Judea and Babylonia* (Tübingen: Mohr Siebeck, 2017), 59.

29. The four named *apkallu* are: Nungalpiriggaldim, Piriggalnungal, Piriggalabsu, and Lu-Nanna. Kilmer ("Mesopotamian Counterparts," 40) lists the four on the basis of several texts edited in four studies, three of which are in German. The English source is Erica Reiner, "The Etiological Myth of the 'Seven Sages,'" *Orientalia* 30 (1961): 1–11.

30. Kilmer, "Mesopotamian Counterparts," 40–41.

31. Ibid., 41.

description is that the post-flood *apkallu* were hybrids. Kilmer draws this same conclusion, and sees its relationship to the *nĕpîlîm* of Genesis 6:1–4 quite clearly:

> Humans and *apkallu* could presumably mate since we have a description of the four post-flood *apkallu* as "of human descent," the fourth being only "two-thirds *apkallu*" as opposed to pre-flood pure *apkallu* and subsequent human sages (*ummanu*).[32]

The implication is that the preflood *apkallu* that were completely divine correspond to the sons of God of Genesis 6:1–4 who cohabit with human women. As has been noted in several places in our own study, the Second Temple Jewish equivalent of the rebellious sons of God were the Watchers. It is significant that Akkadian texts associated with the *apkallu* provide an unmistakable, unambiguous correlation between the *apkallu* and the Watchers. Annus explains:

> Figurines of *apkallus* were buried in boxes as foundation deposits in Mesopotamian buildings in order to avert evil from the house. The term *maṣṣarē*, "watchers," is used of these sets of figurines in Akkadian incantations according to ritual texts. This appellation matches the Aramaic term *ʿyryn*, "the wakeful ones," for both good angels and the Watchers. … The text from Assur, KAR 298, which prescribes the making of apotropaic *apkallu* figurines, often quotes the first line of otherwise unknown incantation *attunu ṣalmē apkallē maṣṣarē* ("You are the *apkallu*-figures, the watchers," e.g. line 14).[33]

In like manner, the unusual offspring that resulted from the forbidden union described in Genesis 6:1–4, the Nephilim, are analogous to the post-flood hybrid *apkallu*. The biblical material has the Nephilim as giants and further describes them as "mighty men" (*gibbōrîm*) and "men of renown" (Gen 6:4). According to Numbers 13:32–33, the giant Anakim (also called Rephaim and Amorites) were descended "from the Nephilim."[34] The correlation of the hybrid *apkallu* with the Nephilim and

---

32. Ibid., 40.

33. Annus, "Origin of the Watchers," 283, 314–15.

34. See Deut 2:10–11, 20–21; 3:8–11; cp. Deut 1:4; 31:4; Amos 2:9–10. I have discussed the nature of the Nephilim at length elsewhere, including the meaning of the term itself. See Heiser, *Unseen Realm*, 105–6, 183–91. As we will discuss in more detail in the next chapter, the Nephilim/Anakim/Rephaim are the biblical counterparts to the Greek Titans. These points are affirmed by a panoply of scholarly

their descendants is reinforced by the description of Gilgamesh in Mesopotamian sources. Gilgamesh is explicitly connected to the *apkallu* in a cylinder which refers to him as "master of the *apkallu*."[35] Gilgamesh is described in the epic that bears his name as two-thirds divine and one-third human. Gilgamesh was also a giant, standing eleven cubits tall (nearly twice as tall as Goliath).[36]

It is not difficult to see how the *apkallu* story contains all the elements of Genesis 6:1–4. Prior to the flood divine beings cohabit with human women. Their offspring are a new generation of culture heroes—"men of renown," in the language of Genesis 6:4. They are also warrior giants. Contrary to Mesopotamian religion, the author of Genesis 6 portrays this event as a horrific transgression of divinely ordained boundaries. We will consider the author's polemic in more detail below. We still have more *apkallu* material to consider that directly relates to Genesis 6, Second Temple Jewish texts, and the New Testament.

THE *APKALLU* UNDER JUDGMENT

We have noted that the *apkallu* from before the flood were viewed very positively by Mesopotamians because their knowledge enabled the flowering and survival of Mesopotamian civilization. But the higher gods who wanted humanity destroyed were displeased. According to the Erra Epic (I.147–162), Marduk sent the offending *apkallu* "down into the Apsû as a consequence of the flood, and ordered them not to come up again."[37] Marduk declared: "I sent craftsmen down to Apsû, I ordered them not to

---

studies. In addition to the sources by Fröhlich, Kvanvig, and Melvin already cited, others include: Amar Annus, "Are There Greek Rephaim? On the Etymology of Greek Meropes and Titanes," *Ugarit Forschungen* 31 (1999): 13–30; Loren T. Stuckenbruck, "Giant Mythology and Demonology: From Ancient Near East to the Dead Sea Scrolls," in *Demons: The Demonology of Israelite-Jewish and Early Christian Literature in Context of Their Environment*, ed. Armin Lange, Hermann Lichtenberger, and Diethard Römheld (Tübingen: Mohr Siebeck, 2003), 31–38; Stuckenbruck, "The 'Angels' and 'Giants' of Genesis 6:1–4 in Second and Third Century BCE Jewish Interpretation: Reflections on the Posture of Early Apocalyptic Traditions," *DSD* 7.3 (2000): 354–77.

35. Greenfield, "Apkallu," 73.

36. Annus, "Origin of the Watchers," 283, 296. Until recently, the eleven cubit height of Gilgamesh had been based on an uncertain reading in the Standard Babylonian version of the Gilgamesh Epic (I 52–58). The eleven cubits has been confirmed by tablets of the epic found at Ugarit. See Andrew R. George, "The Gilgameš Epic at Ugarit," *Aula Orientalis* 25 (2007): 237–54.

37. Annus, "Origin of the Watchers," 282.

come up. I changed the location of *mēsu*-tree and *elmešu* stone, and did not show it to anybody."[38]

The passing note about changing "the location of *mēsu*-tree and *elmešu* stone" meant that Marduk, the high god of Babylon, had taken steps to prevent access to both by the *apkallu*. Annus explains the significance:

> Relocation of a tree and stones is also a motif in the *Erra Epic*, where Marduk during the flood "changed the location of *mēsu*-tree and *elmešu*-stone," in the context of sending the sages down to Apsû (I 147–48). The garden with trees and precious stones in the second dream is comparable to the garden in the end of the hero's journey in the Gilgamesh epic (IX 173–90), with the trees bearing jewels and precious stones.[39]

The *elmešu*-stone was a precious stone or gem of quasi-mythical quality.[40] The *mēsu*-tree was a cosmic tree that reached from the lowest part of the earth to the heavens.[41] Scholars of the book of Ezekiel recognize both items as cosmic-geographical markers of the dwelling place of the gods.[42] The idea being communicated here is that the *apkallu* are barred from Marduk's home and presence for their crime.

The Genesis flood story does not contain the idea that the fallen heavenly sons of God were banned from God's presence in the aftermath. However, the New Testament books of Peter and Jude put forth the idea in very clear terms. Second Peter 2:4 tells us that God did not spare the angels that sinned but instead "cast them into hell [Tartarus],"[43] committing them to "chains of gloomy darkness" until the eschatological judgment. Jude 6 describes those angels in very similar terms: "the angels who did not stay within their own position of authority, but left their proper dwelling" were imprisoned in "eternal chains under gloomy darkness" until the day of judgment. The phrase "cast into Tartarus" is the

---

38. Ibid., 309.

39. Ibid., 310.

40. Daniel Bodi, *The Book of Ezekiel and the Poem of Erra* (Göttingen: Vandenhoeck & Ruprecht, 1991), 92–94.

41. Horowitz, *Mesopotamian Cosmic Geography*, 245.

42. See Wyatt, *Space and Time in the Religious Life of the Near East*, 147–82; Clifford, *The Cosmic Mountain in Canaan and the Old Testament*.

43. We will see in the next chapter that Second Temple retellings of the flood story explicitly parallel the sentence given to the *apkallu* with the judgment handed down against the Watchers.

translation of a verb lemma (*tartaroō*) found in a classical Greek story for the destination of the rebel Titans, a tale well known to have deep roots and clear relationships to the *apkallu* story and Genesis 6:1–4.[44] There the Titans are "hidden under a misty gloom … they cannot go out, for Poseidon has fixed gates of bronze upon it."[45]

The point for our purposes is that these fallen divine beings, cast into the abyss, became associated with demonic activity. This is of course where we would expect to find evil spirits. That the *apkallu* are also related to giants draws our attention to the presence of Rephaim in the underworld. Their offense was preservation of divine knowledge for human benefit.

We will consider all of these points in detail in the next chapter. Each of them was grasped by Second Temple Jewish writers who considered the deeds of the *apkallu* Watchers to be perversions of divine order. As Annus notes, "The Mesopotamian *apkallus* were demonized as the 'sons of God,' and their sons [as] Nephilim (Gen. 6.3–4), who in later Enochic literature appear as Watchers and giants, illegitimate teachers of human-kind before the flood (*1 En.* 6–8)."[46]

THE POLEMIC AIM

The verdict is inescapable. The Mesopotamian *apkallu* story accounts for each element of Genesis 6:1–4. Any interpretation of that passage that fails to account for these transparent correlations cannot be correct.

---

44. See G. Mussies, "Titans," *DDD* 872–74; Mussies, "Giants," *DDD* 343–45; David M. Johnson, "Hesiod's Descriptions of Tartarus (*Theogony* 721–819)," *The Phoenix* 53.1-2 (1999): 8–28; J. Daryl Charles, "The Angels under Reserve in 2 Peter and Jude," *BBR* 15.1 (2005): 39–48; Bradly S. Billings, " 'The Angels Who Sinned … He Cast into Tartarus' (2 Pet 2:4): Its Ancient Meaning and Present Relevance," *Expository Times* 119.11 (2008): 532–37; Birger A. Pearson, "A Reminiscence of Classical Myth at II Peter 2.4," *Greek, Roman, and Byzantine Studies* 10 (1969): 71–80; Jan N. Bremmer, "Greek Fallen Angels: Kronos and the Titans," in *Greek Religion and Culture, the Bible, and the Ancient Near East* (Leiden: Brill, 2008), 73–99. M. L. West notes that the Greek writer Hesiod, whose work is the chief source of the Titans and their rebellion, "put Tartarus far below Hades. … The Titans are bound in Tartarus, far below the earth." See West, *East Face of the Helicon*, 139, 297.

45. Carolina López-Ruiz, *When the Gods Were Born: Greek Cosmogonies and the Near East* (Cambridge, MA: Harvard University Press, 2010), 113. Pages 109–25 of López-Ruiz's work details the relationship of the Titan saga to Ugaritic material. The latter's relationship to the divine council and "sons of God" texts in the Hebrew Bible is equally well known. See Richard A. Parker, "Son of (the) God(s)," *DDD* 794–99; Michael S. Heiser, "Divine Council," *DOTWPW* 112–16.

46. Annus, "Origin of the Watchers," 282, 289.

We have in the *apkallu* saga the long-sought rationale for why Genesis 6:1–4 is in the book of Genesis. The purpose was not to tell us about the godly human line of Seth or to convey an aversion to divinized kings having harems. Rather, Genesis 6:1–4 is part of sacred Scripture because the writer was taking aim at Mesopotamian theology and the myth of Babylonian superiority.

The *apkallu* sought to undermine the wishes of Marduk and his council by ensuring the knowledge that helped create Mesopotamian civilization would survive, allowing humanity to recover from the disaster of the flood. The post-flood *apkallu* warrior-sages were epic heroes to whom Babylon owed its magnificence. The writer of Genesis didn't see it that way. The transgression of the sons of God of Genesis 6:1–4 would eventually produce the greatest threat to capturing the promised land of Canaan, the Nephilim and their descendant giant clans. This point was clearly communicated by linking the Anakim and the giant clans on both sides of the Jordan to the Nephilim (Num 13:32–33; Deut 2–3).[47] As the author of 1 Enoch would later put it, the cohabitation offense was acting in the mode of creators—creating living beings in their own image. In 1 Enoch 68:4–5, the archangels sent to punish the offending sons of God met together:

> Then it happened that when they stood before the Lord of the Spirits, Michael said to Raphael thus, "They shall not prosper before the eye of the Lord; for they have quarreled with the Lord of the Spirits because they make the image of the Lord. Therefore, all that which has been concealed shall come upon them forever and ever; for neither an angel nor a man should be assigned his role; (so) those (evil ones) alone have received their judgment forever and ever."[48]

But the crimes of the sons of God went beyond producing a lethal threat to Yahweh's children, the Israelites. Since, according to the Old Testament, the giant clan lineages expired in the days of David, Second Temple–period Jews were fixated on two other aspects of the Genesis 6:1–4 polemic against the "*apkallu* theology" of Babylon. Our own study

---

47. On how the account of the conquest of Canaan was oriented by the elimination of the giant clans, see Heiser, *Unseen Realm*, 183–214.

48. *OTP*, 1:47.

has already come across the first: the death of the Nephilim and their descendants was the explanation for the origin of demons. The second fixation was that Second Temple writers saw the dispensing of forbidden divine knowledge to humanity as causing the proliferation of human depravity. Unlike modern commentators who lack the *apkallu* story as a frame of reference, ancient Jewish readers understood why the travesty of the sons of God in Genesis 6:1–4 was immediately followed by Genesis 6:5:

> The LORD saw that the wickedness of man was great in the earth, and that every intention of the thoughts of his heart was only evil continually.

Why would the writer connect human wickedness to the transgression of the sons of God? Why would they think that the death of the giants brought forth demons? These beliefs and their connection to the Old Testament are only comprehensible in light of the *apkallu* polemic lurking behind Genesis 6:1–4. It is to both these points of the ancient Jewish theology of the powers of darkness that we now turn.

CHAPTER 6

Depravity and Demons
in Second Temple Judaism

OUR EXPOSURE TO THE ORIGINAL ANCIENT CONTEXT FOR THE SECOND
divine rebellion in the Old Testament storyline prepares us to understand
how both Second Temple period and New Testament writers processed
that rebellion.[1] In our discussion of the point-for-point correlations
between Genesis 6:1–4 and the Mesopotamian *apkallu* story, we briefly
observed that Second Temple Jewish texts like the Book of Giants from
Qumran were informed by the Mesopotamian source material. In this
chapter we will drill down even further into those correlations as a precursor to the New Testament theology of demons we will encounter in
later chapters.

As I noted at the close of the preceding chapter, ancient Jewish writers
and readers of the Second Temple period saw Genesis 6:1–4 and its Mesopotamian backstory as the explanation for the origin of demons. The
"heroic" deeds of the *apkallu* (as the Babylonians saw things) were considered perversions by biblical authors. Amar Annus observes in this regard:

> The Mesopotamian *apkallus* were demonized as the "sons of God,"
> and their sons Nephilim (Gen. 6.3–4), who in later Enochic literature
> appear as Watchers and giants, illegitimate teachers of humankind
> before the flood (see *1 En.* 6–8). … As many kinds of Mesopotamian
> sciences and technologies were ideologically conceived as originat-
> ing with antediluvian *apkallus*, so both Enoch and the Watchers

---

1. That Genesis 6:1–4 was read by Second Temple authors as a divine rebellion is indisputable. See
the lengthy discussion in Wright, *The Origin of Evil Spirits*, 138–65.

were depicted as antediluvian teaching powers. ... By comparison, the *Book of Watchers* 8.1 enumerates the first set of arts forbidden to humanity—a list which consists mainly of useful crafts and technologies. This revelation of forbidden secrets was considered a transgression, because it promoted promiscuity and violence.[2]

This may seem like an interpretive leap, but it is so only to the eyes of modern readers unacquainted with Second Temple Jewish literature— the reading material for generations of Jews leading to and including the New Testament period.[3] In order for us to see what the ancients saw in Genesis 6:1–4 and how their observations cohere with the *apkallu* context, we must begin with their most detailed retelling of Genesis 6:1–4.

THE STORY OF THE WATCHERS IN 1 ENOCH

In the preceding chapter we saw that figurines of the *apkallu* were called *maṣṣarē* ("watchers") in Akkadian. It is no surprise, then, that the book of Daniel (set in Babylon) is where we find the Aramaic equivalent of this term— *ʿîr* (Dan 4:13, 17, 23). The term is qualified by the appositional "holy one" (Dan 4:13, 23), making it clear that a "watcher" (and so, one of the sons of God, a member of the heavenly host) was not by default an evil divine being.[4]

"Watcher" was often the term of choice in Second Temple period retellings of the story of the sons of God. In regard to what "watching" meant

---

2. Annus, "Origin of the Watchers," 282, 289.

3. The notion that the biblical writers avoided this material is deeply flawed. In addition to a handful of instances where they draw material from the books of the Apocrypha and Pseudepigrapha, New Testament writers allude to the content of these books on dozens of occasions (see Heiser, *Reversing Hermon*, 203–56 [Appendix IV: "New Testament Allusions to Books of the Pseudepigrapha"]). Regarding the relationship of the Apocrypha to the New Testament, deSilva writes: "Although it is true that no book of the Apocrypha is quoted or identified as such, recontextualizations and reconfigurations abound. That is, New Testament authors weave phrases and recreate lines of arguments from Apocrypha books into their new texts. They also allude to events and stories contained in these texts. The word 'paraphrase' very frequently provides an adequate description of the relationship" (deSilva, *Introducing the Apocrypha*, 22). DeSilva moves from his statement to a number of clear instances in the New Testament where such re-contextualizing occurs (Ibid., 23–25).

4. The ESV correctly renders the Aramaic phrase *ʿîr wĕqaddîš* as "a watcher, a holy one," as opposed to "a watcher and a holy one." The surrounding context validates the *waw* conjunction being understood as creating an appositional relationship (i.e., only *one* heavenly being converses with Daniel in the passage and when the heavenly figure speaks, singular participles are used by the writer).

and the possible etymological origin of the Aramaic term ʿîr, Nickelsburg notes the likely derivation from a root meaning "be awake, watchful":

> Precisely such an interpretation appears to be presumed in [1 En] 39:12, 13; 40:2; 61:12; 71:7 ("those who sleep not," ʾella ʾiyenawwemu), and it may also be indicated at 14:23. In both cases, these heavenly beings are on twenty-four-hour duty attending God—whether to praise God or to function as a kind of bodyguard in the throne room.[5]

The first thirty-six chapters of 1 Enoch are referred to by scholars as the "Book of the Watchers," a designation that points to their prominence in the book's retelling of events closely preceding and following the flood. Chapters 6–16 are of particular importance for the present study. Collins describes the flow of the story this way:

> Chapters 6–16 tell the story of the Watchers, in which two stories seem to be woven together. In one, the leader of the fallen angels is named Asael (Azazel in the Ethiopic text), and the primary sin is improper revelation; in the other the leader is Shemihazah, and the primary sin is marriage with humans and procreation of giants. ... The Watchers beget giants on earth by their union with human women. Out of these giants come evil spirits that lead humanity astray (1 Enoch 15:11–12; this motif is elaborated further in Jubilees). In the short term, the crisis of the Watchers is resolved when God sends the flood to cleanse the earth.[6]

As Collins's comments suggest, the sin of the Watchers in 1 Enoch expands upon Genesis 6:1–4. Readers should not presume, however, that all of the expansionist material is arbitrary. As we will see, significant

---

5. Nickelsburg, 1 Enoch 1, 140. Nickelsburg's notion of throne guardianship draws immediate attention in light of the original rebel's depiction as a divine throne guardian and the propensity of the writer of 1 Enoch and other Second Temple writers to associate Satan with the leader of the Watchers.

6. J. J. Collins, "Enoch, Books of," DNTB 314. This last comment about the sin of Adam will be explored in the present book in several chapters. This perspective, as one can imagine, affects the reading of certain New Testament passages. See also Kevin Sullivan, "The Watchers Traditions in 1 Enoch 6–16: The Fall of the Angels and the Rise of Demons," in The Watchers in Jewish and Christian Traditions, ed. Angela Kim Harkins, Kelley Coblentz Bautch, and John C. Endres, S.J. (Minneapolis: Fortress, 2014), 91–106.

portions of it are informed by the *apkallu* story. Discerning this will require that we read portions of the salient chapters here.[7]

> 6:1 And when the sons of men had multiplied, in those days, beautiful and comely daughters were born to them. ²And the watchers, the sons of heaven, saw them and desired them. And they said to one another, "Come, let us choose for ourselves wives from the daughters of men, and let us beget for ourselves children." ³And Shemihazah, their chief,[8] said to them, "I fear that you will not want to do this deed, and I alone shall be guilty of a great sin." ⁴And they all answered him and said, "Let us all swear an oath, and let us all bind one another with a curse, that none of us turn back from this counsel until we fulfill it and do this deed." ⁵Then they all swore together and bound one another with a curse. ⁶And they were, all of them, two hundred, who descended in the days of Jared onto the peak of Mount Hermon.[9] And they called the mountain "Hermon" because they swore and bound one another with a curse on it.[10] ⁷And these are the names of their chiefs: Shemihazah—this one was their leader; Arteqoph, second to him; Remashel, third to him; Kokabel, fourth to him; Armumahel, fifth to him; Ramel, sixth to him; Daniel, seventh to him; Ziqel, eighth to him; Baraqel, ninth to him; Asael, tenth to him; Hermani, eleventh to him; Matarel, twelfth to him; Ananel, thirteenth to him; Setawel, fourteenth to him; Samshiel, fifteenth to him; Sahriel, sixteenth to him; Tummiel, seventeenth to him; Turiel, eighteenth to him; Yamiel, nineteenth to him; Yehadiel, twentieth to him. ⁸These are their chiefs of tens.

---

7. The translations of 1 Enoch 6–8 here are from Nickelsburg, *1 Enoch 1* (174, 182, 188). For convenience I have chosen to omit brackets in reconstructed words and names. I have also inserted alternate spellings of Watcher names, and alternate names, found in other passages of 1 Enoch describing the same transgressions.

8. This description is found in the Ethiopic text but is not present in some Greek manuscripts.

9. The direct reference to Mount Hermon is corrupted in the Ethiopic text. Its authenticity is attested in the Aramaic material of *1 Enoch* found among the Dead Sea Scrolls (the first six words of 4QEnᵃ), as well as some Greek manuscripts.

10. In Hebrew (and Aramaic) "Hermon" (*ḥermōn*) is related to *ḥāram* which means (as a verb) "devote to destruction" and (as a noun), "[thing] devoted to destruction." These terms are prominent in the biblical conquest account. See Heiser, *Unseen Realm*, 183–214. Nickelsburg notes that this wordplay "is an explicit and typical etymologizing on the name of Mount Hermon (cf. Gen 4:17; 28:10–19; 31:46–49), possible in both Hebrew and Aramaic. The mutual anathematizing of the watchers (for the verb חרם see 4QEnᵃ 1 3:3) explains the name of the mountain on which it took place (חרמון). The long history of religious activity in the environs of Hermon is well documented" (Nickelsburg, *1 Enoch 1*, 177).

7:1 These and all the others with them took for themselves wives from among them such as they chose. And they began to go in to them, and to defile themselves through them, and to teach them sorcery and charms, and to reveal to them the cutting of roots and plants. ²And they conceived from them and bore to them great giants. And the giants begat Nephilim, and to the Nephilim were born Elioud.¹¹ And they were growing in accordance with their greatness.¹² ³They were devouring the labor of all the sons of men, and men were not able to supply them. ⁴And the giants began to kill men and to devour them. ⁵And they began to sin against the birds and beasts and creeping things and the fish, and to devour one another's flesh. And they drank the blood. ⁶Then the earth brought accusation against the lawless ones. (1 Enoch 6:1–7:6)

To this point the expansion of the biblical material in Genesis 6:1–4 is transparent. But in the next chapter of 1 Enoch, its author draws from material not found in Genesis:

8:1 Asael taught men to make swords of iron and weapons and shields and breastplates and every instrument of war. He showed them metals of the earth and how they should work gold to fashion it suitably, and concerning silver, to fashion it for bracelets and ornaments

---

11. The text as established by Nickelsburg for his translations produces three offspring: giants, *něpîlîm*, and "Elioud." Each succeeding group produces the next. Nickelsburg writes: "The interpretation of this passage, and specifically the relationship between 'the giants' (*něpîlîm*) and 'the mighty ones' (*gibbôrîm*), has long been disputed. Ancient interpreters disagreed, although the varying interpretations may reflect knowledge of the Enochic form of the tradition. An identification of the two groups with one another is as old as the LXX, which translates both nouns with οἱ γίγαντες [*hoi gigantes*] ('the giants'). … Modern interpreters also differ on the referents of the two nouns, and these interpretations are often tied to one's understanding of the history of the tradition. According to Westermann, the two groups are most likely identified with one another in the present state of the Genesis text" (Nickelsburg, *1 Enoch 1*, 184). Nickelsburg is citing Claus Westermann who notes that originally the two terms "did not designate the same object, because Nephilim is a name whereas גברים [*gibbôrîm*] describes a group." See Westermann, *A Continental Commentary: Genesis 1–11* (Minneapolis: Fortress, 1994), 378–79. I agree with Westermann (and others) on this issue. For our purposes (i.e., establishing the Watcher story for the sake of New Testament interpretation), the issue isn't important. The term "Elioud" is enigmatic (see Nickelsburg, *1 Enoch 1*, 185, for a short survey of options). My preference is that the term may derive from the common Semitic root ʿ-l-y ("exalted") and mean something like "arrogant ones." See, for example, Ugaritic *ʿly*—verb: "to rise up" or "attack"; adjective: "exalted" (*DULAT* 1:160–61, s.v. "ʿly").

12. Nickelsburg's preferred text (the Greek version of Syncellus) omits the reference to the height of the Nephilim. The Ethiopic text and some Greek manuscripts read either 3,000 or 300 cubits for their height. It should be obvious that, given Nickelsburg's texts have these giants producing successions of giant offspring (with human women apparently), the heights are absurd, making sexual intercourse impossible.

for women. And he showed them concerning antimony and eye paint and all manner of precious stones and dyes. And the sons of men made them for themselves and for their daughters, and they transgressed and led astray the holy ones.[13] [2]And there was much godlessness upon the earth, and they made their ways desolate.

> [3]Shemihazah taught spells and the cutting of roots.
> Hermani taught sorcery for the loosing of spells and magic and skill.
> Baraqel taught the signs of the lightning flashes.
> Kokabel taught the signs of the stars.
> Ziqel taught the signs of the shooting stars.
> Arteqoph taught the signs of the earth.
> Shamsiel taught the signs of the sun.
> Sahriel taught the signs of the moon.
> And they all began to reveal mysteries to their wives and to their children.

[4](And) as men were perishing, the cry went up to heaven. (1 En 8:1–4)

On the surface the content of 1 Enoch 8 seems straightforward: Watchers taught humanity a variety of skills and practices deemed forbidden by its writer (and Second Temple Judaism more broadly). But the writer's disposition conveys more than pious irritation with pagan culture.

CORRUPTION AND DEPRAVITY

These points of knowledge broadly fall into the categories of skilled crafts and esoteric aptitudes relating to warfare, seduction, sorcery, and divination. But when this list is compared to the knowledge that the *apkallus* taught the people of Babylon before and after the flood, it becomes quite clear that the *apkallu* story is not only the backdrop for the episode

---

13. This line in 1 Enoch 8:2 illustrates why scholars have determined that 1 Enoch is a composite of sources and traditions. Nickelsburg writes: "According to the second clause, these women then led the holy watchers astray. That is, the sin of Shemihazah and his companions, described in chaps. 6–7, was caused ultimately by the instruction of Asael. This idea implies two other ideas not present in chaps. 6–7. First, the original angelic sinner and primary author of the evil under consideration was not Shemihazah but Asael. Second, the angels were seduced by the women" (Nickelsburg, *1 Enoch 1*, 195).

described in Genesis 6:1–4 but also what leads to the verdict of Genesis 6:5 about the corruption of humanity. Annette Yoshiko Reed observes:

> According to *1 En.* 16, the angelic transmission of heavenly knowledge to earthly humans can also be understood as a contamination of distinct categories within God's orderly Creation. As inhabitants of heaven, the Watchers were privy to all the secrets of heaven; their revelation of this knowledge to the inhabitants of the earth was categorically improper as well as morally destructive.[14]

The forbidden knowledge described in 1 Enoch 8 can be divided into "crafts" or technological skills and means of divination. Both are linked to the *apkallu* by Mesopotamian scribal theology. For followers of Yahweh, both categories were considered catalysts to depravity and idolatry.

In regard to the "craft" knowledge disdained by the Enochian writer, it should be recalled that Mesopotamians thought their knowledge was directly from the *apkallu* and therefore to be held in secrecy.[15] This knowledge was to be guarded, for therein lay the wonder of Babylonian civilization. The writer of 1 Enoch, on the other hand, saw the knowledge of the *apkallu* as destructive and intrinsically evil. One reason was that Mesopotamian inscriptions make it clear that knowledge of a particular craft was due to patron deities of the respective skill, whether stone-cutting, metal working, etc.

Other scholars have drawn attention to the relationship between the "craftsmen knowledge" in Mesopotamia, the *apkallu* sages, and Enoch's Watchers. For example, Drawnel observes parallels of organization, knowledge, and activities between the Watchers described in 1 Enoch and the craftsmen in Late Babylonian temples.[16]

---

14. Annette Yoshiko Reed, *Fallen Angels and the History of Judaism and Christianity* (Cambridge: Cambridge University Press, 2005), 46.

15. Lenzi, *Secrecy and the Gods*, 140–62. Lenzi illustrates the point via a number of primary texts (cuneiform tablets). See also Annus, "Origins of the Watchers," 289.

16. Henryk Drawnel, "Professional Skills of Asael (1 Enoch 8:1) and Their Mesopotamian Background," *Revue Biblique* 119.4 (2012): 518–42 (esp. 518, 538). In a separate article, Drawnel objects to a correlation of the Watchers with the *apkallu* instead of priestly and craftsman classes: "Additionally, analyzing the social background of the early Enochic literature, one can hardly speak about the Watchers as representing the mythological *apkallus* because such an approach would deprive the myth of its anchoring in the real life of its author." See Drawnel, "Knowledge Transmission in the Context of the Watchers' Sexual Sin with the Women in 1 Enoch 6–11," *The Biblical Annals* 2.59 (2012): 123–51 (esp. 134, note 18). Annus does not deny these counterparts; that is, he does not deny that the knowledge transmitted in the stories was received by human artisans. Consequently, this is

This connection to Babylonian economic, military, and temple (cultic) activity allows us to read between the lines. For Babylonians who believed that such knowledge came from their gods, connecting between these skills and worldly success and religion would have been expected. The knowledge given would not only serve as a catalyst to human civilization, but that knowledge was also to be employed in the service and worship of the gods. The gods would in turn bless their loyal devotees with military and economic success. The knowledge elements testified to the greatness of Babylon and the greatness of its gods.

The reference to "eye paint and all manner of precious stones and dyes" will seem out of place to the modern reader. While it is clear that the passage links these items to seduction, less apparent is the fact that scholars have successfully connected these terms to Mesopotamian words for magical-medicinal practices known to the intellectual elites of Babylon.[17]

The "magic and divination" category of elite knowledge condemned by 1 Enoch also correlates with the knowledge of Mesopotamian knowledge, this time more directly in terms of divination:

> When one considers this list of forbidden crafts from the point of view of Mesopotamian priests and scholars, almost everything looks familiar. "Spells and the cutting of roots" are relevant to Babylonian medicine (*asûtu*). The skills taught by Hermani are crafts used in exorcism, *āšipūtu*.[18] Baraqel's expertise, whose name means "lightning of God," involves the "signs of Adad," the meteorological omens on the tablets 37–49 in the series *Enuma Anu Enlil*. The first two long sections of this celestial omen series, the "signs of Sin" (tablets 1–22) and the "signs of Shamash" (tablets 23–36), are taught to humankind in the *Book of Watchers* by the angels with appropriate

---

a misguided objection on the part of Drawnel. The correlation of the Watchers with Mesopotamia is not an "either-or" question. Rather, it is a "both-and" issue. Correlations can be drawn to both divine beings and human practitioners.

17. Drawnel, "Professional Skills," 534–37.

18. Annus' footnote on this term is worth reproducing as well: "The Akkadian technical term *āšipūtu* was borrowed into Aramaic as ʾšpʾ, which is frequently used in the book of Daniel. In the Aramaic version of the *Book of Watchers* 7.1, the Watchers teach 'sorcery and charms,' where the second word can be read precisely as ʾšpʾ. ... The sorcery is exercised by 'the seven sages of Eridu' in the Mesopotamian anti-witchcraft collection *Maqlû* V 104." See Annus, "Origins of the Watchers," 290, note 3. Annus cites Nickelsburg, *1 Enoch 1*, 197 in this footnote, as well as T. Abusch and D. Schwemer, "Das Abwehrzauber-Ritual Maqlû ('Verbrennung')," in *Omina, Orakel, Rituale und Beschwörungen*, ed. B. Janowski and G. Wilhelm (Gütersloh: Gütersloher Verlagshaus, 2008), 163.

names, Shamsiel and Sahriel.[19] The "signs of the stars" taught by Kok-abel must be a lore related to *Enuma Anu Enlil*'s tablets 50–70, where the planetary omens are dealt with. … Finally, the "signs of the earth," taught by the angel Arteqoph, are probably not related to geomancy, but to the terrestrial omen series *Šumma ālu*. … In any case, many important Babylonian "antediluvian" sciences are well represented in the above catalogue, which can be taken as *pars pro toto* of all import-ant Mesopotamian sciences. If the list is of independent origin, it may be illuminative to note that it contains seven names, in accordance with the seven antediluvian sages.[20]

Consequently everything 1 Enoch has the Watchers teaching human-ity has some connection to the keepers of Babylonian knowledge, who were connected to Babylonian religion and who credited their knowledge to the *apkallu*.

For Jews acquainted with the history and character of imperial Baby-lon, this matrix of ideas would not have been foreign. Babylon's mystique was powerful well into the Hellenistic era. The ministry of the classi-cal prophets (Isaiah, Jeremiah, Ezekiel) made the important theological argument that the exile of Yahweh's people did not mean the gods of Babylon or any other empire were superior. Rather, those empires were the instruments of Yahweh to chastise his own unfaithful people. Yahweh would redeem his people and, subsequently, judge Babylon and succeed-ing empires and their gods. Yahweh was the one true God.

The Second Temple Jewish writer of 1 Enoch, then, saw the *apkallu* for what they were. There was only one legitimate source of divine knowledge to humankind—Yahweh of Israel, the Creator of all. By definition, then, any dispensing of knowledge to humanity by any other deity was pre-sumptuous at best and a hostile connivance at worst. The Mesopotamian

---

19. Shamsiel corresponds to *shamash*, the word for "sun." Sahriel "is a corruption of *sahri'ēl*, שהריאל" (Nickelsburg and VanderKam, *1 Enoch 2*, 297). The first three consonants of this name correspond to Hebrew and Ugaritic terms for the morning star. See S. B. Parker, "Shahar," *DDD* 754; E. Lipiński, "Shemesh," *DDD* 764.

20. Annus, "Origin of the Watchers," 289–91. Annus (289) cites two sources regarding the Meso-potamian craftsmen and their access to secret knowledge: Christopher Walker and Michael B. Dick, "The Induction of the Cult Image in Ancient Mesopotamia: The Mesopotamian *mīs pî* Ritual," in *Born in Heaven, Made on Earth: The Making of the Cult Image in the Ancient Near East*, ed. Michael B. Dick (Winona Lake, IN: Eisenbrauns), 55–122; A. R. George, "Babylonian Texts from the Folios of Sydney Smith," *Revue d'assyriologie* 82 (1988): 139–62 (esp. 147, lines 19–28).

apkallu story provides the rationale for how the biblical writer could move from Genesis 6:1–4 with its description of the sons of God fathering the Nephilim to conclude in the very next verse, "The LORD saw that the wickedness of man was great in the earth, and that every intention of the thoughts of his heart was only evil continually" (Gen 6:5). Human depravity, sparked in Eden by the original rebel, had been inflamed and accelerated by a new rebellion.[21] Divine rebels—supernatural intelligences—are thus blamed for humanity's descent into self-destruction and idolatry.

THE ORIGIN OF DEMONS: "Bastard Spirits"

As the Watchers' saga continues in 1 Enoch, the four archangels (Michael, Sariel, Raphael, and Gabriel) report the travesty unfolding on earth to the Most High (1 En 9:1–11). God responds by decreeing the coming of the flood (1 En 10:1–3) and ordering the offending Watchers be rounded up for judgment in the abyss:

> [9] And to Gabriel he [God] said, "Go, Gabriel, to the bastards, to the half-breeds, to the sons of miscegenation; and destroy the sons of the watchers from among the sons of men; send them against one another in a war of destruction. And length of days they will not have; [10] and no petition will be (granted) to their fathers in their behalf, that they should expect to live an eternal life, nor even that each of them should live five hundred years." [11] And to Michael he said, "Go, Michael, bind Shemihazah and the others with him, who have united themselves with the daughters of men, so that they were defiled by them in their uncleanness. [12] And when their sons perish and they see the destruction of their beloved ones, bind them for seventy generations in the valleys of the earth, until the day of their judgment and consummation, until the eternal judgment is consummated. [13] Then

---

21. Scholars who focus on Second Temple Jewish thought acknowledge the central importance of Gen 6:1–4, 1 En 6–16, and the transgression of the Watchers (sons of God) in Judaism's doctrine of depravity. See Miryam Brand, *Evil Within and Without: The Source of Sin and Its Nature as Portrayed in Second Temple Literature* (Göttingen: Vandenhoeck & Ruprecht, 2013); Loren T. Stuckenbruck, "The Origins of Evil in Jewish Apocalyptic Tradition: The Interpretation of Genesis 6:1–4 in the Second and Third Centuries BCE," in *The Fall of the Angels*, ed. Christoff Auffarth and Loren T. Stuckenbruck (Leiden: Brill, 2004), 87–118.

they will be led away to the fiery abyss, and to the torture, and to the prison where they will be confined forever. (1 En 10:9–13)

The language of this passage (and others) is the conceptual source of statements in the letters of Peter and Jude regarding the angels who sinned at the time of the flood being sent to Tartarus and chained in gloomy darkness.[22] Sullivan notes, "Because the hybrid offspring were conceived on earth, their spirits are doomed to remain there. ... [T]he conduct of these Watchers was significantly evil as to cause them and their hybrid offspring to be barred from heaven."[23] But Enoch's retelling of the divine rebellion in Genesis 6:1–4 doesn't end there. In 1 Enoch 15 we learn that this episode is at the core of Jewish demonology. God, speaking to Enoch, says:

[2]Go and say to the watchers of heaven, who sent you to petition in their behalf, 'You should petition in behalf of men, and not men in behalf of you. [3]Why have you forsaken the high heaven, the eternal sanctuary; and lain with women, and defiled yourselves with the daughters of men; and taken for yourselves wives, and done as the sons of earth; and begotten for yourselves sons, giants? ... [8]But now the giants who were begotten by the spirits and flesh—they will call them evil spirits upon the earth, for their dwelling will be upon the earth. [9]The spirits that have gone forth from the body of their flesh

---

22. Readers should note that this is not the only passage in 1 Enoch describing the fate of the Watchers and the place of their imprisonment. I mention this due to the absence of a reference to darkness in 1 En 10:9–13. A range of Second Temple period texts describe this cosmic prison in association with the Watchers. Bauckham writes: "The verbs ταρταροῦν [tartaroun] and (rather more common) καταταρταροῦν [katatartaroun] mean 'to cast into Tartarus,' and were almost always used with reference to the early Greek theogonic myths, in which the ancient giants, the Cyclopes and Titans, were imprisoned in Tartarus, the lowest part of the underworld, by Uranos, Kronos and Zeus. ... They are not used in the Greek version of 1 Enoch; though τάρταρος [tartaros] ('Tartarus') is used of the place of divine punishment in 1 Enoch 20:2, as elsewhere in Jewish Greek literature (LXX Job 40:20; 41:24; Prov 30:16; Sib. Or. 4:186; Philo, Mos. 2.433; praem 152). But Hellenistic Jews were aware that the Greek myth of the Titans had some similarity to the fall of the Watchers (though Philo, Gig. 58, rejects any comparison). Sometimes the Watchers' sons, the giants (the Nephilim), were compared with the Titans (Josephus, Ant. 1.73; cf. LXX Ezek 32:27; Sir 16:7) but in Jdt 16:6 (and also the Christian passage Sib. Or. 2:231) the Watchers themselves seem to be called τιτᾶνες [titanes] ('Titans'). ... [T]he author has interpreted Jude's 'chains' (δεσμοῖς [desmois]; see Jude 6) metaphorically of the darkness (ζόθος [zothos] is the gloom of the underworld) in which the angels are confined." See Richard J. Bauckham, 2 Peter, Jude (WBC; Dallas: Word, 1998), 249. In regard to Tartarus, Wright (Origin of Evil Spirits, 116) draws attention to the fact that the leader Watcher (Asa'el) is cast into the darkness of Dudael (1 En 10:4–5), and the Titan Prometheus (who gave forbidden knowledge to humanity) was likewise cast into Tartarus.

23. Sullivan, "The Watchers Traditions in 1 Enoch 6–16," 95, 96.

are evil spirits, for from humans they came into being, and from the holy watchers was the origin of their creation. Evil spirits they will be on the earth, and evil spirits they will be called. ¹⁰The spirits of heaven, in heaven is their dwelling; but the spirits begotten in the earth, on earth is their dwelling. ¹¹And the spirits of the giants lead astray, do violence, make desolate, and attack and wrestle and hurl upon the earth and cause illnesses. They eat nothing, but abstain from food and are thirsty and smite. ¹²These spirits (will) rise up against the sons of men and against the women, for they have come forth from them.

The origin of demons is tied specifically to the incident of the Watchers (Gen 6:1–4).²⁴ Reed summarizes the theology of Second Temple Judaism on the matter:

The birth of the Giants is explored in terms of the mingling of "spirits and flesh" (15:8). Angels properly dwell in heaven, and humans properly dwell on earth (15:10), but the nature of the Giants is mixed. This transgression of categories brings terrible results: after their physical

---

24. See Wright, *Origin of Evil Spirits*, and Loren T. Stuckenbruck, *The Myth of Rebellious Angels* (Tübingen: Mohr Siebeck, 2014) for the most thorough discussions of this topic. In his dissertation, Stokes observes the following in regard to 1 En. 15:7b–16:1: "Some scholars further detect in this passage a second tradition, according to which the children of the watchers were never embodied, but existed as evil spirits from birth. If one removes those statements from the passage that speak of the spirits proceeding from the bodies of the giants (15:9a and 16:1), these scholars argue, one is left with the teaching that evil spirits were never embodied at all but were born as spirits. As further evidence for this etiology, these scholars cite 1 En. 10:15, where God commands the angel Michael, 'Destroy all the spirits of the half-breeds and the sons of the watchers, because they have wronged men.'" Stokes points out why such a perspective lacks coherence: "There are several problems with positing the existence of such a hypothetical tradition, according to which the offspring of the watchers were from the start evil spirits. First, in order to find this idea in 15:7b-16:1, one must remove 15:9a and 16:1 from the passage for no other reason than to arrive at this hypothesized teaching. ... Second, even with the passage reconstructed accordingly, arguments for such a belief amount to no more than an argument from silence. The reconstructed passage does not require one to interpret it in a way that contradicts its context in the *Book of Watchers*, taking it to mean that the children of the watchers were never giants, but were disembodied spirits from birth. Third, they are 'giants who were begotten by the spirits and flesh' (15:8, italics [Stokes']). It is difficult to imagine 'giants' (*gigantes*) who do not have bodies. ... Fourth, the command issued in 10:15 to 'destroy all of the spirits of the half-breeds' is incompatible with an etiology of evil spirits. What a poor etiology it would be if the very beings whose present existence it explains are utterly wiped out in Noah's day! More likely, this command is simply to kill the watchers' gigantic offspring. There is little basis for the hypothesis that an etiology of evil spirits as the children of the watchers ever circulated in the Jewish literature of this period apart from the belief that these beings were at one time embodied in the form of giants." See Stokes, "Rebellious Angels and Malicious Spirits," 71–73.

death, the Giants' demonic spirits "come forth from their bodies" to plague humankind (15:9, 11–12; 16:1).[25]

This passage from 1 Enoch is not unique. Other Second Temple Jewish texts that affirm the supernaturalist perspective of Genesis 6:1–4 and the origin of demons via the Nephilim. Stuckenbruck notes "a number of early Jewish traditions regarded these beings as essentially evil, representative of forces that are inimical to God's original purpose for creation."[26] For example, Jubilees has demons fathered by the Watchers (Jub 10:1, 5). As we saw earlier in our study, demons (the spirits of the giants) "operate under divine permission and, therefore, exist as contained powers (10:3) whose defeat is assured (10:8)."[27]

The Dead Sea Scrolls offer other examples.[28] Thomas identifies numerous texts among the Dead Sea Scrolls "that exhibit familiarity with Watchers and Giants traditions."[29] Certain scrolls refer to demonic powers as "bastard spirits" (*rûḥôt mamzerîm*) precisely because it was presumed that demons were the disembodied Watcher spirits of the Nephilim giants.[30] Thomas further draws attention to Qumran scrolls that contain incantations against evil spirits:

---

25. Reed, *Fallen Angels and the History of Judaism and Christianity*, 46.

26. Stuckenbruck adds: "This picture is, of course, most well-known through apocalyptic and wisdom literature composed prior to the Common Era, remains of some being attested among the Dead Sea Scrolls: the early Enoch traditions—so especially the Book of Watchers and Animal Apocalypse in 1 Enoch, and the Book of Giants—Ben Sira, the Book of Jubilees, Damascus Document, Wisdom of Solomon, 3 Maccabees, 3 Baruch, and several fragmentary texts from previously unknown works (e.g., 4QSongs of the Sage [4Q510–11]; 4QAges of Creation [4Q180–81]; 4QExhortation Based on the Flood [4Q370]; and 11QApocryphal Psalms [11Q11] col. 5)." See Stuckenbruck, "The 'Angels' and 'Giants' of Genesis 6:1–4 in Second and Third Century BCE Jewish Interpretation," 354–55. See also Fröhlich, "Theology and Demonology," 102.

27. Stuckenbruck, "'Angels' and 'Giants,'" 372.

28. On the connection between evil spirits and the Watchers/giants in the Qumran material, in addition to the study already cited (Thomas, "Watchers Traditions in the Dead Sea Scrolls"), see Wright, *Origin of Evil Spirits*, 166–90.

29. Thomas, "Watchers Traditions in the Dead Sea Scrolls," 137. The scrolls Thomas lists in this regard are: 4Q201–202, 204–212 (fragments of 1 Enoch) and 1Q23–24; 2Q26; 4Q203; 4Q206; 4Q530–532; 4Q556; 6Q8 (Ibid., 137–38). He also notes additional fragments of 1 Enoch have been discovered recently that are thought to have come from Qumran (Ibid., 137). Additionally, there are "several other Aramaic compositions from Qumran in which Watchers are mentioned or alluded to: the *Genesis Apocryphon* (1Q20); the so-called 'Elect of God' text (4Q534–36); and the *Visions of Amram* (4Q543–49)" (Ibid., 138). See also Angela Kim Harkins, "Elements of the Fallen Angels Traditions in the Qumran *Hodayot*," in *The Fallen Angels Traditions: Second Temple Developments and Reception History*, ed. Angela Kim Harkins, Kelley Coblentz Bautch, and John C. Endres (Washington, DC: Catholic Biblical Association of America, 2014), 8–24.

30. 4Q510 1 5; 4Q511 35 7; 4Q444 2 i 4. The "bastard" terminology also occurs in 1 En 10:9 (*maze-reoi*). As Wright notes, "The term 'bastard' is defined in the biblical texts as either a person of

[4Q510–511] suggests—even seems to presume—the idea that the spirits of the Giants continued to plague humanity even after the flood. … In a related sectarian, exorcistic text, 4Q444, *mamzerîm* are mentioned in juxtaposition (or apposition?) to a "spirit of impurity" … which may help to clarify the sense of "bastards."[31]

The Genesis Apocryphon from Qumran (1QapGen) is also illustrative as to the prevalence of the Watcher-Nephilim tradition. This text, dated sometime between the first centuries BC–AD, is famous for being one of the first Dead Sea Scrolls published and for its "rewriting" of events included in Genesis, most notably the circumstances of Noah's birth, where Noah's mother is queried by Lamech, his father, as to whether she was impregnated by a Watcher. Thomas observes:

Watchers and Giants are intimately associated in early Jewish Aramaic literature with the story of Noah and the Flood, which in turn is complexly related to older Mesopotamian lore about Gilgamesh and Utnapishtim. The author(s) of the *Book of Giants*, for instance, likely understood Gilgamesh and Hobabish (Humbaba) (and perhaps Atambish = Utnapishtim) to be figures who were in fact Giants themselves—which might help to explain the point made rather defiantly in the Qumran "birth of Noah" materials (1QapGen ar 2–5; *1 En.* 106–107; 1Q19 3; cf. 4Q534–36) that despite any recognizable affinities with hoary Mesopotamian heroes, Noah was *not* the offspring of the Watchers even in light of the aberrant circumstances of his birth.[32]

---

questionable birth (Deut 23:3) or a person whose lineage is pagan (Zech 9:6)" (Wright, *Origin of Evil Spirits*, 150). There are additional fragmentary texts whose context suggests the same idea: 1QHa 24 XVIII 1–16; other scrolls match the content of 1 Enoch (i.e., Aramaic Enoch): 4Q202 IV 5–11 (= 1 En 10:8–12); 4Q204 V 2 (= 1 En 10:13–19 + 12:3). Fröhlich observes of the Hebrew phrase: "The expression *rwḥwt mmzrym* in 4Q510–11 designates demons. Bastard spirits and ravaging angels probably originated in the Enochic tradition where the Watchers had illicit sexual relations with earthly women." See Fröhlich, "Theology and Demonology," 109, as well as Giovanni Ibba, "The Evil Spirits in Jubilees and the Spirit of the Bastards in 4Q510 with Some Remarks on Other Qumran Manuscripts," *Henoch* 31 (2009): 111–16.

31. Thomas, "Watchers Traditions in the Dead Sea Scrolls," 146. The second century BC Visions of Amram (4Q543–49) is another possible text relating to the Watchers, but it is highly fragmentary. See the discussion in Thomas, "Watchers Traditions in the Dead Sea Scrolls," 143–44; Wright, *Origin of Evil Spirits*, 124, 170–71.

32. Thomas, "Watchers Traditions in the Dead Sea Scrolls," 140–41. On the argument between Lamech and his wife (Bitenosh), see Pieter W. van der Horst, "Bitenosh's Orgasm (1QapGen 2:9–15)," *Journal for the Study of Judaism* 43 (2012): 613–28; Stuckenbruck, *Myth of the Rebellious Angels*, 58–77. As noted in the previous chapter, the work of Assyriologists Amar Annus and Andrew George has established that Gilgamesh was a giant. See, in particular, Andrew R. George, "The Gilgameš Epic at

Second Temple Jewish literature thus presents us with a matrix of ideas with respect to evil spirits. The corporate divine rebellion of Genesis 6 was a horrific event aimed at the destruction of the people of God and humanity at large. The fallen sons of God (Watchers) corrupted humanity and turned them toward idolatry. The Nephilim and their descendants wreaked physical destruction and, through their disembodied spirits, ongoing physical and spiritual devastation.[33] Wright summarizes the theological point:

> The giants of the Watcher tradition are described as spiritual beings that were born with a human type of body (*1 Enoch* 15.4, 8 and 16.1). … The giants are seen as categorically evil because they are an illegitimate mixed nature of human and angel (see *1 Enoch* 15). Their function in the physical world of *1 Enoch* was to destroy humanity. Following their death, their purpose as evil spirits was to tempt humans and to draw them away from God.[34]

Early Christian writers were also aware of and embraced this reading of the preflood sons of God/Watchers episode.[35] Stuckenbruck offers examples:

Ugarit," *Aula Orientalis* 25 (2007): 237–54. While the case of Atambish is ambiguous, scholarly work in the Book of Giants has established that several giants (along with Gilgamesh himself) appear in those texts by name: Hobabish (Humbaba), Mahaway, Ohyah, and Hahyah. See Nickelsburg, *1 Enoch 1*, 185; Stuckenbruck, *Book of Giants*, 27. For profiles of these giants, see Stuckenbruck, *Myth of the Rebellious Angels*, 36–57.

33. It should be pointed out that some scholars consider 1 En 19:1 marring the consistency of this picture. That passage reads (translation from Stokes's dissertation): "There stand the angels who mingled with the women. And their spirits—having assumed many forms—bring destruction on men and lead them astray to sacrifice to demons as to gods until the day of the great judgment, in which they will be judged with finality (19:1)." Stokes's comments on this issue are once again pertinent: "Here, as in the previous etiology, these harmful spirits are connected with the watchers who sinned before the flood. In the present passage, however, the evil spirits are referred to as 'their [i.e., the angels'] spirits.' It is possible that this etiology differs from that of *1 En.* 15 in that here the spirits are not thought to be those disembodied spirits of the watchers' half-breed children but are regarded as the spirits of the watchers themselves. Since this understanding of the passage requires the transgressing angels to be simultaneously imprisoned and causing trouble on the earth, it is unlikely that the spirits are the same persons as the angels. The spirits in this passage are likely, as in 15:7b–16:1, thought to be the remnants of the watchers' offspring." See Stokes, "Rebellious Angels and Malicious Spirits," 77.

34. Archie T. Wright, "Some Observations on Philo's *De Gigantibus* and Evil Spirits in Second Temple Judaism," *Journal for the Study of Judaism* 36.4 (2005): 471–88 (esp. 482).

35. In addition to the Stuckenbruck and Schultz sources that follow, for intersections between the Watchers traditions and early Christian theology, see Silviu N. Bunta, "Dreamy Angels and Demonic Giants: The Watchers Traditions and the Origin of Evil in Early Christian Demonology," in *The Fallen Angels Traditions: Second Temple Developments and Reception History*, ed. Angela Kim

In particular [we] see the Christian *Testament of Solomon* 5:3; 17:1. In 5:3 (within the section 5:1–11), the author reinterprets the demon Asmodeus—this is a deliberate reference to the Book of Tobit which follows the longer recension (cf. Codex Sinaiticus at 3:7–8, 17; 6:14–15, 17; 8:2–3; 12:15)—one born from a human mother and an angel. In the latter text (in the passage 17:1–5) the demonic power thwarted by Jesus (in an allusion to Mk 5:3) is identified as one of the giants who died in the internecine conflicts. Similarly, in the *Pseudo-Clementine Homilies* 8.12–18 refers to the giants, which are designated as both "bastards" (18; cf. 15) and "demons" (14; 17) in the ante-diluvian phase of their existence. Here they are said to have survived the deluge in the form of disembodied "large souls" whose post-diluvian activities are proscribed through "a certain righteous law" given them through an angel. … Furthermore, one may consider Tertullian's *Apology* 22, a passage deserving more detailed analysis, in which the offspring of the fallen angels are called a "demon-brood" who "inflict … upon our bodies diseases and other grievous calamities. …" [In] the *Instructions* by the 3rd century North African bishop Commodianus (ch. 3) … the disembodied existence of the giants after their death is linked to the subversion of "many bodies." The implications of the giants traditions for concepts of demonology at the turn of the Common Era have until now been insufficiently recognised.[36]

Harkins, Kelley Coblentz Bautch, and John C. Endres (Washington, DC: Catholic Biblical Association of America, 2014), 116–38; Franklin T. Harkins, "The Magical Arts, Angelic Intercourse, and Giant Offspring: Echoes of Watchers Traditions in Medieval Scholastic Theology," in *The Fallen Angels Traditions: Second Temple Developments and Reception History*, ed. Angela Kim Harkins, Kelley Coblentz Bautch, and John C. Endres (Washington, DC: Catholic Biblical Association of America, 2014), 157–79; Randall D. Chesnutt, "The Descent of the Watchers and its Aftermath According to Justin Martyr," in *The Watchers in Jewish and Christian Traditions*, ed. Angela Kim Harkins, Kelley Coblentz Bautch, and John C. Endres, S.J. (Minneapolis: Fortress, 2014), 167–80; Annette Yoshiko Reed, "The Trickery of the Fallen Angels and the Demonic Mimesis of the Divine: Aetiology, Demonology, and Polemics in the Writings of Justin Martyr," *Journal of Early Christian Studies* 12.2 (2004): 141–71.

36. Stuckenbruck, "The Origins of Evil in Jewish Apocalyptic Tradition," 103, note 35. Stuckenbruck's closing estimation is an understatement. Due to the influence of Augustine, the assent of the early church to the dominant supernaturalist reading of Gen 6:1–4 is virtually unknown today save by specialists. Commenting on the important early church father Irenaeus, D. R. Schultz writes: "Irenaeus sometimes attributes the origin of sin directly to Satan and his forces in terms strongly reminiscent of 1 Enoch, Jubilees, and other late Jewish pseudepigraphical writings. … Sin is directly related to angelic powers and principally to the leader of these powers, Satan. He is the first to sin against God and later lead others to that sin or apostasy. … Thus, the apostasy reaches from Satan to other angels who follow his lead in sin, transgression, and revolt. Moreover, the apostasy which began with Satan and continued through the apostate angels also extends to the whole of mankind.

We have seen how the narrative elements (divine beings cohabiting with mortal women and producing giants) are consistent across the material from Mesopotamian, the Hebrew Bible, and Second Temple texts. But what about this last item, the evil spirits? The *apkallu* were culture heroes. Were they also considered demonic? Is there an association in the Old Testament between the giants and evil spirits?

Readers will recall that the answer to both these questions is yes. We saw earlier that the *apkallu* were exiled from the presence of the high gods for their deed, sent back to the abyss permanently by Marduk. They were also considered evil in Mesopotamian religion:

> It is a little known fact that *apkallu* are occasionally depicted as malevolent beings in Mesopotamian literature, who either angered the gods with their hubris, or practiced witchcraft. ... The *apkallus* occur at least twice in the anti-witchcraft series *Maqlû* as witches, against whom incantations are directed. ... The fact that *apkallu* are born and often reside in Apsu, is not evidence that points to their exclusively positive character, since demonic creatures were also often thought to have their origin in the depths of the divine River.[37]

In like manner, our discussion of the *rephàim* in chapter 1 revealed that the Old Testament not only used that term of giants descended from the Nephilim but also had *rephàim* as underworld inhabitants. Whereas the *rephàim* in the literature and religion of ancient Ugarit (*rp'um*) were only underworld inhabitants, the disembodied spirits of warrior-kings

---

Irenaeus, speaking of all those whom God should punish in the eternal fires, lists 'the angels who transgressed and became apostates, together with the ungodly, and unrighteous, and wicked, and profane among men' (Irenaeus, *Against Heresies*, 1,10,1 [1,2]). ... Irenaeus definitely understands that there exists a causal relationship between Genesis 6:1–4 and the wickedness that follows in Genesis 6:5. ... Further clarification is achieved through an examination of the manner in which Satan's apostasy is extended to mankind. Irenaeus has two different descriptions of the angels defiling mankind. One description is concerned with 'unlawful unions' of angels with offspring from the daughters of men. This 'unlawful union' produces 'giants' upon the earth which cause man's sinfulness; and these giants, which Irenaeus calls the 'infamous race of men', performed fruitless and wicked deeds (Irenaeus, *Proof of the Apostolic Preaching*, 18 and *Against Heresies* 11.4,36,4 [4,58,4])." D. R. Schultz, "The Origin of Sin in Irenaeus and Jewish Pseudepigraphical Literature," *Vigiliae Christianae* 32.3 (1978): 168–69, 172–73.

37. Annus, "Origin of the Watchers," 297–303. The characterization of the *apkallu* as fish-men points to their origin in the watery abyss in Mesopotamian religion. *Apkallu* are also characterized as bird-men, a likely image associated with their divine ("heavenly") nature. The major study on the pictorial iconography of *apkallu* is F. A. M. Wiggerman, *Mesopotamian Protective Spirits: The Ritual Texts* (Leiden: Brill, 1992).

and not giants, the Old Testament puts forth both ideas. This is because Ugaritic literature lacked a corporate divine rebellion story comparable to Genesis 6:1–5, itself a polemic response to the Babylonian *apkallu* traditions. Second Temple Jewish writers had a literary relationship to Babylonian material, not Ugaritic texts, because of the exile in Babylon.

SUMMARY

To this point in our study we have seen that the Second Temple Jewish theology of the powers of darkness draws on the Old Testament and its wider ancient Near Eastern context. Evil powers are present in the world because of an initial divine rebellion in Eden and a subsequent corporate rebellion at the time of the flood. In both instances Second Temple writers connect data points found scattered in the Old Testament. The effect is that one can both see the coherence of connections and the portraits that emerge from them and the creative development of a theology of evil spirits. We will see in later chapters how the New Testament writers draw on the Second Temple material and its source material, the Old Testament, for their own descriptions of the dark powers. But before we move to the New Testament, there is one more divine rebellion in the Old Testament to consider.

CHAPTER 7

The Third Divine Rebellion—
Chaos in the Nations

THE WELL-KNOWN STORY OF THE TOWER OF BABEL IS THE FOCUS POINT of the third divine rebellion in the Old Testament. The story itself is not about divine rebels but, at its core, is the point of origin for yet another defection from Yahweh by members of his heavenly host. Discerning this requires us to begin in Genesis 11:1–9, the scriptural description of the dispersion of the nations, and then to move to a far less-familiar accounting of the event, one that is crucial to understanding how the judgment at Babel ripples through the rest of the Bible.

THE TOWER OF BABEL

The setting of this famous Old Testament story is the post-flood world. After Noah and his family survive the flood (Gen 6–7), God repeats the Edenic command to the remnant of humanity to "be fruitful and multiply and fill the earth. … Increase greatly on the earth and multiply in it" (Gen 9:1, 7). In order to facilitate the subduing of the earth mandated of Adam and Eve much earlier, God tells Noah, "The fear of you and the dread of you shall be upon every beast of the earth and upon every bird of the heavens, upon everything that creeps on the ground and all the fish of the sea. Into your hand they are delivered" (Gen 9:2).

The requirement to spread out over the earth is evident by the words "increase greatly *on the earth* and multiply *in it.*" Readers might presume from Genesis 10 that the sons of Noah and their descendants obeyed

God's reiteration of the Edenic mandate. It is clear that the nations listed in that chapter result from "the generations of the sons of Noah, Shem, Ham, and Japheth" born after the flood (Gen 10:1). But the story of the Tower of Babel directs us to a different conclusion. It is in Genesis 11:1–9 that we learn how the descendants of the sons of Noah were made to obey God's will:

> [1] Now the whole earth had one language and the same words. [2] And as people migrated from the east they found a plain in the land of Shinar and settled there. [3] And they said to each other, "Come, let us make bricks and burn them thoroughly." And they had brick for stone and they had tar for mortar. [4] And they said, "Come, let us build ourselves a city and a tower whose top reaches to the heavens. And let us make a name for ourselves, lest we be scattered over the face of the whole earth." [5] Then Yahweh came down to see the city and the tower that humankind was building. [6] And Yahweh said, "Behold, they are one people with one language, and this is only the beginning of what they will do. So now nothing that they intend to do will be impossible for them. [7] Come, let us go down and confuse their language there, so that they will not understand each other's language." [8] So Yahweh scattered them from there over the face of the whole earth, and they stopped building the city. [9] Therefore its name was called Babel, for there Yahweh confused the language of the whole earth, and there Yahweh scattered them over the face of the whole earth. (LEB)

As in Genesis 1:26–27, the episode at the place that would become known as Babel included the members of the heavenly host, the divine council. In Genesis 11:7 Yahweh exhorts, "Let *us* go down and confuse their language there." Again, in concert with Genesis 1:27, the declaration to the host is followed by the swift judgment of Yahweh alone: "So Yahweh scattered them" (Gen 11:8). The grammatical features in combination connect the two scenes.[1] Miller notes in this regard:

---

1. For a discussion of the plurality language in Gen 1:26–27 and its implications for understanding the concept of the image of God, see Heiser, *Angels*, 28–32; Heiser, *Unseen Realm*, 49–70. The plurality is not coherently interpreted as the Trinity, whose members, being co-eternal and co-omniscient, have no need of such declarations. The plurality language can also not be exegetically limited to three persons. Scenes of God speaking among the members of his heavenly host are equally well known (1 Kgs 22:19–23; Isa 6:1–8; Ps 82:1, 6; Job 1:6; 2:1). For a thorough scholarly grammatical discussion of the plurality language in Gen 1:26; 11:7, see W. Randall Garr, *In His Own Image and Likeness: Humanity, Divinity, and Monotheism* (Leiden: Brill, 2003), 17–94.

As in Gen. 3:22, the building of the tower at Babel is a sin against God as an effort to move into the divine world, the divine domain. The threatened loss of creature limits (3:22a and 11:6–7) leads in both instances to the judging activity of God. In its judgment speech, Genesis 11, like 3:22, reflects a decree within the assembly to create human disorder for the sake of cosmic order, the confusion among humankind to inhibit the breakdown of the orderly relationship between divine and human worlds.[2]

But the Genesis account is only part of the Old Testament theology of the judgment at Babel. There is more to the scattering of humanity and the emergence of the nations. Deuteronomy 32:8–9 adds crucial details:

[8]When the Most High gave to the nations their inheritance,
    when he divided mankind,
he fixed the borders of the peoples
    according to the number of the sons of God.
[9]But the LORD's portion is his people,
    Jacob his allotted heritage.

Many English translations will read "according to the number of the sons of Israel" in verse 8 in place of "according to the number of the sons of God." The difference arises from divergent manuscript readings. The Dead Sea Scrolls demonstrate conclusively that "sons of God" is the correct reading and that the traditional Hebrew text (the Masoretic Text) was altered, mostly likely because of a scribal concern about divine plurality. This textual issue and its implications are well known to Old Testament scholars.[3] For example, in his Deuteronomy commentary, Jeffrey Tigay notes:

---

2. Miller, *Israelite Religion and Biblical Theology*, 435. Miller's reference to Gen 3:22 is in regard to the plurality of *'elōhîm* referenced in the prohibition of eating from the tree of the knowledge of good and evil. This becomes evident when one compares Gen 3:5 ("For God knows that when you eat of it your eyes will be opened, and you will be like *'elōhîm*, knowing good and evil") with Gen 3:22 ("Then the LORD God said, 'Behold, the man has become like one of us in knowing good and evil' "). The phrase "like one of us" clearly informs us that we ought to read *'elōhîm* in v. 5 as a plural ("you will be like the gods" [of God's council]; cp. the plurality language in Gen 1:26–27).

3. The same kind of alteration is present in Deut 32:43, where the Dead Sea Scrolls have (plural) *'elōhîm* ("Rejoice with him O heavens, bow down to him, all *gods*"), a fact that precludes any attempt to justify "sons of Israel" in Deut 32:8 on the basis of the number of Israelites that went down into Egypt (Gen 46:27). The scribal hand is clearly censoring a reference to supernatural beings. As the ensuing discussion of the allotment language in other passages in Deuteronomy makes clear, only a supernatural reading makes sense of that language. Lastly, "sons of Israel" is a reading utterly

The idea stated in the variant reading, that the number of nations equals the number of "sons of the divine," suggests that each of these beings is paired with a nation. Jewish sources of the Hellenistic and talmudic periods elaborate on this picture, indicating that God appointed divine beings to govern the nations on His behalf. Ben Sira paraphrases our passage as follows:

> In dividing up the peoples of all the world,
> Over every people He appointed a ruler,
> But the Lord's portion is Israel.

The "rulers" are Ben Sira's equivalent of Deuteronomy's "sons of the divine." The book of Daniel, from the same period as Ben Sira, refers to them as "governors" or "princes" (Heb. *sarim*) and describes them as angelic patrons and champions of various nations.[4]

Deuteronomy 32:8–9 informs us that the act of judgment enacted on humanity at Babel resulted not only in dividing and scattering them but assigning them to members of Yahweh's heavenly host-council. In this regard the allotment language of verse 9 is significant. Israel is said to be Yahweh's allotted inheritance. This implies that the other nations are "allotted" to lesser gods—"sons of God" among Yahweh's heavenly host.

Old Testament theology puts forth the idea that the gods of the nations were assigned to them by Yahweh, that Israel is forbidden from worshiping those gods since Israel was "taken" (i.e., chosen) by Yahweh as his "allotted inheritance" among humanity. This is confirmed by other passages in Deuteronomy that reference the nations and their gods. Deuteronomy 4:19–20 is the logical place to begin to demonstrate the point:

> [19] And do this so that you do not lift your eyes *toward* heaven and observe the sun and the moon and the stars, all the host of the heaven, and be led astray and bow down to them and serve them, things that Yahweh your God has allotted to all *of* the peoples under all *of* the

---

inconsistent with the flow of biblical history. Israel did not exist at Babel, nor is it listed in the Table of Nations in Genesis 10. For discussion of the issue, see Heiser, "Deuteronomy 32:8 and the Sons of God," 52–74; Paul Sanders, *The Provenance of Deuteronomy 32* (Leiden: Brill, 1996), 156; Emanuel Tov, *Textual Criticism of the Hebrew Bible*, 3rd ed. (Minneapolis: Fortress, 2012), 248–49.

4. Tigay, *Deuteronomy*, 514. The number of the nations (and thus the heavenly princes) derives from the list of nations in Genesis 10, which totals seventy. The number in LXX of Genesis 10 is seventy-two due to the separation of some place names by the translator.

heaven. [20] But Yahweh has taken you and brought you out from the furnace of iron, from Egypt, to be a people of inheritance to him, as it is this day. (LEB)

The passage clearly says that Yahweh, the God of Israel, allotted the "sun and the moon and the stars," worshiped by other people, to those nations and that God took Israel for his own.[5] The sun, moon, and stars are the gods referenced in Deuteronomy 32:8, a point discerned from two other passages in Deuteronomy:

[2] If there is found among you, in one of the settlements that the LORD your God is giving you, a man or woman who has affronted the LORD your God and transgressed His covenant—[3] turning to the worship of other gods ('elōhîm) and bowing down to them, to the sun or the moon or any of the heavenly host, something I never commanded—[4] and you have been informed or have learned of it, then you shall make a thorough inquiry. If it is true, the fact is established, that abhorrent thing was perpetrated in Israel, [5] you shall take the man or the woman who did that wicked thing out to the public place, and you shall stone them, man or woman, to death. (Deut 17:2–5, JPS)

[21] And later generations will ask—the children who succeed you, and foreigners who come from distant lands and see the plagues and diseases that the LORD has inflicted upon that land, [22] all its soil devastated by sulfur and salt, beyond sowing and producing, no grass growing in it, just like the upheaval of Sodom and Gomorrah, Admah and Zeboiim, which the LORD overthrew in His fierce anger—[23] all nations will ask, "Why did the LORD do thus to this land? Wherefore that awful wrath?" [24] They will be told, "Because they forsook the covenant that the LORD, God of their fathers, made with them when He freed them from the land of Egypt; [25] they turned to the service of other gods ('elōhîm) and worshiped them, gods whom they had not experienced and whom He had not allotted to them. (Deut 29:21–25, JPS)

---

5. Scholars often note that this allotment was mutual; that is, that it worked in both directions. Deuteronomy 4:19–20 has the gods allotted to the nations, whereas the language of Deut 32:8 suggests the nations were assigned to the gods.

These portions of Deuteronomy refer to the sun, moon, and stars as *'elōhîm* ("gods"; Deut 17:3; 29:25) allotted to the nations (Deut 29:25). As Deuteronomy 32:8–9 makes clear, these gods were allotted to the nations when God judged humanity at large at Babel. A few verses later in Deuteronomy 32, we read that the Israelites "sacrificed to demons, not God, to deities (*'elōhîm*) they had never known, to new ones recently arrived, whom your ancestors had not feared" (Deut 32:17 NRSV).[6] The point is that, from Israel's inception, Yahweh was the God of their fathers (Abraham, Isaac, and Jacob). As such, Yahweh was Israel's original God; any other god was a latecomer.

PSALM 82—DIVINE REBELLION AND JUDGMENT OF THE NATIONAL GODS

The picture that emerges from the Old Testament is that Deuteronomy 32:8–9 and associated passages are the biblical explanation as to how humanity's direct relationship to the creator God morphed into the worship of other gods. The judgment at Babel altered that relationship. God chose to divorce himself from humanity and begin anew with Israel.

In terms of a human perspective, while Yahweh's judgment was harsh, it was not final. When God chose to raise up a new human family (Israel) in the wake of Babel, he left room for the salvation of the forsaken nations in his covenant with Abram. It would be through Abram's descendants that all the nations of the earth would be blessed (Gen 12:1–3). The promise would, of course, be fulfilled in Christ (Gal 3:16: "Now the promises were made to Abraham and to his offspring. It does not say, 'And to offsprings,' referring to many, but referring to one, 'And to your offspring,' who is Christ"). Prior to the coming of the Promised One, gentiles had to join themselves to Israel, forsaking other gods, to be in right relationship to the true God. Israel was to be a kingdom of priests bearing witness to the goodness of life with Yahweh as their God, but there was no overt attempt to evangelize the inhabitants of the nations. They were under judgment. Yet Paul had a sense that God, "having determined allotted periods and the boundaries" of people in the nations, did so intending

---

6. Deuteronomy 32:17 is poorly translated in some popular Bible versions. See Heiser, "Does Deuteronomy 32:17 Assume or Deny the Reality of Other Gods," 137–45.

"that they should seek God, and perhaps feel their way toward him and find him" (Acts 17:26–27).

What about the divine perspective? While Israel is condemned for worshiping the sun, moon, and stars, there is no indication in the Old Testament that the sons of God allotted to the nations at Babel were "fallen" (i.e., adversaries of Yahweh) when that assignment took place. While the allotment and its punishment context are clear, the Old Testament never indicates that Yahweh was pleased when the allotted sons of God were worshiped. If he had intended the nations to worship the sons of God allotted to them, there would ostensibly be no reason for such worship to offend God. They would be doing what God expected. There are naturally dozens of passages condemning Israelites for the worship of other gods besides Yahweh, but Scripture also condemns such worship in more general terms, inclusive of the peoples in the forsaken nations (Ps 97:7; Isa 2:12–21). God judges the people of the nations and their gods (Deut 12:31; 18:9–14; 20:15–18). The gods allotted to the nations are false (Jer 14:22; 18:15) and their worship worthless (Pss 96:5; 97:7).

What are we to make of this? It would seem that the most coherent perspective is that offered by Paul in Romans 1:18–25, which condemns idolatry as an intentional evil. When we recall Paul's words in Acts 17:26–27, we are led to conclude that God intended his divorce of humanity to be a stimulus to seek him, to return to right relationship with him. Israel alone was the conduit to reestablishing that relationship. But instead the biblical story depicts hostility to Israel, the deliberate worshiping of lesser gods, and Israel's own disloyalty.

One might presume that Yahweh expected better behavior from the other lesser 'elōhîm, that they should have abhorred being worshiped in place of their sovereign. There is no such indication in Scripture. Rather, the expectation seems to have been that, as the God of gods, the Creator, and the sovereign over that creation, Yahweh is the only god worthy of worship by anyone, anywhere. That would in turn mean that the role of the lesser 'elōhîm was administration of the nations. God may have severed the relationship between himself and humanity, but he still wanted those created in his image to be ruled justly, not abused.

At some point, the sons of God transgressed Yahweh's desire for earthly order and just rule of his human imagers, sowing chaos in the nations. This is the distinct trajectory of Psalm 82, where the gods of the nations are excoriated by Yahweh for abusing their charges.

¹God has taken his place in the divine council;
  in the midst of the gods he holds judgment:
²"How long will you judge unjustly
  and show partiality to the wicked? *Selah*
³Give justice to the weak and the fatherless;
  maintain the right of the afflicted and the destitute.
⁴Rescue the weak and the needy;
  deliver them from the hand of the wicked."

⁵They have neither knowledge nor understanding,
  they walk about in darkness;
  all the foundations of the earth are shaken.

⁶I said, "You are gods,
  sons of the Most High, all of you;
⁷nevertheless, like men you shall die,
  and fall like any prince."

⁸Arise, O God, judge the earth;
  for you shall inherit all the nations!

That Psalm 82 has the nations cast aside at Babel in view is apparent from its last verse. The psalmist cries out for God to "inherit all the nations!" The reference to the gods (*'elōhîm*) of Yahweh's council (Ps 82:1, 6) as "sons of the Most High (*'elyōn*)" aligns completely with the apportionment of the nations by the Most High (*'elyōn*) among his sons.⁷ The Hebrew lemma translated "inherit" (*nāḥāl*) is the same as the one translated "inheritance" in Deuteronomy 32:8.⁸

---

7. Some scholars see the language of Deuteronomy 32:8–9 and Psalm 82 as evidence that Yahweh and El (Elyon) were distinct deities, thereby demonstrating early Israelite polytheism. For a scholarly response to that perspective, as well as why the plural *'elōhîm* in Ps 82:1 and the notion of a divine council do not evince polytheism in biblical thought, see Michael S. Heiser, "Are Yahweh and El Distinct Deities in Deut. 32:8–9 and Psalm 82?" *HIPHIL* 3 (2006): 1–9; Heiser, "Divine Plurality in the Hebrew Bible," 1–24. For a less technical discussion of the same points, see Heiser, *Unseen Realm*, 23–37.

8. Deuteronomy 32:8a reads *běhanḥēl 'elyôn gôyim*. The object of the infinitive is *gôyim*. The form in 32:8 (*běhanḥēl*) is pointed as a Hiphil infinitive absolute, but should probably be understood as a defective spelling of the infinitive construct (*běhanḥil*). As Sanders notes, the Hiphil of the verb *n-ḥ-l* can be "connected both with an *accusativus personae* (the inheriting person; hence, 'When the Most High gave the nations their inheritance') or with an *accusativus rei* (the object inherited by this

It is interesting to note the language in verse 5 of Psalm 82. The corruption of the gods of the nations causes chaos on the earth: "all the foundations of the earth are shaken." Several scholars have developed the idea put forth in the Old Testament that creation was "broken and permanently threatened by disorderly, supernatural beings and forces, hostile to God and humankind."[9]

Geyer picks up this theme in his important work on the oracles against the nations, arguing that these oracles, present in all the classical prophets, do not merely have Israel's earthly military enemies in view in the day of the Lord. The apocalyptic vision of the desolation of the nations is also a judgment on the gods of those nations.

> In the so-called Zion Theology when Yahweh is recognised as king he establishes the earth firmly so that it cannot be moved (Ps. xciii 1). But in the time of chaos the world trembles and shakes (Isa. xiii 13) which is the case also in Ps. lx 4 which is part of the festival in the sanctuary (v. 8) and the chaos of v. 4 is identified with the rebellion of the nations (vv. 10–14). Ps. lxviii 9 describes the shaking of the earth at a time when Yahweh overcomes the desert fiend. Ps. lxxvii follows a description of the primaeval waters (v. 17) with the trembling of the earth (v. 19). This element of chaos is mentioned four times in [the oracles against the nations in Isaiah, Jeremiah, and Ezekiel] (Isa. xiii 13; Jer. xlix 21; 1 46; li 29). When Jeremiah extols Yahweh as king over the nations (x 7, 10) he records that the earth trembles. The final stage of the Desolation of the earth is the complete dissolution of the universe. The lords of heaven are thrown into confusion by the general chaos. Sun moon and stars no longer give their light and the world is plunged into darkness (Isa. xiii 10; Ezek. xxxii 7–8).[10]

The gods charged with the rule of the nations became corrupt administrators and, in so doing, sowed chaos in the heavenly realm as well. Yahweh created a world characterized by righteousness (ṣedāqâ) and

---

person; and so rendering, 'When the Most High gave the nations as an inheritance')." See Sanders, *Provenance of Deuteronomy 32*, 154. Other examples include Deut 1:38; 3:28; 21:16; 31:7; Josh 1:6; 1 Sam 2:8; Zech 8:12; and Prov 8:21.

9. Robert Murray, *The Cosmic Covenant: Biblical Themes of Justice, Peace and the Integrity of Creation* (London: Sheed & Ward, 1992), xx.

10. Geyer, "Desolation and Cosmos," 50–51. See also John B. Geyer, "Mythology and Culture in the Oracles against the Nations," *VT* 36 (1986): 129–45.

well-being (*šālôm*). In Psalm 82, "The gods are condemned to death for their failure to carry out justice in the human realm. … [T]he *cosmic* realm also depends upon justice in the social order. Indeed the very foundations of cosmic order are shaken in the presence of injustice."[11]

Patrick Miller applies this idea more fully to the scene in Psalm 82, where the gods over the nations are judged:

> It is against this background that one must look at one of the texts in which the council of Yahweh is most explicitly present, Psalm 82. It takes place entirely in the world of the gods, although what is clear from the story is that that world is totally ruled and controlled by the Lord. The psalm depicts a meeting of the "divine council" (v. 1) in which God rises and pronounces judgment on the gods. The reason for the verdict against them is spelled out in detail and unambiguous. The divine ones, the gods who are supposed to provide for order/ righteousness among the peoples of the earth, have utterly failed to do so. They have shown partiality to the wicked and failed to maintain the right of the poor and the weak. The consequence of this is stated to be a shaking of the foundations of the world. The failure to maintain order, which in this instance is clearly seen to be the maintenance of righteousness in the moral sphere, the resistance to a disorder that does in the poor and gives the rich and the wicked control, is seen to be manifest in a kind of cosmic disorder. The cosmos comes apart when righteousness is not maintained.[12]

The concept is straightforward: when there is disorder in the divine realm, when the members of Yahweh's council are not in harmony with his will, misery, chaos, injustice, and death on earth are the result. Yahweh rules justly and expects the same from those who rule the nations. But what we read in the Old Testament makes it clear that this is not the reality among the nations. Worse, their gods seek to spread chaos to Yahweh's portion, Israel, by seducing his people to worship them instead of the Most High.

---

11. Patrick D. Miller Jr., "When the Gods Meet: Psalm 82 and the Issue of Justice," *Journal for Preachers* 9 (1986): 4–5.

12. Miller, *Israelite Religion and Biblical Theology*, 438–39.

COSMIC GEOGRAPHY AND THE DARK PRINCES OF THE NATIONS

The worldview put forth by Deuteronomy 32 and Psalm 82 is the foundation for what scholars call the "cosmic geography" of Old Testament thought. Israel as a land and people were, in the words of Deuteronomy 32:9, "Yahweh's portion" and his "allotted heritage." As such, Israel was surrounded on all sides by territories inhabited by enemies and under dominion of hostile gods.

This notion is at the heart of the Old Testament story as it unfolds from the Babel event and the subsequent call of Abraham, from which Israel's origin as a people extends. It is no wonder that, given this perspective, the Israelites wandering through the wilderness on the way to Yahweh's land would have associated the journey with demonic powers. The goat for Azazel in Leviticus 16 and the "goat demons" of Leviticus 17:7 make more sense in this light. It is no wonder, as we saw in chapter 1, that desert and barren places were viewed as home to evil spirits associated with the realm of the dead.

A number of episodes in the Old Testament story that have elements that appear odd to modern readers are readily explicable given the backdrop of cosmic-geographical thinking.[13] For example, David describes being driven away from "the inheritance of Yahweh" (1 Sam 26:19 LEB). He angrily complains that Saul and his minions expelled him: "Go, serve other gods!" (1 Sam 26:19 LEB). His words imply a connection between land and deity. When the Syrian military commander Naaman is healed of leprosy following his obedience to the instruction of the prophet Elisha (2 Kgs 5), he asks the prophet for permission to carry dirt back to his home country (2 Kgs 5:17). The request would be inexplicable without understanding that Naaman recognized the lordship of Yahweh over all gods and henceforth pledged to sacrifice only to him. Since Yahweh was to be worshiped in his own land, Naaman asked to carry dirt from Israel to Syria (1 Kgs 5:17–19). When the ark of the covenant was captured by the Philistines and taken to Dagan's temple, the moved proved disastrous. In less than twenty-four hours, Dagan's idol was reduced to a limbless,

---

13. For a more detailed discussion of the examples that follow, see Heiser, *Unseen Realm*, 117–22.

headless stump by an unseen force (1 Sam 5:1–4). The impression left by the obliteration of Dagan's idol was that his priests refused to walk over the ground on which Yahweh had shattered Dagan, even though the space was in Dagan's own temple (1 Sam 5:5). The ground had been conquered and was now under the dominion of Yahweh.

Perhaps the most familiar illustration of cosmic geography is found in Daniel 10:13, 20. That these princes are supernatural beings is confirmed by the fact that they are confronted by Michael, Israel's "prince" and "one of the chief princes" (Dan 10:13; cp. Dan 10:21; 12:1).[14] Commenting on this terminology Collins notes:

> By analogy with Michael it is clear that the "princes" of Greece and Persia are the patron angels of these nations. The notion that different nations were allotted to different gods or heavenly beings was widespread in the ancient world. ... The origin of this [prince] idea is to be sought in the ancient Near Eastern concept of the Divine Council. The existence of national deities is assumed in the Rabshakeh's taunt: "Who among all the gods of the countries have delivered their countries out of my hand that the LORD should deliver Jerusalem out of my hand?" (2 Kgs 18:35 = Isa 36:20).[15]

Some scholars and English translations opt for a human understanding of the "princes" of Persia and Greece due to the statement in Daniel 10:13, "Michael, one of the chief princes, came to help me, for I was left there with the kings of Persia." Stephen Miller's observation is appropriate:

> The Hebrew word translated "king" is plural, and the concept of the angel's being "detained with" the earthly kings of Persia seems

---

14. As we will see when our study turns to the New Testament, this princely language and the wider concept of cosmic geography is the basis for Paul's vocabulary about the powers of darkness (e.g., "principalities"; "rulers"). In his commentary on Daniel, John J. Collins notes, "The title 'prince' does not necessarily imply less than divine status. The 'prince of the host' in Dan 8:11 is apparently the God of Israel. A precedent for the title 'prince' being applied to an angel can be found in the שר צבא יהוה who appears in Josh 5:14. The title is used for the chief angelic powers at Qumran, for example, the 'prince of lights' (1QS 3:20; CD 5:18; compare 'prince of light' in 1QM 13:10) and the 'prince of the dominion of wickedness' (1QM 17:5–6)." See Collins, *Daniel: A Commentary on the Book of Daniel* (Hermeneia; Minneapolis: Fortress, 1993), 375. See also Bampfylde, "The Prince of the Host in the Book of Daniel and the Dead Sea Scrolls," 129–34.

15. John J. Collins, "Prince," *DDD* 663. The term *sār* ("prince") is also used of the supernatural leader of Yahweh's host met by Joshua at the commencement of the conquest (Josh 5:13–15). For the identity of this figure and his relationship (or not) to Michael, see Heiser, *Angels*, 64–65.

untenable. In the context of angelic warfare, these "kings" likely were spiritual rulers who attempted to control Persia.[16]

The nature of the "princes" in Daniel 10 is clear, given the clear precedent of the theology of Deuteronomy. The following assessment by Hartman and Di Lella is representative of the broad consensus among Old Testament scholars as to the princes of the nations:

> "The prince of the kingdom of Persia," mentioned twice in 10:13, and called simply "the prince of Persia" in 10:20 is not King Cyrus of 10:1 or a corporate person representing as a group the kings of Persia, as Calvin and most of the reformers thought, but is rather the tutelary spirit or guardian angel of the Persian kingdom, as the rabbis and most Christian commentators have rightly acknowledged. ... The belief in guardian angels for nations is a survival of an ancient polytheistic theology which held that each city-state or nation or empire had a tutelary god who was in a particular way its protector, enjoying in return special status and cultic recognition. As in former times the patron-god looked after the interests of the nation in his charge, so in orthodox monotheistic circles the guardian angel was thought to be commissioned by the one God to see to it that the affairs of state ran smoothly. If anything went wrong in the nation, then the guardian angel could be blamed for lack of wisdom or skill. In this way, God would be excused from any charge of mismanagement or neglect. To preserve the basic Israelite tenet of monotheism, guardian angels were made subject to God's supreme authority.[17]

Hartman and Di Lella go on to note that Daniel 10 bears an undertone of defiance on the part of the princes of Persia and Greece. This is obvious from the context, as they oppose Michael, Israel's divine guardian under Yahweh (Dan 10:21; 12:1). Daniel 10 coheres with Psalm 82. Second Temple–period writers took note of this third Old Testament circumstance of divine rebellion in the same manner as the earlier rebellions of Genesis 3 and 6:1–4. Second Temple authors affirmed the

---

16. Stephen R. Miller, *Daniel* (NAC; Nashville: Broadman & Holman, 1994), 284.

17. Louis F. Hartman and Alexander A. Di Lella, *The Book of Daniel: A New Translation with Notes and Commentary on Chapters 1–9* (AYB; New Haven, CT: Yale University Press, 1978), 282–83.

cosmic-geographical rule of the nations by powers of darkness and creatively expressed its threat against the people of God. It is to those writers we now turn to complete the theological-conceptual framework for the New Testament's subsequent portrayal of supernatural evil.

CHAPTER 8

Dark Powers over the Nations in Second Temple Judaism

In his study on the Jewish theology of patron deity-angels appointed over the nations, D. Hannah observed that "the ... concept that certain angels served as guardians or patrons of peoples or nations played a [significant] role in the angelology of second temple Judaism."[1] As we saw in the previous chapter, this theology extends from various passages in Deuteronomy, Psalm 82, and Daniel 10. The concept that the nations of the world were allotted to lesser gods as a punishment at Babel and that those gods sowed chaos on earth and were hostile to Yahweh and his people can be seen in a variety of Second Temple texts. This chapter will survey that material with an eye toward establishing the prominence of the concept and its development.

DARK POWERS OVER THE NATIONS:
The Septuagint

The Septuagint (LXX), the Greek translation of the Hebrew Bible, is a Second Temple–period translation. With respect to Deuteronomy 32:8, most manuscripts of the LXX read *angelōn theou* ("angels of God") or *huiōn theou* ("sons of God"). Both translations presuppose a Hebrew text consistent with the Dead Sea Scroll reading for Deuteronomy 32:8, which we discussed in the previous chapter. That earlier discussion relegated

---

1. Darrell D. Hannah, "Guardian Angels and Angelic National Patrons in Second Temple Judaism and Early Christianity," in *Angels: The Concept of Celestial Beings—Origins, Development and Reception*, ed. Friedrich V. Reiterer, Tobias Nicklas, and Karin Schöpflin (Berlin: De Gruyter, 2007), 413.

the related Deuteronomy 32:43 to a footnote. This verse refers to the gods of the nations as well. The wording of the verse in the Dead Sea Scrolls differs from that of the traditional Hebrew Masoretic Text. The LXX is also different, though it aligns conceptually with the Dead Sea Scrolls.

DEUTERONOMY 32:43[1]		
Masoretic Text	4QDeut[q]	Septuagint (adds material for two stanzas)
O nations,	O heavens,	O heavens,
rejoice his people.	rejoice with him	rejoice with him
	Bow to him,	Bow to him,
	all gods (*'elōhîm*).	all sons of God (*huioi theou*).
		O nations,
		rejoice with His people
		And let all angels of God (*angeloi theou*) strengthen themselves in him.
1. Translations of Deut 32:43 here are the author's.		

As was the case in Deuteronomy 32:8, the Masoretic Text omits the divine beings associated with the nations. Deuteronomy 32:8, 43 were both altered when the Masoretic Text was produced, ca. AD 100.[2] Hannah's remark represents the overwhelming scholarly consensus on the matter: "It seems safe to conclude that the original text of the Song of Moses (Deut 32:1–43) affirmed a belief in heavenly guardians, whether lesser deities or angels, set over the nations as a kind of cosmic patron,

---

2. Scholars usually round this number to AD 100 for the creation of what we know as the Masoretic Text. By way of more precision, Brotzman notes, "The multiplicity of text types evident at Qumran between the third to first centuries B.C. was replaced by a single and authoritative text type by A.D. 135 at the latest." See Ellis R. Brotzman, *Old Testament Textual Criticism: A Practical Introduction* (Grand Rapids: Baker Books, 1994), 43–44. Tov summarizes the historical situation at the close of the first century AD this way: "By the end of the 1st century AD the Septuagint had been accepted by Christianity and abandoned by Jews. Copies of the Samaritan Pentateuch were available, but in the meantime that sect had become an independent religion, so that their texts were considered Samaritan, not Jewish any more. The Qumran sect, which had preserved a multitude of texts, did not exist after the destruction of the temple. Therefore the sole texts that existed in this period were the ones that were copied and distributed by the central group in Judaism. ... This situation gave rise to the wrong conclusion that the MT had 'ousted' the other texts." See Emanuel Tov, "Textual Criticism (OT)," *ABD* 6:395, 407. For more information on the Qumran readings of Deut 32:8, 43, see E. Ulrich, F. M. Cross, S. W. Crawford, J. A. Duncan, P. W. Skehan, E. Tov, and J. T. Barrera, *Qumran Cave 4 IX: Deuteronomy, Joshua, Judges, Kings* (Discoveries in the Judaean Desert XIV; Oxford: Clarendon Press, 1996).

although later editors sought to remove this."[3] The point to take away should not be missed: Second Temple–period Jews would have been reading about gods allotted to the nations in their Old Testament.

There are several indications in the apocryphal book of Wisdom of Ben Sira (or Book of Sirach; included in the LXX) that the Deuteronomy 32 worldview was part of Jewish theology. The seventeenth chapter describes humanity in general as God's creation (Sir 17:1–7) and then transitions to the Jew, with whom God entered into a covenant relationship and gave his laws (Sir 17:12–14). Whether Jew or gentile, Ben Sira (Sir 17:15–16)[4] describes

> God's clear knowledge of human acts and thoughts and the divine retribution to be accorded to all men and women as they deserve. The Lord knows human "ways" because "they cannot be hidden from his eyes."[5]

Then, in verse 17 we read, "He [God] appointed a leader for each nation, and Israel is the portion of the Lord" (LES). The word translated "leader" is a participial form of the lemma *hēgeomai*, "to be in a supervisory capacity, lead, guide."[6] In this particular passage and elsewhere in the LXX (e.g., Deut 5:23; Josh 13:21; 2 Sam 6:21; 1 Kgs 16:16; Ezek 43:7) the term clearly denotes "high officials" or someone "of princely authority."[7] Hannah comments of Sirach 17:17, "This parallels exactly the original text of Deuteronomy 32:8–9."[8]

---

3. Hannah, "Angelic National Patrons," 417.

4. Not all manuscripts of the Wisdom of Ben Sira have v. 16 in this chapter.

5. Patrick W. Skehan and Alexander A. Di Lella O.F.M., *The Wisdom of Ben Sira: A New Translation with Notes, Introduction and Commentary* (AYB; New Haven, CT: Yale University Press, 1987), 283.

6. BDAG, s.v. "ἡγέομαι."

7. Ibid.

8. Hannah, "Angelic National Patrons," 418. Hannah adds, "Interestingly, a couple of late Greek manuscripts, minuscule 70 and 248, make the reference at Sir 17:17 more precise, adding at the beginning of this sentence the notice that '[f]or at the division of the nations of all the earth he appointed a ruler.'" Hannah suggests that the gloss in these minuscules (which are medieval manuscripts) was likely added during the rabbinic period in accord with the rabbinic teaching in Targum Pseudo-Jonathan (Gen 11:7–8; Deut 32:8–9) and Pirqe de Rabbi Eliezer 24 that God had appointed angelic guardians over the nations. These references are clear indications that the Dead Sea Scroll reading had survived into the rabbinic period despite the alterations made to create the Masoretic Text of Deuteronomy 32. Box and Oesterley note the rabbinic teaching in this regard as well: "Since He was the God of all the world, His interest in other nations could not be denied (cp. the Midrash *Sifre* 40: 'God doth not provide for Israel alone, but for all men'); thus the belief arose that, while God reserved the Israelites for His special care, He deputed angels to look after, and champion, the cause of other races. It is said, e.g. in the Targum of Pseudo-Jonathan to Gen. 11:7, 8, that every nation has its own

As we noted in chapter 2, LXX material in Daniel 10 is divided. The Theodotion text of LXX Daniel 10:13, 20 allows for a reading of divine beings being rulers of the nations, whereas other LXX texts do not.[9] As noted above, Sirach 17:17 and Deuteronomy 32:43 are clear instances of passages in the LXX outside Theodotion Daniel 10:13, 20 that bear clear witness to the Deuteronomy 32 worldview perspective. The same is true in pseudepigraphical texts from the Second Temple period.

DARK POWERS OVER THE NATIONS:
The Pseudepigrapha

Philo of Alexandria is also in line with this text of Deuteronomy 32:8–9, writing that God "set boundaries of nations according to the number of the angels of God; and the portion of the Lord became his people, Jacob, the lot of his inheritance, Israel."[10]

The Second Temple book of Jubilees makes certain statements in its retelling of Old Testament stories that collectively reflect the Deuteronomy 32 worldview.[11] As we saw in an earlier chapter, in Jubilees 10 the writer has God speaking to the archangels tasked with rounding up and

---

guardian angel who pleads the cause of the nation under his protection before God. It is interesting to observe that in later times even the divine guardianship over Israel was deputed to the archangel Michael; in Ḥagigah 12 b (T. B.) he has the title of 'Advocate of the Jews'; and in the Yalkut Shimeoni, Bereshith 132, Michael is described as the prince over all the angels, because he is the guardian angel of the Israelite nation; he acts as Israel's representative and patron in the presence of God, and he intercedes there on behalf of his people" (APOT, 1:376).

9. As noted earlier, the Theodotion text existed prior to New Testament times and its Daniel text superseded the LXX that had been in use before. See chapter 2 for the full citation of Jobes and Silva, Invitation to the Septuagint, 28, on this issue.

10. Philo, De posteritate Caini 89. The translation is the author's, based on the Greek text from Peder Borgen, Kåre Fuglseth, and Roald Skarsten, The Works of Philo: Greek Text with Morphology (Bellingham, WA: Logos Bible Software, 2005).

11. As Scott points out, Jubilees 8–9 is, in effect, an exposition of Genesis 10 that reflects a world "extending from the Garden of Eden in the east (Jub 8:16) to Gadir (=Cádiz) in Spain (8:23, 26; 9:12)—and Israel's central position in it." See James M. Scott, Paul and the Nations: The Old Testament and Jewish Background of Paul's Mission to the Nations with Special Reference to the Destination of Galatians (Tübingen: Mohr Siebeck, 1995), 15. Scott does not take his discussion into Jubilees 10, as his purpose is not Second Temple Jewish demonology. He references Deut 32:8 while apparently presuming that the geographical centrality of Israel derives from the Masoretic Text reading of that verse. There is nothing about either "sons of Israel" or "sons of God" in Deut 32:8 that specifies geographical orientation. The idea is something an Old Testament writer or reader could presume in light of either textual reading. Scott acknowledges the idea of supernatural beings governing the nations derives from Deut 32:8 (LXX, Qumran) and Daniel 10–11 (Paul and the Nations, 12). Scott's work intersects more of the supernatural elements in his discussion of Pauline literature.

ridding the earth of the demons that were the result of the Genesis 6 debacle (Jub 10:4–5). The leader of the evil spirits, Mastema, requested that a certain number of the demons be permitted to remain on the earth under his charge. Specifically, we must recall that Mastema asked God (Jub 10:8):

> Let them [the spirits] do everything which I tell them, because if some of them are not left for me, I will not be able to exercise the authority of my will among the children of men because they are (intended) to corrupt and lead astray before my judgment because the evil of the sons of men is great."[12]

God's response was to allow a tenth of them to escape judgment (Jub 10:6–11), but the demons left on earth "were restrained from following the sons of Noah" (Jub 10:13). The idea that the demons were prohibited from harassing the "sons of Noah" is odd, as all humanity after the flood extended from the sons of Noah. Jubilees 15 may help explain the author's thinking:

> [30] For the LORD did not draw Ishmael and his sons and his brothers and Esau near to himself, and he did not elect them because they are the sons of Abraham, for he knew them. But he chose Israel that they might be a people for himself. [31] And he sanctified them and gathered them from all of the sons of man because (there are) many nations and many people, and they all belong to him, but over all of them he caused spirits to rule so that they might lead them astray from following him. [32] But over Israel he did not cause any angel or spirit to rule because he alone is their ruler and he will protect them and he will seek for them at the hand of his angels and at the hand of his spirits and at the hand of all of his authorities so that he might guard them and bless them and they might be his and he might be theirs henceforth and forever. (Jub 15:30–32)[13]

12. *OTP*, 2:76. In his recent work on the history of the interpretation of the Tower of Babel account, Sherman clearly perceived the connection of the spirits in the Jubilees version of the episode with the disembodied Watcher-spirits from the Nephilim. However, he curiously fails to take note of the allotment of the gods to the nations elsewhere in Jubilees 10. See Phillip Michael Sherman, *Babel's Tower Translated: Genesis 1–11 and Ancient Jewish Interpretation* (Leiden: Brill, 2013), 107–8. Surprisingly, Deut 32:8–9 doesn't even appear in the index of the book.
13. *OTP*, 2:87.

The key is verse 32. God did not allow "any angel or spirit" to rule over Israel—a clear reference to the Deuteronomy 32 worldview. Israel was Yahweh's allotted inheritance (Deut 32:9), but the other nations were put under the authority of lesser gods (spirit beings). This language, coupled with Jubilees 10:1–13, where one-tenth of the demons sprang forth from the spawn of the Watchers, creates a subtle connection between the sin of the Watchers at the time of the flood and the incident at Babel. Scholars have taken note of this link:

> The evil spirits are not precluded from pursuing *all* of Noah's children, at least not in the long run. ... *Jubilees* wants to claim that national boundaries are essential for understanding the role of demons. Ultimately, the demons are precluded only from pursuing Israel. ... *Jubilees* develops the link between demons and idolatry, and further links demons and idolatry to other nations.[14]

Jubilees 15:31 clearly says that God caused the spirits assigned over the nations "to rule so that they might lead them [the nations] astray from following him." Hannah writes: "The nations are to be led astray from following God because of their sin at the Tower of Babel."[15] While the theology of Deuteronomy 32 is affirmed, the second and third rebellions found in the Old Testament are thus conflated with Satan as the overlord.[16] The notion that the Old Testament does not include that God *wanted* the nations led astray is an inventive thought that makes God's denunciation of the gods of the nations in Psalm 82:2–5 duplicitous.

The Animal Apocalypse (1 Enoch 85–90), a highly symbolic retelling of the history of Israel, also reflects the Deuteronomy 32 worldview. In his scholarly commentary on this portion of 1 Enoch, Patrick Tiller describes it as follows:

> [The Animal Apocalypse] is presented as an allegorical dream of the antediluvian patriarch, Enoch, in which he sees a story about bulls,

---

14. Todd R. Hanneken, "The Watchers in Rewritten Scripture: The Use of the *Book of the Watchers* in *Jubilees*," in *The Fallen Angels Traditions: Second Temple Developments and Reception History*, ed. Angela Kim Harkins, Kelley Coblentz Bautch, and John C. Endres (Washington, DC: Catholic Biblical Association of America, 2014), 23–68 (esp. 48).

15. Hannah, "Angelic National Patrons," 419.

16. As I have noted in an earlier chapter, this conflation of ideas is evident in New Testament thought, though the specific rationale (God intended the nations to be led astray) is not. In fact, Acts 17:26–27 would appear to deny it.

sheep, various animals that prey on the sheep, and humans who interact in various ways with the sheep and bulls. Each element in the story is primarily a sign for some object of human history outside of the story. Cattle represent humans from the time of Adam to Noah, some of the early Shemites, and the restored humanity of the ideal future. Sheep represent Israel. Various unclean predatory and scavenging animals and birds represent the Gentile nations. Stars represent the fallen Watchers, and humans represent other angelic figures, except for the owner of the sheep, who represents God.[17]

The important imagery is that the sheep represent Israel and the owner of the sheep represents God. In the Animal Apocalypse, the owner (God) puts[18] the sheep (Israel) in the control of "seventy Shepherds, that is, to seventy angels, which, of course, recalls the seventy angels of the Angelic Patron Legend."[19] God's abandonment of his sheep (Israel) to the seventy shepherds corresponds to the Davidic monarchy in exile.[20] The period of the seventy shepherds is itself divided into four subperiods, the last of which ends with the dawn of the messianic age.[21] This is one reason why

---

17. Patrick A. Tiller, *A Commentary on the Animal Apocalypse of 1 Enoch* (Atlanta: Scholars Press, 1993), 3.

18. The verb here is literally "cast [threw] away" (*OTP*, 1:67, note 4). As Tiller notes, "One might expect that the owner would *entrust* the sheep to the shepherds to tend them. The owner's action regarding the sheep is even more emphatically negative than his abandoning them in 89:55–56" (Tiller, *Commentary on the Animal Apocalypse*, 325).

19. Hannah, "Angelic National Patrons," 421.

20. According to Hannah, "this period covers the Babylonian captivity (1 En 89:55–71), the limited restoration under Zerubbabel and Joshua (1 En 89:72–77), the Persian and Hellenistic hegemonies (1 En 90:1–7), and especially the crisis under the Seleucids which resulted in the Maccabean revolt (1 En 90:6–19)." See Hannah, "Angelic National Patrons," 421.

21. Ida Fröhlich, "The Symbolic Language of the Animal Apocalypse of Enoch (1 Enoch 85–90)," *Revue de Qumran* 14.4 (1990): 629–36 (esp. 630–31). It should be noted here that Tiller does not believe that the seventy numbering should be tied to Deuteronomy 32:8–9 (Tiller, *Commentary on the Animal Apocalypse*, 53, note 80). He argues instead that the number in the Animal Apocalypse derives from Jer 25:11–12 because the Enochian author links the seventy shepherds to the end of the exile and because the number seventy does not appear in Deut 32:8–9. Tiller admits, though, that the number seventy is derived from the Table of Nations in Genesis 10. Tiller is virtually alone in not connecting the Table of Nations with the Babel event language in Deut 32:8–9. He also neglects entirely the connection of Deut 32:6–7 to El religion at Ugarit. Deuteronomy 32:6–7 links Yahweh to descriptions of El as creator of the seventy gods of Ugarit, fathered by his consort Athirat. I have written about Deut 32:6–7 and the Ugaritic material elsewhere: "These verses clearly contain elements drawn from ancient descriptions of El and attribute them to Yahweh. At Ugarit El is called *'ab 'adm* ('father of mankind'; *KTU* 1.14:I.37, 43) and *ṭr 'il 'abh 'il mlk dyknnh* ('Bull El his father, El the king who establishes him'; *KTU* 1.3:V.35–36; 1.4:I.4–6). Yahweh is described as the 'father' (אָבִיךָ) who 'established you' (וַיְכֹנְנֶךָ). Yahweh is also the one who 'created' Israel (קָנֶךָ) in verse six. The root *qny* denoting El as creator is found in the Karatepe inscription's appeal to *'l qn 'rṣ* ('El, creator of

scholars refer to the allegory as an apocalypse. Many Jews of the Second Temple period, including the author of this portion of 1 Enoch, expected the messianic age to correspond with the ending of exile, still defined as Israel being in subordination to foreign powers.

The seventy shepherds overtly represent the angelic patrons of the gentile nations. Their role is oppression of the sheep (Israel). The writer of 1 Enoch 85–90 cleverly subverts the Deuteronomy 32 worldview, where Israel is Yahweh's exclusive possession and the sons of God were allotted to the nations:

> In turning Israel over to the nations, God in effect turns them over to the nations' heavenly patrons. … [T]he author of the *Animal Apocalypse* has taken the concept of the angelic guardians of the nations and stood it on its head, so to speak. Here the angelic patrons function not so much as guardians of the Gentile nations, although they are that to be sure, nor even as angels charged with leading the Gentiles astray, as in *Jubilees*. Rather, they function as a means of punishing Israel.[22]

The enthusiasm of the shepherds for their task goes too far, however. As Stuckenbruck notes, "The shepherds become disobedient when of their own accord they exceed the limits set by God on the assignment."[23] God responds by commissioning an angelic scribe to monitor the treatment of the sheep and to prevent the shepherds from killing too many of

---

the earth'; *KAI* 26.III.18–19). At Ugarit the verb occurs in the El epithet, *qny w'adn 'ilm* ('creator and lord of the gods'; *KTU* 1.3:V.9), and Baal calls El *qnyn* ('our creator'; *KTU* 1.10:III.5). Genesis 14:19, 22 also attributes this title to El. Deut 32:7 references the עוֹלָם יְמוֹת ('ages past') and דֹר־וָדֹר שְׁנוֹת ('the years of many generations') which correspond, respectively, to El's description ('*lm*) and title '*ab šnm* ('father of years'; *KTU* 1.3 v:2, 25; 1.4 v:4; 1.18 i:12) at Ugarit." See Michael S. Heiser, "Are Yahweh and El Distinct Deities in Deut 32:8–9 and Psalm 82," 8. The idea of the "sons of God" of Deut 32:8 being thought of as seventy is axiomatic for the writers of the Hebrew Bible. Did the writer of 1 Enoch know of these connections? We have already seen in the present study that the author of 1 Enoch was familiar with ancient Near Eastern material. The cosmic mountain of Hermon, where the Watchers descended, has a long history in Ugaritic and Mesopotamian material. See Siam Bhayro, "Noah's Library: Sources for 1 Enoch 6–11," *JSP* 15.3 (2006): 163–77 (esp. 176–77); Edward Lipinski, "El's Abode: Mythological Traditions Related to Mount Hermon and to the Mountains of Armenia," *Orientalia Lovaniensa Periodica* 2 (1971): 13–69. It would seem more judicious to have the writer of 1 Enoch *combining* traditions from Deut 32:8–9 and Jer 25:11–12 than excluding Deut 32:8 from consideration of the number seventy in the Animal Apocalypse.

22. Hannah, "Angelic National Patrons," 421.

23. Loren T. Stuckenbruck, "Angels of the Nations," *DNTB* 30.

them (1 En 89:59–64). This scribe's activity is subsequently described in 1 Enoch 89:70–71, 76–77; 90:14, 17, 22.[24]

The commissioned shepherd-scribe has drawn a good deal of scholarly attention. Stuckenbruck remarks of this passage that "the angelic being appointed to monitor the shepherd's treatment of Israel seems to presuppose a tradition that aligns the people of God with an angel."[25] This, of course, reminds us of the way the book of Daniel describes Michael as Israel's prince (Dan 10:21; 12:1). Hannah's observation reflects the consensus of scholarly suspicion: "As the narrative proceeds, there are a number of clues that this angelic figure is probably to be identified with none other than the archangel Michael."[26] The clues followed by scholars in identifying the shepherd-scribe as Michael include the fact that, as Michael does in the book of Daniel, 1 Enoch 90:13–14 has the shepherd-scribe going to battle for the sheep (Israel) and that Michael is specifically named as the archangel "put in charge of the good ones of the people," a common designation for Israel in the Septuagint.[27]

QUMRAN AND THE "LOT OF BELIAL"

The seemingly secure identification in the Animal Apocalypse provides a conceptual link with an important element of the demonology of the Dead Sea Scrolls. Stuckenbruck summarizes that link concisely:

> In Daniel 10–11 the Persian and Greek empires are each represented by an angelic prince (Dan 10:13, 20) opposed by the angel appearing to Daniel and Michael the prince (Dan 10:13, 20–21; 11:1) and "great captain, who stands guard over" the faithful (Dan 12:1). In a similar

---

24. Nickelsburg, *1 Enoch 1*, 390 (on 1 En 89:61). This is not reflected in the translation in *OTP*, 1:68, that has God "calling another group of shepherds." Nickelsburg (*1 Enoch 1*, 387) and Tiller (*Commentary on the Animal Apocalypse*, 324) have God appointing a single figure in view. The variance is caused by manuscript disagreements. The fact that the wider context describes a single scribe at work makes a single figure far more coherent in 1 En 89:61.

25. Stuckenbruck, "Angels of the Nations," *DNTB* 30.

26. Hannah, "Angelic National Patrons," 421.

27. The translation is from Nickelsburg, *1 Enoch 1*, 294. Several different manuscript readings of this line are known. See Nickelsburg's footnote (a) for a discussion and reason for the coherence of his translation. See Hannah, "Angelic National Patrons," 422, for the observation about LXX. Instances of the lemma *laos* ("people") referring to Israel are numerous (e.g., Exod 8:32; 9:7, 9; Deut 2:4; Josh 4:1).

way, the eschatological struggle between "the sons of light" and "the sons of darkness" in the *War Scroll* is described as a conflict between forces led, respectively, by Michael (probably the one designated "the prince of light") and Belial (1QM 13:9–13; 17:5–8; cf. 1QS 3:20–25).[28]

Belial, along with Mastema, is a name used for the original divine rebel, Satan of the New Testament.[29] We saw a moment ago that Jubilees had the rebellious gods of the nations under the lordship of Satan. This in turn was similar to Second Temple Jewish material we discovered in earlier chapters of our study, which had the rebellious sons of God (Watchers) of the Genesis 6:1–4 episode under the authority of the lead original rebel, called Asael/Azazel/Shemihazah. The Second Temple demonological picture that emerges is one that conceptually unifies the three rebellions with Satan as overlord in command of the fallen sons of God (who are imprisoned for their transgression), demonic disembodied spirits of the giants (a tenth of which are allowed to harass humanity), and the lesser gods allotted to the nations in the judgment at Babel. This portrait closely resembles what we will encounter in the demonology of the New Testament.

The "forces of light" led by Michael in the Qumran War Scroll (1QM) are, not surprisingly, faithful members of the nation of Israel. This logically would mean that the "sons of darkness" led by Belial are from all the other nations. As the Qumran Rule of the Community/Manual of Discipline (1QS) puts the thought, "In the hand of the Angel of Darkness is total dominion over the sons of deceit; they walk on paths of darkness."[30] Collins adds in regard to this passage of 1QS, "In the dualistic world of the Dead Sea Scrolls … God appointed the Prince of light to protect the faithful, while he made Belial to corrupt."[31] This thought is quite in line with the theology of Jubilees, where God caused the spirits assigned over the nations "to rule so that they might lead them [the nations] astray from following him" (Jub 15:31).

---

28. Stuckenbruck, "Angels of the Nations," *DNTB* 30.
29. See the discussion in chapter 4.
30. 1QS 3:20–21. The translation is that of García Martínez and Tigchelaar, *Dead Sea Scrolls Study Edition*, 1:75.
31. J. J. Collins, "Prince," *DDD* 663.

The war described in the War Scroll is not merely a conflict between human "sons of light" representing Israel and men from the forsaken nations. It involves supernatural beings on both sides. Describing the War Scroll as "an eschatological text describing the final war between the 'sons of light' and the 'sons of darkness,'"[32] VanderKam summarizes the theology of the document as follows:

> Other passages term the war the "day of vengeance" (7.5; see 15.3) and "the battle of God" (9.5). Several lines also state that the sons of light, far from fighting alone, battle alongside their allies the angels. Unfortunately, the sons of darkness have their angelic companions as well, so that the conflict is a draw until the last battle (see cols. 12 and 17). The first column speaks of three "lots" during which the sons of light prevail against evil and three in which the sons of darkness gain the upper hand. This material apparently means that each side will be victorious in three engagements. After they have battled to a 3–3 tie, "with the seventh lot, the mighty hand of God shall bring down [the army of Satan, and all] the angels of his kingdom, and all the members [of his company in everlasting destruction]" (1QM 1.14–15; p. 106).[33]

Consequently, the sect at Qumran viewed the nations of the world as under the dominion of supernatural entities, themselves under the authority of Belial/Satan. The War Scroll clearly has divine beings—dark supernatural powers—in charge of Israel's foes. The picture that emerges, while not as explicit as other Second Temple texts, is nonetheless consistent with the Deuteronomy 32 worldview.

The Deuteronomy 32 worldview, extending as it does from the third divine rebellion of the Old Testament, completes our survey of the Second Temple Jewish theology of the powers of darkness. As we proceed to the New Testament, it will be evident that New Testament writers were informed and influenced by Second Temple Jewish thinking about evil spirits in rebellion against God and hostile to humanity.

---

32. James C. VanderKam, *The Dead Sea Scrolls Today* (Grand Rapids: Eerdmans, 1994), 3.
33. Ibid., 65–66.

THE DEMON-HAUNTED WILDERNESS
IN SECOND TEMPLE TEXTS

Readers will recall in chapter 1 that, following Alston's dissertation on the wilderness motif and Talmon's study of the Canaanite god of death (Mōt), we learned that Israelites associated the wilderness with chaos, that part of their world antithetical to life and sustenance which instead was bent on human extinction. The association with death led to "the mythical understanding of the wilderness [being] often denoted by the notion that it is the habitat of strange animals and hostile demons."[34]

This perception is also found in Second Temple Jewish literature.[35] Fourth Maccabees 18:8 has one woman protest, "No seducer of the desert nor deceiver in the field corrupted me, nor did the seducing and beguiling serpent defile my maiden purity." The verse obviously appeals to the tradition of the Watchers and their dalliances with women and associates those "seducers and deceivers" with the desert. However, the reference to the serpent would suggest a reference to Satan. This isn't a surprise given the Second Temple Jewish association of Satan (Azazel) with the Watchers. Emmet concurs in his commentary on 4 Maccabees:

> This verse embodies the well-known Jewish belief that women are in danger of seduction by evil spirits (Gen. 6.; Jub. 4., 5.; Enoch 6.ff.; Test. Reuben 5:6). The descendants of the first union, the giants of Nephilim, became demons who corrupt mankind (Jub. 7:27). … That the desert is the special home of demons is a common idea in the O.T. and elsewhere.[36]

In 1 Enoch 60, referencing the day of judgment, yet another passage associates the desert with supernatural evil:

> [7]On that day, two monsters will be parted—one monster, a female named Leviathan, in order to dwell in the abyss of the ocean over the

---

34. Alston, "The Concept of the Wilderness," 7.
35. It should be noted the community of Qumran, situated out in the desert in response to the perceived theological compromises of the Jerusalem priesthood, chose to emphasize Old Testament content casting the desert wilderness as a place of deliverance and refining.
36. C. W. Emmet, *The Fourth Book of Maccabees: Commentary* (London: Society for Promoting Christian Knowledge, 1918), 73–74.

fountains of water; [8] and (the other), a male called Behemoth, which holds his chest in an invisible desert whose name is Dundayin, east of the garden of Eden, wherein the elect and the righteous ones dwell, wherein my grandfather was taken, the seventh from Adam, the first man whom the Lord of the Spirits created. [9] Then I asked the second angel in order that he may show me (how) strong these monsters are, how they were separated on this day and were cast, the one into the abysses of the ocean, and the other into the dry desert. (1 En 60:7–9)[37]

The passage clearly considers Behemoth as the land (desert) counterpart of the chaos monster Leviathan. This sea-land pairing of twin chaos forces is implicit in Job 40:15–41:34 and continues well into rabbinic literature.[38] Behemoth occupies "an invisible desert" called Dundayin. Nickelsburg and VanderKam note that the spelling of this place varies in the manuscript data. Four of these readings (*dundāyn, dundayin, dunudāyn,* and *duydāyn*) "indicate a connection with the reading 'Doudael' in 1 [En] 10:4."[39] This was the pit in the place of jagged rocks (Dudael/Duda'el) where Azazel (Satan) was cast and imprisoned.

This description is significant since the Old Testament gives every indication that after the fall the garden no longer existed. In the cosmic geography of 1 Enoch, Eden becomes a metaphor for heaven as the destination of the righteous. If, as 1 Enoch 60:8 says, the biblical Enoch was taken to Eden, the meaning must mean "to heaven" where God dwelled (cp. Enoch 5:24; Heb 11:5 ["taken up"]). In 1 Enoch 60:8, the author juxtaposes that heavenly (unseen) realm with its invisible opposite: Dundayin. This suggests a strong connection to Dudael.[40]

---

37. *OTP*, 1:40–41.

38. K. William Whitney, *Two Strange Beasts: Leviathan and Behemoth in Second Temple and Early Rabbinic Judaism* (Winona Lake, IN: Eisenbrauns, 2006).

39. Nickelsburg and VanderKam, *1 Enoch 2*, 233, note 8a (see also page 240). Black echoes this suspicion, that Dundayin and Doudael (= Duda'el) are related. See Matthew Black, *The Book of Enoch or I Enoch: A New English Edition*, vol. 7 of *Studia in Veteris Testamenti Pseudepigrapha*, ed. A. M. Denis and M. de Jonge (Leiden: Brill, 1985), 227.

40. The description that this invisible place was "east of Eden" apparently also creates an intentional link back to the outcast Cain, who went to Nod "east of Eden" after his expulsion.

CONCLUSION

As was the case with the original supernatural rebel of Eden and the transgression of the sons of God in Genesis 6:1–4, Second Temple Jewish thought embraced the sinister cosmic geography of the Old Testament. As we will see in the third and last section of our study, the New Testament writers did as well.

"THE DEVIL AND HIS ANGELS": The Powers of Darkness in the New Testament

OVERVIEW

To this point in our study we've looked at Old Testament terminology for the powers of darkness and sketched the conceptual worldview of ancient Israel, of which those powers were part. The Old Testament describes three divine rebellions: one individual, two corporate. Hostility toward the will of the Most High God began in Eden with a lone rebel. It irrupted again in the days leading to the flood with the transgression of the sons of God. God's punitive rejection and division of the nations and subsequent creation of Israel as his own people precipitated the third rebellion, when the sons of God allotted to the nations went rogue.

Rebellion meant that the relationship of certain members of the heavenly host turned to estrangement and hostility. The original rebel was cast down, expelled from God's presence to earth and under the earth in the realm of the dead. The fallen sons of God were likewise imprisoned in the underworld. The rebellious *'elōhîm* over the nations were destined for the same fate, eternal separation from God, though their end would come only at the day of the Lord. Having committed transgressions that led to the same fate, these rebels were collectively linked in Israel's supernatural worldview. They had all threatened the life, safety, and security of the good order God wanted for humanity.

The conceptual associations between these supernatural protagonists prompted Second Temple Jewish writers to follow certain trajectories and draw particular conclusions about the powers of darkness and their orientation to each other. The namesake of the rebel of Eden eventually became Satan. The term *śāṭān* ("adversary") was a sensible moniker, given the rebel's opposition to God's human imagers and his plan for them. But "Satan" would be only one of several serviceable titles assigned to this figure during this period. The original rebel also came to be viewed as the dark overlord in command of the fallen sons of God, the disembodied spirits ("demons") of their offspring, and the lesser gods allotted to the nations at Babel.

While such a hierarchy between the divine rebels is not put forth in the Old Testament, the data on which it is based were the subject of earlier chapters. The hierarchical perception of these dark powers is consistent with Old Testament impressions. The ranked categorization derives from logical extensions of Old Testament portrayals of divine rebellion. In other words, the relationships have discernible roots in the Old Testament, despite the absence of specific prooftexts. Thoughtful Jews would not have viewed them as theologically aberrant and impermissible.

It is consequently no surprise that the Second Temple portrait of the powers of darkness closely resembles what followed. The New Testament did not arise out of an intellectual vacuum. Rather, New Testament writers show a sound grasp of their Second Temple Jewish heritage. This will become evident as we profile Satan in the New Testament (chapter 9), particularly in terms of his character, the scope of his authority, the place he is encountered by Jesus, and his final destiny. In chapter 10 our focus turns to demons, demonic possession, and the Jewish expectation that the Messiah would have power over demons. Lastly, chapter 11 focuses on the New Testament portrayal of cosmic geography and the delegitimization of the authority of the rebellious sons of God allotted to the nations.

CHAPTER 9

The Devil—
His Dominion and Destiny

THE ORIGINAL REBEL OF EDEN IS A RECURRING FOCUS IN NEW TESTA-
ment theology. New Testament writers follow the Second Temple Jewish
understanding of Satan's character, authority, domain, and final destiny
in transparent ways, embracing the theological mosaic assembled from
disparate data points in the Old Testament.

SATAN'S CHARACTER: Names and Titles
of the Original Rebel

The lead villain of the New Testament went by several names, some of
which are interpretive (i.e., labels extending from his perceived character) and others that have Old Testament roots. Several are found only a
handful of times, such as "the tempter" (*ho peirazōn*, Matt 4:3) and "the
enemy" (*ho echthros*, Matt 13:39; Luke 10:19). Both labels are generic and
reflect the portrayal of the original rebel in both the Old Testament and
Second Temple texts. Others require more attention here and in other
parts of this chapter.

1. Satan (Satanos)

The proper personal name "Satan," a transliteration of the Hebrew noun
śāṭān, occurs thirty-six times in the New Testament, just under half of
which are found in the four Gospels.[1] Satan is said to have a kingdom

---

1. Statistics in this chapter are based on searches in the Nestle-Aland Greek New Testament, 27th
edition (*Novum Testamentum Graece*, ed. Eberhard Nestle, Erwin Nestle, Barbara Aland, Kurt Aland,

(Matt 12:26; Luke 11:18), a detail which presumes an exalted ruling status. The term suggests some of the Old Testament noun's meaning in passages like Mark 4:15 and Luke 22:31, where Satan acts in an adversarial way toward believers. The name is used interchangeably with "devil" three times (Rev 12:9; 20:2; compare Rev 12:7, 10).[2]

2. Devil (diabolos)

The other frequently employed term for God's great enemy is *diabolos* ("devil"), a title that means "slanderer."[3] John's use of the term (John 8:44) followed by the epithet "father of lies" captures the slanderous, accusatory tone. The designation is apparently drawn from the Septuagint, which utilizes *diabolos* as the translation of the supernatural *śāṭān* in Job 1:6, 7, 9, 12; 2:1–4, 6–7; Zechariah 3:1–2; and 1 Chronicles 21:1. True to the contexts of these Old Testament passages, in the Gospels the devil is "portrayed as the adversary of Jesus (Mt 4:1–11; par. Lk 4:1–13) and the enemy of his work (Mt 13:39)."[4] In Matthew 25:41 the devil is cast as the leader of other evil spirits ("angels") in much the same manner as Second Temple Jewish literature describes Satan.[5]

3. Beelzebul (beelzeboul)

The term "Beelzebul" occurs in several places in the New Testament (Matt 10:25; 12:24 [cp. Mark 3:22; Luke 11:15]; Matt 12:27 [cp. Luke 11:18,

---

Johannes Karavidopoulos, Carlo M. Martini, and Bruce M. Metzger, 27th ed. [Stuttgart: Deutsche Bibelgesellschaft, 1993]).

2. Pairing John 13:2, 27 and Rev 2:9–10 produces the same sort of overlap.

3. BDAG, s.v. "διάβολος."

4. Graham H. Twelftree, "Demon, Devil, Satan," *Dictionary of Jesus and the Gospels*, ed. Joel B. Green and Scot McKnight (Downers Grove, IL: InterVarsity Press, 1992), 164. The Gospel of Mark does not use *diabolos*. The lemma is found three times in the Gospel of John (John 6:70; 8:44; 13:2), the first instance of which is not a reference to the chief supernatural enemy.

5. The lemma *diabolos* is found over thirty times in the Greek text of pseudepigraphical books (see Ken Penner and Michael S. Heiser, *Old Testament Greek Pseudepigrapha with Morphology* [Bellingham, WA: Lexham Press, 2008]). However, when the term is used as a proper name, it does so in books that date to the late first century and beyond, strongly suggesting Christian influence. The lone exception may be Jub 10:8, though scholars deem "Mastema" as the better reading since it is believed the book was originally written in Hebrew. See Jacobus van Ruiten, "Angels and Demons in the Book of Jubilees," in *Angels: The Concept of Celestial Beings—Origins, Development and Reception*, ed. Friedrich V. Reiterer, Tobias Nicklas, and Karin Schöpflin (Berlin: De Gruyter, 2007), 585–610 (esp. 600); James C. VanderKam, *Textual and Historical Studies in the Book of Jubilees* (Missoula, MT: Scholars Press, 1977), vi.

19]).[6] Twelftree notes, "The Vulgate and Syriac versions have attempted to explain the term by correcting it to *beelzebub*, the god of Ekron (2 Kings 1:2–3, 6, 16; Josephus *Ant.* 9.19)."[7] MacLaurin (with other scholars) is most likely correct in the opinion that *beelzebub* "is almost certainly secondary ... and probably represents an attempt to replace some honorific title by some disgraceful one just as in the O.T. Ba'al is sometimes replaced by *bosheth*."[8]

There is general consensus that the initial part of the name (*beel-*) represents Semitic *ba'al* ("lord, master") and perhaps the divine name Baal (*Baal*). However, some scholars believe that *zeboul* reflects Hebrew *zebul* ("exalted dwelling"; 1 Kgs 18:33), producing a meaning akin to "lord of heaven" (i.e., ruler in the heavenly realm), a title that would make its bearer the "prince of demons" (*archonti tōn daimoniōn*; Matt 12:24; Mark 3:22; Luke 11:15).[9] This association of the title with an "exalted dwelling" (whether the temple or heaven) is most likely not the case, for reasons suggested by the usage of *zbl* in Ugaritic where the word means "prince" and never seems to be used for a temple. In Ugaritic texts, we sometimes find *zbl bàal* ("prince Ba'al"), but in other "cases we find a proper name followed by the title, as in N.T. Beelzeboul, where Beel is the equivalent of a proper name."[10] This suggests that the name Beelzebul means "Ba'al prince/ruler" and the word *archonti* in Matthew 12:24 (and parallels) was a Greek translation of the Semitic title *zbl*.[11] The phrase *ba'al zebul* would have been well known in the Semitic world as meaning "prince Baal" or "ruler Baal." Attributing such a title to the original rebel of Eden, cast to earth/the underworld after his deception led to the loss of immortality (death) for humanity, makes good sense, as "Ba'al was ruler of the gods,

6. Twelftree notes that a few manuscripts read *beezeboul*, which "represents an assimilation of *l* to the *z*" (Twelftree, "Demon, Devil, Satan," 164).

7. Ibid., 164.

8. E. C. B. MacLaurin, "Beelzeboul," *NovT* 20.2 (1978): 156–60 (esp. 156). The Hebrew *bōšet* means "shame." Certain names in the Old Testament that originally had a "*-baal*" element (e.g., Eshbaal in Saul's genealogy [1 Chr 8:33; 9:39]) apparently had that element changed to "*-bosheth*" (Ish-bosheth) to denigrate and eliminate the reference to Baal (2 Sam 2:8–15). See P. Kyle McCarter Jr., *II Samuel: A New Translation with Introduction, Notes, and Commentary* (AYB; New Haven, CT: Yale University Press, 1984), 86.

9. For example, Twelftree, "Demon, Devil, Satan," 164.

10. MacLaurin, "Beelzeboul," 156–57.

11. Ibid.

the earth and the underworld" in ancient Semitic religion.[12] Beelzebul is therefore best understood as a Greek transliteration of a title of Baal.

4. "The Evil One" (ho ponēros)

This descriptive title occurs nearly a dozen times if one includes the ambiguous references in Matthew 5:37, 6:13, and 13:19 (genitive: *ponērou*), which may also be rendered abstractly ("evil").[13] It is interesting that this designation occasionally shows up paired with the generic *satan* in Second Temple material. For example:

- In the glorious eschatological future, "there will be no satan and no evil (one) who will destroy" (Jub 23:29).
- When Israel is purified in the future, "it will not have any satan or evil (one)" (Jub 50:5).
- "The evil one placed this oath in Michael's hand" (1 En 69:15).

The last example is noteworthy due to the context of swearing an oath—the context of the ambiguous Gospel references. While this wider context is not conclusive, it adds weight to the perspective that *ponērou* in Matthew may rightly be understood as referring to Satan.

SATAN AS RULER OF THE WORLD AND ITS DEMONS

We saw earlier that the title Beelzebul was drawn from a ruling title for Baal (*ba 'al zebul*; "ruler Baal"). Matthew 12:26–27 identifies Beelzebul as Satan who indeed is a ruler:

---

12. Ibid., 158.

13. See Matt 5:37; 6:13; 13:19, 38; John 17:15; Eph 6:16; 2 Thess 3:3; 1 John 2:13–14; 3:12; 5:18–19. On whether "evil" or "evil one" is appropriate in these instances, France notes: "The fact that the genitive form is the same in masculine and neuter allows either 'evil' or 'the Evil One' (the devil). ... In 13:38 a similar ambiguity is probably resolved by the explicit mention of the devil in the following clause, but there is no such indication [in these instances]." See R. T. France, *The Gospel of Matthew* (NICNT; Grand Rapids: Eerdmans, 2007), 193 note 55. Other scholars suggest that the reference in John 17:15 and 1 John might resolve the ambiguity in Matthew in the direction of "Evil One." Glancy writes that Jesus, in his Gethsemane prayer, asks that his disciples "be kept safe from the Evil One (17:14–15). Since the expression is in the genitive (*ek tou ponērou*), we cannot be certain of the gender of *ponērou*. However, a masculine and personal translation is preferred over a neuter and impersonal one because of the clear personal use of *ponēros* in 1 John to refer to the devil [1 John 2:13; 3:12; 5:19], suggesting that the epithet 'Evil One' is known in Johannine circles." See Jennifer Ann Glancy, "Satan in the Synoptic Gospels" (PhD diss., Columbia University, 1990), 254.

And if Satan casts out Satan, he is divided against himself. How then will his kingdom stand? And if I cast out demons by Beelzebul, by whom do your sons cast them out?

Matthew also considered Satan "the prince of demons" (Matt 12:24; cp. Matt 9:34; Mark 3:22; Luke 11:15), allowing us to see clearly that Matthew considered the minions of Satan's kingdom to be demons. This notion makes good sense. Beelzebul derives from the old Semitic title for Baal, lord of the underworld, and Baal was also called "ruler of the earth" in Ugaritic texts nine times.[14] This aspect of an association with Baal dovetails with the Deuteronomy 32 worldview that was part of Second Temple Jewish theology. Each nation was under the dominion of demons, so it is logical to consider a figure associated with Baal, the "ruler of the earth," also to be the ruler of demons. The Gospel writers understood the casting down of the original rebel as conceptually connected to the underworld home of Baal, lord of the dead. The matrix of ideas illustrates how New Testament thinking about Satan, though creative in its articulation, has secure roots in the Old Testament.

A similar title is found three times in the Gospel of John: "ruler of this world" (*ho archōn tou kosmou toutou*; John 12:31; 14:30; 16:11). Glancy, in her lengthy study of Satan in the Synoptic Gospels that includes a comparison with the Gospel of John, believes this unique title in John is part of that Gospel's purposeful portrayal of evil:

> Mark portrays Satan primarily as Jesus' chief adversary in an apocalyptic straggle, and this rivalry is also a theme in other writings of the synoptic tradition. Matthew has a particular interest in Satan's involvement in human sinfulness. Luke intensifies an aspect of Satan's activities already present in Mark, which is Satan's attack on humanity through demon possession and other physical suffering. ... "The ruler of this world (*ho archōn tou kosmou toutou*)," a Johannine title for the devil (12:31; 14:30; 16:11), does not appear in the synoptic Gospels. ... The fourth Gospel, however, employs the title "the ruler of this world" only in contexts where Jesus is referring to his own death and its significance. For John, the crucifixion marks Jesus' upward

---

14. Baal is called "ruler of the earth" (*zbl b'l 'arṣ*) nine times at Ugarit. See N. Wyatt, "Titles of the Ugaritic Storm God," *Ugarit Forschungen* 24 (1992): 403–24.

ascent and return to the Father; in a parallel movement, the devil's rule of the world comes to an end. The cross becomes the signpost of the *archōn's* defeat. The allusions to Satan's dominion in the synoptic Gospels occur in the context of parabolic speech. In a number of instances, John expresses metaphorically ideas similar to those narrated in parables in the first three Gospels. … If we assume that John as well as the synoptic Gospels is heir to traditions concerning Satan's dominion, we may well understand that what the first three Gospels express parabolically, the fourth will sum up in the vivid image of the Ruler of this World.[15]

John's "ruler of this world" is echoed by two Pauline descriptions: "prince of the power of the air" (Eph 2:2) and "god of this world" (2 Cor 4:4). They read as follows (with context):

> [1]And you were dead in the trespasses and sins [2]in which you once walked, following the course of this world (*ton aiōna tou kosmou*), following the prince of the power of the air, the spirit that is now at work in the sons of disobedience. (Eph 2:1–2)

> [3]And even if our gospel is veiled, it is veiled to those who are perishing. [4]In their case the god of this world (*ho theos tou aiōnos toutou*) has blinded the minds of the unbelievers, to keep them from seeing the light of the gospel of the glory of Christ, who is the image of God. (2 Cor 4:3–4)

Several observations are noteworthy. First, the lemma *aiōn* connects this passage to others that speak of an evil supernatural "prince." Second, this figure is in control of unredeemed humankind. Third, the "air" in this passage is best understood as the sky and, therefore, the heavenly (supernatural) realm associated not with the highest heaven above the firmament in Israelite-Jewish cosmology but a lower spiritual realm in close proximity to humanity. The supernatural power mentioned in

---

15. Glancy, "Satan in the Synoptic Gospels," abstract, 216–18. To accentuate the centrality of Satan to John's presentation of supernatural evil, it is interesting to note that, while John makes use of the lemma *daimonion* ("demon") six times, in every case the reference is Jesus' enemies accusing him of being possessed. Köstenberger opines in regard to this observation that "John has eliminated virtually all references to demons (Jesus' opponents' charge that he is demon-possessed is no real exception) … centering the evil supernatural on Satan." See Andreas J. Köstenberger, *A Theology of John's Gospel and Letters: The Word, the Christ, the Son of God* (Grand Rapids: Zondervan, 2009), 281. The six instances of *daimonion* are John 7:20; 8:48–49, 52; 10:20–21.

Ephesians 2:2 would be the same as the one elsewhere referred to as the devil (Eph 4:27; 6:11) or the evil one (Eph 6:16). In other NT passages like John 12:31 and 16:11, he is likewise associated with the "world" (*kosmos*) as in Ephesians 2:2. In 2 Corinthians 4:4, Paul describes him as the "god of this world" (literally, "god of this age" using *aiōn*).[16] Lincoln elaborates on the significance of these labels for the spheres of influence of the powers of evil:

> Here the realm of the ruler's authority is said to be the air. Elsewhere in Ephesians, hostile powers inhabit the heavenly realms (cf. 3:10; 6:12). This notion has its background in OT and Jewish thought where angels and spirit powers were often represented as in heaven (e.g., Job 1:6; Dan 10:13, 21; 2 Macc 5:2; *1 Enoch* 61.10; 90.21, 24); it was also developed in Philo (cf. *De Spec. Leg.* 1.66; *De Plant.* 14; *De Gig.* 6, 7). What is the relationship of "the air" to "the heavenly realms"? It may be that the writer is using terminology from different cosmological schemes, but it is fairly certain that he intends the two terms to indicate the same realm inhabited by malevolent agencies. ... If there is any distinct connotation, it could be that the "air" indicates the lower reaches of that realm and therefore emphasizes the proximity of this evil power and his influence over the world. In later Judaism the air is in fact thought of as the region under the firmament as in *2 Enoch* 29.4, 5, "And I threw him out from the height with his angels, and he was flying in the air continuously above the abyss." (Cf. also *T. Benj.* 3.4; *Targum of Job* 5.7; and *Asc. Isa.* 7.9; 10.29; 11.23 where the firmament is called the air and the ruler of this world and his angels are said to live in it ...).[17]

In his recent work emphasizing Paul's theology of Satan, Brown argues cogently for the coherence of connecting Paul's phrase "god of this world" with his theology of Satan elsewhere, as well as with John's "ruler of this world":

> There are several reasons for regarding ὁ θεὸς τοῦ αἰῶνος τούτου [*ho theos tou aiōnos toutou*; "the god of this age"] as a reference to the same Satan whom Paul mentions in letters to the Romans and

---

16. Andrew T. Lincoln, *Ephesians* (WBC; Dallas: Word, 1990), 94–95.
17. Ibid., 95–96.

Thessalonians. First, other early Christian texts deploy similar expressions and titles to express the theological notion of Satan's role as a powerful ruler in the present age. For example, in John's gospel Satan is referred to as ὁ ἄρχων τοῦ κόσμου τούτου [ho archōn tou kosmou toutou; "the ruler of this world"] three times (John 12:31; 14:30; 16:11). In these passages "the ruler of this world" is spoken of by the Johannine Jesus as having been judged and condemned (12:31; 16:11; cf. 16:33) and therefore powerless against Jesus (14:30). Likewise, the letter to the Ephesians speaks of "the ruler of the power of the air (τὸν ἄρχοντα τῆς ἐξουσίας τοῦ ἀέρος [ton archonta tēs exousias tou aeros]), the spirit that is now at work among those who are disobedient" (Eph 2:2; cf. 6:11–12).[18]

This New Testament profile of Satan has much in common with Second Temple Judaism, in which Satan, or the devil, is leader of all the other evil spirits. His scope of authority is the whole world (i.e., the nations). This perception would effectively assign to Satan ruling authority over the gods allotted to the nations at the Babel event (Deut 32:8; cp. Deut 4:19–20; 17:1–3; 29:23–26). The Old Testament does not attest this power structure, though its logic is discernible.

The "sons of the Most High" who abused the peoples over whom they had charge (Ps 82:2–5) would naturally be considered enemies of Israel, the remnant people of God—Yahweh's nation (Deut 32:9). They were disobedient spirits headed for the realm of the dead at the eschaton

---

18. Brown, *God of This Age*, 133. Brown adds later: "It is clear that Satan is envisioned in 2 Cor 4:4 since in the following verses Paul contrasts the 'blinding' activity of ὁ θεὸς τοῦ αἰῶνος τούτου [ho theos tou aiōnos toutou; 'the god of this age'] with God the Father who said, 'let light shine out of darkness' and who 'has shone in our hearts the light of the knowledge of the glory of God in the face of Jesus Christ' (2 Cor 4:6). For Paul, the roles of 'the god of this age' and God the Father, much like the two ages within apocalyptic thought, are antithetical. It would therefore make little sense if the two 'gods' of vv. 4 and 6 referred to the same figure. Collectively, these points demonstrate the plausibility that Paul's expression ὁ θεὸς τοῦ αἰῶνος τούτου [ho theos tou aiōnos toutou; 'the god of this age'] was not a reference to God the Father but to the same Satan whom Paul charged with hindering his missionary efforts in 1 Thess 2:18." See Brown, *God of This Age*, 134. The notion of binary opposition in Jewish apocalyptic thought is well known from Qumran texts such as the War Scroll (1 QM). This scroll is a textbook illustration of the oppositional theme in that its focus is eschatological warfare between Yahweh's people ("sons of light") and the supernatural spirits sent to aid them and their human ("sons of darkness") and supernatural opponents who oppose them. The figure of Belial/Mastema/Satan is prominent in this and other apocalyptic texts from Qumran. For a general discussion of oppositional thought in apocalyptic, see Bennie H. Reynolds III, "Demonology and Eschatology in the Oppositional Language of the Johannine Epistles and Jewish Apocalyptic Texts," in *The Jewish Apocalyptic Tradition and the Shaping of New Testament Thought*, ed. Benjamin E. Reynolds and Loren T. Stuckenbruck (Minneapolis: Fortress, 2017), 327–46.

(Ps 82:6–7), joining the lord of the dead in his domain.[19] Further, they were of like mind with the original rebel, whose disdain for Yahweh's human family in Eden was transparent. Both the serpent (identified by this time as Satan) and the sons of God allotted to the nations showed their disdain for human life by sowing chaos in the world. Set in contrast to Israel (Zion) was the place of Yahweh's presence, the cosmic mountain where Yahweh intended the revival of Eden, his home and place of rule.[20] This meant that "the world" was the place conceptually opposite Eden and its promise of everlasting life. Opposition to Yahweh meant death. Any spirit standing against him must be like-minded and guided by the lord of the dead in a common agenda.[21]

THE DEVIL'S TEMPTATION OF JESUS IN THE WILDERNESS

In addition to their agreement with Second Temple Jewish writings in regard to the scope of Satan's character and authority, the Gospel writers are also in sync with these sources in regard to the association of the desert wilderness with evil spirits and their leader. This is evident from Matthew 4:1–11:

> [1] Then Jesus was led up by the Spirit into the wilderness to be tempted by the devil. [2] And after fasting forty days and forty nights, he was hungry. [3] And the tempter came and said to him, "If you are the Son of God, command these stones to become loaves of bread." [4] But he answered, "It is written,
>
> > "'Man shall not live by bread alone,
> > but by every word that comes from the mouth of God.'"

---

19. As Brown notes (*God of This Age*, 68), while Paul's writings include no specific connection of Satan with other evil spirits, this eschatological fate that is shared by all evil powers is indeed part of Paul's theology (1 Cor 15:24–28).

20. The seminal study of the cosmic mountain motif in the Hebrew Bible is Clifford, *The Cosmic Mountain in Canaan and the Old Testament*. In ancient Near Eastern thought, the cosmic mountain was the abode of the gods (or God and his heavenly council in Israel's case), the place where heaven and earth intersected, the source of life-giving waters and the earth's life-sustaining fertility. As Monson notes, Zion and its temple were "the archetypal cosmic mountain, the meeting point between heaven and earth" (J. Monson, "Solomon's Temple," *DOTHB* 929; see also *NIDOTTE* 2:333).

21. Paul's terminology for evil spirits (principalities, powers, thrones, etc.) reflect the Deuteronomy 32 worldview in that all such terms denote geographical authority and dominion. See chapter 11.

⁵Then the devil took him to the holy city and set him on the pinnacle of the temple ⁶and said to him, "If you are the Son of God, throw yourself down, for it is written,

"'He will command his angels concerning you,'

and

"'On their hands they will bear you up,
   lest you strike your foot against a stone.'"

⁷Jesus said to him, "Again it is written, 'You shall not put the Lord your God to the test.'" ⁸Again, the devil took him to a very high mountain and showed him all the kingdoms of the world and their glory. ⁹And he said to him, "All these I will give you, if you will fall down and worship me." ¹⁰Then Jesus said to him, "Be gone, Satan! For it is written,

"'You shall worship the Lord your God
   and him only shall you serve.'"

¹¹Then the devil left him, and behold, angels came and were ministering to him.

That Satan tempts Jesus in the desert wilderness is not arbitrary. The Greek term translated "wilderness" (*erēmos*) is used in the Septuagint translation of the destination of the goat for Azazel (Lev 16:10) and the desolate place described by Isaiah that was home to preternatural creatures associated with evil spirits (Isa 13:9). Fitzmyer observes, "By the 'desert' the wilderness of Judea is meant, perhaps as place of contact with God (see Hos 2:14–15), but more so as an abode of wild beasts and demons (Lev 16:10; Isa 13:21; 34:14; Tob 8:3). This double aspect of the desert thus confronts Jesus."[22] Allison's focused comments on the association with supernatural evil are especially appropriate:

In the temptation narratives Jesus confronts Satan in the wilderness. In Luke 8:29 we are told that the Gerasene demoniac was driven into the desert by a demon. And in Matthew 12:43–45 and its parallel Luke 11:24–26 the unclean spirit who has been cast out "passes through waterless places." These texts are illumined by the Jewish belief that the wilderness, being beyond the bounds of society, is the haunt of

---

22. Joseph A. Fitzmyer, *The Gospel according to Luke I–IX: Introduction, Translation, and Notes* (AYB; New Haven, CT: Yale University Press, 1970), 514.

evil spirits (see Lev 16:10; Is 13:21; *1 Enoch* 10:4–5; Tob 8:3; 4 Macc 18:8; *2 Apoc. Bar.* 10:8). The idea dominated later Christian monasticism.[23]

In the previous chapter we learned that in Second Temple Jewish thought, the desert wilderness was where the goat for Azazel was driven and where the demonic Azazel was imprisoned. Consequently, that the Spirit drove Jesus to this place after his baptism seems odd. Why would the Spirit compel Jesus to face the devil?

The answer is to be found in how the New Testament writers wanted to portray Jesus in light of Old Testament history and theology. The Gospels, especially Matthew, cast Jesus' ministry as a new exodus event. Jesus' baptism and temptation in the wilderness parallel Israel's passing through the sea before heading into the wilderness on the way to Canaan, the land promised to them by Yahweh.

> But Israel's faith and loyalty to Yahweh faltered (Judg 2:11–15). They were eventually seduced by the hostile divine powers ("demons") whose domain was the wilderness (Deut 32:15–20). Jesus, the messianic son of God and royal representative of the nation, would succeed where Israel failed.[24]

Consider the imagery of the temptation. Jesus was in the wilderness forty days—a deliberate mirroring of Israel's forty years of wandering in the desert after their failure to believe Yahweh would give them victory over the giant Anakim (evil spawn in Old Testament and Second Temple theology) reported by the spies (Num 13:33–14:35).

This failure was especially shameful because it involved ignoring the earlier incredible deliverance at the Red Sea (Exod 14–15; compare Num 14:11, 22). This is consistent with the observation of many scholars that Matthew's portrayal of Jesus' early life and ministry cast him as the new (superior) Son of God, the central figure of a new exodus.[25]

We must not overlook the fact that the exodus is viewed as a victory over the gods of Egypt—evil spirits in rebellion against Yahweh in the wake of Babel's allotment of the gods over the nations. After the

23. D. C. Allison, Jr., "Mountain and Wilderness," *Dictionary of Jesus and the Gospels*, ed. Joel B. Green and Scot McKnight (Downers Grove, IL: InterVarsity Press, 1992), 565.

24. Heiser, *Unseen Realm*, 277.

25. For a useful summary of the parallels with the exodus story, see Ryken et al., "Matthew, Gospel of," *Dictionary of Biblical Imagery*, 543.

deliverance at the Red Sea, Moses cries out, "Who is like you, O LORD, among the gods?" (Exod 15:11). God himself described the death of the firstborn, the final plague, as a victory over his supernatural enemies:

> I will pass through the land of Egypt that night, and I will strike all the firstborn in the land of Egypt, both man and beast; and on all the gods of Egypt I will execute judgments: I am the LORD. (Exod 12:12; compare Num 33:4)

Jesus' victory over Satan's temptation in the wilderness is also a victory over the gods of the nations. Recall the words of Matthew 4:8–9:

> [8] Again, the devil took him to a very high mountain and showed him all the kingdoms of the world and their glory. [9] And he said to him, "All these I will give you, if you will fall down and worship me."

In effect, Satan was offering Jesus rule over the nations abandoned by Yahweh at Babel (Deut 32:8). That judgment was never intended to be permanent. When Yahweh raised up his own "portion" (Deut 32:9) starting with the covenant with Abraham, he told the patriarch that it would be through his offspring that all the nations would ultimately be blessed (Gen 12:3). Jesus was the specific fulfillment of that promise:

> Now the promises were made to Abraham and to his offspring. It does not say, "And to offsprings," referring to many, but referring to one, "And to your offspring," who is Christ. (Gal 3:16)

Had Jesus failed in the wilderness temptation, the plan to bring the nations back into the family of Yahweh also would have failed. The nature of this temptation and the implications of its outcome presume the Second Temple Jewish perception we discovered earlier, that the rebellious gods of the nations were affiliated with the original rebel of Eden and, in some sense, under his authority. When the Gospels have Satan offering the kingdoms of the world to Jesus in exchange for worship, they presume this affiliation and authority.

THE FINAL FATE OF THE DEVIL
AND OTHER SUPERNATURAL REBELS

The New Testament portrayal of the final judgment of Satan is described in the book of Revelation in unequivocal terms:

> [1]Then I saw an angel coming down from heaven, holding in his hand the key to the bottomless pit and a great chain. [2]And he seized the dragon, that ancient serpent, who is the devil and Satan, and bound him for a thousand years, [3]and threw him into the pit, and shut it and sealed it over him, so that he might not deceive the nations any longer, until the thousand years were ended. After that he must be released for a little while. … [7]And when the thousand years are ended, Satan will be released from his prison [8]and will come out to deceive the nations that are at the four corners of the earth, Gog and Magog, to gather them for battle; their number is like the sand of the sea. [9]And they marched up over the broad plain of the earth and surrounded the camp of the saints and the beloved city, but fire came down from heaven and consumed them, [10]and the devil who had deceived them was thrown into the lake of fire and sulfur where the beast and the false prophet were, and they will be tormented day and night forever and ever. (Rev 20:1–3, 7–10)

Note that this passage does *not* include the demons in the judgment scene. Their inclusion is found only in Matthew 25:41 ("Then he will say to those on his left, 'Depart from me, you cursed, into the eternal fire prepared for the devil and his angels' ").

There are obvious questions raised by these passages. How does Matthew 25:41 align with 2 Peter 2:4 and Jude 6, both of which, as we saw earlier, have the fallen sons of God ("angels that sinned") in "chains of gloomy darkness" in the underworld (Tartarus)? If Satan is to be identified with the original rebel of Eden who was cast down to the underworld after his rebellion, how is being cast into the lake of fire a punishment? Further, what is the relationship with passages like Luke 10:18—where Jesus says, "I saw Satan fall like lightning from heaven," after the kingdom of God was preached by the seventy disciples[26]—and Revelation

---

26. That the seventy are "disciples" is affirmed by synoptic parallels which use that term (Matt 9:35–37; John 4:32–38). English translations variously have Jesus sending out seventy or seventy-two

12:7–10, where Michael and his angels fight Satan, who is thrown down to the earth?

With respect to the renegade sons of God, the Watchers of Second Temple Jewish tradition, it is clear that Second Temple texts have them imprisoned in the abyss for "seventy generations" or "until the day of their judgment … until the eternal judgment is consummated" (1 Enoch 10:11–13).[27] Many scholars believe that the book of Revelation describes their release, a precursor to the return of Christ, the day of the Lord, and their ultimate punishment (with Satan) in the lake of fire. Specifically, the scene in Revelation 9:1–10 of the "unlocking" of the abyss by a "star" who is given the key is construed as the eschatological emancipation of the imprisoned Watchers.[28]

---

disciples in this episode. There is ancient Greek New Testament manuscript evidence for both readings. The number in either reading is not accidental as it references the number of nations listed in Genesis 10 that were dispossessed at Babel. The different numbers in the manuscript evidence arose on account of the Septuagint, which has "seventy-two" for the number of nations in Gen 10, while the Hebrew Masoretic Text has the number of nations as seventy. The number seventy is the best reading on external grounds, given the witness to seventy "sons of El" in the divine council at Ugarit and the El epithets used of Yahweh in Deut 32:6–7 (see the discussion and Ugaritic references in Michael S. Heiser, "Are Yahweh and El Distinct Deities in Deut 32:8–9 and Psalm 82?"). Fitzmyer, noting Deut 32:8, writes that the number "has often been thought to reflect the nations of the world in the table of Gen 10:2–31 and would symbolize the coming evangelization of the Gentiles and diaspora Jews by the disciples, whereas the Twelve would have been sent to Israel itself." Joseph A. Fitzmyer, S.J., *The Gospel according to Luke X–XXIV: Introduction, Translation, and Notes* (AYB; New Haven, CT: Yale University Press, 1985), 846.

27. The translation is Nickelsburg's. See also 1 En 13:1; 14:5; Jub 5:6, 10; 10:7–11.

28. Scholars are in agreement that this "star" is a supernatural being, but disagree as to whether a good or evil entity is in view. In his study of Satan's final end, Thompson argues that the star is an unfallen, loyal member of the heavenly host: "Most commentators, including Charles and Aune, assume that the key was given to the star, who, they then argue, was in fact a fallen angel. But this creates a problem when the star-angel of 9:1 is identified with the angel of 20:1. … The *aggelos* [*sic*] in Rev 9:1 and the *aggelos* in 20:1 have the same heavenly origin and the same responsibility—the key to the abyss. … While the angel keeper of the key of Sheol is not named in Revelation, he is elsewhere. The Greek version of 1 Enoch 20:2 attributes control of Sheol to 'Uriel, one of the holy angels, who is over the world and over Tartarus'. … Elsewhere the angel keeper of Sheol is given a title. In *Sibylline Oracles* book 8 there is an occurrence of the rare Greek *kleidophylax*, 'key-keeper'. Although the sentence is incomplete, the context allows it to refer to an otherwise unidentified key-bearer who is responsible for the enclosure where persons are retained before coming before the judgment seat of God in the final judgment. The concept of the angel keeper(s) of *Sheol* flows into early Christian thinking by use of the Greek term *tartarouchoi aggeloi*, 'angels who keep Tartarus,' in *Apocalypse of Paul* 18; *Gospel of Bartholomew* 4:12; and Hippolytus, *Commentary on Daniel* 2.29.11. The synonymous expression *temelouchos aggelos*, 'angel keeping Tartarus,' is found in Clement of Alexandria, *Prophetic Eclogue* 41.1." See Steven Thompson, "The End of Satan," *Andrews University Seminary Studies* 37.2 (1999): 260–62. Beale is representative of the alternative perspective, that the "star" is a demonic entity: "The main debate is whether this is a good or evil being. It could be either the archangel Uriel, who was chief 'over Tartarus,' or the archangel Saraqael, who was 'over … the spirits, who sin in the spirit' (*1 En.* 19:1; 20:1–6; 21:1–10; *Testament of Solomon* 2). But *1 Enoch* never

Scholars have long noted the similarities between Revelation 9 and Second Temple Jewish texts. Numerous Second Temple texts describe the imprisonment of corrupt, fallen angels, bound in a pit awaiting the final judgment (e.g., 1 En 10:4–14; 18:6–19:1; 21:7; 54:1–6; 88:1–3; 90:23–26; Jub 5:6–14; compare 2 Pet 2:4).[29] Concerning Revelation 9, Aune observes:

> The "star" is obviously some kind of supernatural being, as this verse and the following make clear. ... While the key to the abyss is mentioned again in 20:1, the notion of a shaft that could be locked and unlocked is implied rather than explicitly stated. In the other two references, in Rev 11:7 and 17:8, the abyss is the place from which the beast is said to ascend. ... [The abyss] is sometimes synonymous with the underworld, which is the abode of the dead (*Jos. As.* 15:12; Ps 71:20; Rom 10:7) ... and the place where demons are imprisoned (Luke 8:31; *1 Enoch* 18–21; *Jub.* 10:7) into the abyss until the day of judgment.[30]

The bizarre description of the beings released from the abyss as "locusts" (Rev 9:3) that were "like horses prepared for battle: on their heads were what looked like crowns of gold; their faces were like human faces, their hair like women's hair, and their teeth like lions' teeth" (Rev 9:7–8) does *not* undermine their identification as the fallen Watchers. According to Kulik, the mixture of human and animal features is "widely known" in demonic depictions in Judaism, classical Greek literature, and the ancient Near East.[31] Accordingly, just as in Second Temple tradition, the New Testament has the fallen sons of God imprisoned until the end of days and finally judged at the climax of the apocalyptic day of the Lord.

---

calls those figures 'fallen stars.' Instead, this description is reserved exclusively for fallen angels under the confinement of the archangels. ... In addition to the resemblances with falling star depictions elsewhere (mentioned above), the conclusion that this is not a good angel but a fallen angel is also suggested by v 11. There the 'angel of the abyss' is called 'king over' the demonic locusts and is called 'Abaddon' ('Destruction') and 'Apollyon' ('Destroyer'). The heavenly being who is sovereign over the abyss and the locusts in vv 1–3 is probably the one called their 'king' in v 11. ... Therefore, the angel in v 1 is either Satan or one of his minions (the latter would be parallel with *2 En.* 42:1, which portrays 'those who hold the keys ... of the gates of hell' as 'like great serpents, and their faces like extinguished lamps, and their eyes of fire, their sharp teeth')." See G. K. Beale, *The Book of Revelation: A Commentary on the Greek Text* (NIGTC; Grand Rapids: Eerdmans, 1999), 491, 493.

29. Beale, *Book of Revelation*, 493.
30. David E. Aune, *Revelation 6–16* (WBC; Dallas: Word, 1998), 525–26.
31. See Alexander Kulik, "How the Devil Got His Hooves and Horns: The Origin of the Motif and the Implied Demonology of *3 Baruch*," *Numen* 60 (2013): 195–229 (esp. 215–16).

But questions remain about the original rebel, given the proper name "Satan" (among others) in Second Temple Jewish literature. Earlier parts of our study have established the original rebel's "casting down" in the Old Testament without commentary on that judgment's finality. Only the enduring effect of his transgression and punishment (i.e., death, estrangement from God, chaos) received attention prior to the Second Temple period. Given the post-Eden conditions brought about, ultimately, by the disloyalty of the supernatural serpent figure, it is no surprise that Second Temple Jewish writers presumed the ongoing activity of this figure.

The post-Eden conceptual milieu of the rebel's expulsion helps frame the later conception of Satan's relationship to God and the loyal members of Yahweh's council-host. Though many Bible readers (even scholars) presume otherwise, spirit beings in rebellion against God are not portrayed as remaining in God's service. The presumption confuses God's sovereign status over evildoers with the notion that they are, so to speak, yet in God's employ. To use a human analogy, the state can put people in a position where a behavior or outcome desired by the state comes to pass, but that hardly means those people were employees of the state (or even willing or knowing participants).[32]

After his expulsion from Eden, the original rebel was no longer part of God's council.[33] He is connected to the underworld because death is now a part of God's world. The conception of death as both separation from God and cessation of embodied life are both in play. Eden is no more, which in turn means there is no divine abode on earth. The original rebel (and humanity) are separated from God's abiding presence as Genesis has portrayed it in Eden.

---

32. The above misconception arises from passages that speak of "an evil spirit" being sent by God to trouble people (e.g., Saul, 1 Sam 16:14–16; 18:10–11). The confusion is created by the choice of the word "evil" to translate Hebrew *rā ʿāh* (lemma: *rā ʿ*) in some English translations. The term often has nothing to do with moral evil. It commonly describes something undesirable or contemptible (Gen 41:20, 27; Jer 24:2, 3, 8; 49:23; Ps 112:7; Deut 22:14, 19; Neh 6:13), or some harmful, injurious, or disastrous condition or situation (Gen 19:19; Deut 7:15; 28:35, 59). The "evil spirit" sent by God to trouble Saul therefore may be a mental affliction or psychological disposition. The same ambiguity applies to other passages using the same phrasing in other contexts (Judg 9:22–23; Isa 19:13–14; 37:5–7). Even if spirit beings are in view, it is incoherent to conclude that when God sends these spirits to judge wickedness that they themselves are evil. Such a conclusion would, for example, make absurd certain instances where members of the heavenly host are fighting against unbelievers or wicked enemies of God's people (Judg 5:20; 2 Kings 6:5–19; Ps 78:43–51 [cp. Exod 12:12; Num 33:4]; Matt 13:36–43; Acts 12:21–23). This would be the proverbial "house divided against itself" (Matt 12:25).

33. Recall that the *śāṭān* of Job 1–2 is not the rebel of Eden (the devil, Satan).

Rather than exterminate humanity or allow them to remain in hopeless mortality, God initiates a plan to redeem humanity from death and estrangement—to effectively restore his ruling, fatherly presence on earth. Theologically, that restoration is the concept of the kingdom of God on earth. The heightening of depravity among humanity (Gen 6:5), propelled by more supernatural rebellion (Gen 6:1–4) makes the need for restoration more acute and its obstacles more persistent and insurmountable.[34] The third rebellion at Babel led to the creation of a new human family, the seed of Abraham (Israel) to further this restorative kingdom effort.

The kingdom promises hinged upon the fulfillment of the covenants God made with Abraham and his descendants, particularly David (2 Sam 7). Made with invariably fallible humans, those covenants could only be fulfilled and the kingdom only initiated through the life and ministry of the perfect imager of God—Jesus Christ, God incarnate as a man and descendant of Abraham and David. The inauguration of this kingdom meant the beginning of the end for "the ruler of this world" and the present kingdom under the curse of death.

This is precisely how things play out in the New Testament. It is no coincidence that the presentation of the kingdom in the Gospels is accompanied by the expulsion of demons, which precipitates the defeat of Satan's kingdom.[35] Jesus could not have been clearer in this regard:

> [18] And if Satan also is divided against himself, how will his kingdom stand? For you say that I cast out demons by Beelzebul. [19] And if I cast out demons by Beelzebul, by whom do your sons cast them out? Therefore they will be your judges. [20] But if it is by the finger of God

---

34. God had chosen to transform the entire world into Eden via the participation of human beings. The concept of divine imaging (Gen 1:26–27) meant that humans were God's children, but also his participant-representatives in this transformative process. God was committed to human participation from the beginning, sharing his attributes with his imagers for that purpose. God did not destroy humanity after the fall, nor did he alter this status. One of his attributes God shared with human imagers is freedom. Deepening depravity meant that the agents God was committed to using to restore his good rule would consistently and universally fail to image him. These same agents (in the form of Israel) were the recipients of God's covenants, destined to fail because of human inability. This set of circumstances, along with God's commitment to bring about a return to Eden to accomplish his rule on earth through humans, was why the incarnation of God as man was a necessary element in the biblical epic.

35. For a thorough discussion of these tandem concepts, see Craig A. Evans, "Inaugurating the Kingdom of God and Defeating the Kingdom of Satan," *BBR* 15.1 (2005): 49–75.

that I cast out demons, then the kingdom of God has come upon you. (Luke 11:18–20)

This is the context for Jesus' statement a chapter earlier in Luke. At the return of the seventy disciples who were given the authority to cast out demons, Jesus proclaims, "I saw Satan fall like lightning from heaven" (Luke 10:18).[36] This is not a reference to the primeval past, nor is it the long-overdue expulsion from the council (an assumption driven by mistakenly seeing the śāṭān in Job 1–2 as the devil).[37] The point is that the reversal and demise of Satan's kingdom has begun—for good. From this point forward, linked as it is to what Jesus will accomplish on the cross, there will be no kingdom failure. Jesus will ascend after his resurrection, and the Spirit will come to empower believers to overcome depravity (e.g. Rom 8:2–5) and restore the disinherited nations to the family of God (e.g., Acts 2).

All who are members of the kingdom of Jesus are no longer under the curse of death. By definition this means Satan's kingdom (and the curse of death) no longer has any hold upon them. The "accuser of our brothers" (Rev 12:10) remains active in the world until the final judgment, blinding the minds of people to prevent them from joining the kingdom of Jesus, but he has no accusation to bring against those who belong to Christ. His rightful claim over their lives in the realm of the dead is

---

36. Revelation 12:7–10 is also not a reference to a primeval event (nor a future one). The description of spiritual war—Michael vs. the devil and his angels—is tied to the preceding verses which unambiguously reference the first advent of Jesus. Revelation 12:7–10 is in this sense a parallel to Luke 10:18. They both describe the defeat of the devil at the coming of the Son of God to restore God's kingdom rule. Scholars who do not accept this reading typically decide against it on the basis of higher-critical (source critical) assumptions about how Rev 12:7–10 was originally separated from the earlier portion of the passage. One such scholar nevertheless remarks that "to read Rev 12:7–9 as underscoring Jesus' defeat of Satan through the crucifixion is certainly credible" (Kelley Coblentz Bautch, "The Fall and Fate of Renegade Angels: The Intersection of Watchers Traditions and the Book of Revelation," in *The Fallen Angels Traditions: Second Temple Developments and Reception History*, ed. Angela Kim Harkins, Kelley Coblentz Bautch, and John C. Endres [Washington, DC: Catholic Biblical Association of America, 2014], 69–93). Rather than speculate about a piecemeal history of the text, the view taken by this author accepts the text as it is, noting its congruence to the juxtaposition of the inauguration of Christ's kingdom with the demise of Satan's in the Gospels.

37. It is also partially propelled by the flawed notion that Satan, the original rebel, still works for God. 1 Chronicles 21:1 is usually put forth to defend this idea. As we discussed earlier in chapter 3, the śāṭān of that passage that incites David is none other than Yahweh as the angel of Yahweh (i.e., the second Yahweh figure, God as man in the Old Testament). This is why the parallel passage (2 Sam 24:1) has Yahweh inciting David. A helpful resource on the textual clues that identify this śāṭān with the angel of Yahweh is Paul Evans, "Divine Intermediaries in 1 Chronicles 21: An Overlooked Aspect of the Chronicler's Theology," *Biblica* 85 (2004): 545–58.

nullified through the resurrection of Christ and the union with Christ for all who believe the gospel. In the final judgment, Satan's domicile, the realm of the dead, is transformed into the place of his torment.

The prominence of the expulsion of demons in the Gospels deserves more attention. Not only is the theme a persistent part of announcing the kingdom's restoration, but it is part of the Watchers tradition and, as we will see in the next chapter, the Second Temple Jewish profile of the Messiah.

CHAPTER 10

Evil Spirits—
Demons and Their Destiny

WE'VE COVERED A LOT OF GROUND IN OUR STUDY OF THE OLD TESTA-ment through the Second Temple period. We've seen that the origin of demons was tied to the second supernatural rebellion, in Genesis 6:1–4. Demons were the disembodied spirits of dead Nephilim in Second Temple thought, a conclusion drawn from the Mesopotamian back-story to Genesis 6:1–4 and the presence of Rephaim spirits in under-world scenes in the Old Testament. These data points were then joined by another idea from the Old Testament, that the realm of the dead was the domicile of the original rebel. These scriptural loose ends were tied together in Second Temple Jewish texts to posit a hierarchical relation-ship between Satan and the demons. Our focus in this chapter will be how the New Testament Gospel descriptions of demons show a direct relationship to Second Temple Jewish descriptions, demonic possession, and the matter of exorcism.[1]

DEMONS: Evil/Unclean Spirits

In our discussion of the origin of demons in chapter 6 we saw that "evil spirits" was the predominant term for these entities. The evil spirits were led by Mastema (Jub 10:1–8) or Satan (Jub 1:10–13). These two names

---

1. The terminology of demonic "possession" or demons "possessing" people is problematic. These English word choices, so common in English translations, create unfortunate theological confusion. See the discussion of whether Christians can be possessed in chapter 12. In this chapter I use the terminology only because of its familiarity.

were related linguistically. Mastema in turned overlapped thematically with Beliar/Belial, "the chief of evil spirits, Satan."[2]

The New Testament uses "evil spirits" and similar phrases to speak of demons. "Evil spirits" (or the singular, "evil spirit") are mentioned in eight New Testament passages.[3] More common is "unclean spirits," a descriptive phrase found in over twenty passages.[4] Though "only at Matthew 8:31 is *daimōn* ['demon'] used in the New Testament for an evil spirit,"[5] that "unclean spirits," "evil spirits," and "demons" are interchangeable is evident from Jesus' comments about and acts of power upon these entities in parallel episodes in the Synoptic Gospels. Note the mingled terminology along with the "casting out" verbs:

> As they were going away, behold, a demon-oppressed man who was mute was brought to him. And when the **demon** had been **cast out**, the mute man spoke. And the crowds marveled, saying, "Never was anything like this seen in Israel." But the Pharisees said, "He **casts out demons** by the prince of **demons**." (Matt 9:32–33; compare Mark 3:22; Luke 11:14–23)

> And he called to him his twelve disciples and gave them authority over **unclean spirits**, to **cast them out**, and to heal every disease and every affliction. … These twelve Jesus sent out, instructing them, "Go nowhere among the Gentiles and enter no town of the Samaritans, but go rather to the lost sheep of the house of Israel. And proclaim as you go, saying, 'The kingdom of heaven is at hand.' Heal the sick, raise the dead, cleanse lepers, **cast out demons**." (Matt 10:1, 5–7a; compare Mark 3:13–15; 6:7–13; Luke 6:13; 9:1, 2)

> In that hour he healed many people of diseases and plagues and **evil spirits**, and on many who were blind he bestowed sight. (Luke 7:21)

> Soon afterward he went on through cities and villages, proclaiming and bringing the good news of the kingdom of God. And the twelve

---

2. D. R. A. Hare, "The Lives of the Prophets," in *OTP* 2:90 note c.

3. Matthew 12:45; Luke 7:21; 8:2; 11:26; 19:12–13, 15–16. The Greek lemmas are *ponēros* and *pneuma*.

4. Matthew 10:1; 12:43; Mark 1:23, 26–27; 3:11, 30; 5:2, 8, 13; 6:7; 7:25; 9:25; Luke 4:33, 36; 6:18; 8:29; 9:42; 11:24; Acts 5:16; 8:7; Rev 16:13; 18:2.

5. Twelftree, "Demon, Devil, Satan," 164. Twelftree notes the interchangeability argued for here and elsewhere in the same article: "The Gospels use a variety of terms, often interchangeable, for the Devil and evil spirits" (164).

were with him, and also some women who had been healed of **evil spirits** and infirmities: Mary, called Magdalene, from whom seven **demons** had **gone out**. (Luke 8:1–2)

Then they sailed to the country of the Gerasenes, which is opposite Galilee. When Jesus had stepped out on land, there met him a man from the city who had **demons**. For a long time he had worn no clothes, and he had not lived in a house but among the tombs. When he saw Jesus, he cried out and fell down before him and said with a loud voice, "What have you to do with me, Jesus, Son of the Most High God? I beg you, do not torment me." For he had commanded the **unclean spirit** to **come out** of the man. (Luke 8:26–29)

"When the **unclean spirit** has **gone out** of a person, it passes through waterless places seeking rest, but finds none. Then it says, 'I will return to my house from which I came.' And when it comes, it finds the house empty, swept, and put in order. Then it goes and brings with it seven other **spirits** more **evil** than itself, and they enter and dwell there, and the last state of that person is worse than the first. So also will it be with this evil generation." (Matt 12:43–45; compare Luke 11:24–26)

While the overlap of the terms and phrases is transparent, that the terms are interchanged does not mean that "unclean spirits" has no special nuance. Wahlen has marshaled evidence that suggests "unclean spirits" was used in Second Temple Judaism specifically to draw attention to the origin of these evil spirits as the result of an unnatural mixture and the subsequent emergence from (and contact with) the corpses of the dead Nephilim. These two concepts are at the heart of much of the Levitical uncleanness legislation. Wahlen demonstrates that the description of demons as "unclean" is not about associating demons with ritual impurity or the transmission of such impurity. It is true (see the ensuing discussion in this chapter) that Second Temple Jews associated the spawn of the fallen Watchers with disease, but it is noteworthy that these disembodied spirits of the Nephilim are the focus of that belief.

One of the more puzzling features of early Christian attitudes toward purity is the Gospels' frequent reference to spirits as impure. The absence of similar language in Graeco-Roman literature up through the second century C.E. is striking. ... References to impure spirits in *4QIncantation* and to "unclean demons" in *Jubilees* are clearly based on the Watcher myth of *1 Enoch*, whereby evil spirits proceeded from dead bodies of the fallen giants, who were born as a result of the miscegenation of angels with women. These spirits are called unclean in analogy to the similar classification of unclean animals: an unnatural combination of heavenly and earthly beings, they represent an anomalous mixture of categories. ... Evil spirits, in many Jewish sources, ultimately trace their origins to the defiling union of these heavenly beings with women. Like unclean animals, these "impure spirits" represent an anomalous mixture of categories.[6]

That the phrase "unclean spirit" is found in the New Testament is clear evidence that New Testament writers stood firmly in the Second Temple Jewish tradition regarding the origin of demons. The idea is isolated to Second Temple Judaism and the New Testament before the second century AD.

With respect to the phrase "evil spirit" some elaboration is also in order. As was the case in the Old Testament, there is ambiguity with respect to the phrase "evil spirit" in certain instances in the New Testament. This issue is related to how some modern scholars dismiss the idea of evil spirits. Readers will recall our earlier notes about Old Testament texts that describe "an evil spirit" being sent by God to trouble Saul (1 Sam 16:14–16; 18:10–11) and sow discord or confusion among people (Judg 9:22–23; Isa 19:13–14; 37:5–7). We saw that the term translated "evil" in this phrase (lemma: *rā'*) often does not speak of moral disposition or character, but something contemptible (Gen 41:20, 27; Jer 24:2, 3, 8; 49:23; Ps 112:7; Deut 22:14, 19; Neh 6:13) or harmful (Gen 19:19; Deut 7:15; 28:35, 59). Thus by "evil spirit" the writer may mean that God was the source of an undesirable mental affliction or psychological disposition. As it relates to these and other Gospel passages, the "evil spirit" may therefore be some sort of physical malady or mental illness. Indeed, some of the passages seem to designate "evil spirits" as a sickness:[7]

---

6. Clinton Wahlen, *Jesus and the Impurity of Spirits in the Synoptic Gospels* (Tübingen: Mohr Siebeck, 2004), 1, 66–67, 170.

7. The same connection is found outside the Gospels (e.g., Acts 8:7; 19:12).

And he called to him his twelve disciples and gave them authority over unclean spirits, to cast them out, and to heal every disease and every affliction. (Matt 10:1)

In that hour he healed many people of diseases and plagues and evil spirits, and on many who were blind he bestowed sight. (Luke 7:21)

And he came down with them and stood on a level place, with a great crowd of his disciples and a great multitude of people from all Judea and Jerusalem and the seacoast of Tyre and Sidon, who came to hear him and to be healed of their diseases. And those who were troubled with unclean spirits were cured. (Luke 6:17–18)

The clear connection between these phrases and diseases is among the reasons why many modern scholars argue against the reality of demons. They charge that in the context of the primitive medical knowledge of the first century AD, illnesses of the body and mind were misidentified as the work of demonic entities. This presumption may be workable in some passages, but as Dunn and Twelftree observe, New Testament writers did not attribute all illnesses to demons: "There were well-known maladies like fever, leprosy and paralysis which it was not thought necessary to attribute directly either to Satan or to demons (Mark 1:29–31, 40–4, 2:1–12; cf. Mark 4:19)."[8] Certain New Testament descriptions of evil spirits unmistakably point to an intelligent, conscious spirit entity.[9] For example, certain passages straightforwardly present Jesus in an adversarial stance and in conversation with an evil/unclean spirit, with no hint that Jesus was "playing along" with a deluded, mentally ill individual who only thought he was possessed:[10]

And immediately there was in their synagogue a man with an unclean spirit. And he cried out, "What have you to do with us, Jesus of

---

8. James D. G. Dunn and Graham H. Twelftree, "Demon-Possession and Exorcism in the New Testament," *Churchman* 94 (1980): 217.

9. Aside from the possession episodes noted here, evil/unclean spirits are at times associated with stock vocabulary for demons in Second Temple thought. In Matt 12:43 we read that "when the unclean spirit has gone out of a person, it passes through waterless places seeking rest, but finds none." This is an unmistakable association of demons with the familiar desert wilderness motif.

10. The point here is that words are exchanged between Jesus and the evil/unclean spirit(s). Passages like Mark 9:25 that have Jesus "rebuking" a "mute and deaf" spirit may represent the healing of mere physical conditions, though they can certainly be read otherwise. Instances where words are exchanged do not present the former possibility.

Nazareth? Have you come to destroy us? I know who you are—the Holy One of God." But Jesus rebuked him, saying, "Be silent, and come out of him!" And the unclean spirit, convulsing him and crying out with a loud voice, came out of him. And they were all amazed, so that they questioned among themselves, saying, "What is this? A new teaching with authority! He commands even the unclean spirits, and they obey him." (Mark 1:23–27)

And whenever the unclean spirits saw him, they fell down before him and cried out, "You are the Son of God." And he strictly ordered them not to make him known. (Mark 3:11–12)

The episode with Legion, the cluster of demons possessing the man in the country of the Gerasenes (Mark 5:1), simply cannot be considered a disease. A mental or physical illness does not beg to be transported into a herd of swine nor can it jump from a human into the herd (Mark 5:6–13).[11] This infamous encounter along with others transcends the sorts of diseases and pathologies that are diagnosed and treated medically in today's world.

DEMONIC POSSESSION AND EXORCISM

While certain references to demons ("evil spirits") in the Gospels clearly refer to spiritual entities, the connection between demons and illness is an important one. It is, in certain respects, fundamental to the notion of demonic possession and exorcism. It is in fact another element of a secure conceptual bridge between the demons described as the disembodied spirits of the Watchers and the demons of the Gospels.[12]

---

11. The supernatural nature of the encounter with Legion is also noteworthy for its cosmic-geographical elements. See the next chapter.

12. Our emphasis in this chapter is the Synoptic Gospels. The incident in Acts 16 is also part of this matrix of ideas. In that chapter, Paul delivers a girl from "a spirit of divination" (*pneuma pythōna*). The term translated "divination" is the lemma *pythōn*, an oracular spirit known in the Greco-Roman world. In ancient Greek literature, Python was the serpent or dragon that guarded the shrine of Delphi. The dragon Python was defeated by the god Apollo who then took possession of the oracle at Delphi. In later sources, Python is associated with the oracular spirit of the shrine and the young girl who channeled the oracles of Apollo was called the Pythia. Concerning Acts 16, van Henten notes that, "The passage can be interpreted against the background of the semantic development of *Pythōn*. The Delphic dragon himself became a mantic animal ... and lent his name to predicting demons." See J. W. van Henten, "Python," *DDD* 670. See also J. Fontenrose, *Python: A Study of Delphic Myth and Its Origins* (Berkeley, CA: University of California Press, 1959). The

To discern this link, we must return briefly to the Second Temple Jewish work Jubilees. Recall that, in Jubilees 10:1–13, Satan (Mastema) asked God that a tenth of the demons, the offspring of the Watchers, be allowed to escape imprisonment in the abyss so that they might serve him in afflicting humanity. The passage begins as a prayer of Noah:

> [O Lord] you know that which your Watchers, the fathers of these spirits, did in my days and also these spirits who are alive. Shut them up and take them to the place of judgment. And do not let them cause corruption among the sons of your servant, O my God, because they are cruel and were created to destroy. And let them not rule over the spirits of the living because you alone know their judgment, and do not let them have power over the children of the righteous henceforth and forever. (Jub 10:4–6a)[13]

God begins to answer the prayer by instructing the archangels but then is interrupted. God responds by instructing the archangels to bind the evil spirits but is then approached by their lord with a request:

> And the LORD our God spoke to us [the archangels] so that we might bind all of them. And the chief of the spirits, Mastema, came and he said, "O Lord, Creator, leave some of them before me, and let them obey my voice. And let them do everything which I tell them, because if some of them are not left for me, I will not be able to exercise the authority of my will among the children of men because they are (intended) to corrupt and lead astray before my judgment because the evil of the sons of men is great." And he said, "Let a tenth of them remain before him, but let nine parts go down into the place of judgment." (Jub 10:6b–9)[14]

---

connection to Second Temple "unclean spirits" lies in the fact that, as detailed in earlier chapters of our study, the demons that are the disembodied spirits of the Nephilim were Watcher-spirits and thereby associated with forbidden knowledge (divination) and idolatry. Wahlen comments: "Evil spirits, in many Jewish sources, ultimately trace their origins to the defiling union of these heavenly beings with women. Like unclean animals, these 'impure spirits' represent an anomalous mixture of categories. In 1 Enoch they are linked with idolatry. ... The concerns about apostasy which are found in these books receive greater emphasis and a narrower focus in some of the sectarian documents from Qumran. Another recurrent theme in the literature we examined is the potential which these spirits possess for leading people into impure practices such as idolatry, fornication, and murder or for causing physical harm." See Wahlen, *Jesus and the Impurity of Spirits*, 170.

13. *OTP*, 2:76.
14. Ibid.

Note Mastema's request to leave some of the demons to serve him. God grants Mastema's request, leaving a tenth of the demons to serve him. What ensues is narrated by an archangel:

> And we acted in accord with all of his words. All of the evil ones, who were cruel, we bound in the place of judgment, but a tenth of them we let remain so that they might be subject to Satan upon the earth. And the healing of all their illnesses together with their seductions we told Noah so that he might heal by means of herbs of the earth. And Noah wrote everything in a book just as we taught him according to every kind of healing. And the evil spirits were restrained from following the sons of Noah. (Jub 10:11–13)[15]

Mastema required assistance in his work of corrupting and afflicting humanity. The key item to observe is the reference to healing (Jub 10:13). VanderKam explains, "One way the spirits harmed humans was by causing diseases; so God ordered the angels to teach Noah medicines to counteract their influence."[16] The Second Temple Jewish mind saw a clear connection between illness and demonic activity. This consequentially blurred the line between healing and exorcism and, as we have seen, the overlap is discernible in the Gospels. This link is also discernible in the ways Second Temple writers describe both possession and exorcism. Graham Twelftree, a New Testament scholar who has focused on exorcism, writes:

> Josephus believed that people could be possessed or "overtaken" (*lambanomenos*) by demons causing frenzy (*J.W.* 3.485; 7.120, 389), suffocation and strangling (*Ant.* 6.166). Philo believed that invisible living beings hovered in the air, and that evil spirits among them could be breathed in, or might take over, fill or descend into a person, causing disastrous pestilences. (Philo *Gig.* 6–31)[17]

The fact that physical and mental disease were believed to have been closely associated by many Second Temple–period Jews helps us to understand exorcisms performed before and alongside those of Jesus and the apostles. Specifically, the exorcisms of various ancient sources may

---

15. Ibid.
16. VanderKam, *The Book of Jubilees*, 128.
17. Twelftree, "Demon, Devil, Satan," 165.

reflect no more than healing without a true evil spirit presence. Nevertheless, exorcisms performed in the Jewish community before the arrival of Jesus included an appeal to the power of God.[18] It is likely that New Testament episodes describing exorcism include both situations. Dunn and Twelftree observe:

> Belief in demon-possession and of relief through exorcism was widespread in the ancient world. For example, the popular tale of Tobit, which would have been familiar to Jesus and his contemporaries, relates the expulsion of a demon from Tobias's bride (Tobit 6–8). In the Genesis Apocryphon, one of the Dead Sea Scrolls, Abraham exorcises Pharaoh through prayer and the laying on of hands (1QGA 20). Josephus, the Jewish historian of the second half of the first century AD, relates how he saw a Jew, Eleazar, casting out a demon before the Emperor Vespasian (*Antiquities* 8:45–9). Beyond these we need simply mention the magical papyri which contain traditional incantations, spells and potions for controlling demons and which no doubt reflect beliefs and practices current at the time of Jesus and the Evangelists. We are not surprised when this broader picture is specifically confirmed by the New Testament itself: Matthew 12:27/ Luke 11:19 alludes to Jewish exorcists; Mark 9:38f tells of an exorcist who used Jesus' name (a practice to which Jesus apparently did not object); and Acts 19:13–19 relates the fascinating account of the itinerant Jewish exorcists, the seven sons of a Jewish high-priest named Sceva. For the first Christians to present Jesus as an exorcist, therefore, would have raised no eyebrows among his hearers. The exorcist, not least the Jewish exorcist, was a familiar figure in the ancient world.[19]

---

18. Many modern Christians consider a true exorcism impossible without the invocation of the name of Jesus and the power of the Holy Spirit. As the ensuing discussion notes, ancient episodes referred to as demonic possession and exorcism may not have involved an evil spirit at all (i.e., the problem was medical), thus alleviating the apparent theological difficulty. Nevertheless, the assumption behind such a concern—that the Holy Spirit could not have been present when the name of the God of Israel (or an Old Testament figure thought to have power over demons) was invoked—is not coherent. There is no theological or textual reason to conclude that the Spirit's power in such situations was inoperative prior to the ministry of Jesus. Jews who appealed to the God who is superior to the powers of darkness were in fact depending on that power, despite whatever odd ritual may have accompanied the appeal. It is not unreasonable to think God in his providence would occasionally honor such an appeal. The reality is, though, given the prevalence of the connection between demons and disease in the textual material we have, it is difficult to parse many such episodes.

19. Dunn and Twelftree, "Demon-Possession and Exorcism," 210–11.

The reference in the above to "incantations, spells and potions for controlling demons" is telling, for it makes possible that situations perceived as involving an evil spirit may have been simply medical. "Potions," once administered, would be the actual healing agent. Since they were accompanied by "incantations" and "spells," the perception among people would have been that spiritual powers were being confronted and defeated, though that would not have been the case.

The Synoptic Gospels portray Jesus as a powerful healer and true exorcist.[20] A careful study of Jesus' confrontations with demons reveals both similarities to exorcism techniques found in sources outside the New Testament and insightful differences.

Regarding the similarities, Twelftree and Dunn note, "The actual exorcism stories themselves can be readily paralleled at several points in their form and content."[21] Demons addressing the exorcist (e.g., Mark 1:24; 5:7), verbal demands made of demons (Mark 1:25; 5:9; 9:25; "Come out of him!"; "What is your name?"), and demons being sent from a person into some other object (a herd of pigs; Mark 5:10–13) are all known outside the New Testament.[22]

---

20. Twelftree notes that some scholars have expressed doubt that Jesus was truly an exorcist. This is at least in part apparently motivated by the wish to see Jesus as little more than a wise man. Twelftree has dealt with this issue in detail, both in the sources cited previously in our study and in his book-length studies: *Jesus the Exorcist: A Contribution to the Study of the Historical Jesus* (Eugene, OR: Wipf & Stock, 2011) and *In the Name of Jesus: Exorcism among Early Christians* (Grand Rapids: Baker, 2007). Twelftree establishes the source-critical validity of the Gospel accounts of exorcism, comparisons of techniques known from extrabiblical exorcism texts, and parallels with external sources. With respect to the last item, Twelftree ("Demon, Devil, Satan," 166) notes extrabiblical evidence from Greek magical papyri for "the now-famous incantation intended for use by exorcists: 'I adjure you by the god of the Hebrews, Jesu, …' (*PGM* IV.3019–3020)." Note that *PGM* stands for *Papyri Graecae Magicae* and refers to a Greek papyri collection; see H. D. Betz, ed., *The Greek Magical Papyri in Translation, including the Demotic Spells*, 2nd ed. (Chicago: University of Chicago Press, 1996). The fact that rabbinic literature forbids healing in the name of Jesus is also suggestive that Jesus was remembered as a healer in rabbinic tradition (see t. Hullin 2:22–23; y. Shabbat 14.4.14d; y. Avodah Zarah 2:2.40d–41a; b. Avodah Zarah 27b; Twelftree, "Demon, Devil, Satan," 166).

21. Dunn and Twelftree, "Demon-Possession and Exorcism," 212.

22. Dunn and Twelftree provide some instances: "The unclean spirit addresses Jesus: Mark 1:24, 'What have you to do with us, Jesus of Nazareth? Have you come to destroy us? I know who you are, the Holy One of God'; 5:7, 'What have you to do with me, Jesus, Son of the Most High God? I adjure you by God, do not torment me.' That the demon speaks in such cases was well known, as Lucian of Samosata (second century AD) shows: 'The patient himself is silent, but the spirit answers in Greek or in a language of whatever foreign country he comes from' (*Lover of Lies* 16; cf. Acts 19:15, 'Jesus I know and Paul I know; but who are you?'; Philostratus, *Life of Apollonius* 3:38, 4:20). Jesus addresses the unclean spirit: Mark 1:25, 'Be silent, and come out of him'; 5:9, 'What is your name?'; 9:25, 'You dumb and deaf spirit, I command you, come out of him and never enter him again.' The command, 'Come out (of him)', is again common in other exorcism formulae (cf. Philostratus, *Life* 4:20; Lucian,

The divergences from external exorcism practices and texts serve to highlight the special nature of Jesus as the Son of God. Scholars have taken note that, unlike contemporary exorcists, Jesus did not use any device as part of an exorcism, "a feature common to many other exorcists' technique."[23] Such "tools" for exorcism included incense, potions, rings, bowls of water, amulets, ashes, and various spices.[24] Jesus also never prayed in conjunction with an exorcism nor did he invoke a higher power to bind a demon before commanding it to come out of a person. In short, Jesus never appealed to a higher power to cast out a demon, unlike the common procedure in other exorcism texts. The power to command evil spirits resided within him as God incarnate, the Son of the Most High.[25]

The portrayal of Jesus as needing no aid and seeking no higher power in exorcisms is arguably the most significant theological point to be made in these accounts. In conjunction with this portrayal, the unique

---

Lies 11, 16; PGM [Papyri Graecae Magicae] IV:3013). Similarly, the phrase 'I command you' is familiar in magical incantations seeking to control demons and gods (e.g. PGM I:253, 324; II:43–55; IV:3080; VII:331; XII:171), and the phrase 'Never enter him again' can be paralleled in Josephus, *Antiquities* 8:47 and Philostratus, *Life* 4:20. So, too, examples of an exorcist's request for the name of the demon as a way of gaining control over the demon can also be cited (PGM I:162; IV:3037). In Mark 5 we have the awkward episode in which the demons are given leave to go into a herd of pigs, who then rush down the slope into the lake and drown (5:10–13). This might have been understood as providing confirmation that the demons had left the man, a proof of cure effected—as in Josephus where the cure is proved by the demon disturbing a bowl of water *(Antiquities* 8:48), or in Philostratus when a statue is knocked over *(Life* 4:20). But more likely it would be seen in the light of the ancient idea that in exorcism it was necessary to make the spirit pass from the person into some object (a pebble, a piece of wood) which could then be thrown away." See Dunn and Twelftree, "Demon-Possession and Exorcism," 212.

23. Twelftree, "Demon, Devil, Satan," 167.

24. Examples include burning incense (Tobit 8:3); using medicine (Jub 10:10, 12); use of a finger ring and bowl of water (Josephus, *Ant.* 8.46–49). The Babylonian Talmud and the Greek Magical Papyri include references to amulets, rings, and many natural substances like ashes, branches, and spices. Twelftree notes, "The only thing near a mechanical aid [in Jesus' exorcisms] was the use of the herd of pigs. However, the pigs were not used to exorcise the demons but to provide a habitat for the expelled demons." See Twelftree, "Demon, Devil, Satan," 167.

25. Twelftree elaborates on the contrasts between Jesus and other exorcists in Greco-Roman and rabbinic sources. One significant contrast is that Jesus never calls on the authority of another in his exorcisms. For example, an exorcist might invoke a powerful name like Solomon, but the New Testament reports the sons of Sceva (Acts 19:13) and others trying to cast out demons in *Jesus'* name (Mark 9:38–39; Luke 9:49–50; compare Luke 10:17). Jesus does not even explicitly call on the "Spirit of God," identified as the source of his power over demons in Matt 12:28, in performing exorcisms. Twelftree notes, "Like some of the rabbis (*b. Me῾il.* 17b) and Apollonius (Philostratus *Vit. Ap.* 4.20), Jesus appeared to rely on his own charismatic personal force to subdue and expel the demons." Jesus also never used the usual verb for commanding a demon (*horkizō*; see *PGM* I, 345; Acts 19:13). The key point is that Jesus never acknowledged or appealed to any authority outside of himself, not even through prayer. See Twelftree, "Demon, Devil, Satan," 167–68.

perspective (or lack thereof) of the Gospel of John puts forth the same point. While the Synoptic Gospels have much to say about Jesus and his power over demons, the Gospel of John says nothing about Jesus being an exorcist.

Scholars have offered various explanations for this omission.[26] The most coherent derive from John's unique emphasis among the Gospels on miracles and the centrality of the cross, as opposed to the kingdom of God. As Twelftree notes, "In the Synoptic Gospels the defeat of Satan is linked with Jesus' exorcisms. In John the defeat of Satan is linked with the cross (Jn 14:30; 16:11)."[27] Another scholar elaborates on that point:

> In the Synoptics Jesus' miracles are closely related to his proclamation of the advent of the kingdom of God. … Thus the Synoptists regarded Jesus' miracles, perhaps especially his exorcisms (never mentioned in the Fourth Gospel), as one mode of God's assertion of his royal power, so that while the kingdom in its fullness still lies in the future, it has already become a reality in Jesus' words and works. … Miracle plays a dominant role in the Fourth Gospel, and especially in this domain the distinctive Johannine perspective becomes evident. Jesus' miracles, for example, are set within the context of the one grand miracle, the incarnation of the Logos (Jn 1:14). Thus the Fourth Gospel contains no birth narratives, but in its prologue directs the reader all the way back to the preincarnate Son. … Whereas in the Synoptics the *dynameis* ["mighty deeds"] are closely correlated with the kingdom of God, proclaimed and proleptically established in Jesus' words and deeds, the Johannine *sēmeia* ["signs"] are said to evoke faith in Jesus as the Christ, the Son of God (Jn 20:30–31). … "Signs" are precisely what the Johannine miracles are, for in very concrete, physical ways they point to the deep and crucial truth about Jesus (and God), namely, that he is the absolutely unique Son of God who descended from heaven to reveal the Father and through whose "lifting up" on the cross, resurrection and return to the Father believers receive the Holy Spirit and thus eternal life. The signs, in other words, point to the present glory of the exclusive mediator of eschatological salvation

---

26. See Twelftree, "Demon, Devil, Satan," 171; Dunn and Twelftree, "Demon-Possession and Exorcism," 220–21.

27. Twelftree, "Demon, Devil, Satan," 171.

and also portend the salvation to be enjoyed by the beneficiaries of the completion of his messianic work (cf. Jn 7:37–39).[28]

THE MESSIAH AS EXORCIST?

In the preceding chapter we saw that the expulsion of demons was linked to the inauguration of the kingdom of God. Despite the fact that there are no exorcisms in the Old Testament nor any explicit statement that the Messiah would have power to cast out demons, Jews who witnessed or heard about Jesus' power over demons did not see it at odds with other elements of the messianic profile. Given the apparent silence of the Old Testament on such things, why did exorcism fit the messianic profile? We can only review a portion of the primary source material relevant to answering this question, which is dense. With reference to the parable of the strong man (Matt 12:29 and parallels), Twelftree notes, "In pre-Christian literature there is the expectation that the Messiah would do battle with Satan, but Jesus is the first to make a specific connection between the relatively ordinary events of exorcism and the defeat of Satan, between exorcism and eschatology."[29]

Twelftree alludes to "pre-Christian literature" but does not unpack the issue. His connection with eschatology can be construed as having something to do with the Messiah as king, though he doesn't develop that relationship—which is the key to the coherence of expecting the Messiah, the son of David, to have power over demons. Duling helps us frame the issue:

A comprehensive view of the Son of David in the New Testament requires facing the following problem: on the one hand, Davidic quotations, metaphors, and the descent theme are derived from the Old Testament royal tradition as it is channeled through Jewish texts; on the other, the title Son of David is found only in the synoptic

---

28. B. L. Blackburn, "Miracles and Miracle Stories," *Dictionary of Jesus and the Gospels*, ed. Joel B. Green and Scot McKnight (Downers Grove, IL: InterVarsity Press, 1992), 550, 555.

29. Twelftree, "Demon, Devil, Satan," 168. Twelftree acknowledges the tension in the New Testament between Jesus' evident power over Satan and Satan's continuing power and influence. He states, "This tension is resolved in the light of Isaiah 24:21–22 and 1 *Enoch* 10:4–6 where the defeat of Satan or evil is expected to take place in two stages. Thus, Jesus probably believed that his exorcisms were the first stage of the binding of Satan and the final defeat would take place in the final judgment (Mt 13:30)" (Ibid.).

gospels and is associated primarily with a figure who is so addressed by people in need of exorcism or healing. The usual solution to this problem in works on Christology is to say that a) miracle working is not associated with the Jewish royal Messiah in general or the Son of David in particular in contemporaneous Jewish literature, and b) it is early Christian tradition and/or redaction which has transformed the traditional royal conception and linked it with miracle working.[30]

Duling's explication of the issue focuses on several Second Temple–period Jewish texts that identify Solomon (the "Son of David") as an exorcist, namely, the Testament of Solomon and several Dead Sea Scrolls.[31] In another publication, Duling observes, "The evidence for the Solomonic magical tradition is rather extensive."[32] The Testament of Solomon is a late text, dated between the first and third centuries AD.[33] For our purposes, the earlier material on which its writer drew for his understanding of Solomon as an exorcist is more important. The depiction of Solomon as an exorcist derives from interpretations of 1 Kings 4:29–34 (Heb 5:9–14), which describe Solomon's wisdom and his speaking of thousands of proverbs and songs, including sharing his wisdom about plants and animals. Duling observes that a "number of ancient writers drew on this text for their view of Solomon's magical knowledge, and a few scholars about the turn of the century thought it might be implied. Current OT scholarship, however, does not make this connection."[34]

Elements of this passage (1 Kgs 5:9–14) took on special meaning in light of the Septuagint. First Kings 4:33 records, "[Solomon] spoke of trees, from the cedar that is in Lebanon to the hyssop that grows out of the wall. He spoke also of beasts, and of birds, and of reptiles, and of fish."

---

30. Dennis C. Duling, "Solomon, Exorcism, and the Son of David," *HTR* 68.3/4 (1975): 235. The other major study in English to which Duling points readers is Loren Fisher, "Can This Be the Son of David?" in *Jesus and the Historian: Written in Honor of Ernest Cadman Colwell*, ed. F. T. Trotter (Philadelphia: Westminster, 1968), 82–97.

31. Key studies of the Testament of Solomon include: F. C. Conybeare, "The Testament of Solomon," *Jewish Quarterly Review* 11 (1898–1899): 1–45; C. C. McCown, "The Christian Tradition as to the Magical Wisdom of Solomon," *The Journal of the Palestinian Oriental Society* 2/1 (1922): 1–24.

32. Dennis C. Duling, "Solomon, Testament of," *ABD* 6:118. The additional ancient sources Duling lists for the Solomonic magical tradition include: 11QApocryphal Psalms; Pseudo-Philo, LAB 60; b. Gittin 68ab; Exodus Rabbah 52.4; Midrash Song of Songs 1.1, 5; Numbers Rabbah 11.3; Pesiqta Rabbati 6.7; b. Megillah 11b; Pesiqta of Rab Kahana; Targum of Esther II; and the Nag Hammadi Codex II,5:107,3; V,5:78,30 and 79,3; VII,2:63,11; IX,3:70,6, 27.

33. D. C. Duling, "Testament of Solomon: A New Translation and Introduction," in *OTP*, 1:940–42.

34. Duling, "Solomon, Exorcism, and the Son of David," 237.

The items in this description were commonly associated with magical practices in Hellenistic thought.[35] Further, the Septuagint expanded on the number of Solomon's "songs," crediting him with 5,000 instead of 1,005, and referred to them as "odes" (Greek: *ōdai*, LXX 5:12). Duling and other scholars have noted the close similarity of this term with a common Greek term for "incantations" (*epōdai*) that could have contributed to the notion that Solomon was an exorcist. The Josephus passage reads as follows:

(42) Now the sagacity and wisdom which God had bestowed upon Solomon was so great, that he exceeded the ancients, insomuch that he was no way inferior to the Egyptians, who are said to have been beyond all men in understanding; nay, indeed, it is evident that their sagacity was very much inferior to that of the king's. (43) He also excelled and distinguished himself in wisdom above those who were most eminent among the Hebrews at that time for shrewdness: those I mean were Ethan, and Heman, and Chalcol, and Darda, the sons of Mahol. (44) He also composed books of odes and songs, a thousand and five; of parables and similitudes, three thousand; for he spake a parable upon every sort of tree, from the hyssop to the cedar; and in like manner also about beasts, about all sorts of living creatures, whether upon the earth, or in the seas, or in the air; for he was not unacquainted with any of their natures, nor omitted inquiries about them, but described them all like a philosopher, and demonstrated his exquisite knowledge of their several properties. (45) God also enabled him to learn that skill which expels demons, which is a science useful and Sanative to men. He composed such incantations also by which distempers are alleviated. And he left behind him the manner of using exorcisms, by which they drive away demons, so that they never return, (46) and this method of cure is of great force unto this day; for I have seen a certain man of my own country whose name was Eleazar, releasing people that were demoniacal in the presence of Vespasian, and his sons, and his captains, and the whole multitude of his soldiers. The manner of the cure was this:—(47) He put a ring that had a root of one of those sorts mentioned by Solomon to the nostrils of the demoniac, after which he drew out the demon

---

35. Duling, "Solomon, Testament of," 118.

through his nostrils; and when the man fell down immediately, he abjured him to return into him no more, making still mention of Solomon, and reciting the incantations which he composed. (Josephus, *Ant.* 8.2.5.42–47 [Whiston])

Another Second Temple–period text that connects Solomon with power over demons is the Wisdom of Solomon. It is important to realize that this book was included in the Septuagint, the primary Old Testament source for New Testament writers. In Wisdom of Solomon 7, Solomon, the speaker, claims knowledge of astrology, "powers of roots," and "forces of spirits":

¹Even I am certainly a mortal the same as everyone,
and offspring of the first-formed earthborn;
and I was shaped into flesh in my mother's belly
²in ten months' time, established in blood
from the seed of a man and the pleasure of coming together in sleep.
³And when I was born, I drew in the common air
and fell upon the same earth,
crying with my first sound the same as everyone.
⁴I was nursed in baby clothes and with care.
⁵For no king had any different beginning of existence;
⁶but there is one entrance into life for all and an identical exit.
⁷Because of this I prayed, and understanding was given to me;
I called upon God, and the spirit of wisdom came to me.

[…]

¹⁷For he gave me truthful knowledge of the things that are,
to see the structure of the world and the operation of the elements,
¹⁸the beginning and ending and middle of times,
the changes of cycles and changes of the seasons,
¹⁹the cycles of the year and the positions of stars,
²⁰the nature of animals and the wrath of beasts,
the forces of spirits and the reasonings of humans,
the varieties of plants and the powers of roots.
²¹And I know whatever is hidden and visible,
²²for the artisan of all teaches me wisdom.

(Wisdom of Solomon 7:1–5, 17–22 LES)

Scholars have debated the meaning of the language of verse 20, that Solomon had been given knowledge by God of "the forces of spirits." There are two options: powerful winds or powerful spirit beings. One expert on the Wisdom of Solomon and Second Temple Judaism argues cogently for the latter, bringing the context of the Qumran texts to bear on the matter:

> *The violent force of spirits. pneumatōn bias* may mean either the violent force of winds or of spirits. For the former translation, cf. Philo *Op.* 58 (*nēnemias kai bias pneumatōn*). ... A passage in 1QH, 1.9–11, may help to bridge the two translations: "Thou hast created all the spirits [and hast established a statute] and law for all their works ... the mighty winds (*rûḥôt ʿōz*) according to their laws before they became angels [of holiness] and eternal spirits in their dominions." Cf. Jub 2:2: "the angels of the spirit of the winds" (*angeloi pneumatōn pneontōn, FPG:* 71); "[and the angels] of all the spirits of his creatures (*pantōn tōn pneumatōn tōn ktismatōn autou*) which are in the heavens and on the earth" (*FPG:* 72); 1 Enoch 60:12–22; 41:3*ff*; 18:1–5; 76:1–14; 15:4: *kai pneumata zōnta aiōnia (FPG:* 29); Ps 104:4; Sir 39:28: "There are spirits (*pneumata*) that are created for vengeance. ... Fire and hail, and famine, and death ...";, 1Qap Gen 20:20: "for a spirit (*ruḥāʾ*) smote all of them."[36]

The point is that in Second Temple Jewish thinking, the discussion of winds versus spirits was not a firm intellectual divide. The two were associated, and so it is nigh unto impossible to argue that the author of Wisdom of Solomon would not have had spirit beings in view.

One specific Qumran text that ties the prevalent Solomonic exorcist tradition back to David is 11QPsaᵃ (11Q5):

2 [BLANK] And David, son of Jesse, was wise, and a light like the light of the sun, /and/ learned,

3 [BLANK] and perfect in all his paths before God and men. And

4 [BLANK] YHWH gave him a discerning and enlightened spirit. And he wrote psalms:

---

36. David Winston, *The Wisdom of Solomon: A New Translation with Introduction and Commentary* (AYB; New Haven, CT: Yale University Press, 1979), 175.

5 three thousand six hundred; and songs to be sung before the altar
    over the perpetual

[...]

9 And all the songs which he spoke were four hundred and forty-six.
    And songs
10 to perform over the possessed: four. The total was four thousand
    and fifty.
11 All these he spoke through (the spirit of) prophecy which had been
    given to him from before the Most High. (11Q5 27.2–5, 9–11)[37]

Lines 9–10 assert that David wrote psalms for "the possessed." The
Hebrew behind this translation reads *hpgw ʿym*, a Qal passive participle
of the lemma *pgʿ* (literally, "the assaulted"). This terminology was used in
the rabbinic community of Psalm 91, considered "a song for the stricken"
and "a song for demons." Interestingly, a version of Psalm 91 curiously
appears among the *apocryphal* psalms of Cave 11, a collection of psalms
whose "apparent purpose [is] the exorcism of demons."[38] This is not an
arbitrary judgment, for the rabbis considered Psalm 91 to be a "song
referring to evil spirits" and a "song for demons."[39] This should not be a
surprise, given our study of the terminology for evil spirits in chapter 1.
The evil spirits *deber* ("pestilence") and *qeṭeb* ("destruction") are prominent in that psalm.

While the Old Testament makes no explicit point that the Messiah
would have power over demons, Second Temple Jewish literature certainly pointed readers in that direction. Like Solomon, the Messiah would
be the son of David. Solomon's glory and wisdom were archetypal reference points for the messianic profile, and the Septuagint—the source for
most of the New Testament writers' appeals to the Old Testament—cast
Solomon as an exorcist. Those who witnessed or heard about the exorcisms of Jesus as well as early readers of the New Testament would have
expected this role for the Messiah.

---

37. Translation from Garcia-Martinez and Tigchelaar, *Dead Sea Scrolls Study Edition*, 2:1179.
38. Duling, "Solomon, Exorcism, and the Son of David," 239.
39. Ibid., 239. Rabbinic passages referring to Ps 91 as the "song for the stricken/evil spirits/the
Demons" include b. Shabbat 15b; y. Shabbat 6:8b; and y. Erubin 10:26c.

SUMMARY

The portrayal of demons ("evil spirits"; "unclean spirits") in the Gospels is quite consistent with Second Temple Jewish literature and thought. There is no reason to divorce New Testament demonology from this context, including the Watchers tradition. This is no surprise, given what we read in epistles like 2 Peter and Jude and the discernible connections to the Watchers tradition elsewhere in the New Testament.[40] For New Testament writers, the defeat of evil spirits was firmly linked to the appearance of the Messiah to inaugurate his kingdom, as well as his death and resurrection. As we will see in the next chapter, the resurrection and ascension are the centerpiece of the New Testament understanding of the victory over other supernatural rebels—the gods of the nations from the Deuteronomy 32/Psalm 82 worldview of the Old Testament.

---

40. For a survey of how threads of the Watchers traditions can be found in various places in the New Testament, see Heiser, *Reversing Hermon*.

CHAPTER 11

The Ruling Powers—
Their Delegitimization and Destiny

THE TWO PREVIOUS CHAPTERS FOCUSED ON HOW NEW TESTAMENT writers expressed their understanding of the original supernatural rebel of Eden and the transgression of the sons of God (i.e., the "Watchers") against the backdrop of Second Temple Jewish thought. We now turn to New Testament theology that draws upon the circumstances of the third supernatural rebellion discerned from the Old Testament—the corruption and treachery of the sons of God allotted to the nations at Babel.

In earlier chapters we noted that Second Temple authors affirmed the cosmic-geographical rule of the nations by powers of darkness and creatively expressed its threat against the people of God. As Hannah has observed, the "concept that certain angels served as guardians or patrons of peoples or nations played a role in the angelology of second temple Judaism."[1] As we have seen, this notion was a significant element of Second Temple views about supernatural beings. This concept is just as valid for the New Testament's theology of the powers of darkness.

---

1. Hannah, "Guardian Angels and Angelic National Patrons," 413.

NEW TESTAMENT COSMIC GEOGRAPHY:
Holy and Unholy Ground

Readers familiar with some of my earlier books will know this is a well-worn path in my writing.[2] This chapter will summarize points I have elaborated upon elsewhere and introduce new material.

In chapter 9 we briefly looked at the temptation of Jesus by the devil in the desert wilderness (Matt 4:1–11) and saw how it was in concert with Second Temple Jewish sources in regard to the association of the desert wilderness with evil spirits and their leader. Prior to the arrival of his people in Canaan and the erection of a temple, wherever Yahweh was with his people was holy ground. Hostile supernatural forces occupied the territory beyond the borders of the Israelite camp. The presence of Yahweh with his chosen people defined cosmic geography even before Israel inherited its promised land.

The Day of Atonement ritual (Lev 16) and its goat "for Azazel" illustrated (and reinforced) the idea. Outside the camp was the realm of death, not life, the latter of which was associated with the presence of God. Thus sacrificial remains were taken outside the camp, an idea that prompts the writer of the book of Hebrews to apply Leviticus 16 and its cosmic geography to the crucifixion (Heb 13:10–13). Most commentators on this passage focus on the consumption of sacrifices and the disposition of remains in light of Leviticus 4. However, some have noticed that the Azazel material plays a role here:

> In the ritual of the day of Atonement in chapter 16, it should be noted that in verses 26, 28 the same rule on defilement and purification is applied to the person who handles the Azazel-goat and to the one who handles the remaining flesh of the sin offering. This fact implies that the Azazel-goat ritual is a special form of the burning of the sin offering outside the camp. ... The interpretation that the Azazel-goat ritual constitutes the culminating point of the sin-offering ritual, simultaneously symbolising something beyond the sin offering, seems to be more in line with the other OT prophetic passages such as Psalm 40:6–8, in which no sin offering is said to be necessary (cf. Heb. 10:5–9, 18). Therefore, it is also possible to see the Azazel-goat

2. See Heiser, *Unseen Realm*, 276–87, 296–307; Heiser, *Reversing Hermon*, 87–102.

ritual behind Hebrews 13:12–13. Seen this way, the lifestyle of Christ was compared with that of the Azazel-goat. Since Christ fulfilled the role of the Azazel-goat in a cosmic dimension, believers have no need to bear guilt, whether their own or that of others, in order to make atonement.[3]

Given the absence of any visible postexilic return of the glory that had departed the original Israelite temple of Solomon just before its destruction,[4] New Testament cosmic geography was also discerned by answering the question, "Where is God's presence?" The God of Israel was incarnate in Jesus Christ, and so it should come as no surprise to read his challenge ("Destroy this temple, and in three days I will raise it up"; John 2:19) as ultimately about his own body (John 2:21–22).

After Jesus' ascent to the right hand of the Father, New Testament temple talk focuses on the metaphorical body of Christ and its localized manifestations. In New Testament theology, believers are holy ground, the place where the presence of God resides. This is reflected in New Testament statements referring to believers (corporately and individually) as the "temple of God" (1 Cor 3:16; 2 Cor 6:14–18; cp. 1 Pet 2:4–5) or "a temple of the Holy Spirit" (1 Cor 6:19; Eph 2:19–22). Paul's insistence that an unrepentant believer be expelled from the Corinthian church and that the people "are to deliver this man to Satan" (1 Cor 5:5) illustrates an application of the idea. The church, the visible body of Christ, removes sin "outside the camp" into the world. Sin belongs outside holy ground in the world, the dominion of Satan.

The famous scenes of Peter's confession (Matt 16:13–20) and the transfiguration (Mark 9:2–8) occur, respectively, at the foot of and on Mount Hermon, the place where the Watchers vowed to corrupt humanity in Second Temple Jewish thought. Mount Hermon is in the northernmost

---

3. Nobuyoshi Kiuchi, "Living Like the Azazel-Goat in Romans 12:1b," *TynBul* 57.2 (2006): 260.

4. The departure of the glory of God from the Jerusalem temple is described in Ezek 11:23. Greenberg writes of Ezek 11:23: "The east gate of the temple where the cherubs had previously halted (10:19) was situated in a continuation of the city wall; hence soaring above it might be said to be soaring 'over the city.' The Majesty, leaving the city, takes the direction of King David's flight from Absalom—east to the Mount of Olives (2 Sam 15:23ff.)." Moshe Greenberg, *Ezekiel 1–20: A New Translation with Introduction and Commentary* (AYB; New Haven, CT: Yale University Press, 1983), 191. That the glory left the city and "stood on the mountain that is on the east side of the city" is significant. The location was the Mount of Olives, the mountain to which both Ezek 43:2 and Zech 14:4 prophesy the arrival of the messiah at the end of days.

region of Bashan, associated in the Old Testament and Canaanite literature with the Rephaim giants and entry points to the underworld.[5] While some scholars still accept the traditional identification of Mount Tabor as the site for the transfiguration, many are now convinced that Mount Hermon is the better choice due to the height of Hermon, its proximity to Caesarea Philippi, and its symbolic associations with evil and the underworld.[6] In 1 Enoch, this region is clearly associated with the Watchers. As I noted in *Reversing Hermon*:

> The book of *1 Enoch* identifies Hermon with the region known in Jesus' day as Upper Galilee. When Enoch writes down the confessions and petitions of the Watchers—their pleas to God for forgiveness and clemency, he says, "And I went and sat down upon the waters of Dan—in Dan which is on the southwest of Hermon" (*1 Enoch* 13:7). Of this passage Nickelsburg observes, "This is a clear reference to the immediate environs of Tell Dan in upper Galilee."[7]

It is difficult to miss the implications. When Jesus declares that "the gates of hell" will not be able to withstand the church, he does so in a place deeply rooted in Old Testament and Second Temple–period thinking about Satan and the realm of the dead, his kingdom as it were. Jesus

---

5. Joshua 13:11–12, 30–31 describes Og's general kingdom as the region of Bashan, which encompassed sixty cities. In the Ugaritic language, the location of Ashtaroth and Edrei was not spelled *Bashan* but was pronounced and spelled *Bathan*. The linguistic note is intriguing since Bashan/Bathan both also mean "serpent" so that the region of Bashan was "the place of the serpent." On this point, Ugaritic scholar Gregorio del Olmo Lete observes: "This place 'štrt is also treated in [tablets] *KTU* 1.100:41; 1.107:17; and RS 86.2235:17 as the abode of the god *mlk*, the eponym of the *mlkm*, the deified kings, synonym of the *rpum*. For the 'Canaanites' of Ugarit, the Bashan region, or a part of it, clearly represented 'Hell', the celestial and infernal abode of their deified dead kings, Olympus and Hades at the same time. It is possible that this localization of the Canaanite Hell is linked to the ancient tradition of the place as the ancestral home of their dynasty, the *rpum*" (del Olmo Lete, "Bashan," *DDD* 162). See also James H. Charlesworth, "Bashan, Symbology, Haplography, and Theology in Psalm 68," in *David and Zion: Biblical Studies in Honor of J. J. M. Roberts*, ed. Bernard Frank Batto and Kathryn L. Roberts (Winona Lake, IN: Eisenbrauns, 2004), 351–72. Further, Ashtaroth and Edrei appear together in the Ugaritic text *KTU* 1.108 as the seat of the chthonic deity Rapiu. Hermann writes, "Dietrich and Loretz have shown that Baal is called *rpu* in his capacity as leader of the *rpum*, the Rephaim (1980:171–82). They find the epithet in *KTU* 1.108:1–2 and guess *KTU* 1.113 belongs to the same category of texts. The *Rāpi'ūma* (Hebrew *rĕpā'îm*) are the ghosts of the deceased ancestors, more especially of the royal family. Baal is their lord in the realm of the dead, as shown by the circumlocution *zbl b'l arṣ* ('prince, lord of the underworld')." See W. Hermann, "Baal," *DDD* 139.

6. Heiser, *Reversing Hermon*, 97.

7. Heiser, *Reversing Hermon*, 97, note 175. The Nickelsburg source I cite is George W. E. Nickelsburg, "Enoch, Levi, and Peter: Recipients of Revelation in Upper Galilee," *JBL* 100.4 (1981): 575–600 (esp. 582).

chooses Mount Hermon to reveal his glory—a direct provocation of the demonic realm. For ancient readers, these cosmic-geographical spiritual warfare gestures would be unmistakable. Jesus is essentially picking a fight, as these two events are precursors to the commencement of teaching the disciples that he must die in Jerusalem—the catalyst to God's redemptive plan.

NEW TESTAMENT COSMIC GEOGRAPHY:
Reclaiming the Promised Land

The cosmic geographical significance of the Bashan/Hermon region is at the heart of other passages. Jesus' exorcism of Legion takes place in the region of Bashan.[8] Mark 5:1–13 records the dramatic encounter:

> [1]They came to the other side of the sea, to the country of the Gerasenes. [2]And when Jesus had stepped out of the boat, immediately there met him out of the tombs a man with an unclean spirit. [3]He lived among the tombs. And no one could bind him anymore, not even with a chain, [4]for he had often been bound with shackles and chains, but he wrenched the chains apart, and he broke the shackles in pieces. No one had the strength to subdue him. [5]Night and day among the tombs and on the mountains he was always crying out and cutting himself with stones. [6]And when he saw Jesus from afar, he ran and fell down before him. [7]And crying out with a loud voice, he said, "What have you to do with me, Jesus, Son of the Most High God? I adjure you by God, do not torment me." [8]For he was saying to him, "Come out of the man, you unclean spirit!" [9]And Jesus asked him, "What is your name?" He replied, "My name is Legion, for we are many." [10]And he begged him earnestly not to send them out of the country. [11]Now a great herd of pigs was feeding there on the hillside, [12]and they begged him, saying, "Send us to the pigs; let us enter them."

---

8. The region of ancient Bashan is roughly "the area north of Gilead, west of Salecah and the Jebel Druze Mountains ... south of Mount Hermon, and east of the Jordan and the Sea of Galilee." See Joel C. Slayton, "Bashan (Place)," *ABD* 1:623. Careful study of the boundary descriptions of the tribal allotments has established that Mount Hermon is included in the boundaries of the promised land. See Zecharia Kallai, "The Patriarchal Boundaries, Canaan, and the Land of Israel: Patterns and Application in Biblical Historiography," *Israel Exploration Journal* 47.1–2 (1997): 69–82 (esp. 73); Kallai, "Conquest and Settlement of Trans-Jordan: A Historiographical Study," *Zeitschrift des Deutschen Palästina-Vereins (1953+)* 99 (1983): 110–18.

[13]So he gave them permission. And the unclean spirits came out and entered the pigs; and the herd, numbering about two thousand, rushed down the steep bank into the sea and drowned in the sea.

It is noteworthy that Jesus had limited his ministry to a Jewish audience before Mark 5. This would not be unexpected as Israel's Messiah. His entrance into the country of the Gerasenes—gentile territory—in Mark 5 indicated a departure from that pattern.[9] A close reading of Mark's wording helps us grasp the messaging of Jesus' decision. When Legion asks, "What have you to do with me?" the question echoes Mark 1:24, where Jesus cast out unclean spirits in the Jewish region of Galilee. But there is a subtle difference:

Demons in Galilee (Jewish)	Legion in Bashan (Gentile)
"What have you to do with us, **Jesus of Nazareth**?" (Mark 1:24)	"What have you to do with me, **Jesus, Son of the Most High God**?" (Mark 5:7)

This apparently minor alteration in how Jesus is addressed contains an important theological point. The title "Son of the Most High God" is significant for Old Testament cosmic geography.

Recall that in Deut 32:8–9 the "Most High" had disinherited the nations of the world, assigned them to the dominion of supernatural sons of God, and then created Israel as his own inheritance from nothing. Those sons of God rebelled and became corrupt (Psalm 82:1–4), throwing God's order into chaos (Psa 82:1–5).

The exorcism of Legion is therefore more than a strange tale of suicidal swine. It's about theological messaging. Legion recognizes that Jesus is rightful Lord of the country of the Gerasenes—old Bashan now under Gentile occupation.[10]

While the territory in which this encounter occurs is subsumed in the land promised to Abraham and his descendants, the fact that Jesus

---

9. Some scholars believe that the Legion confrontation is a cryptic call for political liberation. The argument is made on a twofold basis: (1) the Greek term for Legion (*legiōn*) is a direct reference to Roman forces, and (2) the Greek word translated "herd" (*agelē*) was also used of Roman military recruits. The logic is dubious. The region of the Gerasenes was known as gentile territory—that herdsmen were caring for pigs in the region makes that evident. Jews wouldn't have been earnestly seeing Roman expulsion from gentile areas, so a cryptic endorsement of political liberation isn't the point Mark wanted his readers to catch.

10. Heiser, *Reversing Hermon*, 101.

ventured into an area under gentile governance in his day let everyone know that he was not merely the Messiah for Yahweh's portion. He was lord of gentile lands as well.

NEW TESTAMENT COSMIC GEOGRAPHY: Reclaiming the Nations

Pentecost is perhaps the most overt yet hidden instance of cosmic geography in the New Testament. As I described in *The Unseen Realm*, every element of the Pentecost story hearkens back to an Old Testament divine council motif, particularly the reclamation of the nations disinherited at Babel (Gen 11:1–9; Deut 32:8–9).[11] It is a transparent launch of the reversal of the Deuteronomy 32 worldview by the kingdom of God. The list of nations in Acts 2 move from east to west then branches out at the Mediterranean. The list encompasses all the geographical regions reflected in the Table of Nations (Genesis 10) except for Tarshish (Spain), the final location Paul planned on preaching the gospel (Rom 15:24, 28).[12]

After the events at Pentecost in Acts 2, the spread of the gospel extends to those places connected geographically in some way to the land promised to Israel before turning to the gospel taking hold in gentile communities and regions—as Paul would later say, "to the Jew first and also to the Greek" (Rom 1:16). The Jews at Pentecost effectively return to their communities, scattered throughout the known nations, to be catalysts for the gospel of the kingdom in every place. Paul's ministry would build upon that work and blaze new trails. The story of the book of Acts is nothing less than the liberation of the peoples of the world held captive by the gods of the nations who enslaved them in their idolatry and unbelief. Jesus' acts of power in gentile regions and Acts 1:8 were early indications as to what the new covenant entailed (Jer 31:31–33; Ezek 36:25–28).

---

11. Heiser, *Unseen Realm*, 296–306.

12. On Paul's yearning to reach Spain and its connection back to Tarshish to thus complete the gospel infiltration of every nation disinherited at Babel, see Heiser, *Unseen Realm* (302–3) and the sources on which the discussion is based: Harry W. Tajra, *The Martyrdom of St. Paul: Historical and Judicial Context, Traditions, and Legends*, vol. 3 (Tübingen: Mohr Siebeck, 1994); Otto F. A. Meinardus, "Paul's Missionary Journey to Spain: Tradition and Folklore," *The Biblical Archaeologist* (1978): 61–63; Roger Aus, "Paul's Travel Plans to Spain and the 'Full Number of the Gentiles' of Rom XI 25," *NovT* 21.3 (July, 1979): 232–62; John L. Day, "Where Was Tarshish? (Gen 10:4)?" in *From Creation to Babel: Studies in Genesis 1–11*, ed. John L. Day (London: Bloomsbury T&T Clark, 2015).

PAUL'S DEUTERONOMY 32 WORLDVIEW

Paul occasionally used the term *daimonion* for the supernatural powers of darkness; it is found only three times in his letters. Paul used the term twice in 1 Corinthians 10:20 (" ... what pagans sacrifice they offer to demons and not to God. I do not want you to be participants with demons"). Paul was quoting Deuteronomy 32:17 in this instance, which rendered *šēdîm* with *daimonion*. There is little to learn here in terms of theological specificity since, as we noted in chapter 2, *daimonion* was a generic term applied in the Hellenistic era to any spirit being.

The other instance, 1 Timothy 4:1, is a bit more informative: "Now the Spirit expressly says that in later times some will depart from the faith by devoting themselves to deceitful spirits and teachings of demons." The notion that "demons" led people astray by "teaching" arises from the Second Temple Jewish theology of the Watchers, who are repeatedly blamed for leading humanity astray via forbidden knowledge. Recall that the demons of the Gospels were the disembodied Watcher-spirits. Paul's association of false teaching and "demons" is quite consistent with the Second Temple Jewish perspective.

Paul typically does not use *daimonion* when speaking of evil supernatural powers. Paul's vocabulary—predominantly aimed at gentile believers—shows his awareness of the Deuteronomy 32 worldview:[13]

- "rulers" (*archontōn* or *archōn*)
- "principalities" (*archē*)
- "powers"/"authorities" (*exousia*)
- "powers" (*dynamis*)
- "dominions"/"lords" (*kyrios; kyriotēs*)
- "thrones" (*thronos*)
- "world rulers" (*kosmokratōr*)

These lemmas denote *geographical domain authority* in both in the New Testament and other Greek literature. While they can be used of human rulers, they describe evil powers in a number of Paul's letters:

---

13. See Heiser, *Unseen Realm*, 329, and Ronn Johnson, "The Old Testament Background for Paul's Principalities and Powers" (PhD diss., Dallas Theological Seminary, 2004). For brief discussions of individual terms see D. G. Reid, "Principalities and Powers," *DPL* 746–52.

Ephesians 6:12 includes a number of the lemmas listed above: "Our struggle is not against blood and flesh, but against the rulers [*archē*], against the authorities [*exousia*], against the world rulers [*kosmokratōr*] of this darkness, against the spiritual forces [*pneumatikos*] of wickedness in the heavenly places."

Paul refers to these hostile beings in the unseen realm earlier in Ephesians. He wrote that God raised Jesus from the dead and "seated him at his right hand in the heavenly places, far above every ruler [*archē*] and authority [*exousia*] and power [*dynamis*] and dominion [*kyrios*]" (Eph 1:20–21 ESV). It was only after Christ had risen that God's plan was "made known to the rulers [*archē*] and authorities [*exousia*] in the heavenly places" (Eph 3:10 ESV).[14]

Further, Aune notes that "the term *archontes* used as a designation for angelic beings first occurs in the LXX Dan 10:13, and seven times in Theod. Dan 10:13, 20–21; 12:1, where the LXX has *stratēgos*, 'commander,' 'magistrate,' all translations of the Aram *śar*, 'prince.'"[15]

As we saw earlier in our study, Daniel's notion that nations are governed by a spirit "prince" derives from the allotment of the nations to the sons of God described in Deuteronomy 4:19–20; 32:8–9. Paul's use of the term *stoicheia* ("elemental principles") has a subsidiary relationship to the Deuteronomy 32 worldview.[16] In the two passages where this term (at least in part) arguably refers to divine beings (Gal 4:3, 9; Col 2:8, 20) instead of (apparently) the material components of the natural world (2 Pet 3:10, 12) or "first principles" of the Mosaic law (Heb 5:12), the referents would be fallen supernatural beings.

There is no consensus among scholars on Paul's use of the term (Gal 4:3, 9; Col 2:8, 20). The question is whether Paul is using the term of spiritual entities/star deities in Gal 4:3, 9 and Col 2:8, 20. Three of these four instances append the word to "of the world" (*kosmos*; i.e., "*stoicheia* of the world"), but this doesn't provide much clarity. Paul's discussion in Gal 4 and Col 2 includes spiritual forces (angels,

---

14. Heiser, *Unseen Realm*, 330.

15. See D. E. Aune, "Archon," in *DDD* 82–85. Some Septuagint manuscripts have "powers" (*dynamis*; plural: *dynameis*) as the translation for the divine "host" in Dan 8:10. See also Rom 8:38 for supernatural powers.

16. On this term and these passages, see D. G. Reid, "Elements/Elemental Spirits of the World," *DPL* 229–33.

principalities and powers, false gods) in the context, which suggests *stoicheia* may refer to divine beings. He is contrasting *stoicheia* to salvation in Christ in some way. Since Paul is speaking to both Jews and Gentiles, he might also be using the term in different ways with respect to each audience. *Stoicheia* as law would make little sense to Gentiles, though it would strike a chord with Jews. My view is that in Gal 4:3 Paul's use of *stoicheia* likely refers to the law and religious teaching with a Jewish audience in view (cf. Gal 4:1–7). The audience shifts to Gentiles in 4:8–11, and so it seems coherent to see *stoicheia* in Gal 4:9 as referring to divine beings, probably astral deities (the "Fates"). The reference to "times and seasons and years" (4:10) would therefore point to pagan astrological beliefs, not the Jewish calendar. Paul is therefore denying the idea that the celestial *objects* (sun, moon, stars) are deities. His Gentile readers should not be enslaved by the idea that these objects controlled their destiny.[17]

How is this to be reconciled with Old Testament passages that link the heavenly host (i.e., the sun, moon, stars) with divine beings? The Old Testament does not affirm that these celestial objects were in fact spiritual beings. Even if one presumes this is the case, a shift in understanding by Paul's time does not undermine the metaphorical point—that divine beings were spoken of using the language of heavenly objects to ascribe an "otherworldly" (i.e., nonterrestrial) nature to spiritual beings (Job 38:4–8; Isa 14:12–13). The Old Testament forbids the worship of celestial objects as idolatry; whether the objects were conceived of as actual entities or not does not mean their worship is not idolatry.

Paul's thinking is consistent with all these points. Lesser spiritual beings (in rebellion or not) do not control the cycles of time; that is, they are not sovereign. Even passages such as Judges 5:20 ("the stars fought from their courses") or Isaiah 40:26 ("[God] brings out [the heavenly host] by number, calling them all by name") do not have to be taken as evidence that the Old Testament writer thought celestial objects were supernatural beings. The language of the former may suggest propitious heavenly "communication" (compare Ps 19:1–6); observers saw positive portents in the sky during the battle and interpreted them as signs from God. God's ability to signal his intent could certainly be the point

17. Heiser, *Unseen Realm*, 327, note 17.

of Isaiah 40:26—God is in control of the passage of time and history, marked as they are by the movements of the heavens, the reason they were created (Gen 1:14–19).

Orthodox Judaism of the Second Temple period on into late antiquity had a long history of believing that what was observed in the day or night sky had religious meaning. Paul himself cited Psalm 19:4 in Romans 10:18 to make the point that (somehow) the people of the world could have known about Jesus. Paul was not speaking of the gospel per se (there is no sense that he thought Psalm 19 exempted him from preaching Christ). Rather, the idea that signs in the sky portended the arrival of a divine king was in view. This idea was connected to both astronomy and chronological systems (e.g., the mathematical calendar at Qumran) that anticipated a messianic birth. Gentiles (like the Magi) also "read" certain signs the same way. Theologically conservative Jews and Christians believed God did communicate through the heavens. God had created the heavenly objects by which "times and seasons" were measured and was the lone sovereign of human destiny. He could indeed signal his intentions. This idea was a departure from the pagans, who erroneously thought the celestial objects dictated human destiny. Christians made similar distinctions.[18]

The point is that when Paul uses terms of geographical dominion in conversation with gentiles, he is not referring to the demons of the Gospels. He is referring to the corrupt gods allotted to the nations as part of God's punishment of humanity at Babel. Paul's language conveys a theology of cosmic geography.

THE DELEGITIMIZATION OF THE GODS

Paul's cosmic-geographical thought was at the heart of his discussion of the delegitimization of the rule of the gods over the gentile nations and

---

18. See James H. Charlesworth, "Jewish Astrology in the Talmud, Pseudepigrapha, the Dead Sea Scrolls, and Early Palestinian Synagogues," *HTR* 70.3/4 (1977): 183–200; Kocku von Stuckrad, "Jewish and Christian Astrology in Late Antiquity—A New Approach," *Numen* 47 (2000): 1–40; Rachel Hachlili, "The Zodiac in Ancient Jewish Art: Representation and Significance," *BASOR* 228 (1977): 61–77; Bernard R. Goldstein and David Pingree, "Astrological Almanacs from the Cairo Geniza, Part I," *JNES* 38.3 (1979): 153–75; Goldstein and Pingree, "Astrological Almanacs from the Cairo Geniza, Part II," *JNES* 38.4 (1979): 231–56; Timothy Hegedus, *Early Christianity and Ancient Astrology* (New York: Peter Lang, 2007).

their inhabitants as a result of the resurrection and ascension of Jesus Christ. We will begin with Paul's use of Psalm 68:18 in his letter to the Ephesians. Psalm 68:15–18 reads:

> [15] O mountain of God,[19] mountain of Bashan;
>   O many-peaked mountain, mountain of Bashan!
> [16] Why do you look with hatred, O many-peaked mountain,
>   at the mount that God desired for his abode,
>   yes, where the LORD will dwell forever?
> [17] The chariots of God are twice ten thousand,
>   thousands upon thousands;
>   the Lord is among them; Sinai is now in the sanctuary.
> [18] You ascended on high,
>   leading a host of captives in your train
>   and receiving gifts among men,
>   even among the rebellious, that the LORD God may dwell there.

Old Testament scholar J. J. M. Roberts identifies Mount Bashan as Mount Hermon, a logical conclusion since Mount Hermon is the highest peak in the region: "Mount Hermon is rebuked for looking with envy on the mountain of Yahweh."[20] Goldingay explains the coherence of the association this way:

> Rhetorically this further section [of Psalm 68] moves in a new direction as it addresses Mount Bashan, and in content it makes for another form of link between past and present, the reality of God's dwelling. ... It begins by looking across from the mountain chain running through the heartland of Ephraim and Judah to the higher and more impressive mountains on the other side of the Jordan, running south from Mount Hermon through the Golan and Gilead. Mount Hermon in particular is indeed a mighty or majestic mountain, literally, a

---

19. The Hebrew phrase is *har 'elōhîm*. The phrase could be rendered "divine mountain" or "mighty mountain" (taking *'elōhîm* as a superlative). In volume 2 of his series on the psalms, Goldingay observes in a footnote: "J. A. Emerton emphasizes that not least in a context such as the present one, it is unlikely that *'ĕlōhîm* is merely a way of expressing the superlative" (citing J. A. Emerton, "The 'Mountain of God' in Psalm 68:16," in *History and Traditions of Early Israel*, ed. André Lemaire and Benedikt Otzen [Leiden: Brill, 1993], 24–37 [esp. 29–30]). See John Goldingay, *Psalms, Vol. 2: Psalms 42–89* (BCOT; Grand Rapids: Baker Academic, 2006), 323.

20. J. J. M. Roberts, "The End of War in the Zion Tradition: The Imperialistic Background of and Old Testament Vision of World Peace," *Horizons in Biblical Theology* 26.1 (2004): 2–22 (esp. 4).

"mountain of God." It towers into the heavens and thus suggests the possibility of or the claim to a link between heaven and earth.[21]

This backdrop illumines the theology of Paul's citation of Psalm 68:18 in Ephesians 4:

Psalm 68:18	Ephesians 4:8
	Therefore it says,
You ascended on high,	"When he ascended on high
leading a host of captives in your train	he led a host of captives,
and receiving gifts among men.	and he gave gifts to men."

On the surface it seems that Paul changes the meaning of the psalm. Psalm 68:18 describes a military victor (God) taking prisoners, enjoying the booty of war. Paul understands Psalm 68:18 to be about Jesus ascending on high and giving gifts to humanity. In Paul's mind, Jesus is somehow the fulfillment of Psalm 68. The two passages actually are not dissimilar. Many commentators assume that captives are being liberated in Ephesians 4. This assumption leads to the confusion. There is no liberation in Ephesians 4; rather, there is conquest, just as in Psalm 68. Both passages are about conquest. In Psalm 68, Yahweh conquers demonic Bashan. For Paul, Jesus is the conqueror of demonic Bashan. Paul's view of Jesus giving gifts fits well with this context of conquest.

In the ancient world the conqueror would parade the captives and demand tribute for himself. Jesus is the conqueror of Psalm 68, and the booty does indeed rightfully belong to him. But booty was also distributed after a conquest. Paul knows that. He quotes Psalm 68:18 to make the point that after Jesus conquered his demonic enemies, he distributed the benefits of the conquest to his people, believers. Specifically, those benefits are apostles, prophets, evangelists, pastors, and teachers (Eph 4:11).[22]

Paul explains his thinking in Ephesians 4:9-10:

(In saying, "He ascended," what does it mean but that he had also descended into the lower regions, the earth? He who descended is

---

21. Goldingay, *Psalms 42–89*, 323.
22. Heiser, *Unseen Realm*, 293.

the one who also ascended far above all the heavens, that he might fill all things.)

The key to understanding Paul's thinking is parsing the ascent and the descent that he's describing:

There are two possible explanations. The most common view is that, upon his death, Jesus descended into the lower regions *of the earth*. This is the way Ephesians 4:9 is worded in many translations. In this case, the language speaks both of the grave and of cosmic Sheol, the Underworld. This is possible since elsewhere in the New Testament we read that Jesus descended into the Underworld to confront the "spirits in prison"—the original transgressing sons of God from Genesis 6 (1 Pet 3:18–22). But that visitation may not be Paul's point of reference here.

The second view is reflected in the ESV, which is the translation I used for Ephesians 4. Note that instead of "lower parts of the earth" the ESV inserts a comma: "the lower regions, the earth." The effect of the comma is that Jesus descended to "the lower regions, [in other words] *the earth*." This option fits the context better (the gifts are given to people who are of course on earth) and has some other literary advantages. If this option is correct, then the descent of verses 9–10 does not refer to Jesus' time in the grave, but rather to the Holy Spirit's coming to earth after Jesus' conquering ascension on the day of Pentecost.[23]

Once again, the New Testament draws on cosmic-geographical thinking to portray Christ's victory over the powers of darkness. Mount Hermon was being reclaimed as Yahweh's possession. Jesus provoked darkness in Bashan and at Mount Hermon to set the circumstances of his death in motion. The provocation was essential because his sacrificial death was essential. One cannot have a resurrection and an ascension without a death, and the resurrection and ascension are central to the reenthronement of Jesus above all powers (Rom 8:34–39; Heb 1:3; 10:12–13; 1 Pet 3:22).

In Ephesians 4:8 Paul read Psalm 68:18 as describing the conquest of supernatural evil (Bashan), which in turn led to the coming of the

---

23. Ibid., 293–94.

Spirit and the subsequent gifts to the body of Christ. The coming of the Spirit was, of course, contingent on the death, resurrection, and ascension of Christ to the position of rule, the right hand of the Father. Paul more explicitly connects the finished work of Christ and the defeat of evil spirits—in this case, the hostile gods enslaving the nations ("rulers and authorities")—in Colossians 2:8–15:

> [8] See to it that no one takes you captive by philosophy and empty deceit, according to human tradition, according to the elemental spirits of the world, and not according to Christ. [9] For in him the whole fullness of deity dwells bodily, [10] and you have been filled in him, who is the head of all rule and authority. [11] In him also you were circumcised with a circumcision made without hands, by putting off the body of the flesh, by the circumcision of Christ, [12] having been buried with him in baptism, in which you were also raised with him through faith in the powerful working of God, who raised him from the dead. [13] And you, who were dead in your trespasses and the uncircumcision of your flesh, God made alive together with him, having forgiven us all our trespasses, [14] by canceling the record of debt that stood against us with its legal demands. This he set aside, nailing it to the cross. [15] He disarmed the rulers and authorities and put them to open shame, by triumphing over them in him. (Col 2:8–15)

In verse 15 the cosmic forces, the "rulers [*archē*] and authorities [*exousia*]," are disarmed and put to shame. The lemma *archē* is used of divine beings in New Testament (Rom 8:38; 1 Cor 15:24; Eph 1:21; 3:10; 6:12), including earlier in the same letter (Col 1:16). The same is true of the lemma *exousia* (Col 1:13; Eph 2:2). Paul is writing to a gentile church and clearly has gentiles in view when he describes his audience as "dead in your trespasses and the uncircumcision of your flesh" (v. 13). Jews, of course, share the problem of being estranged from God because of sin. Paul makes this clear with language like "our trespasses" and "against us," including himself as a Jew in both the problem and the wonder of forgiveness. But Israel had no supernatural "rulers and authorities" to be disarmed. The nations did, per the Deuteronomy 32 worldview.

Two climactic accomplishments are noted here by Paul. First, "the record of debt that stood against us" (Jew and gentile) was canceled or "set aside" (v.14). Second, the "rulers and authorities" were "disarmed" and "put ... to open shame" (v. 15). The resurrection (v. 12) was the causative agent to both, for if there was no resurrection, the debt against us would still stand and we would not be "made alive together with him."[24]

Scholars have been puzzled by the word choice in v. 15 ("disarmed"; lemma: *apekduomai*). It is found only here and in Colossians 3:9 ("put off, remove, strip off" the old self). It is obvious that the term would not point to the destruction of the rulers and authorities, as Paul elsewhere has the powers of darkness actively engaged against believers (e.g., Eph 6:12). Scholars find the idea of removal or stripping (of something) awkward, and it is—if one lacks the Deuteronomy 32 framework as a reference point.

Paul uses the same verb in Colossians 3:9–10 when he reminds the Colossians that they have "put off the old self with its practices and have put on the new self." The "putting off" and "putting on" speaks of turning from the old way of life to something new. The cognate noun (*apekdysis*)[25] occurs only once in the New Testament, in this very passage (Col 2:11): "In him also you were circumcised with a circumcision made without hands, by putting off [*apekdysis*] the body of the flesh, by the circumcision of Christ." Viewed in tandem, "putting off the body of flesh" is conceptually akin to "putting off the old self." In similar language, Paul elsewhere tells believers that they will someday "put on the imperishable" (1 Cor 15:53). The familiar Pauline binary opposition of the flesh versus the spirit makes it clear that his wording is "overtly metaphoric of spiritual states."[26]

---

24. As the grammar of v. 13 shows, forgiveness of our trespasses and being made alive together are tandem conditions. God "made us alive ... *having forgiven* us ... *canceling* the record of debt." The italicized verbal items are aorist participles whose action is antecedent or contemporaneous to the main (aorist) verb ("made alive"). See Daniel B. Wallace, *Greek Grammar Beyond the Basics: Exegetical Syntax of the New Testament* (Grand Rapids: Zondervan, 1996), 614.

25. James D. G. Dunn, *The Epistles to the Colossians and to Philemon: A Commentary on the Greek Text* (NIGTC; Grand Rapids: Eerdmans, 1996), 167.

26. Ryken et al., *Dictionary of Biblical Imagery*, 319. The discussion of the flesh ("Body," 106) in the same resource includes this observation: "Sarx, 'flesh,' is Paul's common metaphor for inherent human sinfulness. But as one among several Pauline uses of the term, it should not cloud our understanding of the body as the good creation of God that will be redeemed. The *image of sarx* as rebellious human nature occurs most frequently in Romans and Galatians. Particularly in Galatians the image seems to be gauged to subvert the ideology of those who are promoting the circumcision of the 'flesh.' Against these Judaizers, who wish to boast in the Galatians' circumcised flesh, Paul produces this counter-image of flesh as opposed to the 'Spirit' (Gal 3:3) and its fruits (Gal 5:16–17)."

What are we to make of this metaphorical term applied to the rulers and authorities in Colossians 2:15? The idea of "removal" captures the nuance. While not destroyed, the supernatural rulers and authorities have been displaced or removed from the authority they held over the gentiles. Who was it that removed this authority? The Most High himself, on the basis of the death and resurrection of Christ. Lohse comes close to this idea when he writes that the rare verb "means 'to take off,' 'to put aside'. ... The middle, however, can also be used in an active sense. Then it means 'to strip.'"[27] God through Christ "put aside" the old order of the rulers and authorities; he "stripped" them of their authority.

The point of Paul's declaration is that the ruling authority of the gods allotted to the nations (Deut 32:8; cp. Deut 4:19–20; 17:3; 29:23–26) was declared illegitimate and null by the work of Christ. In the past, prior to Christ, the Most High had allotted the nations to the sons of God. Their authority was legitimate because they had been appointed by the true God. They were *supposed* to be in their positions. Psalm 82 tells us that those gods, "sons of the Most High" (Ps 82:6), rebelled and became corrupt. Instead of ruling their people according to the sort of justice God desired, they enslaved them, ultimately becoming the objects of their worship and seducing Yahweh's own people into idolatry. Now, because of the cross, their rule has no legitimacy.

Gentiles would have understood the implications, as early writers like Plato understood the gods had been allotted to the nations:

> In the days of old, the gods had the whole earth distributed among them by allotment. There was no quarrelling; for you cannot rightly suppose that the gods did not know what was proper for each of them to have, or, knowing this, that they would seek to procure for themselves by contention that which more properly belonged to others. They all of them by just apportionment obtained what they wanted, and peopled their own districts; and when they had peopled them they tended us, their nurselings and possessions, as shepherds tend their flocks, excepting only that they did not use blows or bodily force, as shepherds do, but governed us like pilots from the stern of the vessel, which is an easy way of guiding animals, holding our

---

27. Eduard Lohse, *Colossians and Philemon: A Commentary on the Epistles to the Colossians and to Philemon* (Hermeneia; Philadelphia: Fortress, 1971), 111.

souls by the rudder of persuasion according to their own pleasure;—
thus did they guide all mortal creatures. Now different gods had their
allotments in different places which they set in order. Hephaestus
and Athene, who were brother and sister, and sprang from the same
father, having a common nature, and being united also in the love
of philosophy and art, both obtained as their common portion this
land, which was naturally adapted for wisdom and virtue; and there
they implanted brave children of the soil, and put into their minds
the order of government; their names are preserved, but their actions
have disappeared by reason of the destruction of those who received
the tradition, and the lapse of ages.[28]

Consequently, part of the good news of the gospel to those under
the gods' dominion was that they were free to turn from those gods and
embrace Jesus. In fact, God was demanding their return to his family. The
breach caused by the Babel rebellion had been closed; the gap between
them and the true God had been bridged.

That the authority of the rulers and authorities was nullified by the
Most High does not mean that the supernatural forces of darkness allotted to the nations surrender their charges. Paul knew his Old Testament,
specifically that the final judgment of the gods was eschatologically connected to the day of the Lord. Nevertheless their demise is in process.
Paul's language about the cosmic rulers runs parallel to what we saw in
the Gospels with respect to the demons. Jesus' announcement that the
kingdom of God had come was accompanied by exorcisms (Matt 12:28;
Luke 11:18–20). The point wasn't that there were no more demons. Exorcism accounts inform us quite clearly that both the demons and Jesus
knew the fate of the powers of darkness was yet future (Ps 82:6–8; Isa
24:21; 34:1–4). For example, in Matthew 8:29, the demons cry out to Jesus,
"What have you to do with us, O Son of God? Have you come here to
torment us before the time?" The phrase "before the time" points to a
definite, future destiny. Hagner captures the idea succinctly:

---

28. The passage is from Plato, *Critias*, 109 (Plato, *The Dialogues of Plato*, trans. B. Jowett, 5 vols.,
3rd ed. [Oxford: Clarendon, 1892], 3:530). In his book on Greco-Roman appropriation of ancient
Near Eastern thought, West observes, "Tyrtaeus (2.12) states that 'Zeus himself has given this city to
the descendants of Heracles'" (West, *East Face of the Helicon*, 129, note 122).

The demons' subsequent question, "Have you come here to torment us before the time?" (πρὸ καιροῦ), is interesting from at least two aspects: first, in it the demons recognize that at the eschatological judgment they will experience God's judgment and the end of their power (cf. *1 Enoch* 15–16; *Jub.* 10:8–9; TLevi 18:12); and second, they recognize that that καιρός, "time," has not yet come; Jesus has in effect come too early and threatens their realm too soon (for the eschatological judgment of demons, cf *1 Enoch* 55:4; *T. Levi* 18). This, of course, fits in with Matthew's perspective of realized eschatology: the kingdom has come, but in advance of its fullest and final coming (cf. 12:28; 13:30).[29]

In like manner, in declaring to gentiles that the Most High had invalidated the jurisdiction and dominion of their gods, Paul did not intend to claim their eschatological hour had come. Paul linked his mission of evangelism of the gentiles to the restored spiritual fortunes of Israel. The final "mystery" of God's salvation plan would be known when "the fullness of the Gentiles" had become part of the kingdom of God, leading to the salvation of Israel (Rom 11:25–26). Only when the full number of gentiles was saved would the nations and their gods be finally judged.[30]

Other passages in Paul's letters and other New Testament books connect the delegitimization of the authority of the allotted supernatural powers of the nations to Christ's resurrection and ascension.[31] Note the juxtaposition of the two themes in the following instances:

---

29. Donald A. Hagner, *Matthew 1–13* (WBC; Dallas: Word, 1998), 227. France concurs: "The intriguing phrase *pro kairou*, 'before the proper time,' implies a recognition by the demons that their time of opportunity to trouble human beings is limited, and that the arrival of Jesus signals the beginning of the end, which they had hoped would not come yet; for the final judgment of evil spirits as the role of the Messiah see *1 En.* 55:4; *T. Levi* 18:12." See R. T. France, *The Gospel of Matthew* (NIGTC; Grand Rapids: Eerdmans, 2007), 341.

30. The full task of reclaiming the nations in Paul's mind meant the gospel had to reach all the nations listed in Gen 10 that had been divorced by God at Babel. This was what lay behind his urgency to reach Spain (Tarshish; discussed earlier in this chapter), the most remote of those nations. Jewett and Kotansky take note of this point: "At the end of time all Israel will be saved (Rom 11:26) but this cannot occur until 'the fullness of the Gentiles' has been achieved (Rom 11:25). Reckoning backwards from this apocalyptic climax, Paul infers that current Jewish resistance against the gospel provides time for the gentile mission. This is the reasoning behind the Spanish mission project that this letter seeks to advance, for if the gospel can be brought to the end of the known world, the climactic conversion of Israel can occur and the parousia can come as promised." Robert Jewett and Roy David Kotansky, *Romans: A Commentary* (Hermeneia; Minneapolis: Fortress, 2006), 674.

31. There are hints of this theology (the rising of the messiah associated with the defeat of the gods) in the Old Testament.

²⁰ But in fact Christ has been raised from the dead, the firstfruits of those who have fallen asleep. ²¹ For as by a man came death, **by a man has come also the resurrection of the dead**. ²² For as in Adam all die, so also **in Christ shall all be made alive**. ²³ But each in his own order: Christ the firstfruits, then at his coming those who belong to Christ. ²⁴ Then comes the end, when he delivers the kingdom to God the Father **after destroying every rule** [archē] **and every authority** [exousia] **and power** [dynamis]. (1 Cor 15:20–24)

¹⁵ For this reason, because I have heard of your faith in the Lord Jesus and your love toward all the saints, ¹⁶ I do not cease to give thanks for you, remembering you in my prayers, ¹⁷ that the God of our Lord Jesus Christ, the Father of glory, may give you the Spirit of wisdom and of revelation in the knowledge of him, ¹⁸ having the eyes of your hearts enlightened, that you may know what is the hope to which he has called you, what are the riches of his glorious inheritance in the saints, ¹⁹ and what is the immeasurable greatness of his power toward us who believe, according to the working of his great might ²⁰ **that he worked in Christ when he raised him from the dead and seated him at his right hand in the heavenly places, ²¹ far above all rule** [archē] **and authority** [exousia] **and power** [dynamis] **and dominion** [kyriotēs], and above every name that is named, not only in this age but also in the one to come. ²² And he put all things under his feet and gave him as head over all things to the church, ²³ which is his body, the fullness of him who fills all in all. (Eph 1:15–23)

¹⁸ For Christ also suffered once for sins, the righteous for the unrighteous, that he might bring us to God, being put to death in the flesh but made alive in the spirit, ¹⁹ in which he went and proclaimed to the spirits in prison, ²⁰ because they formerly did not obey, when God's patience waited in the days of Noah, while the ark was being prepared, in which a few, that is, eight persons, were brought safely through water. ²¹ Baptism, which corresponds to this, now saves you, not as a removal of dirt from the body but as an appeal to God for a good conscience, through **the resurrection of Jesus Christ, ²² who has gone into heaven and is at the right hand of God, with angels, authorities** [exousia], **and powers** [dynamis] **having been subjected to him**. (1 Pet 3:18–22)

Not surprisingly, Paul's theology linking a rising Messiah to the release of the gentiles from their false worship is anticipated in the Old Testament.[32] Romans 15:8–12 is suggestive in that regard:

> [8] For I tell you that Christ became a servant to the circumcised to show God's truthfulness, in order to confirm the promises given to the patriarchs, [9] and in order that the Gentiles might glorify God for his mercy. As it is written,
>
> > "Therefore I will praise you among the Gentiles,
> > and sing to your name."
>
> [10] And again it is said,
>
> > "Rejoice, O Gentiles, with his people."
>
> [11] And again,
>
> > "Praise the Lord, all you Gentiles,
> > and let all the peoples extol him."
>
> [12] And again Isaiah says,
>
> > "The root of Jesse will come,
> > even **he who arises to rule the Gentiles**;
> > in him will the Gentiles hope."

The key item in the passage is found in verse 12, which has the Messiah (the "root of Jesse") "arising" (lemma: *anistēmi*) to rule the gentiles. Paul's source is Isaiah 11:10 from the LXX. In the context of the Deuteronomy 32 worldview, assuming the rulership described by Isaiah requires withdrawing the authority of the sons of God allotted to the nations at Babel.[33]

---

32. For connections between these two passages in Isaiah and Psalm 82, see Joel Aaron Reemtsma, "Punishment of the Powers: Deut 32:8 and Psalm 82 as the Backdrop for Isaiah 34" (paper presented at the annual meeting of the Evangelical Theological Society, November 19, 2014; San Diego, CA); Ronald Bergey, "The Song of Moses (Deut 32:1–43) and Isaianic Prophecies: A Case of Intertextuality?" *JSOT* 28.1 (2003): 33–54; Thomas A. Keiser, "The Song of Moses as a Basis for Isaiah's Prophecy," *VT* 55 (2005): 486–500.

33. Seifrid observes, "Paul, too, understands the text to speak of the Messiah, the new David, who has arisen to rule over the Gentiles. Yet Jesus rules not by the sword, but rather by his resurrection from the dead (see 1:1–7). The nations enter into the salvation that he brings as they place their hope in him. It is in this way that they submit to him. Paul's mission of effecting [*sic*] the 'obedience of faith' (1:5; 15:18; 16:26) is embedded within this citation. His apostolic 'priestly service' (*hierourgeō* [15:16–18; cf. 1:9]), by which the Gentiles are reclaimed, is thus an echo of the Messiah's 'service' (*diakonos* [15:8])." See Mark A. Seifrid, "Romans," in *Commentary on the New Testament Use of the Old Testament*, ed. G. K. Beale and D. A. Carson (Grand Rapids: Baker Academic, 2007), 690–91.

Of the two Greek verbs (*egeirō*, *anistēmi*) used to describe the resurrection in the New Testament, *anistēmi* (and especially its cognate noun, *anastasis*) has received concentrated attention for its use in describing the resurrection of Jesus:

> The [verb] *anistēmi* occurs in the NT over 100×, but almost always in the Gospels and Acts (the only exceptions are Rom 15:12; 1 Cor 10:7; Eph 5:14; 1 Thess 4:14, 16; Heb 7:11, 15); Luke-Acts accounts for more than 70 instances. In approx[imately] three-fourths of the occurrences the meaning is general, not connected with the concept of resurrection. ... All occurrences in John but one (John 11:31) have to do with resurrection (6:39–40, 44, 54; 11:23–24; 31), whereas Matthew never uses it this way (he prefers *egeirō*; contrast Matt 16:21 with Mark 8:31). Such a meaning occurs a handful of times in Luke and is a bit more freq[uent] in Acts (e.g., Luke 16:31; Acts 2:24, 32), but in the Epistles it is found only 3× (Eph 5:14; 1 Thess 4:14, 16). In contrast, the noun *anastasis*, which occurs c. 40× (incl[uding] 17× in Luke-Acts, but 15× in the Epistles and Revelation), means "resurrection" in virtually every case (the only exception is Luke 2:34). ... Some have thought that *egeirō*, esp[ecially] in the pass[ive], is used predominantly for what happened at Easter, i.e., the wakening of the crucified one to life, while *anistēmi* and *anastasis* refer more esp[ecially] to the recall to life of people during the earthly ministry of Jesus and to the eschat[ological] and universal resurrection. ... There are, however, too many exceptions; e.g., *egeirō* is applied to John the Baptist (Matt 14:2 [and parallels]) and to the dead generally (10:8; Mark 12:26; John 5:21 and freq[uently]), and Paul applies it to both Christ's resurrection and the future resurrection of the dead in the same context (1 Cor 15:15–17). It would be more accurate to say simply that *egeirō* occurs more freq[uently] than *anistēmi* in the sense of resurrection.[34]

The LXX of Zephaniah 3:8 also combines "resurrection language" with reclaiming the nations:

> "On account of this, wait for me," says the Lord,
>   "for the day of my **rising up** [*anastasis*] for a testimony,

---

34. *NIDNTTE*, s.v. "ἀνίστημι," 1:322, 326. In the extract, the Greek has been replaced with transliteration.

because my judgment is for **the gathering of nations,**
    in order to gather the kings,
in order to pour upon them all my angry wrath,
    because in the fire of my zeal all the earth will be consumed." (LES)

Lastly, Psalm 82 itself is part of the matrix of ideas that contribute to Paul's theology of the abrogation of the authority of the allotted powers. Recall that, after castigating the gods (vv. 1–5) and sentencing them to die like humans (vv. 6–7), the psalmist closed the divine council scene with a plea: "Arise, O God, judge the earth; for you shall inherit all the nations!" (v. 8). Scholars have drawn attention to the fact that the Septuagint translator used *anistēmi* for this plea ("Arise, O God … !").[35]

It takes little imagination to see how these passages could be read in hindsight by Paul. After his dramatic encounter with the resurrected Jesus on the road to Damascus and his call to be the apostle to the gentiles, the resurrection of the Messiah would be forever intertwined with the reclaiming of the once-rejected nations.

---

35. David A. Burnett, "A Neglected Deuteronomic Scriptural Matrix for the Nature of the Resurrection Body in 1 Cor 15:39–42?" in *Scripture, Texts, and Tracings in 1 Corinthians*, ed. B. J. Oropeza and Linda Belleville (Minneapolis: Fortress, forthcoming). This author read a prepublication version of this source.

COMMON QUESTIONS AND MISCONCEPTIONS

OVERVIEW

The powers of darkness have captured the attention of millions of people, Christian or not, for millennia. If contemporary popular culture is any indication, this fascination has hardly abated. Unfortunately, a considerable amount of misunderstanding and outright misinformation has accrued to the discussion, even within the church. In my experience, much of what Christians think they know about Satan, demons, and other evil powers is guided far more by Christian tradition and hearsay than exegesis of Scripture in its own context.

This is a problem of both method and translation. Most people interested in what the Bible has to say about the dark powers do not have access to the primary sources that frame the worldview of the biblical writers. English translations often obscure nuances crucial to correctly parsing what the biblical text says (and doesn't say) about the powers of darkness.

To be fair, however, even scholars are not immune to careless statements about the powers of darkness. This is at times quite understandable if, for instance, their expertise is outside the nuts and bolts of textual analysis in ancient context. At other times, scholars uncritically accept a consensus.

CHAPTER 12

Myths and Questions about the Powers of Darkness

WHAT FOLLOWS ARE QUESTIONS AND MISCONCEPTIONS THAT ILLUS-
trate the above. Our study to this point frames my responses, and so I
will not repeat material that can be referenced in earlier chapters.

"THE DEVIL IS A SECOND TEMPLE–PERIOD INVENTION ADOPTED BY THE NEW TESTAMENT."

Scholars commonly suggest that the figure of Satan or the devil as the
archnemesis of God is foreign to the Old Testament. The reason, as we
have seen in our study, is that (1) the Hebrew term śāṭān is not used as
a proper personal name in the Old Testament, and (2) the term śāṭān is
never applied to the original rebel of Eden, the serpent.

These points are obvious and not in dispute in our study. However,
the conclusion that the Satan figure of the Second Temple period and
New Testament is incompatible with the Old Testament is too hasty and
exaggerated. Our study has shown that, while the Old Testament itself
does not evince the profile of the Satan figure that is prominent in these
later texts, the material for that later profile can be found in the Old Testament. In other words, later writers connected data points they found in
the Old Testament and applied those points to the original rebel.

Surprisingly, few scholars seem to have taken this straightforward
approach (i.e., that later Jewish writers used the Old Testament as the
basis for the Satan figure). Rather, it is more common for them to argue

that the Second Temple–period Satan figure was a contrivance that emerged after the exile as the result of the influence of Persian Zoroastrian dualism. Riley's summary is representative:

> During and after the Babylonian Exile, however, Israel was influenced by the cosmological dualism of Persian Zoroastrianism. This system posited two warring camps of spiritual beings headed by twin but opposing siblings, the Zoroastrian God and Devil, who fought for the loyalty of humans in deadly combat. To assist in the battle the two had produced armies of lesser spirits, the angels and the demons. In one important text, "the Evil One" declares to God: "I shall destroy you and your creatures forever and ever. And I shall persuade all your creatures to hate you and to love me." Creation was their battlefield and the present age was the time of spiritual warfare. At the end of this age of conflict, there would be a final battle in which the Devil and his hosts would be defeated and destroyed in a fiery Hell, and a new creation and new age would begin in righteousness.[1]

There is both truth and fallacy in such thinking. On the one hand, it would be foolish to presume that Persian Zoroastrianism contributed nothing to Second Temple Jewish thought. Our study has established that ancient writers, including biblical authors, always were part of their intellectual world. The providence of God in preparing them for the task of producing Scripture meant they were part of their world, not insulated from their own milieu.

On the other hand, it is an overstatement to presume that the core elements of the idea of Satan/the devil we see in Second Temple Judaism *required* Zoroastrian beliefs. Is it really coherent to presume that Israel alone had no conception of an arch-supernatural enemy to Yahweh before the exile? The sort of intolerant monotheism put forth by Old Testament writers requires a binary opposition in the outlook of biblical writers.

The above quotation from Riley further suggests a related idea—that other supernatural evil beings aside from Satan also derive from Zoroastrian influence. This is quite overstated. Is it really unthinkable that an Old Testament writer and his readers would be unable to associate

---

1. G. J. Riley, "Devil," *DDD* 245.

the loss of Eden, initiated by the serpent, with the curse of disease and death? The notion of supernatural powers setting humans up for failure is common in ancient Near Eastern religion. Stories of one or more deities preventing humans from obtaining immortality (i.e., dooming them to death) are equally common. How is it coherent (again) to suppose that these ideas are foreign to the Old Testament writers until they encountered Zoroastrianism?

Rebellion in the divine council by a group of deities is far older than Zoroastrianism. The Mesopotamian *apkallu* story, the polemic target of the second supernatural rebellion of the Old Testament (Gen 6:1–4), predates Zoroastrianism. The notion of geographical rivalry between deities—the concept behind the Deuteronomy 32 worldview, the third divine rebellion of Scripture—is considerably older than (and not dependent upon) Persian Zoroastrianism. To anyone familiar with ancient Near Eastern religion these points are obvious. Should we be astonished that, given the supernatural rebellion of Genesis 6:1–4, which was considered to have proliferated depravity among humanity, and the cosmic geographical worldview of Deuteronomy 32:8–9, Israelites could conceive of an ongoing spiritual conflict that would one day be decided by Yahweh, the Most High? Zoroastrianism might have given expression to these themes, but it is not responsible for their origin. The suggestion that the content we have noted in Second Temple literature could not have been expressed without contact with Zoroastrianism is unwarranted.

"DEMONS ARE FALLEN ANGELS."

This notion is ubiquitous in popular Christian books and preaching. It is both on target and misguided. The statement fails to account for a number of items in the biblical text and the development of biblical thought about the powers of darkness. As we noted early in our study, in the Old Testament "angel" is a functional, not an ontological, term. It is, in effect, a job description. This circumstance changes in the Second Temple period and the New Testament, where "angel" is a term used predominantly to distinguish loyal supernatural beings from evil, rebellious ones. The devil (Satan) can have "angels" on his side (Matt 25:41; Rev 12:9), which, in the totality of good versus evil, would mean that demons, part of Satan's kingdom, can be considered fallen angels. Nevertheless, demons are consistently cast as disembodied spirits of dead Nephilim and their giant-clan descendants. Those spirits are the offspring of the angels that sinned before the flood, so the demons cannot be those fallen angels. Consequently, while a term like "fallen angels" may be used correctly in discussing demons, it is too often used simplistically and inaccurately.

"CAN SATAN AND EVIL SPIRITS BE REDEEMED?"

I have addressed this question in detail elsewhere.[2] Briefly, an offer of redemption to the supernatural rebels (Satan, the offending sons of God of Genesis 6:1–4, and the cosmic-geographical ruling sons of God hostile to Yahweh) is explicitly denied in Scripture:

> And to which of the angels has he ever said,
>
> > "Sit at my right hand
> > until I make your enemies a footstool for your feet"?
>
> Are they not all ministering spirits sent out to serve for the sake of those who are to inherit salvation? (Heb 1:13–14)

The implication of these words is clear in light of the link between the incarnation of the Son as a human and the offer of salvation put forth in Hebrews 2:

> The plan of salvation is focused on human beings because human beings were the original object of eternal life in God's presence on earth. Angels were not the focus, because the fall disrupted *an earthly enterprise*. God's human imagers were corrupted, left estranged from God—left unfit to live in God's presence. In the end, it will be human beings who will share authority with Christ in ruling the new earth, not angels.[3]

---

2. See Heiser, *Angels*, 153.

3. Heiser, *Angels*, 153. Appeals to the language of Rev 1–3 and Col 1:19–20 do not overturn the theology of Hebrews 1–2 and lack exegetical justification. Readers are directed to my earlier book for the details supporting such a conclusion.

"SATAN REBELLED BEFORE THE CREATION OF HUMANKIND AND TOOK A THIRD OF THE ANGELS WITH HIM."

This is an excellent example of how a Christian tradition can become doctrine. There isn't a single verse in the entirety of Scripture that tells us (a) the original rebel sinned before the episode of Genesis 3, or (b) a third of the angels also fell either before humanity's fall or at the time of that fall. There is only one passage that mentions a "third" of the angels (presumably) and Satan/the serpent in tandem (Rev 12:1–9):

> [1] And a great sign appeared in heaven: a woman clothed with the sun, with the moon under her feet, and on her head a crown of twelve stars. [2] She was pregnant and was crying out in birth pains and the agony of giving birth. [3] And another sign appeared in heaven: behold, a great red dragon, with seven heads and ten horns, and on his heads seven diadems. [4] His tail swept down a third of the stars of heaven and cast them to the earth. And the dragon stood before the woman who was about to give birth, so that when she bore her child he might devour it. [5] She gave birth to a male child, one who is to rule all the nations with a rod of iron, but her child was caught up to God and to his throne, [6] and the woman fled into the wilderness, where she has a place prepared by God, in which she is to be nourished for 1,260 days.
>
> [7] Now war arose in heaven, Michael and his angels fighting against the dragon. And the dragon and his angels fought back, [8] but he was defeated, and there was no longer any place for them in heaven. [9] And the great dragon was thrown down, that ancient serpent, who is called the devil and Satan, the deceiver of the whole world—he was thrown down to the earth, and his angels were thrown down with him.

I say that this passage is "presumably" about one-third of God's heavenly host being fallen because it is not clear that the "third of the stars" swept down by the dragon (serpent/Satan) refers to the angels who already are assisting the devil. It could well be that the one-third are good angels who have been defeated by the dragon. There are good reasons to take that position, namely, that Revelation 12:4 appears to be the fulfillment of Daniel 8:10.[4] For the purposes of this discussion, though, we

---

4. Beale writes on this point: "The picture of the dragon's tail sweeping away a third of the stars and casting them to the earth is taken from Dan. 8:10, which describes an end-time enemy

will presume that this third refers to evil supernatural agents in league with Satan.

The passage is clear that the timing of this conflict involving a third of the angels occurred in conjunction with the first coming of the Messiah:

And the dragon stood before the woman who was about to give birth, so that when she bore her child he might devour it. She gave birth to a male child, one who is to rule all the nations with a rod of iron, but her child was caught up to God and to his throne. (Rev 12:4–5)

The birth of the Messiah is clearly in view, as Revelation 12:5 points readers to the messianic theme of Psalm 2:8–9:

Ask of me, and I will make the nations your heritage,
    and the ends of the earth your possession.
You shall break them with a rod of iron
    and dash them in pieces like a potter's vessel.

The reference to the child born to rule the nations as being "caught up to God and to his throne" is an explicit reference to the resurrection and ascension—the key events that result in the defeat of Satan and the inauguration of the kingdom of God on earth. Scores of scholars recognize this point. Beale is representative:

The destiny of the Christ-child is described in an allusion to Ps. 2:7–9, which prophesies that God's Son will defeat all worldly enemies and then be enthroned as ruler over the earth. In fact, Christ is referred to as a "male son" to show that he is the initial fulfillment of the Psalm, which is the decisive event for the successful growth of the church. The last clause, referring to Christ's ascent, implies that the Ps. 2:7–9 prophecy about God's messianic Son has begun to be fulfilled. ... In context, this initial fulfillment means that, as in ancient times, so

---

persecuting the forces of God: 'and it [the horn] grew up to the host of heaven and caused some of the host and some of the stars to fall to the earth, and it trampled them down.' It is debated whether the 'host and some of the stars' in Daniel refers to angels or to Israelite saints. Both are likely true. In Daniel angels represent peoples (cf. Dan. 10:20–21; 12:1; cf. *Assumption of Moses* 10:8–10). The 'stars' in Daniel 8 signify angels who represent saints on earth. The same representational link is present between the Son of man, Michael, angels, and 'saints' in Daniel 7. That 'stars' can represent Israelite saints and not only angels is apparent from Dan. 12:3, where the righteous are compared to 'the firmament and ... the stars' (for this application of Dan. 12:3 see Matt. 13:43; cf. Gen. 15:5; 22:17)." Beale, *Book of Revelation*, 635.

again the dragon has been defeated. This time the defeat has occurred through the resurrection and ascent of Christ.[5]

The first advent context continues into Revelation 12:13–17:

[13] And when the dragon saw that he had been thrown down to the earth, he pursued the woman who had given birth to the male child. [14] But the woman was given the two wings of the great eagle so that she might fly from the serpent into the wilderness, to the place where she is to be nourished for a time, and times, and half a time. [15] The serpent poured water like a river out of his mouth after the woman, to sweep her away with a flood. [16] But the earth came to the help of the woman, and the earth opened its mouth and swallowed the river that the dragon had poured from his mouth. [17] Then the dragon became furious with the woman and went off to make war on the rest of her offspring, on those who keep the commandments of God and hold to the testimony of Jesus. And he stood on the sand of the sea.[6]

The wording of verse 17 is as clear an association of the vision to the first coming of Jesus as the earlier citation of Psalm 2: "Then the dragon became furious with the woman and went off to make war on the rest of her offspring, on those who keep the commandments of God and hold to the testimony of Jesus." This simply cannot be construed as describing a primeval rebellion prior to the creation of humanity in Eden. Since there is no other passage in the Bible that uses the "third" language in conjunction with a satanic conflict, the idea that Satan and one-third of the angels rebelled at that time is a traditional myth.[7]

---

5. Beale, *Book of Revelation*, 639–40.

6. Beale (650, 668) notes that the elements of Revelation 12 from v. 7 onward are connected to vv. 1–6: "John does not make the logical connection between vv 1–6 and vv 7–12 explicit. Such a connection is demanded not only by proximity but also because vv 7–12 continue the vision that began in v 3, as seen by a comparison of the wording of vv 3 and 7: ὤφθη ἄλλο σημεῖον ἐν τῷ οὐρανῷ, καὶ ἰδοὺ ... καὶ ἐγένετο πόλεμος ἐν τῷ οὐρανῷ [*ōphthē allo sēmeion en tō ouranō, kai idou ... kai egeneto polemos en tō ouranō*] ('another sign appeared in heaven, and behold ... and there was war in heaven'). Verses 7–12 are a narration of the defeat of the devil and his angels by Michael and his angels in heavenly combat. ... Verse 13 picks up where both v 6 and v 12 left off. V[erse] 6 narrated only the fact of the saintly community fleeing into a place of divine refuge, and there was no explicit comment about the dragon's persecution of the community. V[erse] 12 explains that the dragon was enraged over losing his heavenly office as a result of his inability to thwart the birth of Christ and especially his ultimate enthronement. Now v 13 shows that he expresses his anger by persecuting the saints."

7. This myth is often defended by means of the so-called gap theory, the belief that Satan rebelled between Gen 1:1 and 1:2. The most exhaustive scholarly refutation of the gap theory is Weston Fields, *Unformed and Unfilled: A Critique of the Gap Theory* (Green Forest, AR: Master Books, 2005). The

"WHAT DID SATAN AND THE DEMONS KNOW ABOUT JESUS?"

It is evident from the Gospel accounts of Jesus' encounters with Satan (Matt 4:1–11; Mark 1:12–13; Luke 4:1–13) and demons (Mark 1:21–24; 5:9–15; Luke 4:31–37; 8:30–33) that the powers of darkness knew who Jesus was. Jesus is identified in these episodes as the "Son of God" or "Son of the Most High" (Matt 4:3, 6; 8:29; Mark 3:11; 5:7; Luke 4:3, 9; 8:28). Such identifications do not mean, however, that Satan and evil spirits knew God's plan for the death of Jesus, his resurrection, and ascension. Passages such as 1 Peter 1:10–12 and 1 Corinthians 2:6–8 make this ignorance evident:[8]

---

gap theory has no exegetical standing. Briefly, there are two Hebrew grammatical-syntactical issues related to Gen 1:1 and 1:2 that destroy the gap theory. First, there is no definite article under the preposition *beth* in *bĕrē'šît*, which suggests that 1:1 does not describe a definite beginning. The absence of the definite article has led many scholars to conclude that Gen 1:1 is a dependent clause circumstantial to 1:3, since 1:2 is certainly a dependent clause. This would mean the first creative act is in Gen 1:3, with Gen 1:1–2 describing preexistent circumstances to Gen 1:3. Other scholars argue that Gen 1:1 is still an independent clause with the absence of the article telegraphing 1:1 is a chapter heading or title. Both options are grammatically viable and undermine a gap theory. Both options destroy a linear sequence of events from 1:1 to 1:2 which is absolutely critical to the gap theory. Second, and most damaging to the gap theory approach, Gen 1:2 begins with a disjunctive *waw* (*waw* + noun). This is indisputable, as a *waw* attached to a noun creates a disjunction when it follows a finite verb, as is the case here. As such, Gen 1:1–3 cannot be read as a linear sequence of events, something the gap theory absolutely requires. This disjunction also ruins the attempt of gap theorists to translate the lemma *hāyâ* ("to be") as "became" in 1:2. If the *waw* disjunctive forbids a linear sequence, then "became" is a nonsensical translation, as that wording presumes 1:2 is the result of some prior event in sequence. See Bruce K. Waltke, "The Creation Account in Genesis 1:1–3: Part II: The Restitution Theory," *BSac* 132 (1975): 136–44; Waltke, "The Creation Account in Genesis 1:1–3: Part III: The Initial Chaos Theory and the Precreation Chaos Theory," *BSac* 132 (1975): 216–28; Victor P. Hamilton, *The Book of Genesis, Chapters 1–17* (NICOT; Grand Rapids: Eerdmans, 1990), 103–15. Lastly the gap theory's notion that "*tōhû wābōhû*" ("formless and empty") speak of a judgment upon evil (the fall of Satan), particularly since "darkness" is a circumstance of Gen 1:2, has been soundly refuted by David Toshio Tsumura, *Creation and Destruction: A Reappraisal of the Chaoskampf Theory in the Old Testament* (Winona Lake, IN: Eisenbrauns, 2005).

8. The wording of 1 Pet 1:12 indicates an ignorance of the plan of salvation on the part of the angels. There is no reason to suppose Satan and demons, hostile to God's plans, knew more. Michaels writes of this wording: "εἰς ἃ ἐπιθυμοῦσιν ἄγγελοι παρακύψαι [*eis ha epithymousin angeloi parakypsai*], 'on these things the angels desire to look.' Like προφῆται [*prophētai*, 'prophets'] in v 10, ἄγγελοι [*angeloi*] is without the article. These are 'angels' in general rather than a particular group; yet as in the case of the prophets Peter evidently has specific traditions in mind. The notion that some heavenly mysteries are hidden even from the angels who dwell in heaven is found both in Jewish apocalyptic literature (e.g., *1 Enoch* 16.3; *2 Enoch* 24.3) and in the NT (e.g., Mark 13:32, and by implication Eph 3:10; 1 Cor 2:6–8 is different in that it focuses on hostile powers in particular). This tradition exists in apocalyptic literature alongside that of the 'interpreting angel' who explains God's mysteries to a prophet or seer (e.g., Zech 1:9; 4 Ezra 4:1; Rev 17:1; 21:9). The very fact that angels know so much enhances the sense of wonder at the things they do not know." See J. Ramsey Michaels, *1 Peter* (WBC; Dallas: Word, 1998), 48. The "rulers" (*archontōn*) of 1 Cor 2:8 are best understood as supernatural

¹⁰ Concerning this salvation, the prophets who prophesied about the grace that was to be yours searched and inquired carefully, ¹¹ inquiring what person or time the Spirit of Christ in them was indicating when he predicted the sufferings of Christ and the subsequent glories. ¹² It was revealed to them that they were serving not themselves but you, in the things that have now been announced to you through those who preached the good news to you by the Holy Spirit sent from heaven, things into which angels long to look. (1 Pet 1:10–12)

⁶ Yet among the mature we do impart wisdom, although it is not a wisdom of this age or of the rulers of this age, who are doomed to pass away. ⁷ But we impart a secret and hidden wisdom of God, which God decreed before the ages for our glory. ⁸ None of the rulers of this age understood this, for if they had, they would not have crucified the Lord of glory. (1 Cor 2:6–8)

As I noted in *The Unseen Realm*, the plan of salvation was scattered and fragmented in dozens of places.⁹ Only in hindsight could the plan be understood as a whole. It is not as though a human or supernatural intelligence could simply consult the Scriptures to find out what would happen. The plan was hidden in plain sight. Even after the resurrection, in the presence of the risen Christ himself, Jesus had to "[open] their minds to understand the Scriptures" (Luke 24:45). The plan of salvation and its relationship to the Old Testament Scriptures had to be revealed supernaturally. There is no reason to expect the powers of darkness to have been given such understanding.

It is not difficult to balance this ignorance with the understanding of the identity of Jesus in the Gospels on the part of Satan and demons. The Old Testament made no effort to conceal God's desire to live among his human creations, to make them participants in governing his creation.

---

beings. "Rulers of this age" makes little sense of human rulers. The context of 1 Cor 2 is that of a divine plan. While *archōn* is found in the New Testament and elsewhere for human rulers, it makes little sense for Paul to see irony in the fact that humans didn't know God's mystery-plan involved the death and resurrection of the Messiah. Such an observation would be palpable. As Aune notes, "The term *archontes* used as a designation for angelic beings first occurs in the LXX Dan 10:13, and seven times in Theod. Dan 10:13, 20–21; 12:1, where the LXX has *stratēgos*, 'commander,' 'magistrate,' all translations of the Aram *śar*, 'prince'" (Aune, "Archon," *DDD* 84). That the rulers here are evil supernatural powers of darkness is an interpretation found in church fathers such as Origen, Tertullian, and Justin (see Aune, "Archon," 82–85).

9. Heiser, *Unseen Realm*, 241, 330.

This was the point of Eden, human creation, and the commands given to humanity (Gen 1:26–28). After the fall, God sought repeatedly (using human agency, in line with his original desire) to restore his rule among his people. Given God's decision to make covenants with fallible humanity, the incarnation was necessary to fulfill those covenants. This is why Jesus occupied the central role of covenant fulfillment as the descendant of Adam, Abraham, and David. It would be perfectly reasonable for Satan and demons to discern that the Son of the Most High had come to earth to inaugurate the kingdom of his Father and reclaim the nations of the earth for membership in that kingdom. In fact, this intent would be difficult to miss. But the mechanism for accomplishing the end game (the cross, resurrection, ascension) was fragmented and cryptic, requiring the Spirit's illumination.

"WHERE DOES THE IDEA OF THE DEVIL HAVING HORNS AND A TAIL COME FROM?"

As we saw in chapter 1, Ugaritic religion knows a deity (ḥby) associated with the realm of the dead that bears such features.[10] However, our discussion took note of the obscure nature of the data in this regard and uncertainties regarding its relationship to biblical passages (Isa 26:20; Hab 3:4) that seem to include this lemma. The Jewish pseudepigraphical work known as 3 Baruch, likely composed in the late first or early second century AD, provides evidence that early Jewish and Christian writer-editors associated these features with the "goat demons" (śĕ'îrîm) of the Old Testament.[11] The devil's horns and tail therefore (in theory) derived from the original enemy's association with a Canaanite underworld deity and the motif of the demonic wilderness with its preternatural creatures. More secure, at least for Christian imagery, is the relationship of the devil to the Greco-Roman deity Pan:

> The worship and the different functions of Pan are derived from the mythology of the ancient Egyptians. This god was one of the eight

---

10. Gordon, "The Devil, ḥby," 15; Xella, "Haby," DDD 377.

11. Kulik, "How the Devil Got His Hooves and Horns," 195–229. Scholars now believe that 3 Baruch was originally a Jewish composition that was later edited and added to by a Christian. One piece of evidence supporting this is the fact that "many of the Christian passages in the Greek version are absent in the Slavonic." See James H. Charlesworth, "Baruch, Book of 3 (Greek)," ABD 1:621–22.

great gods of the Egyptians, who ranked before the other twelve gods, whom the Romans called *Consentes*. He was worshipped with the greatest solemnity all over Egypt. His statues represented him as a goat, not because he was really such, but this was done for mysterious reasons. He was the emblem of fecundity, and they looked upon him as the principle of all things. His horns, as some observe, represented the rays of the sun, and the brightness of the heavens was expressed by the vivacity and the ruddiness of his complexion. The star which he wore on his breast was the symbol of the firmament, and his hairy legs and feet denoted the inferior parts of the earth, such as the woods and plants. Some suppose that he appeared as a goat because when the gods fled into Egypt, in their war against the giants, Pan transformed himself into a goat, an example which was immediately followed by all the deities. When, after the establishment of Christianity, the heathen deities were degraded by the Church into fallen angels, the characteristics of Pan—viz. the horns, the goat's beard, the pointed ears, the crooked nose, the tail, and the goat's feet—were transferred to the devil himself.[12]

We can safely conclude that the grotesque imagery with which Satan was described in early Christian tradition (and Hollywood) is the product of imagination. This should not be interpreted too harshly. The association of Satan/the devil with the underworld, death, disease, and preternatural cosmic geography make good sense in light of the Old Testament conceptions of the effect on humanity of the original rebel's transgression (death) and domicile. Use of pagan imagery to communicate these ideas embedded these theological points in the minds of believers.

"CAN SATAN AND DEMONS READ OUR MINDS?"

There is no scriptural evidence that members of the heavenly host know a person's mind or thoughts the way God does. The question usually arises from presumptions we have about consciousness and its relationship to supernatural beings. The fact that angels appear to people in dreams and

---

12. John M'Clintock and James Strong, "Pan (2)," *Cyclopædia of Biblical, Theological, and Ecclesiastical Literature* (New York: Harper & Brothers, 1894), 7:608. See also Jeffrey Burton Russell, *The Devil: Perceptions of Evil from Antiquity to Primitive Christianity* (Ithaca, NY: Cornell University Press, 1987), 126, 157.

visions (Matt 1:20; 2:13, 19; Acts 10:3) seems to suggest that supernatural beings can tap into one's mind. The assumption is that since evil spirits are fallen angels (see the earlier discussion on that language), then Satan and demons have the ability to "occupy space" in the human mind.

That angels in the New Testament instructed people through such means is not evidence of mind *reading*. If anything, such incidents describe the transmission of information, not reading minds. Such incidents could of course influence human behavior and might conceivably be a line of demonic oppression. That said, there are no scriptural examples of Satan or an evil spirit appearing to someone in a dream. As such, it is impossible to make a *scriptural* argument for a demonic invasion of the mind of the sort that would facilitate mind reading or demonization. An appeal to seeing or interacting with demonic entities in dreams or other altered states of consciousness can teach us nothing about the ontology of those entities until consciousness is understood. The approach is based on speculation.

"CAIN WAS (LITERALLY) FATHERED BY SATAN."

The myth that Cain was the literal spawn of Satan is prevalent among anti-Semitic groups.[13] The idea is extrapolated from several biblical passages. Despite its anti-Semitic connotation, the serpent-seed myth is also defended on the basis of Jewish tradition. The biblical passages referenced to support this myth are as follows:

> Now Adam knew Eve his wife, and she conceived and bore Cain, saying, "I have gotten a man with the help of the LORD." (Gen 4:1)

> And Adam knew his wife again, and she bore a son and called his name Seth, for she said, "God has appointed for me another offspring instead of Abel, for Cain killed him." (Gen 4:25)

> For this is the message that you have heard from the beginning, that we should love one another. We should not be like Cain, who was

---

13. See for example, Michael Barkun, *Religion and the Racist Right: The Origins of the Christian Identity Movement* (Chapel Hill, NC: University of North Carolina Press, 1997), 160–65; Chester L. Quarles, *Christian Identity: The Aryan American Bloodline Religion* (Jefferson, NC: McFarland & Company, 2004), 99–101.

of the evil one and murdered his brother. And why did he murder him? Because his own deeds were evil and his brother's righteous. (1 John 3:11–12)

The references from Genesis 4 seem inexplicable, because they clearly have Adam "knowing" Eve (sexually),[14] after which she bears a child. Proponents of the serpent-seed mythology ignore these parts of both verses and focus on the phrase ending Genesis 4:1, where Eve says, "I have acquired a man with ['*et*] Yahweh."[15] The Hebrew lemma '*et* is most frequently an untranslated particle that marks the direct object of a verb.[16] It may also be a homograph that is a preposition denoting the assistance or participation of the following noun ("with"; "together with").[17]

It is this latter understanding to which serpent-seed proponents appeal. Yet this would leave us with a situation where Yahweh, not the serpent, had sexual relations with Eve, something both verses (Gen 4:1, 25) explicitly deny. The argument is then made that the text originally had the serpent as the object of the preposition, but it was later changed to Yahweh. The myth is thus based on ignoring what the text plainly says about Adam knowing Eve and speculating about scribal tampering.

Most scholars agree that Genesis 4:1 ends with Eve expressing her belief that Yahweh had helped her conceive a child, though she obviously understood she had sexual relations with Adam.[18] This is the most coherent approach since this idea is evidenced elsewhere in the Old Testament. For example, Sarah and Hannah both believed that they were able to conceive and have children due to divine intervention—a point affirmed by the text (Gen 17:19, 21; 18:9–15; cp. Gen 21:2; Heb 11:11; 1 Sam 1:11, 19–20).

---

14. To "know" (*yada*ʿ) a woman is a common Biblical Hebrew idiom for sexual intercourse (cp. Gen 19:5, 8; 24:16; Num 31:17; 1 Kgs 1:4). The idiom is also witnessed in other ancient Semitic languages. See *HALOT*, s.v. ידע.

15. For a dense exegetical and historical discussion of Gen 4:1, including the matter of medieval targums, see Mark William Scarlata, *Outside of Eden: Cain in the Ancient Versions of Genesis 4:1–16* (London: Bloomsbury, 2012), 27–48.

16. *HALOT*, s.v. אֵת (I).

17. *HALOT*, s.v. אֵת (II).

18. Scarlata notes another possibility: "If את ('*et*) taken as a predicative accusative, the sentence could be translated, "I have acquired/created a man, *who is* YHWH," which could signify that Eve believed she had given birth to the promised seed of Gen 3:15." See Scarlata, *Outside of Eden*, 29.

Proponents of the serpent-seed myth support their belief via an Aramaic targum[19] that allegedly puts forth the idea that Eve and Satan copulated and produced Cain. The targum in view is known as Targum Pseudo-Jonathan (Genesis), produced in the seventh or eighth century AD.[20] This targum, composed well over one thousand years *after* the final form of the Hebrew Bible, renders Genesis 4:1 this way: "Adam knew his wife Eve who had conceived from Sammael, the angel of the Lord."[21] "Sammael" is a name for Satan evidenced in the Second Temple period.[22] This targum is known in two editions, one of which omits the reference to Sammael.[23] The translation intentionally omits Eve's declaration at the end of Genesis 4:1, crediting Yahweh for divine assistance. Equally peculiar is its retention of sexual language relative to Adam. The translation may actually be construed as swapping out Yahweh as the divine helper and inserting Satan, making the case for a satanic line of Cain without asserting a sexual relationship between Eve and Satan. In any event, this is the lone manuscript evidence for the serpent-seed myth, and it is demonstrably poor.

Despite the utter lack of exegetical data, we must ask whether 1 John 3:11–12 nevertheless supports the idea that Cain was fathered by Satan. Scarlata summarizes the perspective:

> Since the entire epistle of 1 John deals with the theme of brotherly love, the figure of Cain, the murderer, provides the perfect antithesis to Christ, the one who laid down his life for others. The author exhorts the believers not to be "like Cain, who was of the evil one and murdered his brother. And why did he murder him? Because his own deeds were evil and his brother's righteous." The question of Cain's origins arises from the phrase "who was of the evil one" (ἐκ τοῦ πονηροῦ ἦν; *ek tou ponērou ēn*), which may be considered a reference

---

19. A targum is an Aramaic translation, in this case, of the Hebrew book of Genesis.

20. Michael Maher, *Targum Pseudo-Jonathan: Genesis*, vol. 1B of *The Aramaic Bible*, ed. Kevin Cathcart, Michael Maher, and Martin McNamara (Collegeville, MN: The Liturgical Press, 1992).

21. The translation is from Maher, *Targum Pseudo-Jonathan: Genesis*, 31.

22. The earliest reference appears to be in the Martyrdom and Ascension of Isaiah (Mart. Ascen. Isa. 1:8; 2:1; 3:13; 5:15; 7:9; 11:41). That work is dated between the second century BC and the fourth century AD, as parts of it evince a Christian hand (*OTP*, 2:149).

23. See the discussion in Maher, *Targum Pseudo-Jonathan: Genesis*, 31, note 2 on Gen 4:1; Scarlata, *Outside of Eden*, 69–73. Even more bizarre is the rabbinic tradition from b. Shabbat 146a (738), b. Yebamot 103b (711), b. Abodah Zarah 22b (114), and Pirqe de Rabbi Eliezer 13 (92), 21 (150). These sources have the serpent copulating with Eve and Sammael coming to Eve riding on a serpent.

to his Satanic descent. Following the lesson of Cain, however, v. 15 states in more general terms that "everyone who hates his brother is a murderer." The word for "murderer" (ἀνθρωποκτόνος; *anthrōpoktonos*) is employed only here and in John 8:44, when Jesus calls the scribes and Pharisees children of the devil, who was a "murderer" from the beginning.[24]

The context for verses 11–12, particularly verse 10, is the key to understanding what the Apostle John is saying and exposing the specious reasoning of serpent-seed thinking:

> In vv. 1–9 there is a sharp contrast delineated between the "children of God" as those who no longer sin and those "of the devil" who continue to sin. This polemic is summed up in v. 10 where the author states, "By this it is evident who are the children of God, and who are the children of the devil: whoever does not practise righteousness is not of God, nor is the one who does not love his brother."[25]

The point that must not be missed is that the phrase "children of God" in verse 10 does not mean "those who were physically spawned by God through sexual relations with human women." It refers to spiritual orientation as a result of faith in Christ (cp. 1 John 3:1–3; John 1:12; 11:52). Consequently, those who are set in opposition (Cain; the Pharisees in John 8:44) by John should be viewed in the same way, not as physical spawn of Satan.

"CAN A CHRISTIAN BE DEMON POSSESSED?"

Christian writers have taken both sides of this issue. The disagreement in part derives from semantics, but that is not to imply that the debate lacks substance. The semantic problem derives from English translations of the Greek lemmas in passages describing demonized individuals. Words like "possess" and "possession" denote ownership.

A close reading of the New Testament ought to make it clear that a member of the body of Christ cannot be *owned* by Satan or demons. The body of Christ, the church, has been "obtained with his own blood"

---

24. Scarlata, *Outside of Eden*, 45.
25. Ibid., 46.

(Acts 20:28). The Spirit (Rom 8:9–11, 16–17) and Christ (Col 1:27) dwell within those who believe. Those who are "in Christ" have a new identity as members of the family of God (Gal 3:26). Believers have been "delivered … from the domain of darkness and transferred … to the kingdom of his beloved Son" (Col 1:13). We are God's inheritance (Eph 1:18). The idea that believers described in these ways can be subsequently owned by *lesser* demonic powers is incoherent.[26] Arnold's observations are significant in this regard:

> The word *possession* never even appears in the Bible in the passages where Jesus or the apostles cast evil spirits out of an individual. The expression *demon-possessed* or *demon possession* does occur in some English translations of the Greek text, but there is never a Greek word for "possession" that stands behind it. "Demon possession" is always the translation of a single Greek word, *daimonizomai*. Words for ownership or possession (e.g., *huparchō, echō, katechō, ktaomai,* or *peripoieō*) are absent in the original text. … The expression "he has a demon" *(echei daimonion)* does appear in the Gospels (e.g., Luke 4:33; 8:27), but the inverse, "a demon has him," never occurs.[27]

The point Arnold makes is significant. No Greek word for "possession" or "ownership" appears in passages to clarify or define the activity described by *daimonizomai*. It is English semantics, not the Greek lemma, which have led to the controversy over whether Christians can be possessed by demons.

---

26. Some arguments against Christians being demon possessed are common but not as forceful. For instance, some writers suggest that since believers are the temple of God/the Holy Spirit (1 Cor 3:16–17; 6:19–20; 2 Cor 6:15–18), they cannot be possessed. The temple analogy really does not support this point. Arnold points to New Testament language that undermines its potency. For example, there is the danger of sin reigning in the believer's flesh (Rom 6:12–13). The Old Testament temple was (in theory) holy ground, purged of sin and impurity. This purged status did not prevent subsequent contamination or, in the most extreme cases, introduction of idols into the temple itself. See Clinton E. Arnold, *3 Crucial Questions about Spiritual Warfare* (Grand Rapids: Baker Academic, 1997), 82. As we will note in the ensuing discussion, demonization can include temptation to sin or solicitation of the flesh. It would therefore seem that while demons cannot own the believer, they can cooperate with the sinful propensities of our flesh.

27. Arnold, *3 Crucial Questions about Spiritual Warfare*, 79, including material from footnote 10. Arnold adds on page 80: "Nevertheless, the terms of the current debate have been set by the long-standing tradition of translating the expression *demon-possessed*. Where did English Bible translators get the idea of translating *daimonizomai* as 'demon possession'? The translation was most likely influenced by the Latin Church's tradition of using the term *possessio* to describe a person deeply troubled by a demonic spirit. Interestingly, the Latin Vulgate, however, does not use the term *possessio* to translate *daimonizomai*, but the simple expression *to have a demon* (*habeo* with *daemonia*)."

If "ownership" is not a workable understanding of the Greek lemma *daimonizomai*, how should it be translated and understood? Some translators who have detected the problem caused by English semantics related to words like "possess" have opted for renderings such as "tormented" or "troubled" (i.e., by demons). While these choices may help, there are other Greek lemmas that have these meanings, and so the choices are interpretive. The best alternative seems to be simply to transliterate *daimonizomai* as "demonize." This choice avoids misconceptions (and related theological inconsistencies) that arise from English "possession" semantics.

This decision of course begs an obvious question: Does the New Testament help us understand how a Christian might be "demonized" while not being owned by Satan or an evil spirit? Arnold asks the same question in other ways:

> We might ask, "Can Christians come under a high degree of influence by a demonic spirit?" or, "Is it possible for Christians to yield control of their bodies to a demonic spirit in the same way that they yield to the power of sin?"[28]

The answer to the question, however worded, is "yes." On this the New Testament is clear, as several passages employ language that suggests Christians can fall under the influence of Satan and evil spirits.[29] Paul warned Timothy about certain teachers in this regard: "Now the Spirit expressly says that in later times some will depart from the faith by devoting themselves to deceitful spirits and teachings of demons" (1 Tim 4:1). That those doing so were "departing from the faith" indicates that those Paul had in view were professing believers. For sure, these false teachers did not see what they were doing as out of step with the faith. Paul linked this behavior with the latter days as the Spirit had revealed to the prophets. In his second letter to Timothy, Paul's language was even more foreboding, instructing Timothy to gently correct such opponents so they might "escape from the snare of the devil, after being captured by him to do his will" (2 Tim 2:26). The idea that believers could be

---

28. Arnold, *3 Crucial Questions about Spiritual Warfare*, 80.
29. Arnold devotes considerable space to this reality. While some of my categories differ slightly, readers are encouraged to consult Arnold, *3 Crucial Questions about Spiritual Warfare*, 88–100.

captured by Satan and made servants of his will certainly fits the notion of demonization, though it lacks the bizarre physical torment of episodes in the Gospels.

Less dramatic but equally dangerous are New Testament warnings about "[giving] opportunity to the devil" (Eph 4:27) and habitual, unrepentant sin ("Whoever makes a practice of sinning is of the devil"; 1 John 3:8). While the sinful impulse that gives rise to temptation resides in the flesh (Jas 1:14–15; Rom 7:18–24), the devil is nevertheless called the tempter (1 Thess 3:5). Yielding to temptation enslaves the believer (Rom 6:6, 12–14; 8:3–8), and so such a lifestyle can rightly be construed as a kind of demonization. Aside from enslavement to sin, Satan seeks to control believers by other means, whether mental, emotional, or physical. For example, the context for Peter's familiar portrayal of Satan as a devouring lion is persecution and suffering:

> [8] Be sober-minded; be watchful. Your adversary the devil prowls around like a roaring lion, seeking someone to devour. [9] Resist him, firm in your faith, knowing that the same kinds of suffering are being experienced by your brotherhood throughout the world. (1 Pet 5:8–9)

Paul's equally memorable statement that a "messenger of Satan" was given to him "in the flesh" (2 Cor 12:7) also links suffering with demonization.[30]

The overarching point is that, while Christians cannot be owned by Satan—an idea that derives from the unfortunate "possession" language—they can be demonized. Demonization can take various forms: persecution, harassment, being captivated by false teaching, and enslavement to sin.

"WHAT IS SPIRITUAL WARFARE?"

One of the more popular topics in contemporary Christian interest in the powers of darkness is spiritual warfare. As Arnold notes, "Many

---

30. This point is true whether the messenger was a supernatural being or some physical affliction from Satan. My view is that Paul's "thorn in the flesh ... messenger of Satan" was a demonic being. In this regard, see David Abernathy, "Paul's Thorn in the Flesh: A Messenger of Satan?" *Neotestamentica* 35.1–2 (2001): 69–79; Christopher R. A. Morray-Jones, "Paradise Revisited (2 Cor 12:1–12): The Jewish Mystical Background of Paul's Apostolate: Part 1: The Jewish Sources," *HTR* 86.2 (1993): 177–217; Morray-Jones, "Paradise Revisited (2 Cor 12:1–12): The Jewish Mystical Background of Paul's Apostolate: Part 2: Paul's Heavenly Ascent and Its Significance," *HTR* 86.3 (1993): 265–92.

Christians have come to think of spiritual warfare as a specialized form of ministry—exorcism, deliverance ministry, or certain types of intercession."[31] These ministries place a significant focus on confrontations with evil spirits ("power encounters"). Episodes in the New Testament where Jesus, his disciples, and other apostles (e.g., Paul) cast out demons or challenge evil spirits are taken as template backdrops for passages that talk about the spiritual war in which believers find themselves (Eph 6:10–20; 2 Cor 10:3–6). The Deuteronomy 32 worldview of the Old Testament has also recently become a point of reference for spiritual warfare ministry, specifically what is known as "Strategic Level Spiritual Warfare" (SLSW). Recall that the Deuteronomy 32 worldview emphasizes how God allotted the nations to other spiritual beings while keeping Israel as his possession.[32] This idea that rebellious spiritual beings have power and authority over specific places is central to SLSW. In addition to Deuteronomy 32, advocates of SLSW find biblical support for their approach in Old Testament passages such as Psalm 82, Psalm 96:5, Psalm 106:37–38, and Daniel 10. The latter text is extremely significant because it presents a conflict between rebellious territorial spirits—the "prince of Greece" and the "prince of Persia"—and God's angels, including the "chief prince" Michael. New Testament support for the concept is found in the passages referring to the "ruler(s) or god of this world/age" along with other descriptions of spiritual warfare (e.g., John 12:31; 14:30; 16:11; 1 Cor 2:6–8; 2 Cor 4:4; Eph 6:12; 1 John 5:19; Rev 12:7–9).[33]

The leading figure behind SLSW for many years was C. Peter Wagner, who coined the term. Eddy and Beilby describe Wagner's approach and explain how he developed SLSW

in the process of distinguishing between three levels of activity in the practice of spiritual warfare: "ground-level" (i.e., casting demons out of individual people), "occult-level" (i.e., dealing with demonic forces within Satanism, witchcraft, and other forms of "structured occultism"), and finally "strategic-level" (i.e., direct confrontation of territorial spirits that hold "cities, nations, neighborhoods, people

---

31. Arnold, *3 Crucial Questions about Spiritual Warfare*, 19.
32. See Heiser, *Unseen Realm*, 113–15.
33. Paul Rhodes Eddy and James K. Beilby, "Introduction," in *Understanding Spiritual Warfare: Four Views*, ed. James K. Beilby and Paul Rhodes Eddy (Grand Rapids: Baker Academic, 2012), 41.

groups, religious alliances, industries, or any other form of human society in spiritual captivity"). SLSW commonly involves "spiritual mapping," a process by which the specific territorial spirit(s) of an area is discerned and named. ... SLSW involves focused, aggressive prayer against the territorial spirits themselves.[34]

While it's encouraging to see the Deuteronomy 32 worldview taken seriously, there are some serious flaws with defining spiritual warfare in such terms. Fundamentally, confrontation of the spirit world isn't the pattern that one sees in the New Testament in regard to the defeat of the fallen sons of God ("principalities").

As we saw in the previous chapter, the jurisdictional authority of these sons of God has been nullified by the resurrection and ascension of Christ. That reality is what frames the Great Commission—the call to reclaim the nations ("Go therefore and make disciples of all nations," Matt 28:19). The kingdom of darkness will lose what is essentially a spiritual war of attrition, for the gates of hell will not be able to withstand the church. This is why believers are never commanded to rebuke spirits and demand their flight in the name of Jesus.[35] It is unnecessary. Their

---

34. Ibid., 41–42.

35. SLSW advocates would object to this point, arguing (in part) that the Great Commission passage in Mark 16:9–20 includes casting out demons (Mark 16:17). Several points need to be noted in response. First, most New Testament scholars (evangelical and otherwise) believe that the original text of Mark ended at Mark 16:8. This is why many modern English translations bracket Mark 16:9–20 and include an explanatory footnote. Stein observes: "Although few scholars today argue for the authenticity of either the 'shorter' or 'longer ending' of Mark ... there is continued debate over whether Mark intended to end his Gospel at 16:8. In the first half of the twentieth century, scholars were inclined to argue that 16:8 was not the intended ending of Mark. Later in that century, a reversal of this position took place. Mark was now seen as intending to end his Gospel at 16:8." See Robert H. Stein, *Mark* (BECNT; Grand Rapids: Baker Academic, 2008), 733. The textual problems with the "long ending" of Mark (vv. 9–20) are famous and the bibliography on the issue is copious. Marcus summarizes the manuscript situation: "[Verses 9–20] are found in the overwhelming majority of manuscripts and in all major manuscript families and are attested already by Irenaeus (*Against Heresies* 3.10.5) in 185 C.E and perhaps, even earlier, by Justin (1 *Apology* 45, around 155 C.E). But they were almost certainly not penned by Mark, nor were they the original ending of the Gospel. Matthew and Luke follow Mark's narrative closely up to 16:8, whereas beyond it they diverge radically, suggesting that their version of Mark did not contain anything subsequent to 16:8. Verses 9–20, moreover, do not exist in our earliest and best Greek manuscripts, Sinaiticus and Vaticanus, both of which terminate at 16:8, as do the Sinaitic Syriac, about a hundred Armenian manuscripts, the two oldest Georgian manuscripts (from 897 and 913 C.E.), and all but one manuscript of the Sahidic Coptic. When verses 9–20 *do* appear, moreover, they are often separated from 16:8 by scribal signs (asterisks or obeli) or by notations that state or suggest that what follows is not found in some witnesses." See Joel Marcus, *Mark 8–16: A New Translation with Introduction and Commentary* (AYB;

authority has been withdrawn by the Most High. Believers in turn are commanded to reclaim their territory by recruiting the citizens in those territories for the kingdom of God.

What this means in both theological and practical terms is that spiritual warfare needs to be understood in the context of the conflict between two kingdoms: the kingdom of God and the kingdom of Satan. During Jesus' public ministry we see this binary opposition. Jesus himself articulated it: "If it is by the Spirit of God that I cast out demons, then the kingdom of God has come upon you" (Matt 12:28). It is no coincidence that the expulsion of demons from people and places accompanied the inauguration of the kingdom of God. As the kingdom of God grows, the kingdom of darkness shrinks and loses ground.

Jesus never commanded that his followers confront spiritual entities.[36] Instead he gave the Great Commission. A spiritual entity might be driven away, but that doesn't necessarily result in a new soul entering the kingdom of God. This latter goal is the reason Jesus gave his life and rose from the dead. The work of Christ was not about power encounters with demons. It was much more comprehensive and enduring than that. The goal was to bring Eden full circle—fulfilling God's desire to have a human family with him forever. Punishing fallen spirits does not accomplish God's original Edenic goal. Only the Great Commission accomplishes the ends to which God has been working as well as the defeat and punishment of rebellious evil spirits. The Great Commission is thus a comprehensive plan for spiritual warfare.

A careful reading of the two primary passages used to support power encounter spiritual warfare bears out the preceding assertion that

---

New Haven, CT: Yale University Press, 2009), 1088–89. Consequently, basing any point of doctrine on the content of Mark 16:9–20 is misguided and unwise. Second, one cannot conclude from Mark 16:17 that all believers should be engaging in SLSW. Paul is clear that the gifts of tongues and healing are *not* for every believer. In fact, no supernatural gift is for every believer. They are distributed to some (1 Cor 12:27–31).

36. It is true that the disciples had power to exorcise demons, but even in the instances when Jesus authorized exorcism the context is limited to healing personal harassment and harm. Arnold explains the point: "When Jesus spoke of giving the Seventy authority 'to overcome all the power of the enemy' (Luke 10:19), this did not extend to angelic rulers over cities and nations. This is made clear when the Seventy exclaim to the Lord with excitement, 'even the demons submit to us in your name' (Luke 10:17). They were ministering to people afflicted in various ways by demons. And this is what they continued to do after the day of Pentecost. There is no hint in the text that the Seventy were casting demons out of villages, cities, or temples." See Arnold, *3 Crucial Questions about Spiritual Warfare*, 164.

spiritual warfare is not about confronting supernatural entities but about the furtherance of the gospel by committed believers:

> [10] Finally, be strong in the Lord and in the strength of his might. [11] Put on the whole armor of God, that you may be able to stand against the schemes of the devil. [12] For we do not wrestle against flesh and blood, but against the rulers, against the authorities, against the cosmic powers over this present darkness, against the spiritual forces of evil in the heavenly places. [13] Therefore take up the whole armor of God, that you may be able to withstand in the evil day, and having done all, to stand firm. [14] Stand therefore, having fastened on the belt of truth, and having put on the breastplate of righteousness, [15] and, as shoes for your feet, having put on the readiness given by the gospel of peace. [16] In all circumstances take up the shield of faith, with which you can extinguish all the flaming darts of the evil one; [17] and take the helmet of salvation, and the sword of the Spirit, which is the word of God, [18] praying at all times in the Spirit, with all prayer and supplication. To that end, keep alert with all perseverance, making supplication for all the saints, [19] and also for me, that words may be given to me in opening my mouth boldly to proclaim the mystery of the gospel, [20] for which I am an ambassador in chains, that I may declare it boldly, as I ought to speak. (Eph 6:10–20)

In Paul's explanation of spiritual warfare to the church at Ephesus, he nowhere recommends that believers confront or admonish the supernatural rulers and powers. His list of weapons does not include exorcism against the spiritual forces of evil in the heavenly places. Instead, here is what Paul considered effective in spiritual combat against the forces of darkness:

- truth (v. 14)
- righteousness (v. 14)
- the gospel (v. 15)
- faith (v. 16)
- salvation (v. 17)
- the word of God (v. 17)
- prayer (v. 18)
- perseverance (v. 18)

It is not difficult to see that, instead of power encounters, spiritual warfare in Ephesians 6 is about having persevering faith in the gospel and the word of God and living a holy, prayerful life as a follower of Jesus. The same strategy is evident in the other passage of popular reference for spiritual warfare:

> [3] For though we walk in the flesh, we are not waging war according to the flesh. [4] For the weapons of our warfare are not of the flesh but have divine power to destroy strongholds. [5] We destroy arguments and every lofty opinion raised against the knowledge of God, and take every thought captive to obey Christ, [6] being ready to punish every disobedience, when your obedience is complete. (2 Cor 10:3–6)

Paul's description of how he fights the strongholds of darkness includes neither exorcism nor efforts to evict territorial spirits. There is no confrontation of supernatural powers among his personal strategy.[37] Rather, successful spiritual warfare in this passage "destroys arguments and every lofty opinion raised against the knowledge of God" and "takes every thought captive to obey Christ." In other words, spiritual warfare is being a faithful disciple who is not "tossed to and fro by the waves and carried about by every wind of doctrine, by human cunning, by craftiness in deceitful schemes" (Eph 4:14). Spiritual warfare is about leading a life obedient to Jesus, following his obedient example for the cause of God's vision for a kingdom on earth.

---

37. Peter and Jude take a stance opposite of SLSW. They advocate caution with respect to evil spirits. Both writers warn their readers to not "blaspheme the glorious ones" (Jude 8; 2 Pet 2:10), beings that outrank angels. The term *doxas*, translated "the glorious ones" in Jude 8 and 2 Pet 2:10, most likely refers to beings of the divine council who serve "close to God's glorious presence," a category or rank identified in other Second Temple period texts. For example, the angel Gabriel is identified as one of the "glorious ones" of the Lord in 2 En 21:3. When 2 Pet 2:10–11 warns against blaspheming the "glorious ones," it notes that not even angels, while greater in power than humans, would dare blaspheme these glorious ones. The wording implies some sort of distinction in rank or power between angels and "glorious ones." See Heiser, *Unseen Realm*, 331. For Second Temple parallels, see 1QH 10:8; 2 En 22:7, 10; Martyrdom and Ascension of Isaiah 9:32; Philo, *Spec. Leg.* 1.45; T. Judah 25:2; T. Levi 18:5. See also Richard J. Bauckham, *2 Peter, Jude* (WBC; Dallas: Word, 1998), 57. The Greek verb in these two passages translated "blaspheme" (*blasphēmeō*) means "to speak in a disrespectful way that demeans, denigrates, maligns" (BDAG, s.v. "βλασφημέω"). The point Peter and Jude are making is that even angels have enough sense to avoid speaking disrespectfully to high celestial powers. It seems quite reasonable to conclude that SLSW crosses this line and is therefore ill advised and contrary to the teaching of Peter and Jude. SLSW advocates aren't saying "please" when they allegedly command evil spirits.

While not spectacular, adherence to truth and committed discipleship is what constitutes spiritual warfare in New Testament theology. To be blunt, this is a lot harder than yelling commands in the name of Jesus at a demon (or, more frequently, into the air). As disciples, we need to prepare ourselves to avoid demonization in the form of false teaching, temptation, and sinful life patterns. Paul's characterization of spiritual warfare as adherence to the gospel and other scriptural truths and as a prayerful, persevering life of righteousness are clear headed and on target. Being obedient disciples is what makes us fit soldiers for Christ. The mission of every Christian is to carry out the Great Commission, the means by which the kingdom of God grows and the kingdom of darkness recedes.

"WHY DO SATAN AND THE POWERS OF DARKNESS RESIST THE KINGDOM OF GOD? THEY ARE DEFEATED. DO THEY THINK THEY CAN WIN?"

Our study has laid out the New Testament theology of how the death, resurrection, and ascension of Christ address the three supernatural rebellions. The curse of death brought on by the original rebellion has been overturned. All who embrace the gospel and become members of the kingdom of Jesus will overcome death in their union with him. They will enjoy resurrection and everlasting life in God's family. The Spirit of God residing in believers, sent after the ascension of Jesus, blunts the human depravity proliferated by the transgression of the sons of God before the flood. The territorial authority of the rebellious sons of God, allotted to them by the Most High in the judgment at Babel, has been withdrawn and nullified by the design of the Most High in the work of Jesus. They have no authority over humanity outside the nation of Israel. The gentile is welcomed back into the family of God through Christ. The Great Commission is about awakening all people everywhere to these truths so that they might be embraced by faith.

With the effects and operations of supernatural rebellion being denied and progressively overturned, it would seem logical that the powers of darkness give up. Why do they resist? They must realize that they cannot reverse these things. Surely they know they are not stronger than God.

The powers of darkness do indeed understand these things. Demons, for example, when conversing with Jesus, knew the fate that awaited them (Matt 8:29). When the events of the final stages of the day of the Lord begin to unfold, the devil will understand that his time is short (Rev 12:12). He was powerless to resist being cast down, so he knows the Most High is superior.

Despite the clarity of this point, there are several factors as to why the powers of darkness continue their evil work. Evil spirits are doing what is consistent with their character—they rebel. There is no reason to presume that the rebellious will that launched these entities on their path has diminished. Further, with no opportunity of redemption, there would be no point to a change of course.

These points are fairly obvious. But one more remains. New Testament eschatology links the concept of "the fullness of the gentiles" to the return of Jesus. The second coming immediately precedes the day of the Lord and its final judgment. What is the "fullness of the gentiles"? The phrase refers to the evangelization of the world's nations. Matthew 24:14 says, "And this gospel of the kingdom will be proclaimed throughout the whole world as a testimony to all nations, and then the end will come." The disinherited nations, created at the judgment of Babel, must be reclaimed by virtue of the evangelism of their occupants. Paul reminds us that gentile inclusion operates in tandem with a hardening of the people of Yahweh's portion, Israel (Rom 11:25–29). Paul taught that the completion of gentile evangelism was necessary for a softening and redemption of his people, the Jews. Only when gentile evangelism is completed in God's mind will the restoration of Israel be possible ("in this way all Israel will be saved," Rom 11:26).[38]

What this means for the question under consideration is that the ongoing activity of Satan, demons, and the fallen gods not yet imprisoned

---

38. Paul elsewhere makes it clear that he does not mean by this statement that every last Jew on earth will turn to Jesus as their Messiah. He is speaking of a remnant: "But it is not as though the word of God has failed. For not all who are descended from Israel belong to Israel, and not all are children of Abraham because they are his offspring, but 'through Isaac shall your offspring be named.' This means that it is not the children of the flesh who are the children of God, but the children of the promise are counted as offspring. ... And Isaiah cries out concerning Israel: 'Though the number of the sons of Israel be as the sand of the sea, only a remnant of them will be saved, for the Lord will carry out his sentence upon the earth fully and without delay'" (Rom 9:6–8, 27–28).

makes sense if the goal is impeding and forestalling the fullness of the gentiles. In other words, opposing world evangelism allows them more time to spread misery and destruction among humanity, the objects of God's love and plan. This is the only definable "victory" the powers of darkness can hope to accomplish. It is the only conceivable way they can hurt and grieve God. In this context, their resistance is comprehensible.

"HOW DOES THE DEUTERONOMY 32 WORLDVIEW RELATE TO THE MODERN WORLD?"

This frequent question relates to two issues: (1) Can we identify specific deities with specific nations today? (2) If the nations allotted to the sons of God at Babel were seventy in number, per Genesis 10, and there are more than seventy nations on earth, how do we relate this point of biblical theology to the larger world?

In regard to the first question, the Old Testament does provide some information (far from complete) about what deities were worshiped in specific places. For example, God laments that his people "have forsaken me and worshiped Ashtoreth the goddess of the Sidonians, Chemosh the god of Moab, and Milcom the god of the Ammonites" (1 Kgs 11:33). However, it is common knowledge among archaeologists of the biblical world and scholars of ancient Near Eastern religion that various deities could be (and were) worshiped in the same cities, regions, and nations. Worship of Baal was ubiquitous in this regard. This situation is part of the syncretistic nature of polytheistic systems and the whims of monarchical rulers who would favor different deities and, for example, when changing the nation's capital, import the worship of that deity to a new location.

It is therefore not possible to either biblically or historically aim for precision in this regard. We can presume that since Scripture has no such elucidation, such a listing was not important. The point of how Deuteronomy 32:8–9 describes the judgment at Babel is not to provide a lineup of national deities. Rather, it is to answer the questions of (1) why humanity drifted from recognition of the true God, Yahweh, to the worship of other gods, and (2) to make the point of Israel's uniqueness among the nations and their gods. Readers should take note that the number of the nations listed in Genesis 10, the context for Yahweh's punitive allotment to lesser gods, is seventy.[39] The number seventy is well known as signifying totality in Israelite thought. The number itself reinforces the idea that Israel *alone* was Yahweh's portion and all the rest of the nations in totality were disinherited and under the dominion of rival gods.

This point is useful for addressing the second issue. The fact that biblical writers conceived of the whole world as the nations in Genesis 10 does not blunt the Deuteronomy 32 theology or the coherence of framing the gospel mission to the gentiles in those terms. While it is true that the biblical writers did not know of places like China, Australia, and North and South America, that fact does not overturn a worldview framework with the intention of totality. We cannot confuse God's exhaustive knowledge with the limitations of human knowledge. Biblical theology is not determined by the smallness of human perception in other areas, so it is incoherent to consider that an acceptable hermeneutic here.

For example, the human authors of the Bible devote considerable space to talking about the spiritual world—a world populated by disembodied beings, or beings that have bodies that are not like our bodies, and which exists without spatial qualities, where latitude and longitude do not apply. The human writers do their best to express theological truth by means of the vocabulary and points of analogy at their disposal. God chose men to produce Scripture, preparing them providentially for that task, knowing their deficiencies. God knew what he was getting when calling them to the enterprise. Despite their limitations, they were able to express the theological points God wanted articulated for posterity. Their insufficiencies did not impede completing the assigned tasks in a way that satisfied God.[40]

---

39. As I noted in a footnote in chapter 9 (when discussing Luke 10:1, 18–19), the number in the Septuagint is seventy-two. The divergence between LXX and the traditional Hebrew text arises from joining or dividing one of the names in Genesis 10. The number seventy in the traditional Hebrew text is the best reading on external grounds, given the witness to seventy "sons of El" in the divine council at Ugarit and the El epithets used of Yahweh in Deut 32:6–7 (see the discussion and Ugaritic references in Michael S. Heiser, "Are Yahweh and El Distinct Deities in Deut 32:8–9 and Psalm 82?").

40. This issue is present in regard to a variety of scriptural teachings. God used humans who have little hope of explaining (or even grasping) the nature of things they write about to nevertheless communicate truths about those transcendent realities. Examples include the relationships and workings of the Trinity, the nature of the resurrection body, and even the idea of the cleansing of sin via events in the physical world (i.e., the cross event). How would limited human authors be capable of accurately explaining such things on the basis of their human frame of reference and experience?

What this means for the question at hand is that the Deuteronomy 32 worldview, while reflecting the limited knowledge about the true extent of global land masses, seeks to make the point that *every* nation that was not Israel was alienated from a relationship with the true God. This carries through to the New Testament era. Only Israel had access to the written oracles of God (Rom 3:2). Only Israel could produce the Messiah, Abraham's seed (Gen 12:3; Gal 3:16) to make the people judged at Babel part of God's family once again (Gal 3:7–9, 13–14, 26–29).

We can see this is the correct approach in light of the intended exhaustive totality of various New Testament references to "the world." Certain theological points are attached to an all-encompassing understanding of the "world" despite the limitations of the human authors of Scripture:

- "The field is the world, and the good seed is the sons of the kingdom. The weeds are the sons of the evil one" (Matt 13:38). Evil and evildoers can be found outside the boundaries of the seventy nations of Genesis 10. That requires that the field be the entire world.

- "Jesus said to them, 'Truly, I say to you, in the new world, when the Son of Man will sit on his glorious throne, you who have followed me will also sit on twelve thrones, judging the twelve tribes of Israel'" (Matt 19:28). In the world to come, no one else is ruling the geography outside the parameters of the nations of Genesis 10.

- "And this gospel of the kingdom will be proclaimed throughout the whole world as a testimony to all nations, and then the end will come" (Matt 24:14). The fact the second coming and day of the Lord have not yet occurred is proof that the world being reclaimed is the entire globe. The return of Jesus is held back by God's determination as to when the fullness of the gentiles is complete. If reaching the seventy nations was all that God intended, then the Lord should have returned a long time ago.

- "And he said to them, 'Go into all the world and proclaim the gospel to the whole creation'" (Mark 16:15). The point of the passage is not that the gospel be preached to plants, animals, and inanimate objects. The "whole creation" must refer to every human being, as humans are the part of creation at which God's plan of redemption is aimed (Heb 2:14–18). Wherever humans are, the Great Commission is valid.

- "For God did not send his Son into the world to condemn the world, but in order that the world might be saved through him" (John 3:17). Humans who live outside the scope of the seventy nations are still estranged from God because of sin and subject to death.

- "In these last days [God] has spoken to us by his Son, whom he appointed the heir of all things, through whom also he created the world" (Heb 1:2). Parts of the world outside the seventy nations were not created by some other deity.

The point is that the limitations of the human authors, certainly known to God, did not prevent God from using them to make statements he intended to be understood with global totality.

Select Bibliography

Abegg, Martin G., Jr. *Qumran Sectarian Manuscripts*. Bellingham, WA: Logos Bible Software, 2003.

Abernathy, David. "Paul's Thorn in the Flesh: A Messenger of Satan?" *Neotestamentica* 35.1–2 (2001): 69–79.

Abusch, T., and D. Schwemer. "Das Abwehrzauber-Ritual Maqlû ('Verbrennung')." In *Omina, Orakel, Rituale und Beschwörungen*. Edited by B. Janowski and G. Wilhelm. Gütersloh: Gütersloher Verlagshaus, 2008.

Adams, Sean A. *Baruch and the Epistle of Jeremiah: Commentary*. Septuagint Commentary Series. Leiden: Brill, 2014.

Albani, Matthias. "The Downfall of Helel, Son of Dawn: Aspects of Royal Ideology in Isa 14:12–13." Pages 129–68 in *The Fall of the Angels*. Edited by Christoph Auffarth and Loren T. Stuckenbruck. Leiden: Brill, 2004.

Alston, Wallace M. "The Concept of the Wilderness in the Intertestamental Period." ThD diss., Union Theological Seminary in Virginia, 1968.

Annus, Amar. "Are There Greek Rephaim? On the Etymology of Greek Meropes and Titanes." *Ugarit Forschungen* 31 (1999): 13–30.

———. "On the Origin of the Watchers: A Comparative Study of the Antediluvian Wisdom in Mesopotamian and Jewish Traditions." *Journal for the Study of the Pseudepigrapha* 19.4 (2010): 277–320.

Arnold, Clinton E. *3 Crucial Questions about Spiritual Warfare*. 3 Crucial Questions, edited by Grant R. Osborne and Richard J. Jones Jr. Grand Rapids: Baker Academic, 1997.

Aune, David E. *Revelation 6–16*. WBC. Dallas, TX: Word, 1998.

Aus, Roger. "Paul's Travel Plans to Spain and the 'Full Number of the Gentiles' of Rom XI 25." *Novum Testamentum* 21.3 (July 1979): 232–62.

Baker, David W. *Nahum, Habakkuk and Zephaniah: An Introduction and Commentary*. TOTC. Downers Grove, IL: InterVarsity Press, 1988.

Bampfylde, Gillian. "The Prince of the Host in the Book of Daniel and the Dead Sea Scrolls." *Journal for the Study of Judaism in the Persian, Hellenistic, and Roman Periods* 14.2 (1983): 129–34.

Barker, Margaret. *The Hidden Tradition of the Kingdom of God*. London: Society for Promoting Christian Knowledge, 2007.

Barkun, Michael. *Religion and the Racist Right: The Origins of the Christian Identity Movement*. Chapel Hill, NC: University of North Carolina Press, 1997.

Barr, James. "'Thou Art the Cherub': Ezekiel 28.14 and the Post-Ezekiel Understanding of Genesis 2–3." In *Priests, Prophets, and Scribes: Essays on the Formation and Heritage of Second Temple Judaism in Honour of Joseph Blenkinsopp*. Edited by Eugene Ulrich et al. Sheffield: Sheffield Academic Press, 1992.

Batto, Bernard F. *In the Beginning: Essays on Creation Motifs in the Bible and the Ancient Near East*. Winona Lake, IN: Eisenbrauns, 2013.

Bauckham, Richard J. *2 Peter, Jude*. WBC. Dallas: Word, 1998.

Beale, G. K. *The Book of Revelation: A Commentary on the Greek Text*. NIGTC. Grand Rapids: Eerdmans, 1999.

Benz, F. L. *Personal Names in the Phoenician and Punic Inscriptions*. Rome: Biblical Institute Press, 1972.

Bergey, Ronald. "The Song of Moses (Deut 32:1–43) and Isaianic Prophecies: A Case of Intertextuality?" *Journal for the Study of the Old Testament* 28.1 (2003): 33–54.

Bernstein, M. J. "Noah and the Flood at Qumran." Pages 199–231 in *The Provo International Conference on the Dead Sea Scrolls: Technological Innovations, New Texts, Reformulated Issues*. Edited by D. Parry and E. Ulrich. Leiden: Brill, 1998.

Betz, H. D. *The Greek Magical Papyri in Translation, including the Demotic Spells*. 2nd ed. Chicago: University of Chicago Press, 1996.

Bhayro, Siam. "Noah's Library: Sources for 1 Enoch 6–11." *Journal for the Study of the Pseudepigrapha* 15.3 (2006): 163–77.

Billings, Bradly S. "'The Angels Who Sinned … He Cast into Tartarus' (2 Pet 2:4): Its Ancient Meaning and Present Relevance." *Expository Times* 119.11 (2008): 532–37.

Black, Jeremy, and Anthony Green. *Gods, Demons and Symbols of Ancient Mesopotamia: An Illustrated Dictionary*. Austin: University of Texas-Austin, 2003.

Black, Matthew. *The Book of Enoch or 1 Enoch*. Edited by A. M. Denis and M. de Jonge. Leiden: Brill, 1985.

Block, Daniel I. *The Book of Ezekiel, Chapters 25–48*. NICOT. Grand Rapids: Eerdmans, 1997.

Bodi, Daniel. *The Book of Ezekiel and the Poem of Erra*. Göttingen: Vandenhoeck & Ruprecht, 1991.

Bordreuil, Pierre, and Dennis Pardee. *A Manual of Ugaritic*. Winona Lake, IN: Eisenbrauns, 2009.

Borgen, Peder, Kåre Fuglseth, and Roald Skarsten. *The Works of Philo: Greek Text with Morphology*. Bellingham, WA: Logos Bible Software, 2005.

Box, G. H., and W. O. E. Oesterley. "The Book of Sirach." Pages 1:268–516 in *The Apocrypha and Pseudepigrpha of the Old Testament.* Edited by R. H. Charles. 2 vols. Oxford: Clarendon, 1913.

Brand, Miryam. *Evil Within and Without: The Source of Sin and Its Nature as Portrayed in Second Temple Literature.* Göttingen: Vandenhoeck & Ruprecht, 2013.

Bremmer, Jan N. *Greek Religion and Culture, the Bible, and the Ancient Near East.* Leiden: Brill, 2008.

Brotzman, Ellis R. *Old Testament Textual Criticism: A Practical Introduction.* Grand Rapids: Baker Books, 1994.

Brown, Derek R. *The God of This Age.* Tübingen: Mohr Siebeck, 2015.

Brown, Michael L. "'I Am the Lord, Your Healer': A Philological Study of the Root RAPA' in the Hebrew Bible and the Ancient Near East." PhD diss., New York University, 1985.

———. *Israel's Divine Healer.* Grand Rapids: Zondervan, 1995.

Bunta, Silviu N. "Dreamy Angels and Demonic Giants: The Watchers Traditions and the Origin of Evil in Early Christian Demonology." Pages 116–38 in *The Fallen Angels Traditions: Second Temple Developments and Reception History.* Edited by Angela Kim Harkins, Kelley Coblentz Bautch, and John C. Endres. Washington, DC: Catholic Biblical Association of America, 2014.

Burnett, David A. "A Neglected Deuteronomic Scriptural Matrix for the Nature of the Resurrection Body in 1 Cor 15:39–42?" In *Scripture, Texts, and Tracings in 1 Corinthians.* Edited by B. J. Oropeza and Linda Belleville. Minneapolis: Fortress, forthcoming.

Calvin, John. *Commentaries on the First Book of Moses Called Genesis.* Translated by John King. Edinburgh: The Calvin Translation Society, 1847.

Cathcart, Kevin J. "Ilu, Yariḫu, and the One with the Two Horns and Tail." In *Ugarit, Religion, and Culture: Essays Presented in Honour of John C. L. Gibson.* Edited by N. Wyatt, W. G. E. Watson, and J. B. Lloyd. Münster: Ugarit-Verlag, 1996.

Cathcart, Kevin J., and W. G. E. Watson. "Weathering a Wake: A Cure for Carousal: A Revised Translation of *Ugaritica V* text I." *Proceedings of the Irish Biblical Association* 4 (1980): 35–58.

Charles, J. Daryl. "The Angels under Reserve in 2 Peter and Jude." *Bulletin for Biblical Research* 15.1 (2005): 39–48.

Charlesworth, James H. "Bashan, Symbology, Haplography, and Theology in Psalm 68." Pages 351–72 in *David and Zion: Biblical Studies in Honor of J. J. M. Roberts.* Edited by Bernard Frank Batto and Kathryn L. Roberts. Winona Lake, IN: Eisenbrauns, 2004.

———. "Jewish Astrology in the Talmud, Pseudepigrapha, the Dead Sea Scrolls, and Early Palestinian Synagogues." *Harvard Theological Review* 70.3/4 (1977): 183–200.

Chesnutt, Randall D. "The Descent of the Watchers and Its Aftermath According to Justin Martyr." Pages 167–80 in *The Watchers in Jewish and Christian Traditions*. Edited by Angela Kim Harkins, Kelley Coblentz Bautch, and John C. Endres, S.J. Minneapolis: Fortress, 2014.

Cho, Sang Youl. *Lesser Deities in the Ugaritic Texts and the Hebrew Bible: A Comparative Study of Their Nature and Roles*. Piscataway, NJ: Gorgias Press, 2008.

Chung, Tae Whoe (David). "The Development of the Concept of Satan in Old Testament and Intertestamental Literature." PhD diss., Southwestern Baptist Theological Seminary, 2000.

Clements, Ronald E. "Sacred Mountains, Temples, and the Presence of God." Pages 69–85 in *Cult and Cosmos: Tilting Toward a Temple-Centered Biblical Theology*. Edited by L. Michael Morales. Leuven: Peeters, 2014.

Clifford, Richard J. *The Cosmic Mountain in Canaan and the Old Testament*. Cambridge, MA: Harvard University Press, 1972.

———. "The Temple and the Holy Mountain." Pages 85–98 in *Cult and Cosmos: Tilting Toward a Temple-Centered Biblical Theology*. Edited by L. Michael Morales. Leuven: Peeters, 2014.

Coblentz Bautch, Kelley. "The Fall and Fate of Renegade Angels: The Intersection of Watchers Traditions and the Book of Revelation." Pages 69–93 in *The Fallen Angels Traditions: Second Temple Developments and Reception History*. Edited by Angela Kim Harkins, Kelley Coblentz Bautch, and John C. Endres. Washington, DC: Catholic Biblical Association of America, 2014.

Cohen, C. "The Enclitic *mem* in Biblical Hebrew: Its Existence and Initial Discovery." Pages 231–60 in *Sefer Moshe: The Moshe Weinfeld Jubilee Volume*. Edited by Chaim Cohen, Avi Hurvitz, and Shalom M. Paul. Winona Lake, IN: Eisenbrauns, 2004.

Collins, John J. *Daniel: A Commentary on the Book of Daniel*. Hermeneia. Minneapolis: Fortress, 1993.

Conybeare, F. C. "The Testament of Solomon." *Jewish Quarterly Review* 11 (1898–1899): 1–45.

Cox, Claude. "11.3.1 Septuagint [of Job]." In *Textual History of the Bible: Volume 1C: Writings*. Edited by Armin Lange and Emanuel Tov. Leiden: Brill, 2017.

Craigie, Peter C. *The Book of Deuteronomy*. NICOT. Grand Rapids: Eerdmans, 1976.

———. "Helel, Athtar, and Phaethon (Isa 14:12–15)." *Zeitschrift für die alttestamentliche Wissenschaft* 85 (1973): 223–25.

Dahood, Mitchell. "Enclitic *mem* and Emphatic *lamedh* in Psalm 85." *Biblica* 37.3 (1956): 338–40.

Davila, James R. *The Provenance of the Pseudepigrapha: Jewish, Christian, or Other?* Leiden: Brill, 2005.

Day, John L. *From Creation to Babel: Studies in Genesis 1–11*. London: T&T Clark, 2015.

———. *God's Conflict with the Dragon and the Sea*. Cambridge: Cambridge University Press, 1985.

Day, Peggy. *An Adversary in Heaven: śāṭān in the Hebrew Bible.* Atlanta: Scholars Press, 1988.

deSilva, David A. *Introducing the Apocrypha: Message, Context, and Significance.* Grand Rapids: Baker Academic, 2002.

Dick, Michael B. "Prophetic Parodies of Making the Cult Image." Pages 1–54 in *Born in Heaven, Made on Earth: The Making of the Cult Image in the Ancient Near East.* Edited by Michael B. Dick. Winona Lake, IN: Eisenbrauns, 1999.

Dickson, Keith. "The Jeweled Trees: Alterity in Gilgamesh." *Comparative Literature* 59.3 (2007): 193–208.

Dijk, H. J. van. *Ezekiel's Prophecy on Tyre (Ez. 26:1–28:19): A New Approach.* Rome: Pontifical Biblical Institute, 1968.

Dimant, D. "Noah in Early Jewish Literature. Appendix: The So-Called *Book of Noah.*" Pages 123–50 in *Biblical Figures Outside the Bible.* Edited by M. E. Stone and T. A. Bergren. Harrisburg, PA: Trinity Press International, 1998.

Doak, Brian R. *The Last of the Rephaim: Conquest and Cataclysm in the Heroic Ages of Ancient Israel.* Boston: Ilex Foundation, 2012.

Dodd, C. H. *The Bible and the Greeks.* London: Hodder & Stoughton, 1935.

Ben-Dov, Jonathan. "The Resurrection of the Divine Assembly and the Divine Title El in the Dead Sea Scrolls." Pages 9–31 in *The Comparative Perspective.* Vol. 3 of *Submerged Literature in Ancient Greek Culture: Beyond Greece.* Edited by Giulio Colesanti and Manuela Giordano. Berlin: De Gruyter, 2016.

Draffkorn Kilmer, Anne. "The Mesopotamian Counterparts of the Biblical Nephilim." Pages 39–44 in *Perspectives on Language and Text: Essays and Poems in Honor of Francis I. Andersen's 60th Birthday.* Edited by E. W. Conrad and E. G. Newing. Winona Lake, IN: Eisenbrauns, 1987.

Drawnel, Henryk. "Knowledge Transmission in the Context of the Watchers' Sexual Sin with the Women in 1 Enoch 6–11." *The Biblical Annals* 2.59 (2012): 123–51.

———. "The Mesopotamian Background of the Enochic Giants and Evil Spirits." *Dead Sea Discoveries* 21.1 (2014): 14–38.

———. "Professional Skills of Asael (1 Enoch 8:1) and Their Mesopotamian Background." *Revue Biblique* 119.4 (2012): 518–42.

Duling, Dennis C. "Solomon, Exorcism, and the Son of David." *Harvard Theological Review* 68.3/4 (Jul-Oct 1975): 235–52.

———. "Testament of Solomon: A New Translation and Introduction." Pages 935–87 in *The Old Testament Pseudepigrapha.* Edited by James H. Charlesworth. Vol. 1. New York: Doubleday, 1983.

Dunn, James D. G., and Graham H. Twelftree. "Demon-Possession and Exorcism in the New Testament." *Churchman* 94 (1980): 210–25.

Dunn, James D. G. *The Epistles to the Colossians and to Philemon: A Commentary on the Greek Text.* NIGTC. Grand Rapids: Eerdmans, 1996.

Eddy, Paul Rhodes, and James K. Beilby. "Introduction." In *Understanding Spiritual Warfare: Four Views*. Edited by James K. Beilby and Paul Rhodes Eddy. Grand Rapids: Baker Academic, 2012.

Eichrodt, Walter. *Theology of the Old Testament*. Vol 1. Philadelphia: Westminster John Knox, 1961.

Emerton, J. A. "Are There Examples of Enclitic *mem* in the Hebrew Bible?" Pages 321–38 in *Texts, Temples, and Traditions: A Tribute to Menahem Haran*. Edited by Michael V. Fox et al. Winona Lake, IN: Eisenbrauns, 1996.

Emmet, C. W. *The Fourth Book of Maccabees: Commentary*. London: Society for Promoting Christian Knowledge, 1918.

Engnell, Ivan. *Studies in Divine Kingship in the Ancient Near East*. Uppsala: Almqvist & Wiksell, 1943.

Evans, Craig A. "Inaugurating the Kingdom of God and Defeating the Kingdom of Satan." *Bulletin for Biblical Research* 15.1 (2005): 49–75.

Evans, Paul. "Divine Intermediaries in 1 Chronicles 21: An Overlooked Aspect of the Chronicler's Theology." *Biblica* 85 (2004): 545–58.

Fensham, Charles F. "A Possible Explanation of the Name Baal-Zebub of Ekron." *Zeitschrift für die alttestamentliche Wissenschaft* 79.3 (1967): 361–64.

Fields, Weston. *Unformed and Unfilled: A Critique of the Gap Theory*. Green Forest, AR: Master Books, 2005.

Fisher, Loren. "Can This Be the Son of David?" Pages 82–97 in *Jesus and the Historian: Written in Honor of Ernest Cadman Colwell*. Edited by F. T. Trotter. Philadelphia: Westminster, 1968.

Fitzmyer, Joseph A., S.J. *The Gospel according to Luke I–IX: Introduction, Translation, and Notes*. AYB. New Haven, CT: Yale University Press, 1970.

———. *The Gospel according to Luke X–XXIV: Introduction, Translation, and Notes*. AYB. New Haven, CT: Yale University Press, 1985.

Fleming, David Marron. "The Divine Council as Type Scene in the Hebrew Bible." PhD diss., Southern Baptist Theological Seminary, 1989.

Fontenrose, J. *Python: A Study of Delphic Myth and Its Origins*. Berkeley: University of California Press, 1980.

France, R. T. *The Gospel of Matthew*. NICNT. Grand Rapids: Eerdmans, 2007.

Frankfort, H. *Kingship and the Gods: A Study of Ancient Near Eastern Religion as the Integration of Society and Nature*. Chicago: University of Chicago Press, 1948.

Freedman, David Noel. "Archaic Forms in Hebrew Poetry." *Zeitschrift für die alttestamentliche Wissenschaft* 31 (1960): 101–7.

Frey-Anthes, Henrike. "Concepts of 'Demons' in Ancient Israel." *Die Welt des Orients* 38 (2008): 38–52.

Fröhlich, Ida. "Mesopotamian Elements and the Watchers Traditions." Pages 11–24 in *The Watchers in Jewish and Christian Traditions*. Edited by Angela Kim Hawkins, Kelley Coblentz Bautch, and John C. Endres, S.J. Minneapolis: Fortress, 2014.

———. "The Symbolic Language of the Animal Apocalypse of Enoch (1 Enoch 85–90)." *Revue de Qumran* 14.4 (1990): 629–36.

———. "Theology and Demonology in Qumran Texts." *Henoch* 32.1 (2010): 101–29.

Gallagher, W. "On the Identity of *Helel Ben Shaher* in Is. 14:12–15." *Ugarit Forschungen* 26 (1994): 131–46.

García Martínez, Florentino, and Eibert J. C. Tigchelaar, eds. *The Dead Sea Scrolls Study Edition*. Leiden: Brill, 1997–1998.

Garr, W. Randall. *In His Own Image and Likeness: Humanity, Divinity, and Monotheism*. Leiden: Brill, 2003.

George, Andrew R. "Babylonian Texts from the Folios of Sydney Smith." *Revue d'assyriologie* 82 (1988): 139–62.

———. "The Gilgameš Epic at Ugarit." *Aula Orientalis* 25 (2007): 237–54.

Geyer, John B. "Desolation and Cosmos." *Vetus Testamentum* 49.1 (1999): 49–64.

———. "Mythology and Culture in the Oracles against the Nations." *Vetus Testamentum* 36 (1986): 129–45.

Glancy, Jennifer Ann. "Satan in the Synoptic Gospels." PhD diss., Columbia University, 1990.

Goldingay, John. *Psalms, Vol. 2: Psalms 42–89*. BCOT. Grand Rapids: Baker Academic, 2006.

———. *Psalms, Vol 3: Psalms 90–150*. BCOT. Grand Rapids: Baker Academic, 2006.

Goldstein, Bernard R., and David Pingree. "Astrological Almanacs from the Cairo Geniza, Part I." *Journal of Near Eastern Studies* 38.3 (1979): 153–75.

———. "Astrological Almanacs from the Cairo Geniza, Part II." *Journal of Near Eastern Studies* 38.4 (1979): 231–56.

Goldstein, Ronnie. "A New Look at Deuteronomy 32:8–9 and 43 in the Light of Akkadian Sources." [Hebrew] *Tarbiz* 79.1 (2010): 5–21.

Gordon, C. H. "The Devil, ḥby." *Newsletter for Ugaritic Studies* 33 (1985): 15.

———. "ḤBY: Possessor of Horns and Tail." *Ugarit Forchungen* 18 (1986): 129–32.

Grave, C. "The Etymology of Northwest Semitic ṣapānu." *Ugarit Forschungen* 12 (1980): 221–29.

Green, Joel B., and Scot McKnight, eds. *Dictionary of Jesus and the Gospels*. Downers Grove, IL: InterVarsity Press, 1992.

Greenberg, Moshe. *Ezekiel 1–20: A New Translation with Introduction and Commentary*. AYB. New Haven, CT: Yale University Press, 1983.

Greene, W. C. *Moira. Fate, Good, and Evil in Greek Thought.* Cambridge, MA: Harvard University Press, 1944.

Habel, Norman C. "Ezekiel 28 and the Fall of the First Man." *Concordia Theological Monthly* 38 (1967): 516–24.

Hachlili, Rachel. "The Zodiac in Ancient Jewish Art: Representation and Significance." *Bulletin of the American Schools of Oriental Research* 228 (1977): 61–77.

Hagner, Donald A. *Matthew 1–13.* WBC. Dallas: Word, 1998.

Hallo, William. *Origins: The Ancient Near Eastern Background of Some Modern Western Institutions.* Leiden: Brill, 1996.

Hamilton, Victor P. *The Book of Genesis, Chapters 1–17.* NICOT. Grand Rapids: Eerdmans, 1990.

Handy, Lowell K. *Among the Host of Heaven: The Syro-Palestinian Pantheon as Bureaucracy.* Winona Lake, IN: Eisenbrauns, 1994.

———. "The Authorization of Divine Power and the Guilt of God in the Book of Job: Useful Ugaritic Parallels." *Journal for the Study of the Old Testament* 18.60 (1993): 107–18.

———. "A Solution for Many MLKM." *Ugarit Forschungen* 20 (1988): 57–59.

Hannah, Darrell D. "Guardian Angels and Angelic National Patrons in Second Temple Judaism and Early Christianity." Pages 413–35 in *Angels: The Concept of Celestial Beings—Origins, Development and Reception.* Edited by Friedrich V. Reiterer, Tobias Nicklas, and Karin Schöpflin. Berlin: De Gruyter, 2007.

———. *Michael and Christ: Michael Traditions and Angel Christology in Early Christianity.* Tübingen: Mohr Siebeck, 1999.

Hanneken, Todd R. "The Watchers in Rewritten Scripture: The Use of the *Book of the Watchers* in Jubilees." Pages 23–68 in *The Fallen Angels Traditions: Second Temple Developments and Reception History.* Edited by Angela Kim Harkins, Kelley Coblentz Bautch, and John C. Endres. Washington, DC: Catholic Biblical Association of America, 2014.

Hanson, P. D. "Rebellion in Heaven, Azazel, and Euhemeristic Heroes in 1 Enoch 6–11." *Journal of Biblical Literature* 96 (1977): 221–22.

Haralambakis, Maria. *The Testament of Job: Text, Narrative and Reception History.* London: T&T Clark, 2012.

Hardy, H. H., II, and Charles Otte III. *The Aramaic Inscriptions.* Bellingham, WA: Lexham Press, 2008.

Hare, D. R. A. "The Lives of the Prophets." Pages 379–99 in *The Old Testament Pseudepigrapha.* Edited by James H. Charlesworth. Vol. 2. New York: Doubleday, 1985.

Harkins, Angela Kim. "Elements of the Fallen Angels Traditions in the Qumran Hodayot." Pages 8–24 in *The Fallen Angels Traditions: Second Temple Developments and Reception History.* Edited by Angela Kim Harkins, Kelley Coblentz Bautch, and John C. Endres. Washington, DC: Catholic Biblical Association of America, 2014.

Harkins, Franklin T. "The Magical Arts, Angelic Intercourse, and Giant Offspring: Echoes of Watchers Traditions in Medieval Scholastic Theology." Pages 157–79 in *The Fallen Angels Traditions: Second Temple Developments and Reception History*. Edited by Angela Kim Harkins, Kelley Coblentz Bautch, and John C. Endres. Washington, DC: Catholic Biblical Association of America, 2014.

Harrell, James. "Gemstones." *UCLA Encyclopedia of Egyptology*. Edited by Willeke Wendrich. Los Angeles: UCLA, 2012. http://digital2.library.ucla.edu/viewItem .do?ark=21198/zz002czx1r

———. "Old Testament Gemstones: A Philological, Geological, and Archaeological Assessment of the Septuagint." *Bulletin of Biblical Research* 21.2 (2011): 141–71.

Hartley, John E. *The Book of Job*. NICOT. Grand Rapids: Eerdmans, 1988.

Hartman, Louis F., and Alexander A. Di Lella. *The Book of Daniel: A New Translation with Notes and Commentary on Chapters 1–9*. AYB. New Haven, CT: Yale University Press, 1978.

Hayman, Peter. "Monotheism—A Misused Word in Jewish Studies?" *Journal of Jewish Studies* 42.1 (1991): 1–15.

Healey, John F. "MALKŪ : MLKM : ANUNNAKI." *Ugarit Forschungen* 7 (1975): 235–38.

Heiser, Michael S. *Angels: What the Bible Really Says about God's Heavenly Host*. Bellingham, WA: Lexham Press, 2018.

———. "Are Yahweh and El Distinct Deities in Deut 32:8–9 and Psalm 82?" *Hiphil* 3 (2006): 1–9. https://www.hiphil.org/index.php/hiphil/article/view/29

———. "Co-Regency in Ancient Israel's Divine Council as the Conceptual Backdrop to Ancient Jewish Binitarian Monotheism." *Bulletin of Biblical Research* 26.2 (2016): 195–226.

———. "Deuteronomy 32:8 and the Sons of God." *Bibliotheca Sacra* 158 (2001): 52–74.

———. "The Divine Council in Late Canonical and Non-Canonical Jewish Literature." PhD diss., University of Wisconsin-Madison, 2004.

———. "Does Deuteronomy 32:17 Assume or Deny the Reality of Other Gods?" *Bible Translator* 59.3 (2008): 137–45.

———. "Does Divine Plurality in the Hebrew Bible Demonstrate an Evolution from Polytheism to Monotheism in Israelite Religion?" *Journal for the Evangelical Study of the Old Testament* 1.1 (2012): 1–24.

———. "Giants—Greco-Roman Antiquity." In *Encyclopedia of the Bible and Its Reception*. Vol. 10. Berlin: de Gruyter, 2015.

———. *I Dare You Not to Bore Me with the Bible*. Bellingham, WA: Lexham Press, 2014.

———. "Monotheism and the Language of Divine Plurality in the Hebrew Bible and the Dead Sea Scrolls." *Tyndale Bulletin* 65.1 (2014): 85–100.

———. "Monotheism, Polytheism, Monolatry, or Henotheism? Toward an Assessment of Divine Plurality in the Hebrew Bible." *Bulletin of Biblical Research* 18.1 (2008): 1–30.

———. "The Mythological Provenance of Isaiah 14:12–15: A Reconsideration of the Ugaritic Material." *Vetus Testamentum* 51.3 (Fall 2001): 354–69.

———. "The Name Theology of the Old Testament." In *Faithlife Study Bible*. Bellingham, WA: Lexham Press, 2012, 2016.

———. "Old Testament Godhead Language." In *Faithlife Study Bible*. Bellingham, WA: Lexham Press, 2012, 2016.

———. "Old Testament Theology of the Afterlife." In *Faithlife Study Bible*. Bellingham, WA: Lexham Press, 2012, 2016.

———. *Reversing Hermon: Enoch, the Watchers, and the Forgotten Mission of Jesus Christ*. Crane, MO: Defender, 2017.

———. "Should *'elohim* with Plural Predication Be Translated 'Gods'?" *Bible Translator* 61.3 (2010): 123–36.

———. *The Unseen Realm: Recovering the Supernatural Worldview of the Bible*. Bellingham, WA: Lexham Press, 2015.

Hegedus, Timothy. *Early Christianity and Ancient Astrology*. New York: Peter Lang, 2007.

Hendel, Ronald. "'The Flame of the Whirling Sword': A Note on Genesis 3:24." *Journal of Biblical Literature* 104.4 (1985): 671–74.

Hodge, Zane D. "A Historical and Grammatical Examination of Azazel in Biblical and Extra-biblical Sources with Special Emphasis Given to Its Meaning with the Hebrew Preposition ל." PhD diss., Mid-American Baptist Theological Seminary, 2004.

Holbert, M. Louise. "Extrinsic Evil Powers in the Old Testament." ThM thesis, Fuller Theological Seminary, 1985.

Horowitz, Wayne. *Mesopotamian Cosmic Geography*. Winona Lake, IN: Eisenbrauns, 2011.

Horst, Pieter W. van der. "Bitenosh's Orgasm (1QapGen 2:9–15)." *Journal for the Study of Judaism* 43 (2012): 613–28.

Hummel, Horace D. "Enclitic mem in Early Northwest Semitic, Especially Hebrew." *Journal of Biblical Literature* 76 (1957): 85–107.

Ibba, Giovanni. "The Evil Spirits in Jubilees and the Spirit of the Bastards in 4Q510 with Some Remarks on Other Qumran Manuscripts." *Henoch* 31 (2009): 111–16.

Jeppesen, Knud. "You Are a Cherub, but No God!" *Scandinavian Journal of the Old Testament* 5.1 (1991): 83–94.

Jewett, Robert, and Roy David Kotansky. *Romans: A Commentary*. Hermeneia. Minneapolis: Fortress, 2006.

Jobes, Karen H., and Moisés Silva. *Invitation to the Septuagint*. 2nd ed. Grand Rapids: Baker Academic, 2015.

Johnson, Aubrey R. *The One and the Many in the Israelite Conception of God*. Eugene, OR: Wipf & Stock, 2006.

———. *Sacral Kingship in Ancient Israel*. 2nd ed. Cardiff: University of Wales Press, 1967.

———. *Vitality of the Individual in the Thought of Ancient Israel*. Cardiff: University of Wales, 1964.

Johnson, David M. "Hesiod's Descriptions of Tartarus (*Theogony* 721–819)." *The Phoenix* 53.1–2 (1999): 8–28.

Johnson, Ronn. "The Old Testament Background for Paul's Principalities and Powers." PhD diss., Dallas Theological Seminary, 2004.

Johnston, Philip S. *Shades of Sheol: Death and Afterlife in the Old Testament*. Downers Grove, IL: InterVarsity Press, 2002.

Joines, Karen R. "Winged Serpents in Isaiah's Inaugural Vision." *Journal of Biblical Literature* 86.4 (1967): 410–15.

Jonge, Marinus de, and Johannes Tromp. *The Life of Adam and Eve and Related Literature*. Sheffield: Sheffield Academic Press, 1997.

Josephus, Flavius. *The Works of Josephus: Complete and Unabridged*. Translated by William Whiston. Peabody, MA: Hendrickson, 1987.

Jourdain, E. F. "The Twelve Stones in the Apocalypse." *Expository Times* 22 (1911): 448–50.

Kallai, Zecharia. "Conquest and Settlement of Trans-Jordan: A Historiographical Study." *Zeitschrift des Deutschen Palästina-Vereins (1953+)* 99 (1983): 110–18.

———. "The Patriarchal Boundaries, Canaan, and the Land of Israel: Patterns and Application in Biblical Historiography." *Israel Exploration Journal* 47.1–2 (1997): 69–82.

Kee, Min Suc. "The Heavenly Council and Its Type-Scene." *Journal for the Study of the Old Testament* 31.3 (2007): 259–73.

Keiser, Thomas A. "The Song of Moses as a Basis for Isaiah's Prophecy." *Vetus Testamentum* 55 (2005): 486–500.

Kiuchi, Nobuyoshi. "Living Like the Azazel-Goat in Romans 12:1b." *Tyndale Bulletin* 57.2 (2006): 260.

Knight, Douglas A. "Cosmogony and Order in the Hebrew Tradition." Pages 133–57 in *Cosmogony and Ethical Order: New Studies in Comparative Ethics*. Edited by Robin W. Lovin and Frank E. Reynolds. Chicago: University of Chicago Press, 1985.

Kobelski, P. J. *Melchizedek and Melchiresa*. Washington, DC: The Catholic Biblical Association of America, 1981.

Köstenberger, Andreas J. *A Theology of John's Gospel and Letters: The Word, the Christ, the Son of God*. Grand Rapids: Zondervan, 2009.

Kulik, Alexander. "How the Devil Got His Hooves and Horns: The Origin of the Motif and the Implied Demonology of 3 Baruch." *Numen* 60 (2013): 195–229.

Kvanvig, Helge. "Gen 6: 1–4 as an Antediluvian Event." *Scandinavian Journal of the Old Testament* 16.1 (2002): 79–112.

———. *Primeval History: Babylonian, Biblical, and Enochic: An Intertextual Reading.* Leiden: Brill, 2011.

———. *Roots of Apocalyptic: The Mesopotamian Background of the Enoch Figure and of the Son of Man.* Neukirchen-Vluyn: Neukirchener Verlag, 1988.

Launderville, Dale. "Ezekiel's Cherub: A Promising Symbol or a Dangerous Idol?" *The Catholic Biblical Quarterly* 65.2 (2003): 165–83.

Lee, Lydia. "'You Were the (Divine) Cherub': A Potential Challenge to Yahweh's Sole Divinity in Ezek 28:14." *Journal for the Study of the Old Testament* 41.1 (2016): 99–116.

Lenzi, Alan. *Secrecy and the Gods: Secret Knowledge in Ancient Mesopotamia and Biblical Israel.* Helsinki: The Neo-Assyrian Text Corpus Project, 2008.

Levine, Baruch A., and Jean-Michel de Tarragon. "Dead Kings and Rephaim: The Patrons of the Ugaritic Dynasty." *Journal of the American Oriental Society* 104.4 (1984): 649–59.

Lincoln, Andrew T. *Ephesians.* WBC. Dallas: Word, 1990.

Lioy, Daniel T. "The Garden of Eden as a Primordial Temple or Sacred Space for Humankind." *Conspectus* 10 (2010): 25–57.

Lipinski, Edward. "El's Abode: Mythological Traditions Related to Mount Hermon and to the Mountains of Armenia." *Orientalia Lovaniensa Periodica* II (1971): 13–69.

Lohse, Eduard. *Colossians and Philemon: A Commentary on the Epistles to the Colossians and to Philemon.* Hermeneia. Philadelphia: Fortress, 1971.

López-Ruiz, Carolina. *When the Gods Were Born: Greek Cosmogonies and the Near East.* Cambridge, MA: Harvard University Press, 2010.

MacLaurin, E. C. B. "Beelzeboul." *Novum Testamentum* 20.2 (1978): 156–60.

Maher, Michael. *Targum Pseudo-Jonathan: Genesis.* Vol. 1B of *The Aramaic Bible.* Edited by Kevin Cathcart, Michael Maher, and Martin McNamara. Collegeville, MN: The Liturgical Press, 1992.

———. "Targum Pseudo-Jonathan: Leviticus." In *Targum Neofiti 1: Leviticus and Targum Pseudo-Jonathan: Leviticus.* Vol. 3 of *The Aramaic Bible.* Edited by Kevin Cathcart, Michael Maher, and Martin McNamara. Collegeville, MN: The Liturgical Press, 1994.

Marcus, Joel. *Mark 8–16: A New Translation with Introduction and Commentary.* AYB. New Haven, CT: Yale University Press, 2009.

Martin, Dale Basil. "When Did Angels Become Demons?" *Journal of Biblical Literature* 129.4 (2010): 661.

Mathews, K. A. *Genesis 1–11:26.* NAC. Nashville: Broadman & Holman, 1996.

May, H. G. "The King in the Garden of Eden." Pages 166–76 in *Israel's Prophetic Heritage.* New York: Harpers, 1962.

McCarter, P. Kyle, Jr. *II Samuel: A New Translation with Introduction, Notes, and Commentary.* AYB. New Haven, CT: Yale University Press, 1984.

McCown, C. C. "The Christian Tradition as to the Magical Wisdom of Solomon." *The Journal of the Palestinian Oriental Society* 2/1 (1922): 1–24.

McKay, J. W. "Helel and the Dawn-Goddess: A Re-examination of the Myth in Isa 14:12–25." *Vetus Testamentum* 20 (1970): 450–64.

McKenzie, J. L. "Mythical Allusions in Ezekiel 28:1–28." *Journal of Biblical Literature* 75 (1956): 322–27.

M'Clintock, John, and James Strong, eds. *Cyclopædia of Biblical, Theological, and Ecclesiastical Literature.* 10 vols. New York: Harper & Brothers, 1891–1894.

Meinardus, Otto F. A. "Paul's Missionary Journey to Spain: Tradition and Folklore." *The Biblical Archaeologist* (1978): 61–63.

Melvin, David. "The Gilgamesh Traditions and the Pre-History of Genesis 6:1–4." *Perspectives in Religious Studies* 38.1 (2011): 23–32.

Meyers, Carol L., and Eric M. Meyers. *Haggai, Zechariah 1–8: A New Translation with Introduction and Commentary.* AYB. New Haven, CT: Yale University Press, 1987.

Michaels, J. Ramsey. *1 Peter.* WBC. Dallas: Word, 1998.

Michalowski, Piotr. "The Mortal Kings of Ur: A Short Century of Divine Rule in Ancient Mesopotamia." In *Religion and Power: Divine Kingship in the Ancient World and Beyond.* Edited by Nicole Brisch. Chicago: The Oriental Institute of the University of Chicago, 2008.

Milgrom, Jacob. *Leviticus 1–16: A New Translation with Introduction and Commentary.* AYB. New Haven, CT: Yale University Press, 1991.

Miller, James E. "The Maelaek of Tyre (Ezekiel 28,11–19)." *Zeitschrift für die alttestamentliche Wissenschaft* 105.3 (1993): 497–501.

Miller, Patrick D. *Israelite Religion and Biblical Theology: Collected Essays.* Sheffield: Sheffield Academic Press, 2000.

———. "When the Gods Meet: Psalm 82 and the Issue of Justice." *Journal for Preachers* 9 (1986): 4–5.

Miller, Stephen R. *Daniel.* NAC. Nashville: Broadman & Holman, 1994.

Miscall, Peter D. *Isaiah 34–35: A Nightmare/A Dream.* Sheffield: Sheffield Academic Press, 1999.

Morales, Michael. *The Tabernacle Pre-Figured: Cosmic Mountain Ideology in Genesis and Exodus.* Leuven: Peeters, 2012.

Morray-Jones, Christopher R. A. "Paradise Revisited (2 Cor 12:1–12): The Jewish Mystical Background of Paul's Apostolate: Part 1: The Jewish Sources." *Harvard Theological Review* 86.2 (1993): 177–217.

———. "Paradise Revisited (2 Cor 12:1–12): The Jewish Mystical Background of Paul's Apostolate: Part 2: Paul's Heavenly Ascent and Its Significance." *Harvard Theological Review* 86.3 (1993): 265–92.

Mullen, E. Theodore, Jr. *The Divine Council in Canaanite and Early Hebrew Literature.* Chico, CA: Scholars Press, 1980.

Murray, Robert. *The Cosmic Covenant: Biblical Themes of Justice, Peace, and the Integrity of Creation.* London: Sheed & Ward, 1992.

Newman, Robert C. "The Ancient Jewish Exegesis of Genesis 6:2, 4." *Grace Theological Journal* 5.1 (1984): 13–36.

Nickelsburg, George W. E. *1 Enoch 1: A Commentary on the Book of 1 Enoch, Chapters 1–36; 81–108.* Hermeneia. Minneapolis: Fortress, 2001.

———. "Enoch, Levi, and Peter: Recipients of Revelation in Upper Galilee." *Journal of Biblical Literature* 100.4 (1981): 575–600.

Nickelsburg, George W. E., and James C. VanderKam. *1 Enoch 2: A Commentary on the Book of 1 Enoch, Chapters 37–82.* Hermeneia. Minneapolis: Fortress, 2012.

Nitzan, Bilha. "Evil and Its Symbols in the Qumran Scrolls." Pages 83–96 in *The Problem of Evil and Its Symbols in Jewish and Christian Tradition.* Edited by Henning Graf Reventlow and Yair Hoffman. London: T&T Clark, 2004.

Oldenburg, Ulf. "Above the Stars of El: El in Ancient South Arabic Religion." *Zeitschrift für die alttestamentliche Wissenschaft* 82 (1970): 187–208.

Oort, H. van. "Augustine and Manichaeism: New Discoveries, New Perspectives." *Verbum et Ecclesia* 27.2 (2006): 709–28.

Otzen, Benedikt. "Michael and Gabriel: Angelological Problems in the Book of Daniel." Pages 114–24 in *The Scriptures and the Scrolls: Studies in Honor of A. S. van der Woude on the Occasion of his 65th Birthday.* Edited by F. Garcia Martinez, A. Hilhorst, and C. J. Labuschagne. Leiden: Brill, 1992.

Page, Hugh R. *The Myth of Cosmic Rebellion: A Study of Its Reflexes in Ugaritic and Biblical Literature.* Leiden: Brill, 1996.

Patmore, Hector M. "Adam or Satan? The Identity of the King of Tyre in Late Antiquity." Pages 59–69 in *After Ezekiel: Essays on the Reception of a Difficult Prophet.* Edited by A. Mein and P. M. Joyce. London: T&T Clark, 2011.

———. *Adam, Satan, and the King of Tyre: The Interpretation of Ezekiel 28:11–19 in Late Antiquity.* Leiden: Brill, 2012.

———. "Did the Masoretes Get It Wrong? The Vocalization and Accentuation of Ezekiel XXVIII 12–19." *Vetus Testamentum* 58 (2008): 45–57.

Pearson, Birger A. "A Reminiscence of Classical Myth at II Peter 2.4." *Greek, Roman, and Byzantine Studies* 10 (1969): 71–80.

Penner, Ken, and Michael S. Heiser. *Old Testament Greek Pseudepigrapha with Morphology.* Bellingham, WA: Lexham Press, 2008.

Peters, Dorothy M. *Noah Traditions in the Dead Sea Scrolls.* Atlanta: Society of Biblical Literature, 2008.

Pinero, A. "Angels and Demons in the Greek *Life of Adam and Eve*." *Journal for the Study of Judaism in the Persian, Hellenistic and Roman Period* 24 (1993): 191–214.

Pinker, Aron. "A Goat to Go to Azazel." *The Journal of Hebrew Scriptures* 7 (2007): 18.

Plato. *The Dialogues of Plato*. Translated B. Jowett. 3rd ed. 5 vols. Oxford: Clarendon, 1892.

Provençal, Philippe. "Regarding the Noun Noun שרף [*śārāp*] in the Hebrew Bible." *JSOT* 29.3 (2005): 371–79.

Quarles, Chester L. *Christian Identity: The Aryan American Bloodline Religion*. Jefferson, NC: McFarland & Company, 2004.

Quick, Laura. "*Helēl ben-šaḥar* and the Chthonic Sun: A New Suggestion for the Mythological Background of Isa 14:12–15." *Vetus Testamentum* 68 (2017): 1–20.

Radford, L. B. *The Epistle to the Colossians and the Epistle to Philemon*. London: Methuen, 1931.

Rahlfs, Alfred, and Robert Hanhart, eds. *Septuaginta: SESB Edition*. Stuttgart: Deutsche Bibelgesellschaft, 2006.

Ramantswana, Hulisani. "God Saw That It Was Good, Not Perfect: A Canonical-Dialogic Reading of Genesis 1–3." PhD diss., Westminster Theological Seminary, 2010.

Reed, Annette Yoshiko. "Enochic and Mosaic Traditions in Jubilees: The Evidence of Angelology and Demonology." In *Enoch and the Mosaic Torah: The Evidence of Jubilees*. Edited by Gabriele Boccaccini et al. Grand Rapids: Eerdmans, 2009.

———. *Fallen Angels and the History of Judaism and Christianity*. Cambridge: Cambridge University Press, 2005.

———. "The Trickery of the Fallen Angels and the Demonic Mimesis of the Divine: Aetiology, Demonology, and Polemics in the Writings of Justin Martyr." *Journal of Early Christian Studies* 12.2 (2004): 141–71.

Reemtsma, Joel A. "Punishment of the Powers: Deuteronomy 32 and Psalm 82 as the Backdrop for Isaiah 34." Paper presented at the Annual Meeting of the Evangelical Theological Society. San Diego, CA, 19 November 2014.

Reeves, John C. *Jewish Lore in Manichaean Cosmogony: Studies in the Book of Giants Traditions*. Cincinnati, OH: Hebrew Union College Press, 1992.

Reiner, Erica. "The Etiological Myth of the 'Seven Sages.'" *Orientalia* 30 (1961): 1–11.

Rexine, John E. "Daimon in Classical Greek Literature." *Greek Orthodox Theological Review* 30.3 (1985): 335–61.

Reynolds, Bennie H., III. "Demonology and Eschatology in the Oppositional Language of the Johannine Epistles and Jewish Apocalyptic Texts." Pages 327–46 in *The Jewish Apocalyptic Tradition and the Shaping of New Testament Thought*. Edited by Benjamin E. Reynolds and Loren T. Stuckenbruck. Minneapolis: Fortress Press, 2017.

———. "Understanding the Demonologies of the Dead Sea Scrolls: Accomplishments and Directions for the Future." *Religion Compass* 7.4 (2013): 103–14.

Roberts, J. J. M. "The End of War in the Zion Tradition: The Imperialistic Background of and Old Testament Vision of World Peace." *Horizons in Biblical Theology* 26.1 (June 2004): 2–22.

Robins, Gay. "Cult Statues in Ancient Egypt." Pages 1–12 in *Cult Image and Divine Representation in the Ancient Near East*. Edited by Neal H. Walls. Boston: American Schools of Oriental Research, 2005.

Rochberg, Francesca. *The Heavenly Writing: Divination, Horoscopy, and Astronomy in Mesopotamian Culture*. Cambridge: Cambridge University Press, 2004.

Rudman, Dominic. "A Note on the Azazel Goat Ritual." *Zeitschrift für die alttestamentliche Wissenschaft* 116.3 (2004): 396–401.

Ruiten, Jacobus van. "Angels and Demons in the Book of Jubilees." Pages 585–610 in *Angels: The Concept of Celestial Beings—Origins, Development and Reception*. Edited by Friedrich V. Reiterer, Tobias Nicklas, and Karin Schöpflin. Berlin: De Gruyter, 2007.

Russell, Jeffrey Burton. *The Devil: Perceptions of Evil from Antiquity to Primitive Christianity*. Ithaca, NY: Cornell University Press, 1987.

Ryken, Leland, James C. Wilhoit, and Tremper Longman III, eds. *Dictionary of Biblical Imagery*. Downers Grove, IL: InterVarsity Press, 2000.

Sacchi, Paolo. *Jewish Apocalyptic and Its History*. Translated by William J. Short, O.F.M. Sheffield: Sheffield Academic Press, 1990.

Salters, R. B. "Psalm 82:1 and the Septuagint." *Zeitschrift für die alttestamentliche Wissenschaft* 103.2 (1991): 225–39.

Sanders, Paul. *The Provenance of Deuteronomy 32*. Leiden: Brill, 1996.

Sanders, Seth L. *From Adapa to Enoch: Scribal Culture and Religious Vision in Judea and Babylonia*. Tübingen: Mohr Siebeck, 2017.

Scarlata, Mark William. *Outside of Eden: Cain in the Ancient Versions of Genesis 4:1–16*. London: Bloomsbury, 2012.

Schmid, H. H. "Creation, Righteousness, and Salvation: 'Creation Theology' as the Broad Horizon of Biblical Theology." Pages 102–17 in *Creation in the Old Testament*. Edited by Bernhard W. Anderson. Philadelphia: Fortress, 1984.

Schultz, D. R. "The Origin of Sin in Irenaeus and Jewish Pseudepigraphical Literature." *Vigiliae Christianae* 32.3 (Sep 1978): 168–69, 172–73.

Schwemer, Daniel. "The Storm Gods of the Ancient Near East: Summary, Synthesis, Recent Studies: Part II." *Journal of Ancient Near Eastern Religions* 8.1 (2008): 8–16.

Scott, James M. *Paul and the Nations: The Old Testament and Jewish Background of Paul's Mission to the Nations with Special Reference to the Destination of Galatians*. Tübingen: Mohr Siebeck, 1995.

Seeman, Chris. "The Watchers Traditions and Gen 6:1–4 [MT and LXX]." In *The Watchers in Jewish and Christian Traditions*. Edited by Angela Kim Harkins, Kelley Coblentz Bautch, and John C. Endres, S.J. Minneapolis: Fortress, 2014.

Seifrid, Mark A. "Romans." Pages 607–94 in *Commentary on the New Testament Use of the Old Testament*. Edited by G. K. Beale and D. A. Carson. Grand Rapids: Baker Academic, 2007.

Sherman, Phillip Michael. *Babel's Tower Translated: Genesis 1–11 and Ancient Jewish Interpretation*. Leiden: Brill, 2013.

Shipp, Mark R. *Of Dead Kings and Dirges: Myth and Meaning in Isaiah 14:4b–21*. Leiden: Brill, 2002.

Skehan, Patrick W., and Alexander A. Di Lella, O.F.M. *The Wisdom of Ben Sira: A New Translation with Notes, Introduction and Commentary*. AYB. New Haven, CT: Yale University Press, 1987.

Smith, Mark S. *God in Translation: Deities in Cross-Cultural Discourse in the Biblical World*. Edited by Bernd Janowski, Mark S. Smith, and Hermann Spieckermann. Tübingen: Mohr Siebeck, 2008.

Spronk, K. *Beatific Afterlife in Ancient Israel and in the Ancient Near East*. Neukirchen-Vluyn: Neukirchener Verlag, 1986.

Stadelmann, Luis. *The Hebrew Conception of the World*. Rome: Biblical Institute Press, 1970.

Stein, Robert H. *Mark*. BECNT. Grand Rapids: Baker Academic, 2008.

Stokes, Ryan Evan. "Rebellious Angels and Malicious Spirits: Explanations of Evil in the Enochic and Related Literature." PhD dissertation, Yale University, 2010.

Stuckenbruck, Loren T. "The 'Angels' and 'Giants' of Genesis 6:1–4 in Second and Third Century BCE Jewish Interpretation: Reflections on the Posture of Early Apocalyptic Traditions." *Dead Sea Discoveries* 7.3 (2000): 354–77.

———. *The Book of Giants from Qumran: Texts, Translation, and Commentary*. Tübingen: Mohr Siebeck, 1997.

———. "The Book of Jubilees and the Origin of Evil." In *Enoch and the Mosaic Torah: The Evidence of Jubilees*. Edited by Gabriele Boccaccini et al. Grand Rapids: Eerdmans, 2009.

———. "Giant Mythology and Demonology: From Ancient Near East to the Dead Sea Scrolls." Pages 31–38 in *Demons: The Demonology of Israelite-Jewish and Early Christian Literature in Context of Their Environment*. Edited by Armin Lange, Hermann Lichtenberger, and Diethard Römheld. Tübingen: Mohr Siebeck, 2003.

———. *The Myth of Rebellious Angels*. Tübingen: Mohr Siebeck, 2014.

———. "The Origins of Evil in Jewish Apocalyptic Tradition: The Interpretation of Genesis 6:1–4 in the Second and Third Centuries BCE." Pages 87–118 in *The Fall of the Angels*. Edited by Christoff Auffarth and Loren T. Stuckenbruck. Leiden: Brill, 2003.

Stuckrad, Kocku von. "Jewish and Christian Astrology in Late Antiquity—A New Approach." *Numen* 47 (2000): 1–40.

Sullivan, Kevin. "The Watchers Traditions in *1 Enoch* 6–16: The Fall of the Angels and the Rise of Demons." Pages 91–106 in *The Watchers in Jewish and Christian Traditions*. Edited by Angela Kim Harkins, Kelley Coblentz Bautch, and John C. Endres, S.J. Minneapolis: Fortress, 2014.

Sweeney, Marvin A. "Myth and History in Ezekiel's Oracle Concerning Tyre (Ezekiel 26–28)." Pages 129–48 in *Myth and Scripture: Contemporary Perspectives on Religion, Language, and Imagination*. Edited by Dexter Callender. Atlanta: Society of Biblical Literature Press, 2014.

Tajra, Harry W. *The Martyrdom of St. Paul: Historical and Judicial Context, Traditions, and Legends*. Tübingen: Mohr Siebeck, 1994.

Tallquist, K. "Sumerisch-Akkadische Hymnen der Totenwelt." *Studia Orientalia* 4 (1934): 17–22.

Talmon, Shemaryahu. "The 'Desert Motif' in the Bible and in Qumran Literature." Pages 31–64 in *Biblical Motifs: Origins and Transformations*. Edited by Alexander Altmann. Vol. 3. Cambridge, MA: Harvard University Press, 1966.

Tan, Randall, and David A. deSilva. *The Lexham Greek-English Interlinear Septuagint*. Bellingham, WA: Logos Bible Software, 2009.

Tawil, Hayim. "'Azazel, the Prince of the Steepe: A Comparative Study." *Zeitschrift für die alttestamentliche Wissenschaft* 92.1 (1980): 43–59.

Teixidor, J. *The Pantheon of Palmyra*. Leiden: Brill, 1979.

Thomas, Samuel. "Watchers Traditions in the Dead Sea Scrolls." In *The Watchers in Jewish and Christian Traditions*. Edited by Angela Kim Harkins, Kelley Coblentz Bautch, and John C. Endres, S.J. Minneapolis: Fortress, 2014.

Thompson, Steven. "The End of Satan." *Andrews University Seminary Studies* 37.2 (1999): 260–62.

Tiemeyer, Lena-Sofia. "Zechariah's Spies and Ezekiel's Cherubim." Pages 95–119 in *Tradition in Transition: Haggai and Zechariah 1–8 in the Trajectory of Hebrew Theology*. Edited by Mark J. Boda and Michael H. Floyd. London: T&T Clark, 2008.

Tigay, Jeffrey. *Deuteronomy*. JPS Torah Commentary. Philadelphia: Jewish Publication Society, 1996.

Tiller, Patrick A. *A Commentary on the Animal Apocalypse of 1 Enoch*. Atlanta: Scholars Press, 1993.

Tov, Emanuel. *The Parallel Aligned Hebrew-Aramaic and Greek Texts of Jewish Scripture—Alexandrinus and Theodotion Variants*. Computer Assisted Tools for Septuagint Studies. Bellingham, WA: Logos Bible Software, 2003.

———. *Textual Criticism of the Hebrew Bible*. 3rd ed. Rev. and exp. Minneapolis: Fortress, 2012.

Tsevat, Matitiahu. "God and the Gods in Assembly." *Hebrew Union College Annual* 40–41 (1969–70): 123–37.

Tsumura, David Toshio. *Creation and Destruction: A Reappraisal of the Chaoskampf Theory in the Old Testament*. Winona Lake, IN: Eisenbrauns, 2005.

——. "Genesis and Ancient Near Eastern Stories of Creation and Flood: An Introduction." Pages 44–57 in *I Studied Inscriptions from before the Flood: Ancient Near Eastern, Literary, and Linguistic Approaches to Genesis 1–11*. Edited by Richard S. Hess and David Toshio Tsumura. Winona Lake, IN: Eisenbrauns, 1994.

——. "Janus Parallelism in Hab 3:4." *Vetus Testamentum* 54.1 (Jan 2004): 124–28.

Twelftree, Graham. *In the Name of Jesus: Exorcism among Early Christians*. Grand Rapids: Baker, 2007.

——. *Jesus the Exorcist: A Contribution to the Study of the Historical Jesus*. Eugene, OR: Wipf & Stock, 2011.

Ulrich, E., F. M. Cross, S. W. Crawford, J. A. Duncan, P. W. Skehan, E. Tov, and J. T. Barrera. *Qumran Cave 4.IX: Deuteronomy, Joshua, Judges, Kings*. Oxford: Clarendon Press, 1996.

Vail, Eric M. "Using 'Chaos' in Articulating the Relationship of God and Creation in God's Creative Activity." PhD diss., Marquette University, 2009.

VanderKam, James C. *The Book of Jubilees*. Sheffield: Sheffield Academic Press, 2001.

——. *The Dead Sea Scrolls Today*. Grand Rapids: Eerdmans, 1994.

——. *Enoch and the Growth of an Apocalyptic Tradition*. Washington, DC: Catholic Biblical Association of America, 1984.

Wahlen, Clinton. *Jesus and the Impurity of Spirits in the Synoptic Gospels*. Tübingen: Mohr Siebeck, 2004.

Walker, Christopher, and Michael B. Dick. "The Induction of the Cult Image in Ancient Mesopotamia: The Mesopotamian *mīs pî* Ritual." Pages 55–122 in *Born in Heaven, Made on Earth: The Making of the Cult Image in the Ancient Near East*. Edited by Michael B. Dick. Winona Lake, IN: Eisenbrauns, 1999.

Wallace, Daniel B. *Greek Grammar Beyond the Basics—Exegetical Syntax of the New Testament*. Grand Rapids: Zondervan, 1996.

Waltke, Bruce K. "The Creation Account in Genesis 1:1–3: Part II: The Restitution Theory." *Bibliotheca Sacra* 132 (1975): 136–44.

——. "The Creation Account in Genesis 1:1–3: Part III: The Initial Chaos Theory and the Precreation Chaos Theory." *Bibliotheca Sacra* 132 (1975): 216–28.

Walton, John H. "Demons in Mesopotamia and Israel: Exploring the Category of Non-Divine but Supernatural Enemies." Pages 229–46 in *Windows to the Ancient World of the Hebrew Bible: Essays in Honor of Samuel Greengus*. Edited by Bill T. Arnold, Nancy L. Erickson, and John H. Walton. Winona Lake, IN: Eisenbrauns, 2014.

——. *Genesis 1 as Ancient Cosmology*. Winona Lake, IN: Eisenbrauns, 2011.

——. *The Lost World of Genesis One: Ancient Cosmology and the Origins Debate*. Downers Grove, IL: IVP Academic, 2009.

Watts, John D. W. *Isaiah 1–33*. Rev. ed. WBC. Nashville: Thomas Nelson, 2005.

Wenham, Gordon J. "Sanctuary Symbolism in the Garden of Eden Story." Pages 399–40 in *I Studied Inscriptions from before the Flood: Ancient Near Eastern, Literary, and Linguistic Approaches to Genesis 1–11*. Edited by Richard S. Hess and David Toshio Tsumura. Winona Lake, IN: Eisenbrauns, 1994.

Werman, C. "Qumran and the Book of Noah." Pages 171–81 in *Pseudepigraphic Perspectives: The Apocrypha and Pseudepigrapha in Light of the Dead Sea Scrolls. Proceedings of the International Symposium of the Orion Center for the Study of the Dead Sea Scrolls and Associated Literature*. Edited by E. G. Chazon and M. E. Stone, with the collaboration of A. Pinnick. Leiden: Brill, 1999.

West, D. R. *Some Cults of Greek Goddesses and Female Daemons of Oriental Origin Especially in Relation to the Mythology of Goddesses and Daemons in the Semitic World*. Neukirchen-Vluyn: Neukirchener Verlag, 1995.

West, Martin L. *The East Face of the Helicon: West Asiatic Elements in Greek Poetry and Myth*. Oxford: Clarendon Press, 1997.

White, Ellen. *Yahweh's Council: Its Structure and Membership*. Tübingen: Mohr Siebeck, 2014.

Whitney, K. William. *Two Strange Beasts: Leviathan and Behemoth in Second Temple and Early Rabbinic Judaism*. Winona Lake, IN: Eisenbrauns, 2006.

Wiggerman, F. A. M. *Mesopotamian Protective Spirits: The Ritual Texts*. Leiden: Brill, 1992.

Wildberger, Hans. *A Continental Commentary: Isaiah 13–27*. Minneapolis: Fortress, 1997.

Wilson, J. V. Kinnier. "A Return to the Problems of Behemoth and Leviathan." *Vetus Testamentum* 25 (1975): 1–14.

Winston, David. *The Wisdom of Solomon: A New Translation with Introduction and Commentary*. AYB 43. New Haven, CT: Yale University Press, 1979.

Wright, Archie T. *The Origin of Evil Spirits: The Reception of Genesis 6:1–4 in Early Jewish Literature*. Tübingen: Mohr Siebeck, 2013.

———. "Some Observations on Philo's *De Gigantibus* and Evil Spirits in Second Temple Judaism." *Journal for the Study of Judaism* 36.4 (2005): 471–88.

Wyatt, N. *Religious Texts from Ugarit: The Words of Ilimilku and his Colleagues*. Sheffield: Sheffield Academic Press, 1998.

———. "The Significance of ṢPN in West Semitic Thought." Pages 213–37 in *Ugarit: Ein ostmediterranes Kulturzentrum im Alten Orient*. Edited by M. Dietrich and O. Loretz. Münster: Ugarit-Verlag, 1995.

———. *Space and Time in the Religious Life of the Near East*. Sheffield: Sheffield Academic Press, 2001.

———. "Titles of the Ugaritic Storm God." *Ugarit Forschungen* 24 (1992): 403–24.

Zatelli, I. "Astrology and the Worship of the Stars in the Bible." *Zeitschrift für die alttestamentliche Wissenschaft* 103 (1991): 86–99.

Index of Subjects
and Modern Authors

Index of Scripture and Other Ancient Literature

Proverbs

Ecclesiastes

Isaiah

Jeremiah

Deuterocanonical Works

Tobit

Wisdom of Solomon

Sirach, Wisdom of

Baruch

2 Maccabees

4 Maccabees

Old Testament Pseudepigrapha

Assumption of Moses

2 Baruch (Syriac Apocalypse)

1 Enoch

LEXHAM PRESS

WHAT THE BIBLE REALLY SAYS
ABOUT GOD'S HEAVENLY HOST

ANGELS

MICHAEL S. HEISER

—

WHAT DOES THE BIBLE REALLY TELL US ABOUT THE HEAVENLY HOST?

Everyone knows that angels have wings, usually carry harps, and that each of us has our own personal guardian angel, right? What the Bible really says about angels is overlooked or filtered through popular myths. In his latest book, *Angels*, Dr. Michael Heiser reveals what the Bible really says about God's supernatural servants. *Angels* is not guided by traditions, stories, speculations, or myths about angels. Heiser's study is grounded in the terms the Bible itself uses to describe members of God's heavenly host; he examines the terms in their biblical context while drawing on insights from the wider context of the ancient Near Eastern world.

—

LexhamPress.com/Angels